P9-EDA-978

The Colorado CookBook

A BENEFIT FOR THE UNIVERSITY OF COLORADO LIBRARIES—BOULDER

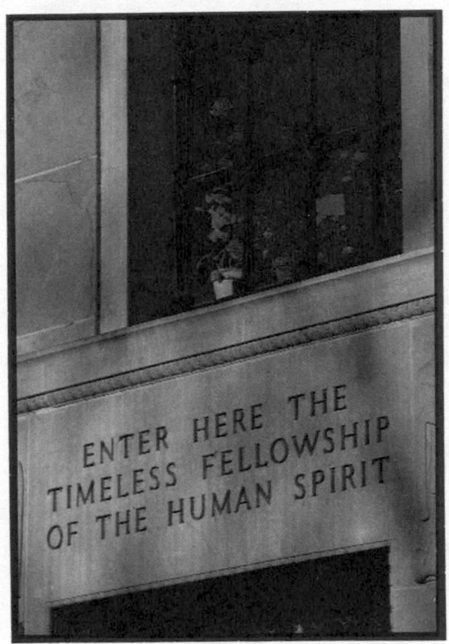
ENTER HERE THE
TIMELESS FELLOWSHIP
OF THE HUMAN SPIRIT

Managed by
Library Volunteer Association

Sponsored by
University of Colorado Women's Club—Boulder
Friends of the Library

Publishers and Editors
Sheryl Kuempel and Nancy Cateora
Boulder, Colorado

The proceeds from the sale of **The Colorado Cook Book** will be used for the purchase of books for the University of Colorado Libraries-Boulder, Boulder, Colorado.

Additional copies of **The Colorado Cook Book** may be obtained by addressing:

The Colorado Cook Book
Campus Box 184—Library Administration
University of Colorado
Boulder, Colorado 80309

Please include a check for $13.95 plus $1.50 postage and handling payable to **Colorado Cookbook.** For your convenience, order blanks are included in the back of this book.

Library of Congress Catalog Card Number: 81-186924

First Printing	August 1981	20,000 copies
Second Printing	September 1982	20,000 copies
Third Printing	October 1987	10,000 copies

ISBN 087081 - 127 - 4

NOTICE: The information contained in this book is true and complete to the best of our knowledge. All recommendations are made without any guarantees on the part of the authors. The authors/publishers disclaim all liability incurred in connection with the use of this information.

THE COLORADO COOK BOOK

EDITORS
Nancy Cateora and Sheryl Kuempel

RECIPE TESTING CHAIRMAN
Eleanor Taylor

WINE CONSULTANTS
James Drevescraft
Wayne Belding
The Boulder Wine Merchant

COPY EDITOR
Marge DeFries

BOOK DESIGN
Michella Clark

PHOTOGRAPHY
Jerry Downs

Printed by
WIMMER BROTHERS
Memphis Dallas

SPECIAL ASSISTANCE

Bob Erisman, Elaine Fowler, Betty Grebe, Janet Lorenzen, Beverly Sterling, Mary Wing

TYPING

Clare Baird, Edith Baumann, Jane Beagle, Phyllis Cateora, Doris Goodrich, Carmen Johnson, Janet Lorenzen, Eleanor Taylor, Julie Wadleigh, Helen Wasley, Ruth Yearns

EDITING

Edith Baumann, Jean Beagle, Carol Bell, Marge DeFries, Mary Jane Husbands, Cicely Kane, Dorothy Lewis, Lois Linsky, Jean Loeffler, Virginia Paddock, Ellie Pollack, Jolene Quigley, Louise Reed, Eleanor Taylor, Helen Wasley, Ruth Yearns, Ethel Zager

PROOF READING

Clare Baird, Martha Campbell, Philip Cateora, Phyllis Cateora, June Dunham, Harold Evjan, Mary Jane Husbands, Cicely Kane, Jean Loeffler, Arlan Norman, Ellie Pollack, Judith Ramsey, Martha Romero, Gail Sachs, Peg Skurnik, Eleanor Taylor, Anne Turner, Bob and Helen Wasley

TESTING

Eleanor Taylor, Chairman
Joyce Price, Assistance Chairman

Millie Anderson, Clare Baird, Frieda Baroway, Eleanor Bartlett, Ellen Boles, Barbara Breternitz, Dorothy Briggle, Thelma Brinton, Jane Byers, Helen Carrasco, Deborah Cateora, Phyllis Cateora, Jean Clark, Edith Del'Apa, Esther deOnis, Janet Desgalier, Fran Dickinson, Herta Dobbins, June Dunham, Peggy Earnest, Corinne Effinger, Norma Ekstrand, Ann Erickson, Elaine Fowler, Britt Garcia, Florence Grieder, Val Havlick, Bette Heimann, Nancy Hodge, Nona Jahsman, Susannah Jordan, Cicely Kane, Caryl Kassoy, Barbara Klemme, Mark Kuempel, June Krantz, Lois Linsky, Jean Loeffler, Linda Loewenstein, Mary Lymberopoulos, Mikki Matheson, Marie McBride, Esther McGuire, Sue McMillan, Sharon Morgan, Janet Nuzum, Jan Osterweil, Doris Ostwald, Audrey Palmer, Melinda Parks, Priscilla Peale, Roslyn Pfaff, Rosemary Plane, Ellie Pollack, Elizabeth Porter, Joyce Price, Judith Ramsey, Susan Randa, Carol Reese, Lyn Robinson, Alvena Rogers, Norma Schattke, Eleanor Shulls, Gwen Shurm, Peg Skurnik, Joyce Smith, Jan Sumek, Joanne Steele, Deborah Taylor, Linda Toomre, Denyce Towle, Anne Turner, Helen Wasley, Florence White, Ruth Yearns, Ethel Zager

PREFACE

Truly, it is a pleasure for me to have this opportunity to write a word or two about The Colorado Cook Book. Many people have helped collect and test the recipes, particularly members of the University Women's Club. There is no way to measure the hours spent to bring this volume to publication, although we know that the number is immense. And so, for this single-minded dedication, our Libraries express sincere thanks.

I hope you like The Colorado Cook Book, for after all, how often can you enjoy the food prepared from this book and at the same time make a contribution to our Libraries—a contribution which will enrich the educational opportunities available to our students? Surely the owner of The Colorado Cook Book has, at least momentarily, the best of two worlds!

Clyde C. Walton
Director of Libraries
University of Colorado, Boulder

This collection of favorite recipes has come from friends of the University of Colorado. It is brought to you with the hope that you will enjoy new taste treats and at the same time support the concept of excellence for our University Libraries. We hope this effort will continue to aid the library for many years. We sincerely thank everyone involved in putting this book together. It has required countless hours from many people to gather, sort, test, and type over 2,000 recipes from which we selected the 600 plus included in the book.

A project of this magnitude also required support and encouragement from the Library Administration and others. So our special thanks to Clyde Walton, Director of Libraries; Leo Cabell, Associate Director of Libraries; and J.K. Emery, Director of Publication Services. And to Richard Emerson, Alumni Director and Charles McCord, Director of Development.

Special medals for patience and understanding go to Philip, Deborah, Phyllis and Hank Cateora and to Peter and Mark Kuempel.

CONTENTS

FROM THE EDITORS

These recipes were tested in home kitchens and carefully proofread to give you excellent results. We have tried to offer an appealing choice of recipes that are a little different and very exciting. We hope you find the format clear and easy to follow. Each recipe indicates the number of servings plus the preparation time. These are highly variable factors so they are offered here only as guidelines to help you assess whether your available time permits starting a recipe. And always read each recipe through completely before starting. Enjoy!

APPETIZERS

SESAME SEED WAFERS

Yields 5 Dozen
Chill 30 Minutes

Preparation 20 Minutes
Bake 15 Minutes at 350°F

2 cups flour
1 teaspoon salt
Dash of cayenne pepper
1/2 cup butter or margarine
1/2 cup sesame seeds, toasted and cooled
1/4 cup water

1. Place flour, salt, and cayenne in bowl of a food processor fitted with a steel blade. Turn on for a few seconds to mix dry ingredients.
2. Add butter in 4 or 5 pieces and process until the consistency of corn meal. Add sesame seeds and process briefly.
3. Pour water through the top with machine running. Process only long enough to form a ball. If this takes more than a few seconds; add more water by the teaspoonful.
4. Form dough into a roll about 2 inches in diameter, wrap in waxed paper and chill at least 30 minutes. Preheat oven to 350 degrees.
5. Slice dough 1/8-inch thick using a very sharp knife. Bake 15 to 20 minutes on ungreased baking sheet after pricking rounds with a fork several times. Salt lightly while still hot.

NOTE:

Freeze well-wrapped roll; thaw slightly before slicing and baking.

Sally Adams
Piedmont, California

CEREAL-NUT MIX

Serves 6 to 8

Preparation 10 Minutes
Bake 1 Hour at 250° F

1/4 cup oil
2 to 3 small fresh, hot chilies, chopped
4 ounces cashew nuts
4 ounces peanuts
1 cup shredded coconut
4 tablespoons sesame seeds
3/4 teaspoon turmeric
1 teaspoon oregano
1 tablespoon ground ginger
4 cups crisp rice cereal
1 cup crisp corn cereal
1 teaspoon salt
1 tablespoon sugar

1. Heat oil in large pan and saute' chili peppers. Stir in nuts and saute' a few minutes more over low heat.
2. Add coconut, sesame seeds, spices, and cereals. Sprinkle with salt and sugar. Stir to mix well. Transfer to a baking sheet.
3. Bake in preheated 250-degree oven for 1 hour.

Naryan Patel
Cleveland, Ohio

SPICED NUTS

Yields 4 Cups

Preparation 15 Minutes
Bake 45 Minutes at 275°F

2 tablespoons butter
1 egg white
1/2 cup sugar
1 teaspoon cinnamon
1/2 teaspoon each salt, ground cloves, and nutmeg
1/4 teaspoon ground ginger
1/4 teaspoon allspice
2 tablespoons water
1 cup pecan halves
1 cup almonds, whole
1 cup walnut halves
1 cup peanuts

1. Melt butter on baking sheet in 275-degree oven. Remove from oven.
2. Beat egg white until stiff. Combine sugar and spices and gradually beat into egg white. Stir in water and then nuts.
3. Spread nut mixture in a thin layer on baking sheet. Bake at 275 degrees for 45 minutes. Cool and break into pieces.

CHICKEN-ALMOND PUFFS

Yields 4 to 5 Dozen

Preparation 45 Minutes
Bake 10 Minutes at 450°F
5 to 10 Minutes at 350°F

1/2 cup butter or margarine
1 cup chicken broth
1 cup flour
1/4 teaspoon salt
4 eggs
1/2 cup finely diced cooked chicken
2 tablespoons chopped almonds, toasted
Dash of paprika

1. Combine butter and chicken broth in a saucepan and keep over low heat until butter has melted.
2. Add flour and salt all at once. Stir vigorously over low heat until the mixture forms a ball and pulls away from the sides of the saucepan. Remove from heat and cool slightly.
3. Add the eggs one at a time, beating thoroughly after each addition. Continue beating until a thick glossy dough is formed.
4. Stir in chicken, almonds, and paprika.
5. Drop by small teaspoonful onto a greased baking sheet. Bake at 450 degrees for 10 minutes, then reduce heat to 350 degrees and bake 5 to 10 minutes more or until golden brown.

NOTE:

Homemade chicken broth (see Index) gives the puffs a stronger chicken flavor. Puffs may be frozen in plastic bags and reheated just before serving. These puffs should not be filled.

Nona Jahsman
Palo Alto, California

TOMATO TOAST

Serves 24 to 40

Preparation 40 Minutes
Broil 5 Minutes

1/2 to 3/4 pound bacon slices
1 pound bread slices
1/4 cup chopped green onion
1/4 cup chopped bell pepper
1/2 cup mayonnaise
1/2 cup grated Cheddar cheese
1/4 teaspoon salt
4 to 5 small tomatoes, thinly sliced

1. Cut each bacon slice into 5 pieces. Fry carefully to retain shape.
2. Roll bread very thin and press into greased cupcake tins. Toast lightly.
3. Mix onion, pepper, mayonnaise, cheese, and salt.
4. Assemble by placing tomato slice in toast cup, then scant spoonful of cheese mixture. Top with cooked bacon piece. Broil.

NOTE:

You may prepare and freeze after assembling toast cups. Broil directly from freezer.

Trisha Gallagher
Piedmont, California

SPINACH BALLS

Yields 8 Dozen
Chill 2 Hours

Preparation 30 Minutes
Bake 15 Minutes at 350°F

10 ounces fresh or frozen spinach, chopped
1/2 large onion, minced
2 eggs, beaten
1/3 cup butter, melted
1/4 cup Parmesan cheese
1/2 clove garlic, minced
1/2 teaspoon thyme
1/2 teaspoon pepper
1 cup stuffing mix, crushed

1. Cook spinach and squeeze dry.
2. Mix together the spinach, onion, eggs, butter, cheese, garlic, thyme, and pepper. Add stuffing crumbs and mix thoroughly.
3. Shape into 1/2-inch balls and chill for several hours to blend flavors or freeze for later use.
4. Bake in a 350-degree oven for 15 minutes or for 20 minutes if frozen.

Ruth F. Stewart
San Antonio, Texas

STUFFED MUSHROOMS

Mushrooms are a versatile and elegant appetizer. Prepare mushrooms according to general directions, then choose a filling. Plan 2 to 3 mushrooms for each guest. These fillings will fill 12 to 15 large mushrooms.

GENERAL DIRECTIONS:

Select large, firm mushrooms with the underside still tightly closed. (They will keep several days, refrigerated, if they are stored in a paper sack instead of plastic.) Wash mushrooms in cold water, lifting them *out* of the wash water several times and drying. Carefully remove stems and reserve for use in fillings, sauces, or soups.

BACON-CHEESE

Serves 6 to 8

Preparation 30 Minutes
Bake 25 Minutes at 350°F

7 slices bacon
8 ounces cream cheese
1 bunch green onions, finely chopped
Dash of garlic salt
1/3 cup mushroom stems, minced
3 tablespoons butter, melted

1. Fry bacon, drain, and crumble.
2. Mix softened cream cheese, onions, garlic salt, mushroom stems, and crumbled bacon.
3. Brush prepared mushroom caps with melted butter, fill, and place in shallow baking dish with 2 to 4 tablespoons water. Bake 20 to 25 minutes at 350 degrees.

Deborah Taylor
Boulder, Colorado

BLEU CHEESE

Serves 6 to 8

Preparation 15 Minutes
Broil 5 Minutes

1/2 cup finely minced mushroom stems
1/4 cup finely chopped green onion
2 tablespoons margarine
8 ounces cream cheese
1/2 package bleu cheese salad dressing mix
2 tablespoons milk

1. Saute' mushroom stems and onion in margarine for 5 minutes.
2. Combine softened cream cheese, dressing mix, and milk. Add mushroom-onion mixture. Stir.
3. Fill prepared mushroom caps. Broil until browned and bubbly.

Sonia K. Plisco
Golden, Colorado

CRAB-CHEESE

Serves 6 to 8

Preparation 15 Minutes
Broil 4 Minutes

1 package (6-ounce) frozen crab, thawed and drained or 1 can (4 1/2 ounce) shrimp, drained and chopped
3 tablespoons mayonnaise
2 tablespoons chopped green onions
2 tablespoons golden raisins
1/4 cup shredded sharp Cheddar cheese
1 teaspoon curry powder
Freshly grated Parmesan cheese

1. Combine crab or shrimp, mayonnaise, onions, raisins, Cheddar cheese, and curry powder. Mix well.
2. Fill prepared mushroom caps. Sprinkle with Parmesan cheese and broil about 6 to 8 inches from source of heat.

PORK

Serves 6 to 8

Preparation 30 Minutes
Cook 30 Minutes

1/2 pound lean pork, minced
1 small green onion, minced
1 slice ginger root
1 tablespoon sherry
1 tablespoon soy sauce
1 teaspoon sugar
1 teaspoon cornstarch
1 teaspoon peanut oil

1. Grind together pork, onion, and ginger root.
2. Blend in sherry, soy sauce, sugar, cornstarch, and peanut oil.
3. Fill prepared mushroom caps and steam 30 minutes.

Margaret Riddle
Boulder, Colorado

STUFFED ARTICHOKES

Serves 10 to 12

Preparation 30 Minutes
Bake 30 Minutes at 350°F

4 cans (14-ounce each) artichoke hearts
6 ounces cream cheese with chives
2 eggs, beaten
3/4 cup grated Parmesan cheese

1. Dig out center of the artichoke with grapefruit spoon. Fill artichoke with cream cheese, dip in egg, then roll in Parmesan cheese.
2. Place on cookie sheet and bake at 350 degrees for 30 minutes.
3. Cut into quarters to serve as an appetizer.

Betty Quarnstrom
Avalon, California

STUFFED CELERY
(*Apio relleno*)

Serves 6 to 12

Preparation 15 Minutes

1 bunch celery
1 avocado
1 to 2 tablespoons cream cheese
1 banana
1 tablespoon sugar
Juice of 1 lemon
Salt to taste
3 tablespoons chopped nuts
Chili powder or paprika

1. Clean and trim celery for stuffing.
2. Mix avocado, cream cheese, banana, sugar, juice, salt, and nuts. Fill celery stalks, dust with chili powder or paprika. Cut in 2- to 4-inch lengths.

NOTE:

The banana imparts a very unusual flavor which is seldom identified.

Betty Quarnstrom
Avalon, California

SPICY HAM ROLL-UPS

Serves 15 to 20

Preparation 40 Minutes
Refrigerate 2 Hours

6 ounces cream cheese, softened
4 tablespoons milk
2 tablespoons grated onion
4 tablespoons horseradish
1 teaspoon Tabasco
1/2 teaspoon cayenne pepper
1 pound ham, very thinly sliced

1. Combine softened cream cheese, milk, onion, horseradish, Tabasco, and cayenne. Refrigerate for several hours to allow flavors to develop. Adjust flavor to taste.
2. Spread cream cheese mixture on a slice of ham. Roll-up and cut each roll into 3 pieces. Refrigerate until ready to use.

Carol Kuempel
Boston, Massachusetts

SWEET AND SOUR MEAT BALLS

Yields 5 Dozen

Preparation 20 Minutes
Cook 1 Hour

1 pound ground chuck (or any meat)
1/4 cup milk
1 medium onion, grated
1 teaspoon salt
1 egg
2 slices white bread, cubed
1 medium onion, diced
1/3 cup lemon juice
1 can (8-ounce) tomato sauce
1/2 cup water
1/2 cup brown sugar
1/2 cup white sugar
A few gingersnaps (optional)

1. In a large bowl, mix together ground chuck, milk, grated onion, salt, egg, and bread.
2. In a large pan, combine diced onion, lemon juice, and tomato sauce. Rinse can with the water and add to pan. Taste liquid; it should be slightly sour. Add equal amounts of brown and white sugar until the mixture tastes slightly sweeter than you would like when finished.
3. Roll meat mixture into small balls and add to tomato mixture. Cook approximately one hour.
4. A few crumbled gingersnaps may be added for thickening and flavor. May also be served with rice as an entree.

Betty Berger
Los Angeles, California

SPICY COCKTAIL MEATBALLS

Yields 5 Dozen
Refrigerate Overnight

Preparation 25 Minutes
Bake 20 Minutes at 350°F

3/4 pound ground beef
4 3/4 ounces liver spread
1 teaspoon Dijon mustard
1/2 teaspoon salt
1/4 teaspoon white pepper
1/4 cup fine dry bread crumbs
1 egg, beaten
3/4 cup crushed corn chips

1. Combine ground beef, liver spread, mustard, and seasonings. Blend well. Add crumbs and egg. Mix thoroughly.
2. Shape into 1-inch balls.
3. Cover tightly and refrigerate overnight.
4. Just before baking, roll in crushed corn chips.
5. Bake on rack in shallow pan at 350 degrees for 10 minutes. Turn once and bake 10 minutes more.

Deborah Frances
Denver, Colorado

GLAZED SAUSAGE BALLS

Yields 5 Dozen

Preparation 25 Minutes
Cook 8 to 10 Minutes

- **1/3 pound sausage**
- **3/4 pound ground pork or ground beef**
- **1/2 teaspoon salt**
- **1/2 teaspoon dry mustard**
- **1/2 teaspoon crushed coriander**
- **1/4 teaspoon ground allspice**
- **1 egg**
- **1/4 cup fine dry bread crumbs**
- **1/4 cup sliced green onions**
- **1/2 cup apple jelly**
- **1/2 cup chopped chutney**
- **1 teaspoon lemon juice**

1. Combine sausage, pork or beef, salt, mustard, coriander, allspice, egg, crumbs, and onions. Shape into 1-inch balls.
2. On a shallow pan bake 6 to 8 minutes in 500-degree oven until brown. Drain on paper toweling.
3. In large frying pan over low heat combine jelly, chutney, and lemon juice. Stir until melted.
4. Add meat balls and simmer 8 to 10 minutes until glazed. Transfer to chafing dish to keep hot.

Sue McMillan
Boulder, Colorado

CHINESE BARBECUED BABY DRUMSTICKS

Serves 25
Marinate 2 Hours

Preparation 30 Minutes
Bake 1 Hour at 350°F

- **3 pounds chicken wings**
- **1/2 cup soy sauce**
- **3 tablespoons sugar**
- **3 tablespoons brown sugar**
- **3 tablespoons vinegar**
- **1 teaspoon ground ginger**
- **2 garlic cloves, chopped**
- **1/2 cup chicken broth**
- **Freshly ground pepper**

1. Separate wings into three pieces, discarding tips.
2. Marinate wings in soy sauce, sugar, brown sugar, vinegar, ginger, garlic, broth, and pepper for two hours. Turn once.
3. Bake uncovered for 1 hour or more in a 350-degree oven.

Vera Gale
Foster City, California

GREEK MUSHROOMS
(*Champignons à la Greque*)

Serves 8
Refrigerate 3 Hours

Preparation 20 Minutes
Cook 20 Minutes

2 pounds (or more) mushrooms of uniform size
3 cups dry white wine
1 cup water
4 tablespoons tomato paste
White peppercorns
Paprika
20 whole coriander seeds
4 tablespoons olive oil
1 bouquet garni (thyme leaves and bay leaves)
Juice of one lemon
Salt
Pepper

1. Clean mushrooms and remove stems, reserving for another use.
2. Put mushrooms in heavy pot with remaining ingredients. Bring to boil, stir, and reduce heat. Cover and cook mushrooms until almost tender. Remove mushrooms with slotted spoon.
3. Boil until sauce is reduced and slightly thickened. Return mushrooms to sauce and chill before serving, or marinate overnight.

NOTE:

This is served as a first course in France. Boiling onions can be substituted for mushrooms.

Arlette Sinobad
Orsay, France

MARINATED GREEN OLIVES

Serves 6 to 8

Preparation 10 Minutes
Marinate Overnight

1/2 bottle (10-ounce) tarragon white wine vinegar
1 cup water
2 small cloves garlic
1/2 teaspoon leaf oregano
Dash Tabasco sauce
1 can (7 3/4-ounce) green olives, drained

1. Combine vinegar, water, whole garlic, oregano, and Tabasco.
2. Pour over drained olives. Marinate overnight.

NOTE:

Marinade may be reused or used for salad dressing.

Mary Gerlitz-Garnett
Boulder, Colorado

PICKLED BELL PEPPERS

Serves 10 to 12

Preparation 15 Minutes
Marinate 24 Hours

9 large green peppers
1 cup vinegar
1 cup water
1/2 cup salad oil
1 tablespoon whole allspice
2 cloves garlic
1 tablespoon salt
1 tablespoon sugar

1. Cut green peppers into large pieces, removing ribs and seeds. Steam until tender but not soft.
2. Mix vinegar, water, oil, allspice, garlic, salt, and sugar and pour over peppers in a large jar. Marinate at least 24 hours.

NOTE:

Will keep in refrigerator for weeks.

VARIATION:

Use a thin slice of ham wrapped around pepper slices and held with a toothpick for variety and color. Also, use the marinade to marinate meat or chicken.

Betty Berger
Los Angeles, California

SWEDISH PICKLED SHRIMP

Serves 10 to 15

Preparation 1 Hour
Refrigerate 24 Hours

3 pounds fresh or frozen shrimp in shells
1/2 cup celery leaves
1/4 cup mixed pickling spices
1 tablespoon salt
2 cups sliced onion
6 bay leaves
1 1/2 cups salad oil
1 cup white vinegar
3 tablespoons capers with juice
2 1/2 teaspoons celery seed
1 1/2 teaspoons salt
4 drops bottled hot pepper sauce

1. Cover shrimp in saucepan with boiling water. Add celery leaves, pickling spices, and salt. Cover pan, simmer 5 minutes, and drain. Peel and devein shrimp under cold water.
2. Layer shrimp, onion, and bay leaves in shallow dish.
3. Combine remaining ingredients. Pour over shrimp. Cover. Chill at least 24 hours, spooning the marinade over shrimp occasionally.

Nancy Cateora
Boulder, Colorado

SHRIMP APPETIZER

Serves 4

Preparation 1 1/2 Hours
Cook 10 Minutes

1 pound (16 to 18) large shrimp, with tails, deveined and shelled
1/2 cup dry sherry
2 tablespoons butter
Garlic salt
1/2 cup freshly grated Parmesan cheese

1. Soak shrimp in sherry for one hour.
2. Drain and saute' in butter until just cooked (use a pan that can go under a broiler.)
3. Sprinkle shrimp with garlic salt and Parmesan cheese and put under broiler until lightly browned. Watch carefully.
4. Serve right out of pan with crunchy French bread.

VARIATION:

Swordfish, shark, halibut, or bass can be used instead of shrimp.

Marge Berger
Berkeley, California

MUSSELS MARINIÈRE

Serves 6
Soak 2 Hours

Preparation 10 Minutes
Cook 5 Minutes

1 1/2 cups white wine
4 shallots, minced
2 cloves garlic, minced
4 to 6 sprigs parsley
3 tablespoons butter
1/8 teaspoon thyme
Pepper to taste
3 quarts mussels, scrubbed and soaked

1. In a large pot, boil the wine with shallots, garlic, parsley, butter, thyme, and pepper for several minutes.
2. Add mussels and steam for 5 minutes or until mussels just open. Discard any unopened shells.
3. Remove mussels to large soup bowls. Pour liquid over mussels, taking care to leave any sand in the cooking pot.

NOTE:

Follow cleaning instructions for mussels from Garlic Mussels Florentine (see Index).

Leon Peters
San Francisco, California

GARLIC MUSSELS FLORENTINE

Serves 4
Soak 2 Hours

Preparation 45 Minutes
Cook 10 Minutes

2 quarts mussels, scrubbed and soaked
8 ounces butter, softened
4 shallots, minced
3 cloves garlic, minced
2 tablespoons bread crumbs
3 tablespoons minced parsley
1/4 teaspoon dried basil
2 tablespoons minced spinach

1. Wash the mussels by scrubbing off the beards and soaking in cold water for several hours. This will rid the mussels of sand. Discard any mussels that are partially open. Drain and rinse again.
2. Arrange mussels in one layer on a baking sheet. Place in a preheated 400-degree oven for 6 to 8 minutes or until the shells have opened. Discard any that do not open. Remove top shell.
3. Mix softened butter with shallots, garlic, bread crumbs, parsley, basil, and spinach. Beat well.
4. Spread the butter mixture on the mussels. Refrigerate until ready to use.
5. Broil for 2 to 3 minutes or until the butter has melted, or bake at 400 degrees, if you prefer. Serve immediately with French bread for dipping in the butter.

NOTE:

Chop all ingredients except mussels in a food processor. Mussels may be steamed instead of baked before stuffing. This is a good dish to prepare well in advance as it will keep for at least 24 hours.

Sheryl Kuempel
Boulder, Colorado

GREEK PASTRY HORS D'OEUVRES

Yields 5 Dozen
Refrigerate 2 Hours

Preparation 1 1/2 Hours
Freeze 3 Hours
Bake 15 Minutes at 450°F

PASTRY
8 ounces cream cheese
1 cup butter, softened
2 cups sifted flour
FILLING
1 onion, finely diced
3 tablespoons olive oil
1 teaspoon salt
Pepper, tarragon, and Tabasco to taste
1 package (10-ounce) frozen chopped spinach, thawed
1/4 pound feta cheese
1/2 cup cottage cheese
1 egg, beaten

1. Blend cream cheese, butter, and flour to form a smooth dough. Shape into a ball, wrap in plastic wrap, and refrigerate for 2 hours.
2. Sauté onion in olive oil until tender. Add salt, pepper, tarragon, Tabasco, and thawed spinach.
3. Mix remaining cheeses and add beaten egg. Stir, then add to spinach mixture.
4. Roll chilled pastry dough on a floured surface to 1/8-inch thickness. Cut with 2 1/2-inch cookie cutter.
5. Place 1/2 teaspoon filling in center of each round, moisten edges, and fold in half. Press edges with fork and prick top.
6. Freeze on a baking sheet before baking. If they are not to be used immediately, wrap in plastic bags or store in a freezer container. Keep frozen until ready to bake. Do not thaw. Bake for 15 minutes in 450-degree oven. Serve warm.

Millie Anderson
Boulder, Colorado

TIROPETES

Make plenty per person . . . they go like crazy!

Yields 12 Dozen

Preparation 1 Hour
Bake 10 to 15 Minutes at 400°F

3 eggs, beaten
1 pound feta cheese, crumbled
1 pound small curd cottage cheese
1 pound *filo* pastry
1 pound butter, melted

1. Combine beaten eggs and cheeses.
2. Using a wide, soft paint brush, spread a sheet of *filo* pastry with melted butter. (Don't be fussy, but do be quick.) Cut lengthwise into 6 equal strips.
3. Place 1 teaspoon of the cheese mixture at the bottom of the strip about an inch from the edge. Fold one corner over the filling making a triangle, then fold the angle over again and again until the whole strip is folded.
4. Place on ungreased cookie sheet and bake at 400 degrees for 10 to 15 minutes or until puffy and golden brown. Serve piping hot.

NOTE:

Tiropetes can be fully prepared ahead of time and frozen, preferably unbaked. Do not defrost before baking.

VARIATION:

To cheese mixture add sautéed green onion, green pepper, finely chopped garlic, mushrooms, and/or cubed cooked chicken.

Ellen Denton
Piedmont, California

SPRING ROLLS
(*Chả Giò*)

As any housewife will tell you in any language the world over, substitutions are the name of the game. The cook uses what she likes, and what she can find at home, in the garden, and the local market. When it comes to spring rolls, there are all kinds of ingredients which taste good together. Just remember that in Vietnam the tastes of fish and garlic are especially well liked.

Yields 5 Dozen

Preparation 2 Hours

1 to 2 pounds ground pork (or less, depending upon the amounts of other ingredients)
ANY OR ALL OF THE FOLLOWING:
Canned crabmeat, flaked
Canned shrimp pieces
Chinese mushrooms, soaked in hot water 1/2 hour and sliced
Bean threads (cellophane noodles), soaked 1/4 to 1 hour and cut into short lengths (2 ounces dry makes 1/2 cup soaked)
Green onions and tops, chopped
Carrot, shredded
Turnip, peeled, sliced thin, and diced
Bean sprouts, washed, drained, and chopped
Eggs, beaten, cooked like an omelet, chopped
Garlic, crushed
Salt and pepper
Pinch of sugar
Vietnamese rice paper, Philippine pastry wrappers, or Chinese spring roll wrappers
***Nuốc mam* sauce (see Index)**

1. Mix your choice of ingredients thoroughly and let sit for a few minutes to 1/2 hour for tastes to blend.
2. If using rice paper, lightly wet wrapper all over on both sides and lay it gently on a board.
3. Carefully cut wrapper into quarters. Put a little filling near one corner of one piece of wrapper. Roll it in, turning in the sides after the first roll-over so that the filling is entirely enclosed. Continue rolling. Cut off ragged outside edge of rice paper. A little beaten egg may help seal the ends.
4. There are two ways of frying: first, in deep vegetable fat at 350 to 400 degrees several at a time, for 8 to 10 minutes; or second, in 1/2-inch medium-hot oil, turning over often to brown all sides, about 15 minutes until golden and crispy (if the oil is too hot, the filling will not cook through).
5. Drain. Serve hot with *nuốc mam.*

VARIATION:

Serve each roll wrapped individually in a leaf of soft lettuce, with a bit of fresh mint leaf, cucumber strip, and Chinese parsley. Dip each roll in *nuớc mam* sauce just before eating.

NOTE:

1. Chinese dried mushrooms, bean threads, *nuớc mam* sauce, Chinese parsley, and all of the wrappers can be found in an Oriental market or large supermarket.
2. Rolls may be frozen before or after frying.
3. For wetting wrapper, use cold water, warm water, or water with a little egg white. Or use 1/2 cup beer and 1 tablespoon sugar.
4. Spring rolls may be kept warm in oven until ready to eat.
5. Vietnamese rice paper is delicate and much harder to handle than Chinese spring roll wrappers, which are smaller, stronger, and made of wheat dough. While not so tidy, the rice paper roll is definitely superior in crispness and crunchiness.

Indo-China Mobile Education Project
Washington, D.C.

MEXICAN EGG ROLLS

Serves 10 to 12 — Preparation 1 Hour

1 package 6-inch egg roll wrappers or 1 package wonton wrappers
3/4 cup grated Monterey Jack cheese
1/4 cup chopped green chilies
1 tablespoon chopped Jalapeño chili
Oil for deep fat frying

1. If using egg roll wrappers, cut into quarters. Combine cheese and chilies.
2. Turn wrapper with corner pointing toward you. Place one teaspoon of cheese filling in center. Fold in sides first, then roll the wonton away from you.
3. Fry in two inches of oil at 360 degrees a few at a time until they are golden brown. Drain on paper toweling. Serve hot with guacamole (see Index).

NOTE:

The egg roll may be frozen after Step 2 until ready to cook and serve.

Audrey Benedict
Ward, Colorado

VARIATION:

Prepare 1 pound hamburger with taco seasoning mix. Drain meat and cool. Use 1 teaspoon meat and 1/2 teaspoon grated Monterey Jack cheese. Fill, roll, and cook as above.

DANISH-STYLE LIVER PÂTÉ

Serves 10 to 20

Preparation 45 Minutes
Bake 3 Hours at 400°F

1 pound chicken livers, uncooked
3/4 pound pork fat, raw
1 small onion, cut up
1 tablespoon salt
3/4 teaspoon pepper
1/2 teaspoon allspice
1/4 teaspoon ground cloves
2 eggs, beaten
2 cups milk
2 tablespoons cornstarch
2 tablespoons butter

1. Grind together liver, fat, and onion at least three times, or puree in a food processor.
2. Mix into ground ingredients salt, pepper, allspice, cloves, and eggs.
3. Add milk to cornstarch slowly, stirring until smooth.
4. Melt butter in small saucepan, then add cornstarch-milk mixture slowly over medium heat. Cook, stirring constantly, until it boils. Add to ground meat mixture.
5. Shape into 2 pyrex 8 1/2 x 4 1/2 x 2 1/2-inch loaf pans. Cover with foil. Place in larger baking pan filled with 1 to 2 inches hot water.
6. Bake 3 hours at 400 degrees or until pink color is almost gone. Remove foil the last 15 minutes.

NOTE:

Don't pour off liquid after baking. This will soak in and is necessary for a moist pâte'.

Harold Coombes
Avalon, California

OYSTER PÂTÉ

Serves 6 to 8

Preparation 8 Minutes
Bake 30 Minutes at 350°F

1/2 pint oysters, drained
1/2 small onion
Pinch of nutmeg
Salt and pepper to taste
1 egg
4 tablespoons heavy cream
1 tablespoon lemon juice
1 teaspoon butter

1. Combine oysters, onion, nutmeg, salt, pepper, egg, cream, lemon juice, and butter. Blend in a food processor or blender until smooth.
2. Place in a buttered oven-proof dish and cover. Bake in a 350-degree oven for 30 minutes. Serve cold.

Bette Heimann
Boulder, Colorado

SALAMI PÂTÉ

Serves 16 to 20

Preparation 30 Minutes
Refrigerate Overnight

2 pounds salami (Kosher)
1 bunch green onions, cut into small pieces
4 large sprigs parsley
1 cucumber, peeled and grated
16 ounces cream cheese, softened
2 envelopes unflavored gelatin
6 ounces V-8 juice
1/4 cup milk
Cucumber, thinly sliced for garnish

1. Blend salami, onions, and parsley in blender, food processor, or food mill until very fine.
2. Drain the grated cucumber and squeeze dry. Blend with 8 ounces cream cheese. Set aside.
3. Sprinkle 1 1/2 envelopes gelatin over juice. Place over low heat and stir until dissolved. Combine with meat mixture.
4. Oil a loaf pan. Using half the salami mixture, spread a layer on the bottom of the pan, then spread all the cucumber-cream cheese mixture on top. Cover with the remaining salami mixture.
5. Sprinkle remaining 1/2 envelope gelatin over milk in small pan. Over low heat, stir until dissolved. Add remaining cream cheese, beating until smooth. Spread over salami. Chill overnight.
6. Remove from loaf pan for serving and decorate with thin cucumber slices. Serve with pita, rye, or pumpernickel bread.

Frances Kretschmann
Boulder, Colorado

VEGETARIAN PÂTÉ

Serves 8 to 10

Preparation 25 Minutes

1 1/2 to 2 cups French-style green beans, cooked
2 hard-cooked eggs
1/2 cup toasted walnuts
2 tablespoons plain yogurt
1/2 cup minced onion, sauteéd
1 to 2 tablespoons sherry (optional)
Salt and pepper to taste
Dash of nutmeg

1. Combine all ingredients in a blender, food processor, or food mill. Blend until smooth. Chill.

NOTE:

Serve as a dip with crackers. This makes an interesting sandwich sprinkled with chopped fresh onion.

Ilene Kaspar
Boulder, Colorado

CAMEMBERT SPREAD

Serves 12 to 14

Soak Overnight
Preparation 20 Minutes

4 ounces Camembert cheese
1/8 cup dry sherry
4 ounces unsalted butter, room temperature
Chopped parsley

1. Soak Camembert cheese in dry sherry at room temperature overnight.
2. Drain sherry from cheese and save.
3. Beat butter and cheese together until smooth, adding reserved sherry gradually. Chill and decorate with chopped parsley.
4. Serve with thin toast, Norwegian flatbread, and apple slices.

Nancy Cateora
Boulder, Colorado

CHEESE BALL

Serves 12 to 15

Preparation 30 Minutes
Refrigerate 3 Hours

16 ounces cream cheese
1 tablespoon seasoned salt
2 tablespoons finely chopped onion
1/4 cup chopped green pepper
1 can (8 1/4-ounce) crushed pineapple, well drained
1/2 cup chopped nuts

1. Cream cheese with mixer. Add seasoned salt, onion, green pepper, and drained pineapple. Refrigerate 3 hours.
2. Sprinkle nuts on plastic wrap or wax paper. Shape cheese mixture into a ball. Roll in nuts until completely covered.
3. Serve with crackers.

Ruth J. Fink
Boulder, Colorado

SMOKED FISH PÂTÉ

Yields 2 Cups

Preparation 15 Minutes

1/2 pound smoked fish, flaked
1/2 to 3/4 cup butter, melted
Juice of 1/2 lemon or to taste
1/2 teaspoon horseradish sauce, or to taste
1 cup heavy cream, whipped
Salt and pepper to taste
Melba toast or crackers

1. Mix and slightly mash fish, butter, lemon juice, and horseradish sauce or blend briefly in a food processor or blender.

2. Fold in whipped cream. Add salt and pepper to taste.
3. Serve with melba toast or crackers.

NOTE:

1. Use any kind of smoked fish such as mackerel, salmon, whiting, herring or trout.
2. May be made ahead and frozen for later use.

Ann Roberts
Edinburgh, Scotland

SHRIMP SPREAD

Serves 12 to 14

Preparation 30 Minutes
Refrigerate 2 Hours

2 tablespoons unflavored gelatin
1/2 cup cold water
1 can (10 3/4-ounce) tomato soup
6 ounces cream cheese
Salt to taste
1 cup mayonnaise
3/4 cup finely chopped green onions
3/4 cup finely chopped celery
9 ounces shrimp, canned or frozen, cooked, cleaned, and deveined

1. Soak gelatin in cold water.
2. Bring soup to boil and add gelatin, cream cheese, and salt. Stir until smooth. Cool.
3. Fold in mayonnaise, onions, celery, and crumbled shrimp.
4. Pour into oiled 1 1/2-quart mold and refrigerate 2 hours.

Rose Arno
Avalon, California

CRAB SPREAD

Serves 12

Preparation 20 Minutes
Refrigerate 24 Hours

12 ounces cream cheese
2 tablespoons Worcestershire sauce
2 teaspoons mayonnaise
1 tablespoon lemon juice
6 ounces chili sauce
1 can (6 1/2-ounce) crab meat, canned or frozen
Parsley flakes

1. Blend cream cheese, Worcestershire sauce, mayonnaise, and lemon juice and spread on round platter.
2. Top with chili sauce and crumble crab on top. Sprinkle with parsley flakes. Cover and refrigerate 24 hours.

Ginger Resseguie
Boulder, Colorado

CAVIAR SPREAD

Serves 8

Preparation 20 Minutes
Chill 2 Hours

8 ounces cream cheese
1/4 cup sour cream
2 tablespoons finely chopped onion
1 jar (3 1/2-ounce) black lump fish caviar
2 hard-cooked eggs
2 tablespoons chopped parsley
Melba toast

1. Cream together cream cheese, sour cream, and onion.
2. Carefully fold in caviar, reserving 1 teaspoon for garnish.
3. Spread on shallow bowl or plate (about 8-inch diameter). Cover with plastic wrap and chill 2 hours.
4. Finely chop egg whites and set aside. Press yolks through fine sieve. Chill separately.
5. To serve, garnish top of spread with circles of parsley, egg whites, and yolks. Place reserved caviar in center. Serve with melba toast or Norwegian flat bread.

NOTE:

To make delicious melba toast, cut crusts off very thin sliced bread. Cut each slice into thirds and place on baking sheet in a single layer. Put in 200-degree oven for 1/2 hour. Increase to 250 degrees for another 1/2 hour. They should be nicely brown. Cool and store well wrapped.

Cicely Kane
Boulder, Colorado

HUNGARIAN CHEESE SPREAD (*Korozott*)

Serves 12

Preparation 10 Minutes

8 ounces cream cheese, softened
1/2 cup butter, softened
3 tablespoons sour cream
4 ounces feta cheese, crumbled
1 tablespoon prepared mustard
4 green onions, chopped
2 teaspoons Hungarian paprika
1 teaspoon caraway seeds
1/2 teaspoon salt
1 teaspoon capers to garnish

1. Mix together cream cheese and butter. Add sour cream, feta cheese, mustard, onions, paprika, caraway seeds, and salt. Blend well.
2. Shape into a smooth mound on a serving plate. Garnish with capers.

Marilyn Peltzer
Boulder, Colorado

CURRY DIP

Yields 3 Cups

Preparation 5 Minutes

2 cups mayonnaise
1/2 cup sour cream or yogurt
1/4 teaspoon turmeric
2 tablespoons curry powder
2 cloves garlic, crushed, or 1/2 teaspoon garlic powder
4 teaspoons sugar
2 teaspoons salt
2 teaspoons lemon juice
1/4 cup parsley, minced

1. Stir together mayonnaise, sour cream, turmeric, curry powder, garlic, sugar, salt, lemon juice, and parsley.

NOTE:

Best prepared two hours ahead. Serve with vegetables such as cauliflower, zucchini, cherry tomatoes, radishes, celery, carrots, mushrooms, eggplant slices, turnip slices, Brussels sprouts, etc. Keeps well in refrigerator.

Mikki Matheson
Boulder, Colorado

EGG DIP

Serves 8 to 10

Preparation 20 Minutes

3/4 cup mayonnaise
2 tablespoons butter
3/4 teaspoon Worcestershire sauce
1 tablespoon lemon juice
Dash of Tabasco
3 teaspoons Dijon mustard
1 tablespoon grated onion
1/4 teaspoon pepper
1 1/4 teaspoon celery salt
8 hard-cooked eggs

1. Using a food processor, blender, or food mill, mix mayonnaise, butter, Worcestershire sauce, lemon juice, Tabasco, mustard, onion, pepper, and celery salt. Add eggs and blend until very smooth. Chill.
2. Serve as a dip with fresh vegetables.

NOTE:

This is an excellent appetizer for a summer barbecue. This dip can also be used as a deviled egg filling or as a sandwich spread.

Deborah Taylor
Boulder, Colorado

GREEK *SKORDALIA* SAUCE

Skordalia *means garlic.*

Serves 8 to 10 | Preparation 40 Minutes

1 pound (3 medium) potatoes
2 teaspoons crushed garlic
1/2 teaspoon salt
1/2 cup oil
1/2 cup olive oil
1/3 to 1/2 cup vinegar
Cooked beets or raw vegetables

1. Boil potatoes until tender. Peel.
2. Mash potatoes together with garlic and salt until smooth.
3. Alternately, one teaspoon at a time, whip in oils and vinegar. Chill. Serve with cooked beets or as a dip with raw vegetables.

NOTE:

Instant potatoes may be substituted. This sauce may be made a few days before serving. If oil separates, beat again.

Bette Heimann
Boulder, Colorado

GUACAMOLE

Serves 6 | Preparation 10 Minutes

2 ripe avocados, finely diced
1 tomato, peeled and finely diced
1 tablespoon finely chopped onion
1 clove garlic, minced (optional)
1 tablespoon green chilies
1 1/2 teaspoon salt
1/4 teaspoon black pepper
1/4 teaspoon cayenne pepper
1 teaspoon chopped fresh coriander
2 tablespoons lemon or lime juice
Flour tortillas, fried

1. Mix together avocados, tomato, onion, garlic, green chilies, salt, peppers, and fresh coriander. Add lemon or lime juice. Stir and chill. Serve with fried flour tortillas.

Jay Marks
Houston, Texas

MEXICAN LAYERED DIP

Serves 10 to 20

Preparation 1 Hour

1 can (30-ounce) refried beans
1 package (1 1/2-ounce) dry taco mix
3 avocados, mashed
1 tablespoon lemon juice
1 cup sour cream
1/4 teaspoon salt
1/8 teaspoon pepper
3 medium tomatoes, chopped
12 green onions, diced
1 can (4-ounce) diced green chilies
1 cup grated Cheddar cheese
1 cup grated Monterey Jack cheese
1 head lettuce, shredded
1 can (6-ounce) olives, sliced
Crisp tortilla chips

1. Mix refried beans with dry taco mix and set aside. Mix avocados with lemon juice, sour cream, salt, and pepper. Set aside. Mix tomatoes with green onions and chilies. Mix cheeses.
2. Layer ingredients on a large platter in the following order: shredded lettuce, bean mixture, avocado-sour cream mixture, tomato mixture. Top with cheeses and olives. Serve with tortilla chips.

Ellen Denton
Piedmont, California

BLEU CHEESE CHEESECAKE

Serves 15 to 20
Refrigerate 3 Hours

Preparation 20 Minutes
Bake 50 to 55 Minutes at 300°F

16 ounces cream cheese
8 ounces bleu cheese
2 cups sour cream
3 large eggs
1/8 teaspoon white pepper
Crackers

1. In a large bowl, beat cream cheese and bleu cheese with electric mixer until well blended.
2. Add 2/3 cup sour cream, eggs, and pepper and beat until smooth.
3. Pour into 9-inch spring-form pan and bake 40 to 45 minutes at 300 degrees or until a toothpick inserted in center comes out clean. Cool 5 minutes.
4. Stir remaining sour cream and spread carefully on top of cheese cake.
5. Bake 8 to 10 minutes longer. Cool completely. Chill 3 hours or more. Serve with crackers.

NOTE:

To freeze, cut into quarters and wrap tightly in freezer wrap. Will keep up to 6 weeks. Return to room temperature before serving.

Marcia Cutter
Lubbock, Texas

HOT SPINACH DIP

Serves 12 to 15

Preparation 20 Minutes

- **2 packages (10-ounce each) frozen, chopped spinach**
- **2 tablespoons chopped onion**
- **4 tablespoons butter or margarine, melted**
- **4 to 6 ounces hot pepper cheese, grated**
- **2 tablespoons flour**
- **1/2 cup evaporated milk**
- **1/2 teaspoon pepper**
- **3/4 teaspoon garlic salt**
- **1 teaspoon Worcestershire sauce**
- **1/2 cup water from spinach**
- **3/4 teaspoon celery salt**
- **Corn chips, crackers or fried flour tortillas**

1. Cook spinach following package directions, drain, and reserve water.
2. Cook onion in butter, add to spinach along with cheese, flour, milk, and remaining ingredients except corn chips. Heat, stirring occasionally over low heat in medium saucepan until cheese is melted and mixture is creamy.
3. Serve hot with chips or crackers or fried flour tortillas.

NOTE:

The dip can be made ahead and reheated. It also freezes well.

Vallie Burke
Avalon, California

SAUSAGE DIP

Yields 4 Cups

Preparation 25 Minutes

- **1 pound ground pork sausage**
- **1 medium onion, chopped fine**
- **1/2 pound mushrooms, sliced thin**
- **1 cup sour cream**
- **1 1/2 tablespoons flour**
- **3/4 cup milk**
- **1 tablespoon Worcestershire sauce**
- **1 teaspoon soy sauce**
- **1 teaspoon paprika**
- **Potato or corn chips**

1. Cook sausage in skillet, crumbling with fork until sausage is browned. Drain on paper toweling.
2. Add onions and mushrooms to fat in skillet, and cook until onions are soft, stirring well. Drain fat and add drained sausage.
3. In small bowl, gradually add sour cream to flour (this prevents curdling). Stir in milk and seasonings then add to sausage in skillet.
4. Cook over moderate heat until thickened.
5. To serve, transfer to a chafing dish and serve hot with potato chips or corn chips.

Deborah Taylor
Boulder, Colorado

SOUPS

BASIC CHICKEN BROTH

Preparation 25 Minutes
Cook 3 Hours

2 chickens, 3 pounds each, whole or pieces
3 1/2 to 4 quarts water
4 carrots, sliced
4 stalks celery, including tops, sliced
4 onions, sliced
2 leeks, white part only, sliced
Salt and pepper
Bouquet Garni
2 whole cloves

1. Put chicken into 8- to 10-quart pot and cover with water. Bring to a boil and skim foam that may appear.
2. Add vegetables and seasonings. Simmer uncovered for 2 to 2 1/2 hours.
3. Strain. Discard vegetables. Remove meat, discard skin, and save for salad or casserole. Freeze if not used within a day or two.
4. Chill strained stock and remove fat.
5. Freeze in 1- or 2-cup portions any stock you do not use within a week. Always bring stored stock to a boil before using in a recipe.

NOTE:

Bouquet Garni is used to flavor soups, stocks, and sauces. Fold fresh parsley around thyme and a bay leaf and tie with cotton string. If only dried herbs are available, tie the parsley, thyme, and bay leaf in a small piece of cheesecloth.

BEEF BROTH

Preparation 40 Minutes
Cook 6 Hours

8 pounds beef soup bones, with or without meat, cut into 2-inch pieces
1 pound beef marrow bones
3 tablespoons butter
3 onions, chopped
3 large carrots, chopped
1 clove garlic
8 quarts water
1 turnip, peeled, quartered
3 whole cloves
2 stalks celery, chopped
8 peppercorns
1 medium bay leaf
1/2 teaspoon dried thyme leaves
6 parsley sprigs

1. Using large shallow roasting pan, brown bones in 500-degree oven. Turn occasionally. Brown to a deep rich color but do not burn.
2. In 12-quart pot, melt butter and brown onion, carrot and garlic. Add water, turnip, cloves, celery, peppercorns, bay leaf, thyme, and parsley. Bring to a boil, reduce heat and simmer, uncovered, for 4 hours. Skim foam as it forms.
3. Strain broth into 4- to 5-quart sauce pan. Return to a simmer, reduce to about one half. Cool then refrigerate.
4. Store in refrigerator 2 to 3 days. Freeze any unused portion in 1 cup quantities. Remove fat before freezing.

HOT AND SOUR SOUP

Serves 6

Preparation 45 Minutes
Cook 15 Minutes

4 dried Chinese mushrooms
2 tablespoons tiger lily buds
2 tablespons dried cloud ears
1/4 pound pork or chicken
3 tablespoons cornstarch
2 teaspoons dry sherry
1/2 cup water
1 cake bean curd
4 tablespoons Chinese rice-wine vinegar
1/2 teaspoon ground white pepper
1/2 teaspoon Chinese hot oil
2 teaspoons Chinese or Japanese sesame oil
1 quart chicken broth
1 tablespoon soy sauce
1 egg, beaten
3 scallions, chopped

1. Soak mushrooms, lily buds, and cloud ears in warm water for about 20 minutes. Drain.
2. While dry ingredients are soaking, cut meat into matchstick-size pieces. Mix one tablespoon cornstarch with dry sherry. Add to pork or chicken.
3. Slice mushroom caps in thin strips, shred cloud ears, and cut tiger lily buds into thirds.
4. Mix remaining cornstarch with water and set aside.
5. Cut bean curd into small cubes.
6. Mix together vinegar, pepper, hot oil, and sesame oil and set aside.
7. Bring chicken broth and soy sauce to a boil in a 2- to 3-quart saucepan.
8. Add pork or chicken mixture and boil for 2 minutes. Add cloud ears, tiger lily buds, mushrooms, and bean curd. Boil 1 minute more.
9. Add cornstarch and water mixture and stir to thicken.
10. Add vinegar mixture. Slowly stir in beaten egg. Garnish with scallions.

NOTE:

The Chinese ingredients for this soup are available in most large supermarkets or in Oriental grocery stores.

Sheryl Kuempel
Boulder, Colorado

VIETNAMESE SOUR SOUP
(*Canh Chua*)

Serves 6 to 10

Preparation 15 Minutes
Cook 30 Minutes

- **1 tablespoon oil**
- **1 small onion, chopped**
- **1 clove garlic, finely chopped**
- **1 can (8-ounce) crushed unsweetened pineapple**
- **1 can (16-ounce) tomatoes**
- **1 small bunch celery including leaves, sliced diagonally**
- **5 cups water or chicken broth**
- **1/4 cup fish sauce or soy sauce**
- **1 teaspoon salt**
- **1 teaspoon sugar**
- **1 teaspoon crushed fresh ginger root**
- **2 teaspoons basil**
- **3 ounces (or more) fresh tomatoes, cut in wedges**
- **3 green onions, including tops, chopped**

1. Heat oil in soup pot. Saute' onion until golden. Add garlic and saute' another minute.
2. Add pineapple, first batch of tomatoes, celery, and water. Bring to boil.
3. Season with fish or soy sauce, salt, sugar, ginger root, and basil. Cook 10 to 15 minutes or until celery is barely cooked and not limp.
4. Add fresh tomatoes and green onions and remove from heat.

VARIATION:

Fresh tomatoes (cut into wedges) and small cubes of fresh pineapple may be used in place of canned ingredients. If desired, fresh bean curd cut into squares may be added at the last minute, or add shrimp and cook until just done.

NOTE:

Fish sauce is an essential ingredient to Vietnamese cooking and is used in much the same way as light soy sauce. It is produced by fermentation of salted fresh fish. Fish sauce is available in most Oriental groceries and supermarkets in large cities.

Indo-China Mobile Education Project
Washington, D.C.

ENDIVE SOUP

Serves 6 to 8

Preparation 20 Minutes
Cook 1 1/4 Hours

1 pound hot Italian sausage
1 large or 2 small heads of endive
4 cloves garlic, finely chopped
Salt, pepper, oregano to taste
Parsley (optional)
8 eggs
Parmesan cheese, grated

1. Cut sausage in bite-size pieces and boil in water to cover in a 4-quart soup pot for 1/2 hour.
2. Add cleaned and broken endive, garlic, salt, pepper, oregano, and parsley. Cook 1/2 hour.
3. Beat eggs and add Parmesan cheese until consistency of heavy cream.
4. Add to soup mixture and heat. It may look curdled, but it is not.

Joanne Steele
Boulder, Colorado

SAUERKRAUT SOUP

This is a traditional Polish recipe, usually served on Christmas Eve (Wiglia). It is also a terrific cold weather dish.

Serves 8

Preparation 25 Minutes
Cook 2 1/2 Hours

1 pound sauerkraut, rinsed
4 quarts water
1 pound fresh pork butt, fresh pork hocks, or spareribs (cut up)
1 small onion, chopped
1 tablespoon butter
1/4 cup barley
4 medium potatoes, peeled and cubed
Salt and pepper to taste
Pinch of caraway seed (optional)

1. Add sauerkraut to 2 quarts water in a 3-quart pot and bring to boil. Reduce heat, simmer for 5 minutes, and drain.
2. Bring remaining 2 quarts water to a boil in a 4- to 5-quart pot and add the meat. Skim off any foam that forms after water boils. Reduce heat.
3. Saute' chopped onion in butter.
4. Add sauerkraut, barley, and saute'ed onion to soup. Simmer approximately 2 hours, adding cubed potatoes during last hour of cooking. Add salt and pepper to taste; add caraway seed, if desired.

Mary Juszynski
Louisville, Colorado

TEXAS (HOT) VEGETABLE SOUP

Serves 6 to 8

Preparation 40 Minutes
Cook 10 Hours

3/4 to 1 pound beef soup bones with some meat
1 large onion, chopped
1 can (46-ounce) V-8 juice
3 stalks celery, chopped
1 turnip, diced
3 carrots, sliced
1 tablespoon Worcestershire sauce
1/2 teaspoon Tabasco (optional)
1 teaspoon beef bouillon granules
1/2 teaspoon oregano
2 small potatoes, cubed

1. In a large frying pan, brown soup bones. Transfer to a 3 1/2-quart crockpot. Then brown onion in same pan and add to soup bones.
2. With crockpot turned to high, pour V-8 juice over meat. Add celery, turnip, carrots, Worcestershire sauce, Tabasco, beef granules, potatoes, and oregano. Cover. After soup comes to a boil, reduce heat to low and continue to cook 8 to 10 hours (overnight or all day).
3. Skim off excess fat and remove bones. Return all meat to soup.

NOTE:

Bones may be browned in a very hot oven, turning occasionally.

LIMA MINESTRONE

Serves 6 to 8

Preparation 10 Minutes
Cook 30 Minutes

1/2 cup chopped onion
1 tablespoon butter or margarine
5 cups chicken broth
3/4 teaspoon salt
1/2 teaspoon Italian herb seasoning
1/4 teaspoon basil, crumbled
1 package (10-ounce) frozen chopped spinach or 10 ounces fresh spinach
1 package (10-ounce) frozen baby lima beans
1/4 cup small pasta
1 can (16-ounce) tomatoes

1. Saute' onion lightly in butter.
2. Add broth, salt, herb seasoning, and basil. Heat to boiling.
3. Add spinach and lima beans. Heat until vegetables can be broken.
4. Add pasta and simmer 10 minutes or until pasta is done.
5. Add tomatoes, breaking up large pieces. Heat through.

NOTE:

Italian herb seasoning is a commercial product. One-eighth teaspoon each of oregano, thyme, rosemary, and marjoram may be substituted.

MINESTRONE SOUP

Serves 8 to 10
Soak Overnight

Preparation 40 Minutes
Cook 2 Hours

- 3/4 cup large white beans, soaked overnight
- 1 quart water
- 1/4 pound salt pork, chopped
- 1/4 cup lentils
- 2 quarts beef broth
- 1 medium onion, chopped
- 3/4 cup tomato puree
- 2 stalks celery, diced
- 1 zucchini, sliced
- 3/4 cup diced carrots
- 1/2 cup canned garbanzo beans, drained
- 1 bay leaf
- 1 1/4 cups diced potatoes
- Salt and pepper to taste
- 1 cup green peas, fresh or frozen
- 1/4 cup ditali or thin spaghetti
- Parmesan cheese (optional)

1. Combine water and salt pork in a large kettle. Bring to a boil, reduce heat, and simmer 10 to 15 minutes.
2. Add soaked beans and lentils and simmer approximately 1 hour or until beans are tender.
3. Add beef broth, onion, tomato puree, celery, zucchini, carrots, garbanzo beans, and bay leaf and cook 20 minutes.
4. Add potatoes and salt and pepper to taste. Simmer until vegetables are tender.
5. Add peas and ditali during the last 10 minutes of cooking time. If soup becomes too thick, thin with water. Serve hot or cold, sprinkled with Parmesan cheese if desired.

Barbara Moore
Avalon, California

OXTAIL SOUP

Serves 8 to 10

Preparation 30 Minutes
Cook 51/2 Hours

- 2 pounds oxtail
- 2 to 4 tablespoons butter
- 1/2 cup diced onion
- 4 cups water
- 2 beef bouillon cubes
- 21/2 cups tomato juice
- 1 teaspoon salt
- 4 peppercorns or 1/8 teaspoon pepper
- 1 cup chopped parsley
- 1 cup sliced carrots
- 1 cup sliced celery
- 1 bay leaf
- 1 can (6-ounce) tomato paste or 1/2 cup catsup
- 1/2 teaspoon each thyme, marjoram, and basil
- 2 tablespoons butter
- 1 tablespoon flour
- 1/4 to 1/2 cup Madeira

1. Brown oxtail in butter in a 4- to 5-quart pot, push to one side, add onion and brown.
2. Add water, beef bouillon, tomato juice, salt, and pepper. Simmer a minimum of 41/2 hours.

3. Skim off excess fat and add parsley, carrots, celery, bay leaf, tomato paste, thyme, marjoram, and basil. Simmer until vegetables are tender.
4. Remove oxtail and take meat off bones. Return meat to soup.
5. In a small pan, melt butter, add flour, and stir until brown. Add some broth to the flour-butter and mix. Pour into soup and stir.
6. Correct seasoning. Add Madeira. Serve.

NOTE:

Serve with bread and salad. May be frozen and reheated.

Jan Osterweil
Boulder, Colorado

LENTIL SOUP

Serves 10 to 12 — Preparation 25 Minutes
Soak Overnight — Cook 1 3/4 Hours

1 1/2 cups dry lentils, soaked overnight
5 slices bacon, finely chopped
1 medium onion, chopped
1 cup diced carrots
2 cups chopped celery
1/2 clove garlic, finely chopped
2 cups diced potatoes
1/2 cup tomato puree
2 whole cloves
2 bay leaves
6 cups cold water
4 cups beef broth
1 tablespoon salt
Dash white pepper
1 large smoked ham hock, cut in three pieces by butcher
2 tablespoons red wine vinegar
1 cup thinly sliced leeks

1. Cover lentils with water and soak overnight. Drain.
2. In a 6-quart kettle, sauté the bacon. Add onion, carrots, celery, and garlic and cook for a few minutes.
3. Add the drained lentils, potatoes, tomato puree, cloves, bay leaves, water, beef broth, seasonings, and smoked ham hock.
4. Simmer, covered, for about 1 1/2 hours or until lentils are tender.
5. Remove the ham hock and add vinegar and leeks.
6. Shred the meat from the ham hock and add to soup. Correct seasonings if necessary.

VARIATION:

1 1/2 pounds *kielbasa* (Polish sausage) in one-inch slices may be substituted for the smoked ham hock.

NOTE:

Serve with French bread and salad for a hearty, quick supper. Leftovers freeze beautifully.

Joan Mason
Boulder, Colorado

MEXICAN SOUP

Serves 4

Preparation 10 Minutes
Cook 30 Minutes

2 tablespoons margarine
2 medium potatoes, diced
1/2 cup chopped onion
1 can (4-ounce) green chilies cut into strips
2 cups water
1 can (16-ounce) whole tomatoes
1 egg
1/2 pound Longhorn cheese, cut into strips
Salt and pepper to taste

1. Melt margarine in large saucepan. Add potatoes, onion, and green chilies. Fry for 5 minutes.
2. Add water, cover, and simmer until potatoes are almost done (about 15 minutes).
3. Add tomatoes with juice, crushing them with a spoon. Stir in egg, breaking yolk.
4. Simmer 2 to 3 minutes, then add cheese strips. Stir until cheese melts.
5. Add salt and pepper to taste.

Karen MacDonald
Golden, Colorado

TORTILLA SOUP

Serves 8 to 10

Preparation 10 Minutes
Cook 30 Minutes

1 can (16-ounce) tomatoes
1 large onion, quartered
2 cloves garlic
3 tablespoons fresh cilantro leaves or parsley
1/4 teaspoon sugar
6 cups chicken broth
1/2 teaspoon chervil
Salt to taste
Oil for frying
9 8-inch corn tortillas
8 ounces Monterey Jack cheese, grated

1. Combine canned tomatoes (including juice), onions, garlic, cilantro or parsley, and sugar in blender or food processor. Blend until almost smooth.
2. Pour into 3- to 4-quart saucepan, add chicken broth and chervil, and bring to a simmer. Cover and cook 20 minutes. Salt to taste.
3. While soup is cooking, cut tortillas into 1/2-inch-wide strips. Fry strips in hot oil 1/2-inch deep until crisp and lightly browned. Drain on paper toweling.

4. Divide fried tortilla strips and cheese among soup bowls and ladle in soup. Serve immediately.

NOTE:

Cilantro has a unique flavor and is also sold as coriander, Chinese parsley and Italian parsley. Never substitute coriander powder or coriander seed in a recipe that calls for fresh coriander. The flavors are not the same.

Barbara Ogarrio
Half Moon Bay, California

LEON'S CHICKEN CURRY SOUP

Serves 10 to 12

Preparation 30 Minutes
Cook 2 1/2 Hours

1 chicken, 2 pounds
1 quart water
4 teaspoons chicken bouillon granules
3 onions, coarsely diced
1 celery stalk, coarsely diced
1 carrot, diced
1 teaspoon chopped parsley
Pinch of thyme
3/4 cup crushed vermicelli
3 cups milk
1/2 teaspoon salt
2 tablespoons butter or margarine
3 teaspoons curry powder
2 tablespoons cornstarch

1. Using a 5-quart pot, combine chicken, water, and bouillon granules. Cover and simmer 1 1/2 hours.
2. Remove chicken, cool slightly, debone, and set aside.
3. To the broth add 2 diced onion, celery, carrot, parsley, and thyme. Bring back to simmer, and cook 30 minutes.
4. Add vermicelli and cook 10 minutes.
5. Stir in 2 cups milk and salt, bring back to a boil, then remove from heat.
6. In medium skillet, sauté remaining onion in butter or margarine until lightly browned. Add curry powder, stir, then add to soup along with deboned chicken.
7. Stir cornstarch into remaining milk, add to soup. Return to heat and bring to a boil stirring constantly. Adjust seasonings.

NOTE:

Curry fans will enjoy this soup with the stronger, imported curry powders.

Leon Karels
Aurora, Colorado

CARROT AND ORANGE SOUP

Serves 8 to 10

Preparation 30 Minutes
Cook 30 Minutes

2 ounces butter (or 4 tablespoons olive oil if soup is to be served cold)
10 to 12 medium carrots, coarsely chopped
2 medium onions, coarsely chopped
2 large leeks (white part only), coarsely chopped
10 cups chicken broth
2 oranges, juice of both and grated rind of one
1 1/2 to 2 teaspoons curry powder
2 cloves garlic, crushed
Salt and freshly ground pepper
2 teaspoons brown sugar

1. Gently heat the butter (or oil) in large heavy pan. Add vegetables and gently "sweat" them for 10 minutes with pan covered. Do not let them brown.
2. Add broth, orange juice, rind, curry powder, and garlic. Season lightly with salt and pepper. Continue to cook until carrots are tender.
3. Puree soup in blender, food processor, or food mill. Soup should not be too thick.
4. Reheat and add brown sugar.
5. Chill well if serving cold.

Deborah Taylor
Boulder, Colorado

POTATO AND GARLIC SOUP

Serves 6 to 8

Preparation 20 Minutes
Cook 1 Hour

4 tablespoons butter
2 leeks (white part only), cleaned and sliced
15 large cloves of garlic, peeled
2 pounds potatoes, peeled and cubed
6 cups chicken broth (or part water)
1 teaspoon salt (or to taste)
1 cup milk or cream

1. Melt 2 tablespoons of butter in a large, heavy-bottomed pot and sauté leeks and garlic. Cook over low heat for several minutes.
2. Add potatoes, broth, and salt and allow to come to a boil. Cover pot and simmer 45 minutes to an hour.
3. Remove potatoes and garlic cloves from pot, reserving broth. Puree a small amount at a time in a blender, food processor, or food mill. When smooth, return to broth, adding water if too thick.
4. Add milk or cream and heat. Add remaining 2 tablespoons butter and mix into soup.

Caryl Kassoy
Boulder, Colorado

CLAM CHOWDER

Serves 6 to 8

Preparation 25 Minutes
Cook 25 Minutes

6 slices lean bacon, diced
2 large onions, diced
3/4 cup butter
3 potatoes, peeled and finely diced
2 tablespoons minced parsley
1/8 teaspoon pepper
1 bottle (8-ounce) clam juice
5 cans (6 1/2-ounce each) chopped clams
1 quart half-and-half or milk

1. In a 4-quart saucepan, brown bacon, add onions, and cook in the bacon drippings until translucent. Drain.
2. Add half of the butter, potatoes, parsley, pepper, bottled clam juice, and the drained juice from canned clams. Simmer until potatoes are soft.
3. Add clams, stir until heated.
4. Add half-and-half and remaining butter. Stir until very hot but do not boil.

Jacqui Goeldner
Boulder, Colorado

CREAM OF AVOCADO SOUP

Serves 5

Preparation 10 Minutes

2 large or 3 small avocados
2 cups half-and-half
2 cups chicken broth
1 tablespoon lemon juice
1/2 teaspoon salt
1/8 teaspoon white pepper
Dillweed, fresh or dried, to garnish

1. Peel avocados and remove seeds.
2. In blender or food processor add avocados, half-and-half, chicken broth, lemon juice, salt, and pepper and blend until smooth.
3. Chill well and garnish with dillweed.

NOTE:

Wonderful served as first course for any chicken entrée.

Alison Husted
Boulder, Colorado

LEEK SOUP

This is a delicious Belgian soup.

Serves 4

Preparation 30 Minutes
Cook 45 Minutes

6 leeks, cut in 1/2-inch lengths
2 cups chicken or beef broth
2 cups water
4 medium potatoes, quartered
1 head Boston lettuce, finely shredded
1/2 cup chopped sorrel or spinach
1/4 cup chopped fresh chervil or 1 tablespoon dried chervil
1/8 teaspoon dried savory
Salt and pepper to taste
4 tablespoons heavy cream

1. Wash leeks by placing cut lengths in a bowl of cold water and swish around. Repeat until there is no more dirt in bowl. Drain.
2. In a soup pot cook leeks in broth and water for 30 minutes.
3. Add potatoes; cook 15 minutes, then mash coarsely.
4. Add lettuce, sorrel, chervil, savory, salt, and pepper. Heat to boiling but do not boil.
5. Taste to correct seasoning.
6. Serve very hot with one tablespoon heavy cream at the bottom of each bowl.

Marilyn Peltzer
Boulder, Colorado

CHEESY MUSHROOM SOUP

Serves 6

Preparation 20 Minutes
Cook 20 Minutes

6 tablespoons margarine or butter
1 cup diced onion
1/2 pound mushrooms, sliced
4 tablespoons flour
3/4 tablespoon dry mustard
1/2 teaspoon pepper
2 cups beef broth
2 cups milk
1/2 pound Cheddar cheese, grated
1 large carrot, finely shredded
3 tablespoons chopped parsley
Salt and pepper to taste

1. Melt margarine or butter in 4-quart pot; add onion and mushrooms. Cook, stirring until onion is limp and mushroom liquid evaporates.
2. Mix flour, mustard, and pepper and stir into mushroom mixture.
3. Add beef broth, bring to boil, and stir until thickened.
4. Off heat, stir in milk, cheese, carrot, and parsley. Add salt and pepper to taste.

Frances Kretschmann
Boulder, Colorado

ZUCCHINI BISQUE

Serves 12

Preparation 15 minutes
Cook 30 minutes

2 cups chicken broth
2 1/2 pounds unpeeled zucchini, sliced
1 medium onion, chopped
1/4 pound margarine
Dash of nutmeg
Salt and pepper to taste
1/2 cup half-and-half

1. In 3- to 4-quart saucepan, bring chicken broth to a gentle boil and add zucchini, onion, margarine, nutmeg, salt, and pepper. Cook 20 to 30 minutes.
2. Puree in blender or food processor in 2 batches.
3. Add half-and-half. Stir to blend.
4. Serve hot or cold.

VARIATION:

1. Add 1/4 to 1/3 cup white wine in Step 1.
2. For spinach soup, use two 10-ounce packages frozen spinach in place of zucchini.
3. For broccoli soup, use 1 1/4 pounds broccoli, chopped. Save a few flowerets for garnish.
4. You may also substitute cauliflower, carrots, and celery, using about 2 pounds of any vegetable.

Frances T. Newberry
Boulder, Colorado

CHEESE-VEGETABLE CHOWDER

Serves 8

Preparation 20 Minutes
Cook 30 Minutes

1 cup thinly sliced carrots
1/2 cup margarine
2 cups chopped cabbage
1 cup sliced onion
1 cup chopped celery
1 cup frozen peas
1 can (16-ounce) cream style corn
2 1/2 cups milk
1 teaspoon salt
Dash pepper
1/4 teaspoon thyme
10 ounces Cheddar cheese, shredded

1. In a large Dutch oven, sauté carrots in margarine 5 minutes, then add cabbage, onion, celery, and peas and sauté 8 to 10 minutes more or until tender, stirring often.
2. Add corn, milk, and seasonings.
3. Heat at low temperature, stirring frequently. Add cheese, stir until melted.

Jane Wilson
Boulder, Colorado

MIDDLE EASTERN COLD SUMMER SOUP

Serves 6 to 8 | Preparation 15 Minutes

1/4 cup chopped walnuts
1/2 cup raisins, chopped
1/4 cup chopped green onions
1 cup finely chopped, peeled cucumbers, including small seeds
3 cups plain yogurt
2 sprigs mint, or 1/4 teaspoon dried mint
2 sprigs basil, or 1/4 teaspoon dried basil
1/4 teaspoon dried savory
1/2 teaspoon salt

1. Mix walnuts, raisins, onions, and cucumbers together.
2. Beat yogurt until smooth. Add cucumber mixture, mint, basil, savory, and salt. Chill.

NOTE:

Cold Summer Soup makes a good light lunch when small pieces of pumpernickel bread are added just before serving. Using only enough yogurt to moisten mixture, this recipe may be served as a summer salad.

Colleen K. Garnsey
Boulder, Colorado

VARIATION:

To the same amount of walnuts, raisins, onions, cucumbers (grated), and yogurt, add 1 cup water, 1/2 cup half-and-half, and the following spices for those mentioned above: 1 tablespoon chopped fresh dill weed (1 teaspoon dry), 1 tablespoon chopped fresh parsley (1/4 teaspoon dry), 1/2 teaspoon pepper, and 2 teaspoons salt.

NOTE:

For a heartier soup, add 1 or 2 hard-cooked eggs, chopped, and increase the chopped walnuts to 1/2 cup. Soup may be made one day in advance. If sour cream is preferred to yogurt, substitute 1 1/2 cups sour cream and enough water to make a good consistency.

Larry Chartrand
Boulder, Colorado

GAZPACHO

Serves 6 or more

Preparation 45 Minutes
Refrigerate 2 Hours

6 large ripe tomatoes
1 sweet red pepper or 1 green pepper
4 small cucumbers, unpeeled
2 tablespoons grated carrots
2 tablespoons fresh lemon juice
1 clove garlic, mashed
2 tablespoons finely grated onion
Dash of cayenne and black pepper
Salt to taste
Watercress to garnish

1. Chop tomatoes and red or green pepper.
2. Cut cucumbers lengthwise, scoop out and discard seeds. Chop cucumbers and mix with the remaining ingredients in a 2-quart glass bowl, adding cayenne, black pepper, and salt to taste.
3. Chill and serve very cold, preferably in glass bowls.
4. Garnish with sprigs of watercress.

NOTE:

A food processor will reduce preparation time.

Esther deOnis
Boulder, Colorado

CHILLED PAW PAW SOUP

Serves 8

Preparation 15 Minutes
Refrigerate 2 Hours

1 quart chicken broth
1 pint sour cream
1 can (12-ounce) papaya nectar
1/2 cup finely chopped fresh papaya
1 tablespoon lemon rind
1 tablespoon lemon juice
1 teaspoon salt
Slices of papaya to garnish

1. Mix broth, sour cream, nectar, papaya, lemon rind, lemon juice, and salt. Chill thoroughly.
2. Serve in soup cups garnished with papaya slices.

NOTE:

Apricot nectar can be substituted for papaya nectar and melon for papaya.

Susannah Jordan
Jamestown, Colorado

COLD RASPBERRY SOUP

Serves 6 to 8
Refrigerate 2 Hours

Preparation 10 Minutes
Cook 20 Minutes

1 tablespoon cornstarch
1 cup cold water
1 1/2 cups rose'wine
2 packages (10-ounce each) frozen raspberries
1/2 cup sour cream

1. Combine cornstarch and water, stir in wine, and bring to a simmer over low heat. Cook until thickened.
2. Add frozen raspberries and stir until raspberries are thawed and soup is cool. Refrigerate at least 2 hours.
3. Serve soup cold with a dollop of sour cream.

Willie Rautenstraus
Boulder, Colorado

HUNGARIAN CHERRY SOUP

Serves 6 to 8
Refrigerate 2 Hours

Preparation 10 Minutes
Cook 15 Minutes

2 cans (16-ounce) sour cherries, pitted
Reserved juices from cherries
Water
1 cup sugar
1 cinnamon stick
1 tablespoon arrowroot
1/4 cup heavy cream
3/4 cup red wine

1. Drain juices from canned cherries and add enough water to make 3 cups liquid.
2. In a 3-quart saucepan, combine liquid, sugar, and cinnamon stick. Bring to a boil. Add cherries and simmer 10 minutes.
3. Make a paste of arrowroot and 2 tablespoons cold water. Add to soup and simmer 2 minutes. Remove from heat and chill 2 hours.
4. When ready to serve, stir in cream and wine.

Deborah Taylor
Boulder, Colorado

VARIATION:

If you have access to a cherry tree, make your cherry soup with fresh, *unpitted* cherries. The pits intensify the flavor. Eat with care!

SALADS • AND • SALAD DRESSINGS

SOME NOTES ON SALADS AND DRESSINGS

1. All leafy greens are suitable for salads. They can be used alone or in combination with other greens, vegetables, and/or fruits. Variety should be the keynote when making a salad. Only fresh, crisp greens should be used, and they must be washed and then dried (a salad spinner is easy and very effective for this).
2. Vinegars also add variety to salads. Experiment with the many flavored vinegars on the market. Lemon juice is frequently used in addition to vinegar and just as often to replace it.
3. Oils used in salad dressings must be carefully considered in order to obtain the right flavor and not mask others in the salad. French, Greek, or Spanish olive oils are strong in taste, while Italian olive oil is lighter in flavor. Peanut oil and corn oil are also very light. Nut oils, such as walnut and hazelnut, give an exciting flavor to your salads.
4. The proportion of oil to vinegar is 3-to-1 for olive oil and 4-to-1 for peanut and corn oils. In vinaigrette for provincial French dishes, use all olive oil and all lemon juice.
5. Besides the flavor of the oil and the vinegar, additional flavors come from adding herbs and mustards. Mustard is especially good on strong tasting greens, such as endive, escarole, watercress, chicory, and romaine.
6. When using soft lettuce leaves, mix with dressing immediately before serving. Mixing it earlier will "cook" the leaves.

INDONESIAN BEAN SPROUT SALAD

Serves 4 to 6

Preparation 10 Minutes
Refrigerate 1 Hour

2 cups fresh bean sprouts
1/4 cup chopped green onion
1/4 cup chopped green pepper
1/4 cup chopped celery
1/4 cup chopped pimiento
Sesame Dressing (see Index)

1. Toss bean sprouts, onions, peppers, celery, and pimiento with dressing. Chill 1 hour.

Kathy Van Arsdale
Denver, Colorado

HUNGARIAN PICKLED BEET SALAD
(*Cekla Saláta*)

Serves 8

Preparation 45 Minutes
Marinate 2 Hours

2 pounds beets
2 tablespoons white vinegar
2 tablespoons water
1 teaspoon salt
1 tablespoon sugar
1/2 teaspoon caraway seeds
1 teaspoon prepared horseradish
4 hard-cooked eggs, sliced (optional)

1. Cook beets until tender. Peel and slice.
2. Mix vinegar, water, salt, sugar, caraway seeds, and horseradish and pour over beets. Let stand several hours.
3. Store covered and refrigerated until ready to serve. Garnish with hard-cooked eggs.

Marilyn Peltzer
Boulder, Colorado

CAULIFLOWER AND EGG SALAD

Serves 4 to 6

Preparation 30 Minutes
Marinate Overnight

1 small head cauliflower, broken into flowers
2 tablespoons red wine vinegar
1/4 teaspoon salt
1/8 teaspoon pepper
Pinch each of basil tarragon, and parsley
4 tablespoons oil
3 hard-cooked eggs
3/4 cup mayonnaise
Paprika for garnish

1. Cook cauliflower until just tender. Drain well and add vinegar, salt, pepper, basil, tarragon, parsley, and oil while still hot. Refrigerate for several hours or overnight.
2. Separate yolks from whites of hard-cooked eggs. Slice whites only and mix them with cauliflower and mayonnaise. Save yolks.
3. Place mixture in a shallow serving bowl and sprinkle with grated egg yolks and paprika.

VARIATION:

This salad can also be prepared with cooked and sliced leeks.

Sheryl Kuempel
Boulder, Colorado

CORN-DATE SALAD

Serves 4 to 6

Preparation 15 Minutes
Refrigerate 2 Hours

1 can (17-ounce) whole kernel corn, well drained
12 dates, chopped
1 small onion, finely chopped
2 tablespoons chopped pimiento
4 tablespoons vinegar
Salt and pepper
4 tablespoons oil

1. Put corn, dates, onion, and pimiento into a shallow bowl.
2. Mix vinegar, salt, pepper, and oil. Pour over corn mixture. Refrigerate several hours.

Sheryl Kuempel
Boulder, Colorado

AUSTRIAN EGGPLANT SALAD

Serves 4 to 6

Preparation 1 Hour

1 large eggplant, cut off top
3 large green peppers, cut in half
Vinaigrette Dressing I (see Index)

1. Preheat oven to 350 degrees. Bake eggplant and peppers for 25 minutes. Remove peppers, but continue to bake eggplant for another 15 to 20 minutes. Wrap eggplant in a damp towel for 10 minutes to loosen skin.
2. Meanwhile, peel peppers, remove seeds and ribs, and chop very fine.
3. Peel eggplant and mince. Squeeze dry in kitchen towel. Add to peppers.
4. Toss eggplant and pepper mixture with dressing.

Ulla Taylor
Goff's Oak, England

HEARTS OF PALM

Serves 4

Preparation 15 Minutes

1 can (14-ounce) hearts of palm, drained and thinly sliced
1 jar (2-ounce) pimientos, sliced
1 avocado, sliced
Lettuce for garnish
Vinaigrette II (see Index)

1. Line a medium bowl or individual plates with lettuce. Arrange hearts of palm, pimientos, and avocado attractively on the lettuce.
2. Add dressing.

SWEET AND SOUR RADISH SALAD

Serves 3 to 4

Preparation 25 Minutes

2 bunches radishes
1/2 teaspoon salt
2 tablespoons light brown sugar
2 tablespoons cider vinegar
1/2 teaspoon Oriental sesame oil

1. Trim both ends of radishes, wash, and drain. Crush radishes gently by using side of blade of cleaver or bottom of jar. Cut large ones in half.
2. Sprinkle salt on crushed radishes and let stand for 15 minutes.
3. Drain liquid from radishes. Mix sugar with vinegar and pour over radishes.
4. Garnish with sesame oil and serve.

NOTE:

Although radishes will taste better by soaking longer in the sugar and vinegar, they will be discolored and less crisp.

Margaret Mason
Boulder, Colorado

MARINATED RED PEPPERS

Serves 4

Preparation 1 Hour
Refrigerate 2 Hours

6 red sweet peppers, cleaned and halved
6 tablespoons red wine or sherry wine vinegar
1/2 teaspoon salt
1/4 teaspoon black pepper
1/2 teaspoon each dried basil, tarragon, parsley, and chervil
3/4 cup oil
4 shallots or 1 small onion, finely minced

1. Roast peppers, cut side down in oven at 425 degrees for 20 to 30 minutes. The skins should be almost black, split and puckered. Peel and cut into strips.
2. Mix vinegar, salt, pepper, basil, tarragon, parsley, and chervil. Let sit until salt dissolves, about 10 minutes. Add oil and shallots and mix well.
3. Pour over red peppers and chill.

VARIATION:

Roast and peel 3 large green peppers in the above manner, marinate in 2 tablespoons vinegar, 1 teaspoon each sugar and salt for 12 hours then drain and serve with 1/2 cup homemade mayonnaise.

Marguerite Cateora
Dallas, Texas

SAUERKRAUT SALAD

Serves 8 to 10

Preparation 20 Minutes
Refrigerate 1 Hour

1 cup sugar
1/2 cup vinegar
3 1/2 cups sauerkraut, lightly washed
1/2 cup chopped celery
1/2 cup finely chopped green pepper
1 jar (2-ounce) pimientos, drained

1. Cook sugar and vinegar just to boil and then cool.
2. Pour cooled mixture over sauerkraut, celery, green pepper, and pimientos and refrigerate. Flavor improves with age.

Marian A. Wightman
Lincoln, Nebraska

TOMATO TANGERINE SALAD

Serves 6

Preparation 30 Minutes

1 head Boston lettuce, washed and dried
1 bunch watercress, trimmed and washed
2 medium tomatoes, diced
4 tangerines, rind and pith removed
Zesty Lemon Dressing (see Index)

1. Line a bowl with lettuce and arrange tomatoes, tangerines, and watercress on top.
2. Just before serving add dressing and toss.

Marcia Rothstein
Beverly Hills, California

SALAD ITALIANO

Serves 8 to 10

Preparation 30 Minutes

2 cucumbers, peeled and thinly sliced
2 bunches radishes, thinly sliced
3 oranges, peeled, sliced, and halved
2 tablespoons red wine vinegar
3 tablespoons light olive oil
1 teaspoon chervil
Lettuce leaves to garnish

1. Toss cucumbers, radishes, and oranges together.
2. Mix vinegar, oil, and chervil together. Just before serving pour over salad and toss. Serve on lettuce leaves.

Nancy Cateora
Boulder, Colorado

ZUCCHINI SALAD

Serves 6

Preparation 30 Minutes

2 pounds small zucchini
1 lemon, juiced
Salt and pepper
1/4 cup red wine vinegar
1 teaspoon salt
2 tablespoons finely minced fresh basil or 1 teaspoon dried basil
1 large clove garlic, minced
4 tablespoons minced green onions
4 tablespoons minced green pepper
2 tablespoons chopped parsley
2 tablespoons chopped pimiento
1/2 cup oil
Romaine or other lettuce to garnish

1. Wash zucchini, slice off tips and cook in boiling, salted water for 10 to 15 minutes or until easily pierced with the tip of a sharp knife. Do not overcook.
2. Run the zucchini under cold water. Drain and place on a layer of paper towels. Cut in half lengthwise, sprinkle with lemon juice, salt, and pepper.
3. Prepare dressing in a small bowl by combining vinegar, salt, basil, garlic, onions, green pepper, parsley, pimiento, and oil.
4. Spread dressing over zucchini and chill. Serve chilled but not cold on romaine or other lettuce leaves.

Pat Wright
Boulder, Colorado

ZUCCHINI IN SALSA VERDE

Serves 4

Preparation 45 Minutes
Marinate 1 Hour

1 1/2 pounds small zucchini
1/2 cup flour
1 1/2 teaspoons salt
2 cups (or more) salad oil
1/4 cup olive oil
1/4 cup minced *fresh* parsley
3 tablespoons white wine vinegar
3 anchovies, minced
1 small clove garlic, crushed
1/2 teaspoon black pepper
1 lemon, thinly sliced for garnish

1. Wash zucchini and cut into slices 1/4 inch thick.
2. Mix flour and salt in paper bag. Toss zucchini slices a handful at a time in bag to coat.

3. Pour salad oil into a large skillet about 1 inch deep. Use more than 2 cups if necessary. Fry zucchini slices in batches until lightly browned on both sides. Do not crowd. Allow 5 to 8 minutes to brown each batch. Drain slices on paper towels and allow to cool.
4. Mix oil, fresh parsley, vinegar, anchovies, garlic, and pepper.
5. Arrange cooled zucchini slices in a bowl and pour sauce over them. Marinate for at least 1 hour at room temperature. Serve garnished with lemon slices.

NOTE:

Because it takes time both to fry the zucchini, and then to cool it, salad must be made early in the day or the night before serving. If using an electric skillet, heat oil to 375 degrees.

Jane Abbott
Albuquerque, New Mexico

VIETNAMESE CABBAGE SALAD

Serves 6 — Preparation 45 Minutes

1/4 medium head white cabbage
1/8 small head red cabbage
1/4 cup chopped green onion with tops
1 carrot, shredded
3 fresh mint leaves, chopped (optional)
2 tablespoons vinegar
Pinch each salt and black pepper, to taste
1 teaspoon fish sauce
1 teaspoon sugar
1 egg, made into a small omelet, cooled, and cut into thin strips
1/4 cup dry roasted peanuts, crushed
A few coriander leaves (Chinese parsley) (optional)

1. Slice white and red cabbages into long, thin slivers. Add green onion (saving some green for garnish), carrot, and mint.
2. Mix together vinegar, salt, pepper, fish sauce, and sugar. Pour over salad only 10 to 15 minutes before serving. Mix in well with hands, squeezing cabbage firmly.
3. Place strips of egg on top and sprinkle with remaining onion greens, crushed peanuts, and coriander leaves.

NOTE:

Fish sauce may be purchased at most specialty food shops and large supermarkets.

Indo-China Mobile Education Project
Washington, D.C.

APPLE, PEANUT, AND CABBAGE SALAD

Serves 4 to 6

Preparation 20 Minutes

1 1/2 cups finely chopped cabbage
2 apples, cored and finely chopped
1/3 cup mayonnaise
1 teaspoon fresh lime juice
1/4 cup dry roasted peanuts, finely chopped

1. Mix together cabbage and apples. Add mayonnaise and lime juice.
2. Add peanuts to cabbage mixture. Mix thoroughly and chill.

Lisa Loeffler
Boulder, Colorado

CASHEW NUT SALAD

Serves 8 to 10

Preparation 20 Minutes

1 head lettuce, torn into bite-sized pieces
1 cup cashew nuts
4 ounces Swiss cheese, cubed
Poppy Seed Dressing (see Index) or Celery Seed Dressing (see Index)

1. Mix lettuce, nuts, and cheese.
2. Toss with your choice of dressings.

Pat Wright
Boulder, Colorado

UNUSUAL SALAD

Serves 4 to 6

Preparation 30 Minutes
Refrigerate 1 1/2 Hours

1 small head lettuce, cut into chunks
Mayonnaise
1 medium Bermuda onion, very thinly sliced
Sugar
1 can (17-ounce) peas, (or less) or 1 package (10-ounce) frozen peas, cooked and cooled
6 ounces Swiss cheese, cut in julienne strips
1/4 pound bacon (or more), cooked and crumbled

1. Place a layer of crisp lettuce in large salad bowl. Spread thinly with mayonnaise.
2. Add a layer of onion. Sprinkle lightly with sugar. Add a layer of peas and then a layer of Swiss cheese. Repeat layers to quantity desired. Use no salt or pepper. Do not toss.
3. Refrigerate for no more than 1 1/2 to 2 hours. When ready to serve, sprinkle with crumbled bacon.

NOTE:

The amounts of ingredients are only approximate. Prepare as much as desired. This salad is not sweet. The sugar causes the onion to weep, which—together with the mayonnaise—makes the dressing. The lettuce stays crisp and does not wilt. Serve with plain barbecued meat and buttered rye or pumpernickel bread.

Ethel Zager
Avalon, California

SPINACH-PECAN SALAD

Serves 6 to 8 — Preparation 30 Minutes

1 package (10-ounce) fresh spinach, cleaned and dried
1 cup pecans, coarsely broken
12 ounces dry curd cottage cheese
1 cup sour cream
1/2 cup sugar
3 tablespoons vinegar
1 1/4 teaspoon dry mustard
1/2 teaspoon salt
4 teaspoons horseradish

1. Tear leaves into bite-sized pieces and toss with pecan pieces and cottage cheese.
2. Mix sour cream, sugar, vinegar, mustard, salt, and horseradish. Shake.
3. Add to salad and toss gently just before serving.

NOTE:

If dry curd cottage cheese is not available in your area, substitute small curd cottage cheese.

Jane Beagle
Boulder, Colorado

SPICY SPINACH SALAD

Serves 8 — Preparation 30 Minutes

1 package (10-ounce) fresh spinach, dried
1/2 pound mushrooms, sliced
1 can (8-ounce) water chestnuts, sliced
2 tablespoons sesame seeds, toasted
Spicy Spinach Dressing (see Index)

1. Tear spinach leaves into bite-sized pieces.
2. Toss spinach, mushrooms, water chestnuts, and sesame seeds lightly with dressing. Serve immediately.

Debby Oliger
Palo Alto, California

GERMAN POTATO SALAD

This is a family recipe from Germany.

Serves 6 to 8 | Preparation 1 Hour

6 large red potatoes
1 pound bacon
3/4 cup white vinegar
1/2 cup sugar
1 tablespoon salt
1 teaspoon pepper
1 large onion, finely chopped
2 to 3 tablespoons celery seed

1. Boil potatoes until done but not mushy. Cool and peel.
2. While potatoes are cooling, dice bacon and sauté until crisp. Remove bacon and drain on paper towel. Reserve drippings.
3. Add vinegar, sugar, salt, and pepper to bacon drippings and simmer until sugar has dissolved.
4. Slice potatoes. Add onion and vinegar-sugar mixture to potatoes. Mix carefully.
5. Add bacon pieces and celery seed.

NOTE:

This dish may be kept in the refrigerator for over two weeks. It may be served warm or cold.

Rosemary Jones
San Francisco, California

HERRING SALAD

Serves 8 | Preparation 45 Minutes

1 1/2 pints pickled herring
2 dill pickles, diced
1 can (16-ounce) sliced beets, drained
2 medium green apples, cored, peeled, and diced
6 medium boiled potatoes, diced and cooled
Mayonnaise
Capers
4 hard-cooked eggs, sliced

1. Drain herring, reserving onions. Cut herring into bite-sized pieces.
2. Combine herring and onions with pickles, beets, apples, and potatoes.
3. Add enough mayonnaise to bind ingredients together. Garnish with capers and eggs.

Barbara Smith
Boulder, Colorado

DANISH POTATO SALAD

Serves 6 to 8

Preparation 45 Minutes
Refrigerate 2 Hours

4 to 5 potatoes, boiled in jackets
4 tablespoons oil
4 tablespoons tarragon vinegar
1 teaspoon salt
1 teaspoon sugar
1 garlic clove, crushed
1 tablespoon fresh dill or 1 teaspoon dried dill
1/4 cup mayonnaise
3 green onions, chopped
6 to 8 radishes, thinly sliced
3 hard-cooked eggs
Parsley to garnish

1. Peel potatoes and cut into 1/2-inch cubes.
2. Mix oil, vinegar, salt, sugar, and garlic. Pour over warm potatoes. Chill.
3. When ready to serve, mix dill and mayonnaise. Toss lightly with onions, radishes, and potatoes. Garnish with eggs and parsley.

Sheryl Kuempel
Boulder, Colorado

SALADE NICOISE

Serves 6

Preparation 45 Minutes
Marinate 2 Hours

1/2 pound green beans
2 large potatoes, cooked and sliced
***Nicoise* Dressing (see Index)**
1 head lettuce or other salad greens
3 hard-cooked eggs, quartered
12 pitted ripe olives
2 large tomatoes, quartered or 6 cherry tomatoes, halved
1 can (7-ounce) tuna fish or 1 can (2-ounce) anchovy filets

1. Cook green beans until slightly tender, slice diagonally and cool.
2. Marinate cooled green beans and potato slices for 2 hours in 2/3 recipe of dressing.
3. Arrange greens to cover bowl. Place beans and potatoes in a sunburst design around edge of bowl. Add egg quarters, olives, tomatoes, and tuna in center.
4. Add remaining 1/3 dressing.

NOTE:

A few sliced onions (separated into rings) and a sliced green pepper may be added. Decorate with a few anchovy filets even if you use tuna.

Ann Deschanel
Boulder, Colorado

HOLIDAY TROUT BRUNCH

Serves 4

Preparation 20 Minutes

2 cups cooked, flaked trout
1/4 cup smoked crushed almonds
1/4 cup diced green onion
1/4 cup chopped celery
1/2 cup mayonnaise
Parsley flakes
Garlic salt
2 avocados, peeled
Lettuce
Paprika, lemon wedges

1. Combine trout, almonds, onions, celery, and mayonnaise. Season with parsley and garlic salt. Fill avocado halves.
2. Serve on lettuce garnished with paprika and lemon wedges.

The All Trout Cookbook
Grand Junction, Colorado

INDONESIAN MIXED VEGETABLE SALAD WITH PEANUT BUTTER DIP

Serves 6

Preparation 30 Minutes
Chill 2 to 3 Hours

1/4 pound fresh green beans, cooked
1/4 pound shredded cabbage, cooked 5 minutes
1 can (4-ounce) bamboo shoots
1/4 pound fresh bean sprouts
6 green onions
1/4 pound carrots, cooked
2 potatoes, cooked, sliced or diced
1 cucumber, sliced
1 tablespoon oil
1/2 small red chili, (fresh or dried), chopped
1 medium onion, chopped
1 tablespoon brown sugar
Juice of 1 lemon
1 teaspoon lemon rind
2 tablespoons water
1/2 cup chunky peanut butter
Shrimp crackers

1. Select 4 to 8 of listed vegetables and prepare. Chill.
2. Stir-fry chili (if fresh) and onion in oil until soft. Put in a blender.
3. Add sugar, lemon juice, and rind with 2 tablespoons water. Blend.
4. Add peanut butter and blend again. Chill.
5. Serve prepared vegetables with chilled dip and shrimp crackers.

NOTE:

Canned green beans may be used when fresh are not available. Shrimp crackers are available in the deli or gourmet section of grocery stores. This salad may be served with hot food or as an appetizer with an Indonesian meal (see Menu Section).

Kathy Van Arsdale
Denver, Colorado

COLORADO BULGAR SALAD

Serves 8 to 10 — Preparation 1 Hour

4 cups boiling water
2 cups bulgar wheat
3/4 cup salad oil
1/4 cup olive oil
Salt and pepper to taste
Garlic powder
Juice of 3 to 4 lemons
1 onion, chopped
4 ounces fresh spinach, chopped
2 avocados, cubed
1/4 cup almonds or walnuts, coarsely chopped
1 stalk celery, chopped
2 hard-cooked eggs, sliced

1. Pour boiling water over bulgar and soak 1 hour. Drain any water that has not been absorbed. Squeeze dry.
2. Mix salad oil, olive oil, salt, pepper, garlic powder, and lemon juice. Add to bulgar.
3. Add spinach, onion, avocados, nuts, celery, and eggs.

Jan Sumek
Boulder, Colorado

TABBOULEH

Serves 4 — Preparation 1 1/2 Hours

1/2 cup *bulghúr* (crushed wheat), medium grade
1 cup boiling water
1 tomato, minced
1 cup parsley or cilantro, finely chopped
1/2 cup chopped green onion tops
1 to 2 teaspoons salt
1/4 teaspoon cinnamon (optional)
Sugar to taste (optional)
1/4 to 1/3 cup fresh lemon juice
1/3 cup olive oil
2 tablespoons fresh mint, finely chopped or 1 tablespoon dried mint

1. Put *bulghur* in bowl and cover with water. Allow to stand 1/2 to 1 hour until all water is absorbed. Squeeze dry. Put in salad bowl.
2. To *bulghur* add tomato, parsley, onion, salt, cinnamon, and sugar.
3. Mix lemon juice, olive oil, and mint. Add to salad and mix well. Refrigerate.

NOTE:

The salad can be served on cooked vine leaves, lettuce, or tender cabbage leaves. It is traditionally served on individual platters. It can also be served as an appetizer, when it is piled high on a large platter.

Victoria S. Barker
Boulder, Colorado

ORANGE CHICKEN SALAD

Serves 4 to 6

Preparation 1 Hour

1/2 cup mayonnaise
1/4 cup undiluted orange juice concentrate
Grated rind of 1 orange
Dash or two of Tabasco
3 cups cooked chicken, cubed
3/4 cup walnuts, chopped
3/4 cup water chestnuts, sliced
1 can (11-ounce) mandarin oranges, drained
1 cup seedless green grapes
1/2 cup heavy cream, whipped

1. Prepare the dressing by combining mayonnaise, orange juice concentrate, grated orange rind, and Tabasco. Can be refrigerated up to 12 hours.
2. Toss together chicken, walnuts, water chestnuts, mandarin oranges, and green grapes just before serving.
3. Whip cream and fold into mayonnaise mixture. Pour most of dressing over salad and toss. Use rest to garnish salad.

HOI SIN CHICKEN SALAD

Serves 4

Preparation 30 Minutes

1 pound chicken breasts
1/2 cup *hoi sin* sauce
1/2 teaspoon mustard
4 teaspoons sesame seeds, toasted
6 teaspoons toasted almonds, finely chopped
5 green onions, chopped
Pinch of salt
Oil for frying
1/3 package rice sticks
1/2 head iceberg lettuce, shredded
5 sprigs Chinese parsley, chopped

1. Deep fry chicken breasts about 5 to 8 minutes. Drain on paper towels and cool. Cut or pull apart chicken into long strips.
2. In a large salad bowl mix *hoi sin* sauce, mustard, sesame seeds, almonds, onions, and salt. Mix well. Add chicken and mix again.
3. Heat oil and fry rice sticks, a small handful at a time. They will swell and brown immediately. Remove and drain.
4. When ready to serve add shredded lettuce, fried rice sticks, and parsley to chicken mixture.

NOTE:

This recipe may be prepared ahead through step 2. *Hoi sin* sauce may be found at most specialty food shops and large supermarkets.

Jonas S. Brooks
Los Angeles, California

CHINESE CHICKEN SALAD

Serves 6 to 8
Stand 2 Hours

Preparation 40 Minutes

6 tablespoons sugar
3 teaspoons salt
1 1/2 teaspoons black pepper
3/4 cup salad oil
9 tablespoons red wine vinegar with garlic
2 pounds chicken breasts, baked and cubed
1 medium head lettuce, shredded
1 bunch green onions, sliced
1 package (2 1/4-ounce) blanched almonds, toasted
8 tablespoons sesame seeds, toasted
1/2 package rice sticks, fried per package directions

1. Combine sugar, salt, pepper, oil, and vinegar and let stand for several hours.
2. Combine chicken, lettuce, onions, almonds, sesame seeds, and rice sticks and toss with dressing immediately before serving.

NOTE:

All cutting and toasting may be done the day before, but *do not* mix together until ready to serve. You may want to double dressing recipe. If rice sticks are not available, substitute cooked rice or 1 large can crisp chow mein noodles.

Joy Rousso
Woodland Hills, California

VARIATION:

For a change of flavor, use 1 medium head of cabbage, shredded, in place of lettuce. If the rice noodles are hard to find, use the noodles, uncooked from a package (3-ounce) of Top Ramen oriental soup mix. In the dressing, the flavor packet may be used to replace the salt and Japanese rice-vinegar substituted for the wine vinegar.

BLUSHING APPLE SALAD

Serves 4 to 6

Preparation 30 Minutes
Refrigerate 2 Hours

1/2 cup red cinnamon candies
1/2 cup water
3 apples, cored, peeled and cut into thick slices
Lettuce leaves
3 ounces cream cheese
3 tablespoons mayonnaise
Parsley for garnish

1. Dissolve candies in water, add apple slices, and simmer until tender. Chill.
2. Arrange chilled slices on lettuce leaves and fill centers with cream cheese softened with mayonnaise. Garnish with parsley.

PINEAPPLE FRUIT SALAD

Serves 8 to 10

Preparation 1 1/2 Hours

1 can (20-ounce) crushed pineapple
1 cup sugar
1 tablespoon flour
3 bananas
1 or 2 Delicious apples
3 oranges, peeled and divided into segments
1 can (29-ounce) peach halves, drained
1 can (29-ounce) pear halves, drained
1 pint strawberries, washed and halved
1 to 2 stems green grapes, washed and halved
Sweetened coconut (optional)

1. Combine crushed pineapple, sugar, and flour and cook over medium heat, stirring constantly, until smooth. Cool and refrigerate.
2. Slice bananas and dice apples directly into cool pineapple mixture. Mix well. Refrigerate and hold at this step until ready to serve.
3. Dice the orange segments, peach and pear halves. Add these with the strawberries and grapes to the pineapple mixture. Fold gently.
4. Transfer to a clear glass salad bowl. Serve with a side dish of sweetened coconut if desired.

Ellen Doenges
Austin, Texas

CHRISTMAS EVE SALAD
(*Ensalada de Noche Buena*)

Serves 6 to 8

Preparation 1 Hour

3/4 cup sugar
6 tablespoons wine vinegar
2 medium beets, cooked and cubed
3 oranges, peeled and sliced
1 medium jicama, peeled and diced
3 bananas, sliced
3 slices fresh pineapple, cut into cubes
1/2 cup chopped peanuts
Lettuce to garnish

1. For dressing, dissolve sugar in vinegar and let stand for at least 1 hour.
2. Mix beets, oranges, jicama, bananas, and pineapple. Chill. Add peanuts.
3. Place salad in a bowl lined with lettuce leaves and serve dressing separately.

NOTE:

Two tart apples, diced, may be used for the jicama. Also delicious with *Noche Buena* II (see Index).

TARRAGON FROZEN FRUIT SALAD

Serves 8 to 10

Preparation 30 Minutes
Freeze 12 Hours

2 tablespoons tarragon vinegar
2 tablespoons sugar
2 egg yolks
2 egg whites, beaten stiff
1 can (8 1/4-ounce) crushed pineapple, drained
1/2 cup pecan halves
2 1/2 cups quartered marshmallows
1 bottle (3-ounce) maraschino cherries
1 cup heavy cream, whipped

1. Cook vinegar, sugar, and egg yolks in double boiler until a thick cream, stirring constantly. Cool.
2. Fold in beaten egg whites. Add pineapple, pecans, marshmallows, and cherries, then fold in whipped cream.
4. Freeze in ice cube tray. Cover with wax paper and then aluminum foil.

Ann L. McDowell
Boulder, Colorado

AVOCADO MOUSSE

Serves 6 to 8

Preparation 25 Minutes
Refrigerate 2 Hours

1 envelope unflavored gelatin
2 tablespoons cold water
2 tablespoons boiling water
3 medium avocados (very ripe, about 2 cups)
2 tablespoons lemon juice
1 teaspoon grated onion
3/4 teaspoon salt
3/4 cup mayonnaise
3/4 cup heavy cream
Butter lettuce for garnish

1. Soften gelatin in cold water. Add boiling water and stir to dissolve. If gelatin is not completely dissolved, set over hot water and stir occasionally until completely dissolved.
2. Meanwhile, puree avocado meat and blend in lemon juice, onion, salt, and mayonnaise.
3. Add dissolved gelatin. Stir thoroughly.
4. Whip cream to stiff peaks and gently fold in avocado mixture. Pour into rinsed 6-cup mold (use cold water for rinsing). Refrigerate until firm. Unmold on butter lettuce.

Frances W. Wilson
Omaha, Nebraska

MOLDED CUCUMBER SALAD

Serves 6 to 8

Preparation 30 Minutes
Refrigerate 2 Hours

1 box (3-ounce) lime gelatin
1 box (3-ounce) lemon gelatin
2 cups boiling water
1 1/2 tablespoons vinegar
1 1/2 tablespoons finely chopped onion
1 large cucumber, finely chopped
2 tablespoons horseradish
2 cups mayonnaise or salad dressing

1. Dissolve gelatin in boiling water. Add vinegar and refrigerate until mixture is slightly thickened.
2. Stir in onion, cucumber and horseradish, folding in the mayonnaise or salad dressing last.
3. Pour into a 13 x 19-inch pan or 6-cup mold and chill until firm.

NOTE:

Instead of 2 cups mayonnaise or salad dressing, one cup mayonnaise and one cup sour cream or yogurt may be substituted.

Marian A. Wightman
Lincoln, Nebraska

TOMATO RASPBERRY MOLD

Serves 8 to 12

Preparation 15 Minutes
Refrigerate 3 Hours

3 boxes (3-ounce each) raspberry gelatin
3/4 to 1 cup hot water
3 cans (16-ounce each) stewed tomatoes
2 to 4 dashes Tabasco (or to taste)
Sour cream in desired quantity
Horseradish to taste

1. Dissolve gelatin in hot water. Add stewed tomatoes and Tabasco. Mix, pour into 2-quart mold, and refrigerate until set.
2. Mix sour cream and horseradish.
3. Unmold salad and serve with dressing.

NOTE:

This salad is a magnificent red color. It is especially pretty if made in a 2-quart ring mold and unmolded onto parsley or watercress.

Cathy Bickell
Boulder, Colorado

TOMATO ASPIC

Serves 6

Preparation 1 Hour
Refrigerate 2 Hours

1 envelope unflavored gelatin
1/4 cup cold water
2 1/2 cups tomato juice
2 bay leaves
5 whole cloves
1/4 cup chopped onion
1/2 teaspoon salt
1/4 teaspoon Tabasco
1 cup finely chopped celery
1 medium avocado, cubed

1. Soften gelatin in cold water.
2. Boil tomato juice with bay leaves, cloves, onion, salt, and Tabasco for 5 minutes. Strain.
3. Add gelatin to hot spiced tomato juice and stir to dissolve. Chill until slightly thickened.
4. Add celery and avocado. Pour into 4-cup mold and chill until firm.

VARIATION:

Use a pre-seasoned tomato juice instead of plain tomato juice and omit Tabasco.

Jane Wilson
Boulder, Colorado

ZESTY SHRIMP ASPIC

Serves 6 to 8

Preparation 30 Minutes
Refrigerate 3 Hours

2 1/2 cups tomato juice
1 box (6-ounce) lemon gelatin
1 can (7-ounce) green chili salsa
1 to 3 teaspoons horseradish
1/4 cup lemon juice
1 1/2 cups shrimp, cooked
1/2 cup chopped celery

1. Heat tomato juice to boiling. Add gelatin and stir until dissolved.
2. Stir in salsa, horseradish, and lemon juice. Chill mixture until slightly thickened.
3. Cut shrimp into bite-sized pieces, mix with celery, and add to slightly thickened gelatin. Turn into a 1 1/2-quart mold and chill until firm.

Ethel Zager
Avalon, California

RED SALMON MOUSSE

Serves 6 to 7

Preparation 35 Minutes
Refrigerate 3 Hours

1 can (15 1/2-ounce) red salmon (sockeye)
1 envelope unflavored gelatin
1/2 cup cold water
1 teaspoon salt
1 1/2 teaspoons sugar
Dash red pepper
1/4 cup white vinegar
3/4 cup milk
2 teaspoons flour
1 teaspoon dry mustard
4 egg yolks, slightly beaten

1 large cucumber, peeled and diced
4 tablespoons lemon juice
1 cup mayonnaise
1 cup sour cream
2 tablespoons paprika
1/2 teaspoon salt
1 teaspoon sugar
3 teaspoons mustard
Green olives, parsley, and lemon wedges to garnish

1. Drain salmon, reserving liquid. Clean off bones and black skin.
2. Add gelatin to cold water to soften.
3. Mix salt, sugar, pepper, vinegar, milk, flour, mustard, and egg yolks in top of double boiler. Add salmon liquid and cook over hot water. Stir frequently. When mixture thickens enough to glaze a wooden spoon, remove from stove. Add gelatin and stir to dissolve.
4. If a smooth mousse is desired, whirl gelatin mixture with salmon in blender or food processor. If not, flake salmon and stir in gelatin mixture.
5. Pour into 8 1/2 x 4 1/2 x 3-inch loaf pan or desired mold rinsed in cold water or sprayed with Pam. Cool, then refrigerate.
6. For the sauce, combine cucumber, lemon juice, mayonnaise, sour cream, paprika, salt, sugar, and mustard.
7. When ready to serve, run spatula or knife around edge of pan or mold and unmold mousse on plate. Garnish as desired with green olives, parsley, lemon wedges. Serve with sauce.

NOTE:

This mousse is also excellent served with Tangy Cucumber Sauce (see Index). Some may prefer to cut the sauce quantity in half. May be made a day or two ahead.

Willie-Fan Mayo Stovall
Denver, Colorado

MOLDED TUNA SALAD

Serves 6

Preparation 30 Minutes
Refrigerate 3 Hours

- 1 box (3-ounce) lemon gelatin
- 1 cup boiling water
- 1 cup cold water
- 1 can (6 1/2-ounce) tuna fish
- 1 1/2 cups chopped celery with leaves
- 2 teaspoons chopped onion
- 1 teaspoon chopped green pepper
- 2 hard-cooked eggs, chopped, salted to taste
- 3/4 cup mayonnaise
- Lettuce or spinach leaves to garnish

1. Dissolve gelatin in boiling water. Stir in cold water and refrigerate.
2. Drain tuna. If packed in oil, rinse with boiling water, drain, and flake.
3. When gelatin has slightly thickened, add celery, onion, green pepper, and eggs. Stir in mayonnaise. Carefully fold in tuna.
4. Pour into an 8 x 8-inch pan that has been rinsed in cold water. Refrigerate until set.
5. To serve, cut into rectangles and place on lettuce or spinach leaves.

Jean K. Clark
Boulder, Colorado

RED RIBBON SALAD

Serves 16

Preparation 2 Hours
Refrigerate 2 Hours

- 2 boxes (3-ounce each) black cherry gelatin
- 2 1/2 cups boiling water
- 1 can (7-ounce) crushed pineapple in heavy syrup
- 1 can (8-ounce) jellied cranberry sauce
- 2 cups sour cream
- 2 boxes (3-ounce each) raspberry gelatin
- 2 1/2 cups boiling water
- 2 boxes (10-ounce each) frozen raspberries

1. Dissolve black cherry gelatin in boiling water. Add crushed pineapple and cranberry sauce. Some lumps of cranberry sauce will remain. Chill until firm in 9 x 13-inch pyrex dish.
2. Spread sour cream over first layer.
3. For top layer dissolve raspberry gelatin in boiling water and add frozen raspberries. Pour cooled mixture over sour cream layer. Chill until firm.
4. Serve with a dollop of sour cream on top.

Laura Dussart Leman
Sacramento, California

PINEAPPLE MOLD

Serves 20

Preparation 1 Hour
Refrigerate Overnight

1 can (20-ounce) crushed pineapple
2 envelopes unflavored gelatin
3 tablespoons fresh lemon juice
1/2 cup honey
1 cup grated Cheddar cheese
1/2 cup heavy cream
3 tablespoons finely chopped celery
3 tablespoons finely chopped green pepper
3/4 cup mayonnaise
40 white grapes, washed and dried
20 pecan or walnut halves

1. Drain off 1/2 cup pineapple juice and add gelatin to dissolve.
2. Bring to boil in a saucepan. Remove from heat and add lemon juice and honey. Stir until dissolved.
3. Cool slightly and add cheese and drained pineapple. Cool completely.
4. Whip cream. Fold into pineapple mixture and put into buttered 9 x 13-inch pan. Cool for 8 hours or overnight.
5. Mix celery, green pepper, and mayonnaise. Spread evenly over salad. Chill again. Cut into 20 squares and garnish each one with 2 white grapes and a nut half.

NOTE:

Will keep several days under refrigeration. Freezes well. Do not garnish until ready to serve.

Athena Clement
Denver, Colorado

SALAD DRESSINGS

VINAIGRETTE I

Yields 1/2 Cup

Preparation 10 Minutes

6 tablespoons olive oil
2 tablespoons lemon juice
2 tablespoons chopped parsley
1/2 teaspoon minced garlic
1 teaspoon salt
Pepper to taste

1. Mix olive oil, lemon juice, parsley, garlic, salt, and pepper. Shake well.

Ulla Taylor
Goff's Oak, England

VINAIGRETTE II

Yields 3/4 Cup

Preparation 10 Minutes

4 tablespoons oil
2 tablespoons finely chopped onion
1 teaspoon dried chervil
1 tablespoon vinegar
1 tablespoon lemon juice
1/4 teaspoon salt
1/8 teaspoon dry mustard
1 finely chopped hard-cooked egg

1. Mix oil, onion, chervil, vinegar, lemon juice, salt, dry mustard, and hard-cooked egg thoroughly.

Evelyn Logan
Santa Cruz, California

VINAIGRETTE III

Yields 1/2 Cup

Preparation 5 Minutes

3 tablespoons wine vinegar
1/2 teaspoon each sugar, dry mustard, and salt
1/4 teaspoon pepper
1 garlic clove, peeled and split
6 tablespoons olive oil

1. Mix vinegar, sugar, mustard, salt, pepper, garlic, and olive oil. Blend well.

NOTE:

This dressing lends itself very well to a salad of cooked, diced, fresh beets with a liberal sprinkling of freshly grated nutmeg.

Deborah Taylor
Boulder, Colorado

NICOISE SALAD DRESSING

Yields 3/4 Cup

Preparation 5 Minutes

1 clove garlic, minced
1/2 cup olive oil or salad oil
2 tablespoons lemon juice
2 tablespoons vinegar
Sprinkling of salt, basil, rosemary, fresh parsley, and freshly ground pepper

1. Mix all ingredients.

Ann Deschanel
Boulder, Colorado

CREAMY VINAIGRETTE DRESSING

Yields 3/4 Cup

Preparation 10 Minutes

Salt and pepper to taste
1/4 teaspoon mustard
3 tablespoons vinegar or lemon juice
6 tablespoons salad oil
2 tablespoons milk or cream

1. Combine salt, pepper, mustard, and vinegar. Add salad oil and milk. Beat until thick. Refrigerate.

Margit Staehelin
Boulder, Colorado

TOMATO MARINADE

Yields 1/2 Cup

Preparation 5 Minutes

1/4 cup red wine vinegar
1/4 cup olive oil
1/2 teaspoon sugar
1/2 teaspoon salt
1 1/2 teaspoons oregano
1/2 teaspoon pepper

1. Combine ingredients. Shake well.

NOTE:

Use on fresh sliced tomatoes, crumbled Feta cheese, and thinly sliced red onion.

Pat Wright
Boulder, Colorado

LEMON MUSTARD DRESSING

Yields 1 3/4 Cups

Preparation 5 Minutes

1 teaspoon English mustard
2 teaspoons brown mustard
1/2 teaspoon white pepper
1 1/2 teaspoons salt
2 teaspoons chopped chives
1/2 cup lemon juice
1 teaspoon Worcestershire sauce
1/2 cup olive oil
1/2 cup salad oil
1/2 teaspoon mixed herbs

1. Mix all ingredients and shake well.

Dorothy Ridgeley
St. Louis, Missouri

ZESTY LEMON DRESSING

Yields 1/2 Cup

Preparation 10 Minutes

- 1 lemon, juiced and zested
- 1 teaspoon Dijon mustard
- 1 teaspoon sugar
- Salt to taste
- Freshly ground black pepper, to taste
- 1 tablespoon chopped parsley
- 5 tablespoons olive oil

1. Mix lemon juice, lemon zest, mustard, sugar, salt, pepper, parsley, and olive oil thoroughly.

Marcia Rothstein
Beverly Hills, California

COLORADO CAESAR DRESSING

Yields 1 1/2 Cups

Preparation 15 Minutes

- 1 egg
- 3/4 cup oil
- 1/4 cup lemon juice
- 1 teaspoon Worcestershire sauce
- 1/4 cup Parmesan cheese
- 1/2 teaspoon salt
- 1/4 teaspoon pepper, freshly ground

1. Pierce egg with a needle and cook for one minute in boiling water. Break egg, drop into blender and mix.
2. Add oil slowly.
3. Add lemon juice, Worcestershire sauce, Parmesan cheese, salt, and pepper. Mix well.
4. Serve immediately. Will keep for two days in refrigerator but best fresh.

NOTE:

Two to 4 anchovies may be added to the salad greens with this dressing.

Mary J. McArthur
Louisville, Colorado

SPICY SPINACH SALAD DRESSING

Yields 1/2 Cup

Preparation 5 Minutes

- 1/3 cup salad oil
- 1/4 cup lemon juice
- 2 tablespoons soy sauce
- 1 teaspoon salt
- 1/8 teaspoon Tabasco

1. Combine ingredients and mix well.

Debbie Oliger
Palo Alto, California

SESAME DRESSING

Yields 2/3 Cup

Preparation 5 Minutes

1 clove garlic, minced
1/4 cup peanut oil
2 tablespoons vinegar
2 tablespoons soy sauce
1/2 teaspoon salt
1/4 teaspoon cayenne pepper
2 tablespoons sesame seeds

1. Blend all ingredients. Shake thoroughly.

Kathy Van Arsdale
Denver, Colorado

CELERY SEED DRESSING

Yields 2 Cups

Preparation 10 Minutes

1 cup salad dressing
1/3 cup sugar
1/4 cup vinegar
1 tablespoon celery seed
1 teaspoon dry mustard
1 teaspoon salt
1/4 cup minced onion
Dash of pepper

1. Mix well. Refrigerate.

Pat Wright
Boulder, Colorado

POPPY-LIME DRESSING

Yields 2 Cups

Preparation 15 Minutes
Refrigerate 1 Hour

1/3 cup lime juice
1/4 cup vinegar
3/4 cup sugar
1 teaspoon dry mustard
1 teaspoon poppy seeds
1 teaspoon paprika (optional)
1 cup salad oil

1. Heat lime juice and vinegar to boiling.
2. Combine sugar, mustard, poppy seeds, and paprika and add to hot mixture. Stir until sugar is dissolved.
3. Gradually beat in oil until well mixed and slightly thickened. Chill. Serve on fresh fruit.

Marilyn Peltzer
Boulder, Colorado

POPPY SEED DRESSING

Yields 2 Cups | Preparation 15 Minutes

1/2 cup sugar
1 teaspoon dry mustard or Dijon mustard
1 teaspoon salt
1/3 cup vinegar
1 1/2 tablespoons onion juice
1 cup oil
1 1/2 tablespoons poppy seeds

1. Mix together sugar, mustard, salt, and vinegar. Add onion juice and stir.
2. Add oil slowly and beat with a wire whisk until thick and creamy. Add poppy seeds.

NOTE:

This dressing is delicious as a sauce for Fondue Bourguignon. Use this dressing on peeled and sliced cucumbers combined with equal parts sliced bananas; a good salad for East Indian foods.

Diane Gayer
Denver, Colorado

CREAMY POPPY SEED DRESSING

Yields 1 1/2 Cups | Preparation 10 Minutes

1/4 cup sugar
1 tablespoon onion juice
1/3 cup vinegar
1 teaspoon salt
1 teaspoon dry mustard
1 tablespoon poppy seeds
1 cup cottage cheese (or less to taste)

1. Combine sugar, onion juice, vinegar, salt, and dry mustard in covered jar and shake well.
2. Add poppy seeds and cottage cheese, shaking after each addition.

Virginia Thaemert
Denver, Colorado

AUNT PEGGY'S SWEET FRENCH DRESSING

Yields 2 1/2 Cups | Preparation 10 Minutes

2 to 3 tablespoons grated onion
1/2 to 1 cup sugar
1/4 cup cider vinegar
1/3 cup catsup
1/2 teaspoon salt
1 teaspoon Worcestershire sauce
1 cup salad oil

1. Mix together in a quart jar and shake well. Refrigerate.
2. Serve on greens, vegetables, or fruits.

Libby Lipstreu
Boulder, Colorado

KAREN'S DRESSING

Yields 2 1/2 Cups

Preparation 10 Minutes

1 cup white tarragon wine vinegar
1 cup salad oil
1/2 medium onion
1 teaspoon salt
1 teaspoon dry mustard
5 tablespoons sugar
Juice of 1/2 lemon
3 tablespoons papaya seeds

1. Mix all ingredients in blender until papaya seeds look like coarse pepper.

NOTE:

Excellent on a spinach, avocado, and grapefruit or orange salad, sprinkled with toasted sesame seeds. Chunks of papaya are an added attraction.

Peg English
Costa Mesa, California

AVOCADO DRESSING

Yields 1 1/2 Cups

Preparation 10 Minutes

1/2 cup mashed avocado
1 tablespoon lemon juice
1/2 cup sour cream
1/3 cup salad oil
1 garlic clove, crushed
1/2 teaspoon sugar
1/2 teaspoon chili powder
1/4 teaspoon salt
1/4 teaspoon Tabasco

1. Combine ingredients in container of blender, food processor, or electric mixer. The flavors improve upon standing.

NOTE:

This dressing is excellent used on a mixture of tomato, lettuce, Cheddar cheese, crushed corn chips, and black olives along with tuna or hamburger (cooked and well drained), and/or kidney beans.

Deborah Taylor
Boulder, Colorado

COLESLAW DRESSING

Yields 1 1/2 Cups

Preparation 5 Minutes

1 cup mayonnaise
1/4 cup cider vinegar
1 teaspoon salt
1 tablespoon sugar
1/4 teaspoon white pepper

1. Blend all ingredients. Refrigerate

NOTE:

For a quick coleslaw dressing, blend in food processor the above dressing but reduce vinegar to 2 tablespoons and add seasoned salt to taste instead of regular salt. Pour over finely chopped cabbage with a touch of carrot and radish.

Marlene J. Thomas
Boulder, Colorado

BLEU CHEESE DRESSING

Yields 1 1/2 Cups

Preparation 10 Minutes

4 ounces bleu cheese
1/2 cup mayonnaise
1/2 cup sour cream
1 tablespoon sugar
1 tablespoon cider vinegar
Few drops of Tabasco

1. Crumble bleu cheese. Add mayonnaise, sour cream, sugar, vinegar, and Tabasco. Refrigerate.

Loyceine Grier
Parker, Colorado

PEPPER AND ONION DRESSING

Yields 3 1/4 Cups

Preparation 15 Minutes

2 cups mayonnaise
4 tablespoons chopped parsley
6 tablespoons chopped green pepper
2 tablespoons chopped onion
4 tablespoons chopped pimiento
3/4 teaspoon paprika
4 teaspoons lemon juice
1/4 teaspoon pepper
1/2 teaspoon salt

1. Mix all ingredients thoroughly.
2. Refrigerate several days to develop flavor. Excellent with seafood salads or aspics.

Esther deOnis
Boulder, Colorado

HOUSE DRESSING

Yields 3 Cups | Preparation 10 Minutes

1 to 2 cloves garlic, minced
1 teaspoon white vinegar
1 teaspoon steak sauce
1/2 teaspoon Worcestershire sauce
1 teaspoon dry mustard
6 tablespoons grated Parmesan cheese
3 cups mayonnaise
3 tablespoons sour cream (optional)

1. Mix together garlic, vinegar, steak sauce, Worcestershire sauce, mustard, cheese, mayonnaise, and sour cream. Refrigerate.

NOTE:

Flavor improves with time (up to two weeks). An excellent dip for cooked whole artichokes or other vegetables.

Ethel Zager
Avalon, California

GREEN GODDESS DRESSING

Yields 3 3/4 Cups | Preparation 10 Minutes

2/3 cup heavy cream
1 1/2 cups mayonnaise
1 can (2-ounce) flat anchovies, drained
1/2 cup chopped parsley
1 cup chopped green onion
2 tablespoons chopped chives

1. Combine all ingredients in blender and blend until smooth. Refrigerate.

Susan Branigan
Arlington, Virginia

SUDAN SALAD DRESSING

Yields 1 1/2 Cups | Preparation 10 Minutes

1 cup yogurt
1 tablespoon vinegar
1/4 cup vegetable oil
1 to 2 teaspoons salt
1/2 teaspoon crushed red pepper
1 clove garlic, crushed

1. Stir together yogurt, vinegar, oil, salt, red pepper, garlic.

NOTE:

This is an excellent dressing for a salad of lettuce, tomatoes, green onions, and cucumbers. It also compliments African food.

Susannah Jordan
Jamestown, Colorado

HERB DRESSING

Yields 1 Cup

Preparation 5 Minutes

- **1 cup yogurt**
- **1 tablespoon lemon juice**
- **1 teaspoon onion powder**
- **1 teaspoon dry chives**
- **1 teaspoon vegetable salt**
- **1 teaspoon honey**
- **Pinch of dill**

1. Mix all ingredients, stir well, and refrigerate. Flavor improves after 24 hours.

NOTE:

Good on bean sprouts, coleslaw, or cucumber salad. This also is an excellent vegetable dip.

Ilene Kasper
Boulder, Colorado

NOCHE BUENA DRESSING II

Yields 1 1/2 Cups

Preparation 5 Minutes

- **1 cup mayonnaise**
- **1 teaspoon grated lime peel**
- **1/4 cup honey**
- **3 1/2 tablespoons lime juice**

1. Mix mayonnaise, lime peel, honey and lime juice thoroughly. Cover and chill, if made ahead.
2. Serve with *Ensalada de Noche Buena* (see Index).

Serena Dubach
Boulder, Colorado

FRUIT SALAD DRESSING

Yields 1 1/4 Cups

Preparation 10 Minutes

- **1/2 cup mayonnaise**
- **2 tablespoons concentrated orange juice**
- **1 teaspoon lemon juice**
- **1 tablespoon sugar**
- **1/2 cup heavy cream, whipped**

1. Fold mayonnaise, orange juice, lemon juice, and sugar into whipped cream. Refrigerate.

NOTE:

Use on a Waldorf salad variation containing 4 apples, chopped; 1/2 cup chopped celery; 1/2 cup seeded and halved red grapes; and 1/2 cup chopped walnuts.

John Taylor
Boulder, Colorado

ELEGANT FRUIT SALAD DRESSING

Yields 2 1/2 Cups

Preparation 20 Minutes
Cook 10 Minutes

1/2 cup sugar
1 teaspoon flour
1 egg yolk
2 1/2 tablespoons lemon juice
1/2 cup unsweetened pineapple juice
1 cup heavy cream, whipped

1. Combine sugar, flour, and egg yolk. Add fruit juices and cook in a double boiler until thick.
2. Cool and fold in whipped cream.

Elaine Fowler
Boulder, Colorado

LEMON DRESSING

Yields 2/3 Cup

Preparation 15 Minutes

1 egg
Juice of 1 lemon
1/2 cup sugar

1. Slightly beat egg. Combine with lemon juice and sugar.
2. Cook, stirring constantly, until dressing thickens and becomes clear.
3. Cool before serving.

NOTE:

Best made with fresh lemon juice. Can be made a day or two ahead if stored tightly sealed in refrigerator, but the flavor is better if used soon after preparing.

Ann E. Cavender
Lakewood, Colorado

MOLDED GELATIN DRESSING

Yields 1/2 Cup

Preparation 5 Minutes

1/4 cup salad dressing
1/4 cup half-and-half
Fresh lemon juice to taste

1. Mix salad dressing and half-and-half.
2. Add lemon juice to taste.

NOTE:

Use on any gelatin salad.

Loyciene Grier
Parker, Colorado

EGGS
•
AND
•
CHEESE

TWO CHEESE QUICHE

Serves 6

Preparation 30 Minutes
Bake 35 to 40 Minutes at 375°F

1/2 pound sliced bacon
9-inch unbaked pie crust (see Index)
3/4 cup grated Swiss cheese
3/4 cup grated Cheddar cheese
3 eggs
1 1/2 cups half-and-half
3/4 teaspoon salt
Dash each cayenne pepper, nutmeg, and pepper

1. Fry bacon crisp. Drain and crumble on bottom of pie crust.
2. Mix grated cheese, eggs, half-and-half, salt, cayenne, nutmeg, and pepper. Pour into pie crust and add extra seasoning to taste.
3. Bake at 375 degrees for 35 to 40 minutes. Cool 10 minutes.

VARIATION:

Spinach [1 package (10-ounce), frozen and chopped] may be added (cook according to directions). Other ingredients may be added if desired.

Joyce Edelson
Sepulveda, California

YOGURT AND CHEESE QUICHE

Serves 6

Preparation 1 Hour
Bake 55 Minutes at 375°F

12-inch unbaked pie crust (see Index)
5 eggs
2 cups plain yogurt
1 teaspoon salt
1/2 teaspoon white pepper
1/2 teaspoon oregano
1/8 teaspoon sage
1/8 teaspoon leaf thyme
1 1/2 cups grated Swiss cheese
1/2 cup finely chopped fresh chives
Paprika
Parsley, chopped

1. Place pastry in lightly buttered quiche dish, prick bottom and sides with a fork and bake 10 minutes in preheated 375-degree oven. Set aside to cool.
2. In a large bowl, lightly beat eggs and stir in yogurt, whisking well until mixture is creamy and smooth. Add salt, pepper, oregano, sage, and thyme.
3. Using a wooden spoon, fold cheese and chives into mixture. Pour into pastry shell.
4. On center rack of oven, bake 55 minutes at 375 degrees. Let cool 5 minutes. Garnish with paprika and parsley.

Lee L. Swanstrom
Boulder, Colorado

BRIE QUICHE

Serves 8 to 10
Chill Overnight

Preparation 1 Hour
Bake 40 Minutes at 375°F

12-inch baked pie crust (see Index)
5 to 6 ounces Brie, very old
12 ounces cream cheese
4 tablespoons butter
1/3 cup heavy cream
4 eggs
Salt, white pepper, and cayenne pepper to taste
1 tablespoon minced fresh chives

1. Scrape white crust from surface of Brie and weigh out the rest to the amount desired. If very strong, use less.
2. Soften cream cheese, Brie and butter. Blend in mixer approximately 3 minutes until light and fluffy. Add the cream and blend. Add eggs, one at a time, blending after each. Add salt and peppers to taste. Add chives, blend, and cover.
3. Refrigerate for at least one hour, preferably overnight. Remove from refrigerator and whip for several minutes in mixer. Pour gently into prebaked quiche shell and bake on middle shelf for 35 to 40 minutes at 375 degrees.

NOTE:

Quiche will puff and brown and be very slightly soft in the center. Serve immediately as it will deflate slightly as it cools. Can be reheated but will not puff again.

Jan Osterweil
Boulder, Colorado

CHILI QUICHE

Serves 8 to 10

Preparation 20 Minutes
Bake 1 Hour at 350°F

1 can (7-ounce) diced chilies
1 pound Monterey Jack cheese, grated
1 can (4-ounce) bacon bits
6 eggs, lightly beaten

1. Butter a 9-inch square pan.
2. Layer with half of chilies, grated cheese, and bacon bits. Repeat.
3. Beat eggs and pour over all.
4. Bake approximately 1 hour at 350 degrees or until knife inserted in center comes out clean.
5. Let stand 15 minutes before cutting. Good hot or cold and *easy*.

NOTE:

Cut into 1-inch pieces and serve as an appetizer.

Betty Quarnstrom
Avalon, California

VEGETARIAN SPECIAL QUICHE

Serves 3 to 4

Preparation 30 Minutes
Bake 40 Minutes at 425°F
25 Minutes at 325°F

1 deep-dish pie crust, unbaked
1 package (10-ounce) frozen chopped broccoli
1/4 cup bacon bits
3/4 cup shredded Jarlesburg cheese
4 eggs
1 cup half-and-half
1/2 teaspoon salt
Dash pepper

1. Cook broccoli as directed on package. Drain well, squeezing with paper towels to remove as much moisture as possible.
2. Sprinkle bacon bits on pie crust, then drained broccoli, and top with cheese.
3. Mix eggs, half-and-half, salt, and pepper together, stirring well. Pour into pie shell.
4. Bake 40 minutes at 425 degrees. Reduce heat to 325 degrees and continue to bake until quiche is set (about 25 minutes more).

Bonnie M.J. Schriner JD
Denver, Colorado

ZUCCHINI QUICHE

Serves 4

Preparation 15 Minutes
Bake 45 Minutes at 350°F

9-inch unbaked pie crust (see Index)
1 cup peeled and shredded zucchini
2 1/2 cups shredded sharp Cheddar cheese
1/2 cup shredded Monterey Jack cheese with Jalapeño peppers
3 eggs, beaten
4 teaspoons dry minced onion or 1/4 onion, chopped
4 slices bacon, crisply fried and crumbled
1/2 teaspoon salt

1. Combine zucchini, cheeses, eggs, onion, bacon, and salt.
2. Pour into unbaked 9-inch pie shell and bake at 350 degrees for 45 minutes.

NOTE:

Dry onion has a more subtle flavor.

Kathy Said
Nederland, Colorado

CRAB QUICHE

Serves 8

Preparation 25 Minutes
Bake 45 to 60 Minutes at 375°F

10-inch unbaked pie crust (see Index)
1 cup grated Swiss cheese
1 can (7 1/2-ounce) or 1 package (5 3/4-ounce) frozen crab, thawed
2 tablespoons chopped green onion
3 eggs, slightly beaten
1 cup half-and-half
1/2 teaspoon salt
1/2 teaspoon grated lemon peel
1/4 teaspoon dry mustard
Dash of nutmeg
1/4 cup sliced almonds, toasted

1. Roll dough thin and line a 10-inch pie plate. Chill 5 to 10 minutes.
2. Sprinkle cheese over bottom of pie crust. Add crab meat and green onion.
3. Combine eggs, half-and-half, salt, lemon peel, mustard, and nutmeg.
4. Pour over crab. Top with almonds.
5. Bake at 375 degrees for 45 to 60 minutes.

Jane Mahoney
Boulder, Colorado

SALMON QUICHE

Serves 6

Preparation 45 Minutes
Bake 45 to 60 Minutes at 350°F

9-inch unbaked pie crust (see Index)
1 can (15 1/2-ounce) red sockeye salmon
3 large eggs
1 cup cottage cheese
2 teaspoons Dijon mustard
3/4 teaspoon salt
1/2 cup half-and-half
1 cup sliced mushrooms
1/2 cup shredded carrots
1/4 cup thinly sliced green onions
Parsley, chopped

1. Partially bake pastry shell on lower rack of oven for 15 minutes at 350 degrees.
2. Drain salmon, reserving 2 tablespoons liquid. Break salmon into chunks.
3. Beat eggs with cottage cheese, mustard, and salt. Add half-and-half, salmon liquid, and mushrooms. Stir in carrots, onions, and salmon. Spoon into partially baked pastry shell.
4. Return to oven. Bake 45 to 60 minutes at 350 degrees until set in center. Let stand 10 minutes before serving. Garnish with parsley.

Ann Chirikos
Boulder, Colorado

FRESH CAROLINA-APPLE QUICHE

A different combination with a delicious flavor and aroma.

Serves 6 to 8

Preparation 1 Hour
Bake 15 Minutes at 425°F
30 Minutes at 350°F

10-inch unbaked pie crust (see Index)
1/2 pound bulk pork sausage
1/2 cup chopped onion
1/4 teaspoon dried leaf thyme
1 tablespoon lemon juice
1 tablespoon sugar
1 1/2 cups apple (tart, firm variety), pared and cut into 1/2-inch cubes
1 cup shredded Cheddar cheese
3 eggs, well beaten
1 1/2 cups half-and-half

1. Crumble sausage into a large skillet, add onion and thyme, breaking up sausage with fork, and cook over medium heat until browned and onion is tender, about 15 to 20 minutes. Remove from heat and drain off excess fat.
2. In large bowl, toss lemon juice, sugar, and apple. Add sausage mixture and cheese.
3. Blend eggs with half-and-half and pour into the apple-sausage mixture, mixing well.
4. Line 9 3/4-inch quiche dish or other container with pastry. Turn apple mixture carefully into the dish. Bake in lower third of 425-degree oven for 15 minutes. Reduce heat to 350 degrees and continue baking 30 minutes or until custard is set. May be served hot or cold.

Marcia W. Keleher
Denver, Colorado

RICOTTA OMELET

Serves 2

Preparation 15 Minutes
Cook 3 Minutes

4 large mushrooms, sliced
1 slice ham, chopped
1 green onion, sliced
1 tablespoon chopped hot green pepper
1 cup diced tomatoes
1/4 teaspoon basil
1 clove garlic, crushed, or garlic salt to taste
4 eggs
4 heaping teaspoons ricotta cheese

1. Saute' mushrooms, ham, green onion, and green pepper. Add tomatoes and spices. Cook until slightly thickened. Keep warm.
2. Make omelet with eggs, adding ricotta cheese. Fold and cook enough for cheese to soften. Serve topped with sauce.

Sue McMillan
Boulder, Colorado

FRESH ARTICHOKE OMELET

Serves 6

Preparation 2 Hours
Bake 25 Minutes at 325°F

4 or 5 artichokes
Oil
3 garlic cloves
6 eggs, beaten
Garlic powder to taste
Onion powder to taste
Salt to taste
1 cup Parmesan cheese

1. Cook artichokes. Strip out all meat and cut heart into small pieces.
2. Fry garlic cloves in oil in pan until brown. Remove garlic and put in artichoke meat. Fry for 5 minutes. Remove from heat and place in a 9-inch baking dish.
3. Break eggs into bowl. Add garlic and onion powders and salt. Mix.
4. Add to baking dish with artichokes. Spread flat. Sprinkle Parmesan cheese on top.
5. Bake in oven at 325 degrees for 25 minutes.

Barbara Loskutoff
Solana Beach, California

ARTICHOKE FRITTATA

Serves 4

Preparation 15 Minutes
Bake 40 Minutes at 325°F

4 eggs, beaten
6 soda crackers, crumbled
1/2 pound grated sharp Cheddar cheese
2 or 3 jars (6-ounce each) artichokes
3 green onions, chopped
1 tablespoon chopped parsley
1 clove garlic, finely chopped
Salt, pepper, and Tabasco to taste

1. Mix eggs, crackers, cheese, artichokes, onions, parsley, garlic, salt, pepper, and Tabasco. Bake in an oiled 8 x 10-inch pan for 35 to 40 minutes at 325 degrees.

Sally Adams
Piedmont, California

POTATO FRITTATA

Serves 6 to 8

Preparation 35 Minutes
Cook 15 Minutes

1/4 cup olive oil
1/4 cup butter
12 ounces frozen hash brown potatoes
1 large yellow onion, thinly sliced
1 teaspoon salt
1/4 to 1/2 teaspoon freshly ground black pepper
8 eggs
1/4 cup chopped parsley
1/2 teaspoon salt
1 jar (4-ounce) chopped pimientos, drained

1. In a 10-inch skillet, heat oil and butter over medium heat. Add partially thawed potatoes and onions. Cook over medium heat until potatoes are thawed and onions are limp.
2. Sprinkle with salt and pepper. Continue cooking, turning occasionally to brown evenly.
3. Beat eggs with parsley, salt, and pimientos and pour over potatoes and onions. Stir slightly, lower heat, cover, and cook 10 minutes.
4. Remove cover from skillet and put under a broiler, 4 inches away from heat, and broil until set, about 4 minutes.
5. Slide onto a platter and serve.

NOTE:

Can be served hot or cold. Cut into squares for appetizers.

Nancy Cateora
Boulder, Colorado

SPINACH CASSEROLE

Serves 4

Preparation 10 Minutes
Bake 60 Minutes at 300°F

5 ounces Cheddar cheese, cut into small pieces
1 package (10-ounce) spinach, thawed and drained
1 pint cottage cheese, rinsed
3 eggs, beaten

1. Mix all ingredients together. Bake in greased 9-inch square casserole for 1 hour at 300 degrees.

Helen Fullerton
Denver, Colorado

ZUCCHINI FRITTATA

Serves 4

Preparation 30 Minutes
Bake 30 Minutes at 350°F

1 large onion, minced
2 cloves garlic, minced
3 tablespoons olive oil
2 tablespoons chopped fresh parsley
2 tablespoons Italian seasoning
1 tablespoon Maggi seasoning
1 tablespoon salt
1 teaspoon pepper
10 small zucchini
8 eggs
3/4 cup grated Parmesan cheese
1 tomato, peeled and chopped for garnish

1. Saute' onion and garlic in oil until onion is limp. Add herbs and seasonings.
2. Slice zucchini very thin. Add to onion mixture and saute' 5 minutes.
3. Mix eggs and cheese, pour over zucchini, and mix thoroughly.
4. Pour mixture into baking dish. Bake for 30 minutes at 350 degrees or until eggs are set. Garnish with chopped tomato.

Rosemary Jones
San Francisco, California

HARVEST SOUFFLÉ

Serves 6 to 8

Preparation 1 Hour
Bake 40 Minutes at 350°F

1/4 cup butter
1/4 cup flour
1/4 teaspoon salt
1/8 teaspoon garlic salt
1 can (16-ounce) cream-style corn
1/3 cup milk
1/2 teaspoon Worcestershire sauce
1 1/2 cups shredded sharp Cheddar cheese
1/2 cup shredded Provolone cheese
6 eggs, separated

1. Melt butter in saucepan. Blend in flour, salt, and garlic salt. Cook until mixture bubbles, then remove from heat. Blend in corn, milk, and Worcestershire sauce. While stirring constantly, bring mixture to a boil. Cook 1 to 2 minutes longer. Remove from heat and cool slightly. Add cheeses all at once and stir rapidly until melted.
2. Beat egg yolks until thick and lemon colored. Slowly spoon sauce into egg yolks, stirring vigorously after each addition.
3. Using clean beater, beat egg whites until rounded peaks form and egg whites do not slide when bowl is partially inverted. Gently spread egg yolk mixture over beaten egg whites. Carefully fold together until just blended.
4. Turn mixture into ungreased 2-quart souffle' dish. Bake about 40 minutes at 350 degrees. Serve immediately.

CHILI-CHEESE BAKE

Serves 8 to 10

Preparation 35 Minutes
Bake 60 Minutes at 350°F

1 can (4-ounce) chopped green chilies, drained
1 can (4-ounce) chopped mushrooms, drained
1 pound Monterey Jack cheese, coarsely grated
1 pound sharp Cheddar cheese, coarsely grated
4 eggs, separated
2/3 cup evaporated milk, undiluted
1 tablespoon flour
1/2 teaspoon salt
1/4 teaspoon pepper
2 medium tomatoes, sliced
Parsley for garnish

1. Combine chopped chilies, mushrooms, and grated cheeses by tossing together. Turn into well-greased 21/2- or 3-quart casserole.
2. Beat egg whites to stiff peaks. Combine yolks, milk, flour, salt, and pepper. Blend until smooth. Fold gently into egg whites.
3. Pour over cheeses and "ooze" in with fork.
4. Bake 30 minutes at 350 degrees. Arrange tomato slices around edges and bake 30 minutes longer. When done, a knife will come out clean as in a custard. Garnish with parsley.

COMPANY STRATA

Serves 6 to 8
Chill 6 Hours

Preparation 30 Minutes
Bake 55 Minutes at 325°F

12 slices white bread, crusts removed
12 ounces sharp Cheddar cheese, sliced
1 package (10-ounce) frozen broccoli, steamed briefly
2 cups diced cooked ham or 2 cups shrimp, diced
2 tablespoons instant minced onion
6 eggs, slightly beaten
31/2 cups milk
1/2 teaspoon salt
1/4 teaspoon dry mustard

1. Cut bread into desired shapes. Arrange 1/2 of bread on bottom of 12 x 8 x 2-inch buttered baking dish. Layer cheese slices, broccoli, and ham or shrimp over bread.
2. Arrange remaining bread on top; sprinkle with minced onion.
3. Combine eggs, milk, salt, and mustard. Pour over broccoli mixture. Cover with foil and refrigerate 6 hours.
4. Bake uncovered for 55 minutes at 325 degrees. Let stand 10 minutes before serving.

Anne Binkley
Laxeuburg, Austria

EGGS AND CHEESE HOLLANDAISE

Serves 4 to 6

Preparation 20 Minutes
Bake 40 Minutes at 375°F

1/2 pound Cheddar cheese, shredded
1 pound sausage links, cooked
1 pound fresh mushrooms, saute'ed
8 eggs, beaten
Hollandaise sauce (see Index)

1. Line buttered 2-quart casserole with cheese. Drain cooked sausage and cut into bite-sized pieces. Put into casserole on cheese and sprinkle with mushrooms. Pour well-beaten eggs over all.
2. Place pan of boiling water in preheated 375-degree oven. When it bubbles again, place casserole in pan and bake 35 to 40 minutes or until well puffed and lightly browned on top.
3. Serve with Hollandaise sauce.

VARIATION:

Sprinkle Parmesan cheese over casserole or add thinly sliced tomatoes to the beaten eggs before they are poured into casserole.

Beth Poynter
Boulder, Colorado

EGGS PACIFIC

Serves 6

Preparation 45 Minutes
Bake 15 Minutes at 425°F

12 hard-cooked eggs, shelled, sliced
1 pound shrimp or crab, cooked and shelled
3 tablespoons butter
3 tablespoons flour
1 2/3 cups half-and-half, heated
1 teaspoon prepared mustard
1 teaspoon salt
Dash pepper
2 tablespoons dry white wine
2 tablespoons chopped parsley
1/4 teaspoon leaf thyme
1/2 cup shredded Swiss cheese

1. Grease shallow 2-quart casserole. Arrange 6 sliced eggs on bottom.
2. Sprinkle shrimp or crab over eggs and top with remaining eggs.
3. Melt butter, then stir in flour. Allow to bubble while whisking for 2 minutes but do not brown.

4. Add hot half-and-half all at once. Bring to a boil and continue boiling, while whisking for 30 seconds. Stir in mustard, salt, pepper, wine, parsley, and thyme.
5. Pour sauce over eggs, sprinkle with cheese.
6. Bake 15 minutes in a 425-degree oven until bubbly. Serve immediately.

NOTE:

This dish may be prepared in advance, refrigerated, brought back to room temperature, then baked. Serve over toasted English muffins (sauce may be doubled for topping each serving).

Victoria Smith
Boulder, Colorado

SCOTCH EGGS

Serves 8
Refrigerate 2 Hours

Preparation 30 Minutes
Cook 7 to 10 Minutes

1 pound bulk pork sausage
1/2 teaspoon rubbed sage
2 tablespoons snipped parsley
1/2 teaspoon dried thyme, crushed
8 hard-cooked eggs
1/4 cup flour
1/4 teaspoon salt
Freshly ground pepper
1 egg, slightly beaten
1/2 cup fine dry bread crumbs
Cooking oil for deep-fat frying

1. In mixing bowl, blend together sausage, sage, parsley, and thyme.
2. Shape into 8 patties, 4 inches in diameter, using about 1/4 cup mixture for each.
3. Wrap one sausage patty around each hard-cooked egg, completely covering the egg. Cover and chill several hours.
4. Combine flour, salt, and pepper. Roll sausage-covered eggs first in flour mixture, next in beaten eggs, and then in crumbs.
5. Fry in deep oil at 350 degrees until very brown all over. Serve hot or cold.

NOTE:

May make ahead. To serve, heat in oven 15 to 30 minutes.

Mary Angela Eccles
Redondo Beach, California

EGGS IN BURGUNDY SAUCE
(*Oeufs en Meurette*)

Serves 4

Preparation 1 Hour
Cook 15 Minutes

8 slices lean bacon
1 carrot, very finely chopped
1 onion, very finely chopped
1 *bouquet garni* (see Index)
4 cloves garlic, crushed
2 1/2 cups red Burgundy wine
3/4 cup beef or chicken broth
9 tablespoons butter
1/4 pound mushrooms, sliced
1 lemon slice
Salt and pepper to taste
4 slices of firm white bread, crusts trimmed
8 eggs
1 tablespoon flour
2 teaspoons chopped fresh parsley

1. Cut 3 slices of bacon into small pieces. Cut remaining 5 slices into narrow strips and set aside.
2. In a heavy saucepan, saute′ small bacon pieces. Add carrot, onion and cook until they are golden.
3. Add the *bouquet garni*, garlic, wine, broth and simmer for 40 minutes.
4. Meanwhile, saute′ bacon strips in 2 tablespoons butter. Set aside.
5. Saute′ mushrooms with lemon slice in 2 tablespoons butter, salt, and pepper. Set aside.
6. Melt 4 tablespoons butter and fry bread slices on both sides until golden and remove to a serving dish.
7. Strain the sauce, pressing the vegetables. Return sauce to pan and bring to boiling point. Poach eggs in sauce, 4 at a time, pushing the whites over the yolks. Drain eggs and put 2 on each slice of toast.
8. Mix 1 tablespoon softened butter with flour and add to sauce. Cook until thickened.
9. Add cooked bacon strips and mushrooms and pour over eggs. Sprinkle with parsley.

Sheryl Kuempel
Boulder, Colorado

SWISS ONION PIE

Serves 6

Preparation 15 to 30 Minutes
Bake 30 Minutes at 350°F

1 cup crushed soda crackers
1/4 cup butter, melted
2 cups grated Swiss cheese
3/4 cup sour cream
2 eggs, beaten
Dash of salt
1/2 cup bacon bits
1 cup chopped onions, saute'ed
2 teaspoons brown sugar

1. Combine soda crackers with butter. Pat into pie pan.
2. In a mixing bowl, combine cheese, sour cream, eggs, salt, bacon bits, and onions.
3. Pour into crust, top with brown sugar. Bake 30 minutes at 350 degrees.

NOTE:

Increase butter by 2 tablespoons if a richer crust is desired. May be prepared the day before and refrigerated. If so, baking time will vary. Good served with smoked pork chops and asparagus.

Sheryl Henderson
Boulder, Colorado

ZUCCHINI FINGER FOOD

Serves 6 to 8

Preparation 15 Minutes
Bake 30 Minutes at 375°F

3 cups grated zucchini (2 large or 3 medium)
1 onion, finely chopped
2 cloves garlic, pressed
1/2 cup corn oil
1/2 cup grated Monterey Jack cheese
1 cup Bisquick
4 eggs
Salt and pepper to taste

1. Mix zucchini, onion, garlic, oil, cheese, and Bisquick. Add eggs one at a time. Season to taste.
2. Pour into 9 x 9 x 2-inch baking pan. Bake for 30 minutes at 375 degrees or until top is golden brown.

NOTE:

May be served as a vegetable dish or cut into squares for hors d'oeuvres. The dish may be cooled and frozen. After thawing, reheat at 400 degrees for 15 or 20 minutes.

Delores Wong
Los Angeles, California

CHEESE BREAD
(*Bulgarian Totmanick*)

Serves 12

Preparation 30 Minutes
Bake 1 Hour at 350°F

1 cup butter, melted
1/4 cup oil
3 cups Bisquick
1 package dry yeast
8 eggs
1 cup warm water
12 ounces dry curd cottage cheese
1/2 cup crumbled feta cheese

1. Pour 1/2 cup melted butter into a 9 x 13-inch pan. Combine remaining 1/2 cup butter with oil and set aside.
2. Combine Bisquick and yeast.
3. Beat 2 eggs and water, then stir in butter-oil mixture.
4. Add egg mixture to dry ingredients and mix with fork until well blended. Set batter aside.
5. In another bowl, mix cottage cheese, feta cheese, and 6 eggs.
6. Spread 2/3 of batter in prepared pan and cover with cheese mixture.
7. Spoon remaining batter evenly over cheese layer. Batter will spread during baking even though cheese layer is not completely covered.
8. Bake 1 hour at 350 degrees. Can be served hot or cold.

Sonia K. Plisco
Golden, Colorado

BRUNCH BLINTZES

Serves 6 or more

Preparation 10 Minutes
Bake 60 Minutes at 375°F

12 frozen cheese blintzes
1/2 cup orange juice
1/4 pound butter or margarine, softened
4 eggs
1/2 cup sugar
Pinch of salt
1 teaspoon vanilla
12 ounces sour cream

1. Place frozen blintzes close together in a buttered 9 x 13-inch pan.
2. Blend orange juice, butter, eggs, sugar, salt, vanilla, and sour cream in a blender for 1 to 2 minutes.
3. Pour over blintzes and bake at 375 degrees for 1 hour or until top is golden.,

Betty Berger
Los Angeles, California

GREEN TOMATO ENCHILADAS

Serves 4 to 6

Preparation 15 Minutes
Bake 15 Minutes at 350°F

1 can (4-ounce) green chilies
1 can (10-ounce) tomatillas (Mexican green tomatoes)
3 sprigs parsley
1 small white onion, chopped
1 clove garlic, chopped
10 ounces Monterey Jack cheese, grated
1/2 cup sour cream
Oil for frying
12 to 14 corn tortillas

1. For sauce, blend chilies, tomatillas, parsley, onion, and garlic together in a blender or food processor.
2. Moisten 6 ounces cheese with sour cream for filling. Set aside remaining 4 ounces cheese.
3. Dip tortillas in hot oil until limp. Dip in sauce. Fill with 1 tablespoon filling, roll up and place in a 1-quart baking dish.
4. Pour remaining sauce over top, sprinkle with reserved cheese, and bake 15 minutes at 350 degrees.

AVOCADO ENCHILADAS

Serves 4 to 6

Preparation 1 Hour
Bake 20 to 30 Minutes at 350°F

2 or 3 fresh yellow chili peppers
1 can (4-ounce) chili peppers
1 clove garlic, crushed
1 teaspoon salt
1/2 cup oil
2 cups milk
1 dozen corn tortillas
2 avocados, mashed
1 cup chopped onion
2 cups grated Monterey Jack cheese
1 can (3-ounce) black olives, sliced (optional)

1. Roast and peel fresh chilies.
2. Mash chilies until pulpy, add garlic and salt. Saute' mixture in 1 tablespoon oil, then add milk. Heat just to boiling, do not boil.
3. In another skillet, heat remaining oil and dip tortillas to soften.
4. Mix avocados, onion, and 1 1/2 cups cheese. Dip each tortilla in chili sauce and then fill with avocado-cheese mixture.
5. Pour a little chili sauce in bottom of a 9 x 13-inch pan, add filled tortillas in a single layer.
6. Pour remaining sauce over enchiladas and sprinkle with remaining cheese.
7. Top with sliced black olives if desired and bake at 350 degrees for 20 to 30 minutes or until cheese has melted.

Sue Bray
Avalon, California

CHILIES STUFFED WITH CHEESE
(*Chiles Rellenos con Queso*)

Serves 4

Preparation 30 Minutes
Cook 20 Minutes

1/2 pound Monterey Jack cheese
1 can (6-ounce) whole peeled green chilies
Flour
2 eggs, separated
2 tablespoons flour
Oil for frying
1/2 medium onion, chopped
1 clove garlic, crushed
1 small, fresh chili pepper, chopped
1 tablespoon oil
1 can (16-ounce) stewed tomatoes
2 teaspoons chicken bouillon granules
Salt, pepper, and oregano
1/2 cup shredded Cheddar cheese

1. Cut cheese in rectangles about 1/2-inch thick and 3-inches long. Stuff each chili with a piece of cheese. Roll in flour. At this point, these may be covered and refrigerated until ready to use.
2. Make the batter by beating egg whites until stiff. Beat yolks slightly. Fold yolks into whites, then fold in the flour.
3. Drop the stuffed and floured chilies into batter one at a time. Slide into about 1 1/2 inches of moderately hot oil in frying pan. Baste with the hot oil but work quickly!
4. Fry until golden brown on each side. Drain well on absorbent paper. Keep warm or reheat in low oven until hot.
5. To prepare sauce, heat oil and cook onion, garlic, and chili pepper until soft. Add tomatoes and heat until bubbling. Add bouillon, salt, pepper, oregano, and cheese and stir until smooth. Serve with or over fried chilies.

NOTE:

This makes an unusual and eye-opening breakfast or brunch. Serve with Refried Beans (see Index), warmed corn tortillas, and a tequila based drink.

Red Windham
Anchorage, Alaska

ENTREES

ZESTY STEAK

Serves 4

Preparation 5 Minutes
Cook 10 Minutes

2 pounds sirloin steak
Salt and pepper to taste
1 tablespoon Cognac
1/4 cup half-and-half
1 tablespoon chopped green chilies
1/2 teaspoon Dijon mustard

1. Pan fry steak to desired degree of doneness. Add salt and pepper to taste. Transfer to a platter and keep warm.
2. Remove excess fat from skillet, add Cognac, heat 5 seconds. Then add half-and-half, chilies, and mustard. Simmer, stirring, a few seconds and pour over steak.

Pat Wright
Boulder, Colorado

Serve with a Beaujolais or an Oregon Pinot Noir.

CARBONNADES FLAMANDE

Serves 6

Preparation 30 Minutes
Bake 2 Hours at 325°F

2 pounds round steak, 1/2-inch thick, cut into 1 x 2-inch strips
1/2 cup flour
1/2 cup oil or margarine
3 large onions, thickly sliced
3 cloves garlic, minced
3 tablespoons dark brown sugar
1/2 cup chopped fresh parsley
1/4 cup red wine vinegar
2 small bay leaves
2 teaspoons thyme
1 teaspoon salt
Freshly ground pepper
2 cups beef broth
1 bottle (12-ounce) dark beer

1. Dredge steak strips in flour. Brown in oil a few pieces at a time. Remove to ovenproof baking dish.
2. Add onions to skillet and brown, adding more oil if necessary. Add to meat along with garlic, sugar, parsley, vinegar, bay leaves, thyme, salt, and pepper.
3. Pour off excess oil and add beef broth. Heat and scrape the browned particles and meat juices. Pour over meat, add beer and cover. Bake at 325 degrees for 2 hours or until meat is tender. Add more beer if necessary.

NOTE:

Serve with *Haluski* (see Index).

Mary Kerkhoff
Ann Arbor, Michigan

Serve with dark beer or a California Merlot.

ROUND STEAK PARMESAN

Serves 4 to 5

Preparation 20 Minutes
Bake 1 1/2 Hours at 350°F

1 egg, beaten
2 tablespoons water
1/3 cup grated Parmesan cheese
1/4 cup bread crumbs
2 pounds round steak cut into 1-inch pieces
3 tablespoons oil
2 tablespoons minced onion
Salt and pepper to taste
1/2 teaspoon sugar
1/2 teaspoon marjoram
1 can (24-ounce) tomato sauce
Mozzarella cheese slices

1. Combine egg and water. Combine Parmesan cheese and bread crumbs.
2. Dip meat into egg mixture, then into Parmesan mixture. In large skillet, brown meat on both sides in oil. Transfer to greased, shallow casserole. In the same skillet, cook onion until soft. Stir in salt, pepper, sugar, marjoram, and tomato sauce. Simmer 5 minutes and pour over meat.
3. Cover and bake 1 1/4 hours in 350-degree oven. Uncover and top with cheese slices. Bake until cheese melts.

Virginia Thaemert
Denver, Colorado

Serve with a Chianti Classico Reserva or a Vino Nobile di Montepulciano.

STUFFED STEAK WITH SOUR CREAM SAUCE

Serves 4 to 6

Preparation 1/2 Hour
Bake 2 Hours at 350°F

2 pounds round steak
3 slices bacon
3 slices bread, cubed
1 cup apple slices
1/4 cup chopped onion
1 teaspoon salt
1/2 teaspoon sage
1/4 teaspoon thyme
1/4 teaspoon pepper
1 1/2 cups apple juice
1 cup sour cream
1 tablespoon Worcestershire sauce
1/2 teaspoon onion salt
3 tablespoons cornstarch
3 tablespoons water

1. Tenderize meat. Lay bacon lengthwise across steak.
2. Mix bread, apples, onion, salt, sage, thyme, and pepper and place over bacon. Fold ends of meat over filling, roll from side, fasten with skewers or food picks, and lace with string.
3. Place in baking pan, add apple juice, cover tightly. Bake at 350 degrees for 2 hours or until tender. Uncover pan last 15 minutes of baking.
4. Remove skewers and string and place meat on platter.
5. Combine sour cream, 1 1/2 cups pan drippings, Worcestershire sauce, and salt in saucepan. Beat until smooth.

6. Mix cornstarch with water, add gradually to sour cream mixture. Bring to boil over medium heat, stirring constantly. Serve immediately with stuffed steak.

Barbara Moore
Avalon, California

Serve with a Cotes-du-Rhone or a California Cabernet Sauvignon.

BARBECUE POT ROAST

Serves 6 to 8

Preparation 10 Minutes
Bake 3 to 4 Hours at 350°F

1/2 to 1 green pepper, chopped
1 onion, coarsely chopped
1 cup catsup
1 tablespoon mustard
1 teaspoon celery seed
1 cup red wine
3 tablespoons brown sugar
2 tablespoons lemon juice
1 teaspoon salt
1/2 teaspoon pepper
4- to 5-pound chuck roast

1. Mix together green pepper, onion, catsup, mustard, celery seed, wine, sugar, lemon juice, salt, and pepper.
2. Pour over meat in large roasting pan. Cover tightly and bake at 350 degrees until fork tender (3 to 4 hours).
3. Skim fat from sauce and serve sauce with meat.

Bob Berger
Berkeley, California

Serve with beer or an Australian Shiraz.

ESTOUFFAT DE NOEL

Serves 6 to 8

Preparation 30 Minutes
Cook 6 Hours

4-pound beef round roast
1 clove garlic
1 ham rind, 4-inch square
Salt and pepper to taste
Pinch nutmeg and cinnamon
2 slices bacon
***Bouquet Garni* (see Index)**
4 onions, chopped
4 carrots, julienned
1/4 cup brandy
2 cups red wine
1 cup beef broth
Water to cover meat

1. Brown beef, garlic, and ham rind in small roasting pan.
2. Add remaining ingredients. Cover with foil and bake in 250-degree oven for 6 hours.

Marguerite Cateora
Dallas, Texas

FRENCH DRIP BEEF

Serves 10 to 15

Preparation 20 Minutes
Simmer 8 to 9 Hours

1 6- to 8-pound boneless chuck roast
2 to 3 bouillon cubes
1 tablespoon each garlic powder, savory, whole rosemary, and crushed oregano
2 bay leaves
Salt and cracked pepper to taste
Pumpernickel, poppy seed or whole wheat buns
Hot Mustard Sauce (see Index)

1. Place roast in Dutch oven or roaster and cover halfway with water. Add bouillon cubes and spices, cover, and bring to a boil.
2. Reduce heat to barely a simmer, and cook for 8 to 9 hours. (The meat may be cooked on top of the stove or in the oven at 250 degrees so it is just barely bubbling.)
3. Check every 1 to 2 hours, sprinkling with salt and pepper to taste each time. Do not add more water. If too much juice remains when meat is tender, remove cover and cook at slightly higher temperature to reduce juices.
4. Just before serving, remove any fat and shred meat with 2 forks. Serve on pumpernickel, poppy seed, or whole wheat buns with Hot Mustard Sauce.

Ellen Doenges
Austin, Texas

Serve with an Italian Dolcetto or a Chateauneuf-du-Pape.

PEPPERED BEEF

Serves 8
Marinate Overnight

Preparation 20 Minutes
Bake 3 Hours at 300°F

1/4 cup coarsely ground black pepper
1 teaspoon ground cardamom
1 3- to 4-pound boneless brisket of beef
Tomato-Soy Marinade (see Index)
Thinly sliced rye bread
Mustard Horseradish Sauce (see Index)

1. Combine pepper and cardamom and spread evenly on sheet of waxed paper. Place beef over mixture and press down. Turn beef over.
2. With heel of hand, press pepper mixture firmly down into the meat. Cover both sides evenly and thoroughly, using all the pepper mixture.
3. Place meat in shallow dish and add Tomato-Soy Marinade. Cover and refrigerate overnight, turning meat occasionally.

4. When ready to bake, remove meat from marinade and wrap securely in aluminum foil. Place in shallow pan and bake at 300 degrees for 3 hours or until meat is quite tender.
5. Slice very thin and serve hot or cold on thin-sliced rye bread with Mustard Horseradish Sauce.

Nancy Cateora
Boulder, Colorado

Serve with a Cotes-du-Rhone or an Australian Shiraz.

BEEF MOLE

Serves 8

Preparation 1 Hour
Cook 1 Hour

2 pounds chuck roast, cubed
2 tablespoons salad oil
2 medium onions, chopped
2 cloves garlic, chopped
1 1/4 cups water
1 teaspoon vinegar
1 3/4 teaspoons salt
1 bay leaf
2 to 3 tablespoons chili powder
1/2 teaspoon coriander
Dash of cinnamon
Dash of cayenne
2 medium tomatoes, peeled and seeded
2 tablespoons sesame seeds, toasted
1/3 cup dark raisins
1 ounce unsweetened chocolate
1/2 cup dry roasted peanuts

1. In Dutch oven, brown meat in oil. Remove with slotted spoon and set aside.
2. Add onion and garlic and sauté 15 minutes. Return meat, add water, vinegar, salt, bay leaf, chili powder, coriander, cinnamon, and cayenne. Cover and simmer 45 minutes.
3. Puree, in blender or food processor, tomatoes, sesame seeds, and raisins until almost smooth. Add to beef mixture.
4. Add chocolate and peanuts and simmer 10 minutes longer, stirring occasionally.

Ruth Stewart
San Antonio, Texas

Serve with Mexican beer.

BEEF SALAMI

Serves 18 to 20
Refrigerate 3 Days

Preparation 15 Minutes
Bake 8 Hours at 200°F

3 pounds ground beef
1 tablespoon + 3/4 teaspoon Tenderquick salt
1 tablespoon mustard seed
1 1/2 teaspoons pepper or peppercorns
1 1/2 teaspoons garlic salt

1. Mix all ingredients and refrigerate. Knead briefly each day for three days.
2. On the fourth day, shape into rolls and bake at 200 degrees for 8 hours.
3. Cool, wrap in foil and refrigerate or freeze.

Florence E. Hamblen
Avalon, California

Serve with a premium beer, a young Chianti or a Cabernet d'Anjou.

TAMALE PIE

Serves 6 to 8

Preparation 30 Minutes
Bake 20 Minutes at 375°F

1 onion, minced
1 clove garlic, minced
1 green pepper, minced
2 tablespoons salad oil
1 pound ground round
1/4 pound ground pork
1 can (28-ounce) tomatoes
1/2 cup ripe olives
1 1/2 teaspoons salt
Dash pepper and cayenne
1/2 cup grated American or Cheddar cheese
1 cup plus 2 tablespoons yellow corn meal
1 teaspoon chili powder
3 cups boiling water

1. Saute' onion, garlic, and green pepper in oil until light brown. Add beef and pork and brown lightly. Add tomatoes, olives, 1/2 teaspoon salt, pepper, and cayenne and cook slowly for one hour.
2. Add cheese, 2 tablespoons corn meal and chili powder. Cook until cheese melts, stirring occasionally. (Mixture should be consistency of baked hash.)
3. In a separate pan, gradually add 1 cup corn meal and 1 teaspoon salt to boiling water, stir constantly until thickened (about 5 minutes).
4. Pour corn meal mixture into greased casserole. Add meat mixture and bake at 375 degrees for 20 minutes.

Lillie Malork
Vallejo, California

Serve with Mexican beer or a robust Zinfandel.

SOUTH AFRICAN *BOBOTEE*

Serves 4 to 6

Preparation 30 Minutes
Bake 50 Minutes at 350°F

1 slice white bread
1 pound hamburger
1 onion, chopped
2 tablespoons butter or margarine
1 tablespoon curry powder
Juice of 1 lemon or 1 tablespoon vinegar
1/4 cup slivered almonds
Salt and pepper to taste
Grated rind of 1 orange
2 tablespoons apricot jam
2 tablespoons sour cream
2 eggs, beaten
1 cup milk
Yellow Rice (see Index)

1. Soak bread in a little water and squeeze dry. Add to meat and stir.
2. Fry onion in butter and add to meat.
3. Mix curry powder with lemon juice and add to meat mixture along with almonds, salt, pepper, orange rind, apricot jam, and sour cream. Mix well.
4. Place in 1 1/2-quart casserole and bake 30 minutes at 350 degrees.
5. Beat eggs and milk with a pinch of salt and pour over baked meat. Return to oven (350 degrees) and bake until egg sets—about 20 minutes. Serve with Yellow Rice.

NOTE:

This is Africa's answer to our chili dish; therefore, the list and amounts of ingredients vary widely—depending on the region and availability.

Susie Quick
Boulder, Colorado

VARIATION:

The jam and orange rind may be replaced by 8 dried apricots, soaked and chopped, and 1/4 cup chutney. Also add 2 bay leaves broken into small pieces.

Victoria Barker
Boulder, Colorado

Serve with beer or a California Gamay Beaujolais.

PERSIAN MEATLOAF

Serves 6 to 8

Preparation 15 Minutes
Bake 35 to 45 Minutes at 325°F

- **1 1/2 pounds ground beef**
- **3 tablespoons melted butter**
- **1 large onion, chopped**
- **3 whole pimientos, sliced**
- **2 cups or 1 package (10-ounce) frozen chopped spinach**
- **1/2 cup chopped green onions**
- **1/3 cup chopped parsley**
- **1 teaspoon curry powder**
- **1/2 teaspoon cinnamon**
- **1/2 cup chopped walnuts**
- **Salt and pepper to taste**
- **4 eggs, slightly beaten**
- **Plain yogurt**

1. Lightly mix beef, butter, onion, pimientos, spinach, green onion, parsley, curry powder, cinnamon, walnuts, salt, pepper, and eggs.
2. Put in buttered 9-inch casserole and bake 45 minutes at 325 degrees. Pour off excess grease. Slice and serve with yogurt garnish.

Sue McMillan
Boulder, Colorado

Serve with a North African red wine.

POLYNESIAN MEATBALLS

Serves 6 to 8

Preparation 10 Minutes
Cook 20 Minutes

- **1 1/2 pounds ground beef**
- **3/4 cup quick cooking oats**
- **1 can (8-ounce) water chestnuts, drained, finely chopped**
- **1/2 teaspoon onion salt**
- **1/2 teaspoon garlic salt**
- **2 tablespoons soy sauce**
- **1/8 teaspoon Tabasco**
- **1 egg**
- **1/2 cup milk**
- **1 can (8 1/2-ounce) crushed pineapple**
- **1 cup packed brown sugar**
- **2 tablespoons cornstarch**
- **1 cup beef broth**
- **1/2 cup vinegar**
- **1/3 cup chopped green pepper**

1. Combine beef, oats, water chestnuts, onion salt, garlic salt, 1 tablespoon soy sauce, Tabasco, egg, and milk. Mix thoroughly.
2. Form into meatballs 1 or 1 1/2 inches in diameter (smaller for appetizers). Place on cookie sheet and brown under broiler, 5 minutes on a side.
3. Drain pineapple, reserve juice. Mix sugar and cornstarch thoroughly in a large pan. Add pineapple juice, broth, vinegar, remaining 1 tablespoon soy sauce, and mix well. Bring mixture to a boil, stirring constantly. Boil for 1 minute.
4. Stir in peppers and pineapple. Add meatballs, cover, and simmer for 20 minutes.

Betty McBride
Denver, Colorado

Serve with a Vouvray or a young Beaujolais-Villages.

MEXICAN BAR-B-QUE

Serves 6 to 8

Preparation 1 Hour
Bake 1 to 1 1/2 Hours at 325°F

4 pounds lamb shoulder or leg
1 bay leaf
1 onion, cut in half
1 teaspoon salt
2 red onions, sliced
1/2 cup plus 2 tablespoons red wine vinegar
1 1/2 cups catsup
1 cup orange juice
1 cup red wine
1 teaspoon oregano
Salt and pepper to taste
2 cloves garlic, crushed
Refried beans (see Index)
Guacamole (see Index)
Shredded lettuce
Corn tortillas softened in hot oil

1. Boil meat, bay leaf, onion, and salt for 1 hour. Drain.
2. Meanwhile, marinate red onions in 1/2 cup red wine vinegar, salt, and pepper 1 hour.
3. Mix catsup, orange juice, wine, oregano, salt, pepper, garlic, and 2 tablespoons vinegar together. Pour over cooked lamb.
4. Bake 1 to 1 1/2 hours at 325 degrees in uncovered pan, baste every 10 minutes.
5. Slice and serve with refried beans, guacamole, lettuce, marinated onions, or in soft corn tortillas.

Barbara Aldrete
Denver, Colorado

Serve with Mexican beer.

SMOKY LAMB CHOPS

Serves 4

Marinate Overnight
Cook 8 to 10 Minutes

2 tablespoons chopped parsley
2 tablespoons minced onion
1 tablespoon lemon juice
1 tablespoon salad oil
1 teaspoon liquid smoke
2 tablespoons sugar
1/2 teaspoon salt
1/4 teaspoon pepper
6 lamb chops

1. Mix parsley, onion, lemon juice, oil, liquid smoke, sugar, salt, and pepper.
2. Spread marinade over meat. Refrigerate overnight, turning once.
3. Charcoal broil chops 8 to 10 minutes or to desired degree of doneness.

Marcee Shwartz Kutner
Denver, Colorado

Serve with a California Cabernet Sauvignon or a red Graves from Bordeaux.

LAMB DIJON

Serves 8 to 10

Marinate 2 to 24 Hours
Broil 1 to 1 1/2 Hours

5 to 6 pound leg of lamb, boned and butterflied
1 jar (8-ounce) Dijon mustard
1 teaspoon ginger
1 teaspoon dry or 1 tablespoon fresh rosemary
1/2 cup soy sauce
1 clove garlic, minced
2 tablespoons olive oil

1. Have butcher prepare lamb; remove any excess fat.
2. Combine mustard, ginger, rosemary, soy sauce, garlic, and oil in small saucepan. Heat and whisk until mustard is fairly well blended with other ingredients.
3. Pour mixture over meat. Marinate all day, or at least 2 hours, turning 2 or 3 times.
4. Broil or barbecue about 6 inches from heat or hot coals 30 to 40 minutes on each side. Meat should be pink inside after cooking.

Pat Wright
Boulder, Colorado

Serve with a Cote Rotie or a Barbaresco.

LAMB STEW
(South African *Karoo Bredie*)

Serves 4 to 6

Preparation 45 Minutes
Cook 2 Hours

1/2 pound fresh pork fat, diced
3-pound leg of lamb, cubed
1/2 cup brandy
2 1/2 cups broth
1/2 cup red wine
1/2 cup white wine
Pepper to taste
1 large bay leaf
2 cloves garlic, mashed
8 whole small onions
4 large carrots, halved
1/2 pound fresh mushrooms, washed
4 tablespoons flour
1/2 cup cold water

1. Fry pork fat until crisp. Remove from pan, reserving grease.
2. Saute' lamb in grease. Pour brandy over hot meat and set alight. This removes excess fat as well as leaves a nice flavor.
3. Place meat, broth, wines, pepper, bay leaf, garlic, and crumbled browned pork fat in 4-quart, heavy-bottomed pan. Cover and simmer 1 hour.
4. Add onions, carrots, and mushrooms. Simmer 30 minutes or until tender.
5. Mix flour and water. Add a little hot cooking liquid and mix well. Pour flour mixture back into pan. Cook and stir until thickened.

NOTE:

Serve with rice, green salad, and stewed dried peaches flavored with cinnamon.

Susie Quick
Longmont, Colorado

Serve with a California Cabernet Sauvignon or Merlot.

TAS KEBOB

Serves 4 to 6

Preparation 30 Minutes
Cook 2 1/2 Hours

1 1/2 pounds cubed lamb or 8 chicken pieces
3 1/2 cups sliced onions
4 cups thinly sliced potatoes
1 1/2 cups thinly sliced carrots
3 tomatoes, sliced 1/2-inch thick

Salt and pepper to taste
8 to 12 prunes
1/2 to 1 teaspoon curry powder
1 cup V-8 juice
1/2 cup water

1. Brown meat and set aside. Add sliced onion and saute' until onions are transparent; drain and set aside.
2. In a 3-quart pot, layer potatoes, carrots, half of tomato slices and onions, sprinkling each layer with salt and pepper.
3. Add prunes and remaining tomatoes. Arrange meat on top.
4. Combine curry powder and V-8 juice; blend into water, mixing until smooth.
5. Pour liquid around edge of pan. Bring to boiling, reduce heat and simmer, tightly covered, about 2 hours. As mixture steams, more liquid will accumulate.
6. Do not stir during cooking period. Serve in bowls.

NOTE:

To use the crockpot, cook for 6 to 8 hours on low. One can (16-ounce) tomatoes, undrained, may be substituted for fresh tomatoes.

Trev Lewis
Denver, Colorado

Serve with a young Valpolicella or a Spanish Rioja.

ŞIŞ KÖFTE

Serves 6

Preparation 20 Minutes
Cook 5 to 10 Minutes

2 slices stale bread
1/2 cup red wine
1 pound ground lamb
1/2 pound ground beef
1/2 cup chopped onion
2 eggs
2 teaspoons paprika
1 teaspoon salt

1. Soak bread in wine; squeeze dry.
2. Combine lamb, beef, onion, eggs, paprika, salt, and bread. Mix thoroughly.
3. Divide mixture into small finger-like portions. Thread onto greased skewers.
4. Charcoal broil or grill 3 inches from heat source, turning slowly, for 5 minutes or longer. All sides should be browned evenly.

NOTE:

Serve with Turkish Pilaf (see Index). Skewered meat may be prepared and stored in refrigerator up to 2 hours before broiling.

Roslyn Pfaff
Boulder, Colorado

Serve with a Chianti or a California Zinfandel.

KÖFTE CURRY

Serves 6 to 8

Preparation 1 Hour
Cook 25 Minutes

1 1/2 pounds ground lamb
3 tablespoons ground coriander
2 teaspoons salt
1 1/2 teaspoons minced ginger root
1/8 teaspoon cloves
1/8 teaspoon cinnamon
1 tablespoon flour
1 egg, beaten
6 tablespoons oil
1 onion, sliced
1 teaspoon paprika
1/2 teaspoon pepper
1/4 teaspoon turmeric
2 cloves garlic, minced
2 tablespoons grated coconut
3 tomatoes, peeled and sliced
1/2 cup boiling water
1 teaspoon lemon juice

1. Combine lamb, 2 tablespoons coriander, 1 teaspoon salt, ginger root, cloves, cinnamon, flour, and egg. Mix well and shape into 24 meatballs (wet hands for easier handling). Brown in 3 tablespoons oil. Drain and set aside.
2. For curry sauce, saute′ onion in remaining 3 tablespoons oil and add 1 tablespoon coriander, paprika, pepper, turmeric, garlic, coconut, and 1 teaspoon salt. Saute′ 3 minutes and add tomatoes and water. Simmer 15 minutes.

3. Add meatballs and simmer 10 minutes. Just before serving add lemon juice.

Kathy Van Arsdale
Denver, Colorado

Serve with beer.

HUNGARIAN PAPRIKA PORK
(*Bakonyi Pork*)

Serves 4

Preparation 20 Minutes
Cook 25 Minutes

1 pound boneless pork, thinly sliced
2 tablespoons flour
Salt and pepper
4 tablespoons vegetable oil
2 small onions, thinly sliced
1/4 teaspoon celery seed
1 teaspoon Hungarian paprika
1 cup beef broth
3/4 pound fresh mushrooms, sliced
1/2 teaspoon Dijon mustard
1/2 cup sour cream
Chopped parsley
***Haluski* (see Index)**

1. Pound pork slices as thin as possible. Dredge in mixture of flour, salt, and pepper. Reserve flour.
2. Heat 3 tablespoons oil in skillet. Cook pork lightly on both sides. As it becomes golden, transfer meat to two-quart covered casserole. Cover and cook over low heat.
3. Add onion to skillet used for browning meat. Cook, stirring, on low heat, until golden.
4. Add celery seed, paprika, and beef broth. Simmer three minutes and pour over pork.
5. Add remaining oil to skillet. Saute' mushrooms lightly and add to meat-onion mixture. Salt and pepper to taste.
6. Combine remaining flour and mustard with sour cream, dilute with a little liquid from meat, and blend well. Stir sour cream mixture into meat.
7. Simmer gently for five minutes. Do not boil. Garnish with parsley.
8. Serve with *Haluski.*

Susannah Jordan
Jamestown, Colorado

Serve with an Australian Chardonnay or a California Chenin Blanc.

PORK CHOPS WITH WILD RICE

Serves 6

Preparation 30 Minutes
Bake 2 Hours at 350°F

6 large loin pork chops
6 tablespoons washed, raw wild rice
6 onion slices
6 tomato slices
6 green pepper rings
2 to 3 cups tomato juice
1 cup water

1. Lightly brown pork chops in skillet. Transfer to roasting pan.
2. Layer each chop with wild rice, onion slice, tomato slice, and pepper ring. Season to taste.
3. Pour on tomato juice and water. Cover and bake 2 hours at 350 degrees.
4. After 1 hour, baste and add more juice and water if needed.

Dorothy Gould
Los Angeles, California

Serve with a Brunello di Montalcino.

PORK AND SAUERKRAUT GOULASH
(*Székely Gulyás*)

Serves 8 to 10

Preparation 30 Minutes
Cook 2 Hours

2 large onions, chopped
2 tablespoons bacon fat
2 cloves garlic, mashed
2 tablespoons Hungarian sweet paprika
1 1/2 teaspoons caraway seed
2 to 3 cups water or broth
2 pounds pork shoulder, cut in 1-inch cubes
1/2 teaspoon salt
1 pound sauerkraut, well washed
1 cup sour cream
1 tablespoon flour
Buttered noodles

1. In large casserole, sauté onions in fat until lightly browned.
2. Add garlic, paprika, and caraway seed. Mix well and add 1 cup water or broth. Bring to boil.
3. Add pork and salt, reduce heat and cover. Simmer 1 hour.
4. Add sauerkraut and 1 cup water or broth. Simmer 45 minutes until meat is tender, adding more liquid as necessary.
5. Blend sour cream and flour and add to goulash. Mix well. Simmer 5 to 10 minutes longer.
6. Serve over buttered noodles.

Sheryl Kuempel
Boulder, Colorado

Serve with a Rheinpfalz *kabinett* or a California Johannisberg Riesling.

PORTUGUESE SAUERBRATEN
(*Vinha D'Alhos*)

Serves 8 to 10
Marinate Overnight

Preparation 15 Minutes
Bake 2 Hours at 350°F

3/4 cup cider vinegar
1 1/2 cups water
2 to 3 cloves garlic, mashed
1 to 2 dried chili peppers
1 teaspoon salt
2 ounces whiskey or sherry
1/4 cup chopped parsley
4 pounds pork butt
4 potatoes (optional)

1. Mix vinegar, water, garlic, chilies, salt, whiskey, and parsley.
2. Add whole pork butt and marinate 12 to 14 hours or overnight, turning occasionally.
3. Place pork butt and marinade in roasting pan.
4. Bake at 350 degrees for 2 hours, turning meat as it browns. If desired, add potatoes during last hour of baking.

VARIATION:

Cut pork into cubes and boil in marinade. When liquid is gone, add oil and fry meat. Makes an excellent appetizer.

Sheryl Kuempel
Boulder, Colorado

Serve with a Portuguese red Dão or a Cotes-du-Rhone.

CHINESE SPARERIBS

Serves 4

Preparation 1 Hour
Bake 25 Minutes at 450°F
20 Minutes at 350°F

1 slab pork spareribs (3 1/2 to 4 pounds)
1 1/2 to 2 teaspoons salt
1/2 cup catsup
1/4 cup soy sauce
3/4 cup sugar

1. Rub spareribs with salt. Let meat stand for 1/2 hour to absorb salt.
2. Combine catsup, soy sauce, and sugar. Add spareribs and marinate at least 1/2 hour.
3. Bake in uncovered 9 x 13-inch baking pan at 450 degrees for 25 minutes. Turn ribs over, lower heat to 350 degrees and bake another 20 minutes.

NOTE:

May be prepared and left in marinade up to 3 hours before cooking. Ribs are also delicious when barbecued over charcoal. Marinade may also be used on chicken.

Friends of the Chinatown Library
Los Angeles, California

Serve with Chinese beer or an Alsatian Gewurztraminer.

DANISH SPARERIBS

Serves 4 to 6

Preparation 2 Hours
Bake 20 Minutes at 450°F
1 to 1 1/2 Hours at 350°F

1 cup dried prunes
Warm water
2 tablespoons butter
1/3 cup currant jelly
1/4 teaspoon dry mustard
1 teaspoon Worcestershire sauce
2 tablespoons vinegar
3 pounds pork ribs in two equal-sized racks
Salt and pepper to taste
2 to 3 medium apples, peeled and quartered

1. Cover prunes with warm water and soak 2 hours.
2. Meanwhile, prepare basting sauce. Melt butter in saucepan, add jelly, mustard, Worcestershire sauce, and vinegar. Heat until jelly melts, stirring constantly. Set aside.
3. Sprinkle ribs with salt and pepper. Drain prunes and discard liquid.
4. Place apples and prunes on one rack of pork. Top with remaining rack. Sew edges together with heavy thread or tie with string.
5. Place in drip pan. Do not add water; do not cover.
6. Bake at 450 degrees for 20 minutes; reduce heat to 350 degrees. Continue baking until tender, approximately 1 to 1 1/2 hours, basting with sauce.

Serve with Danish beer.

Crede Dever
Boulder, Colorado

HUNGARIAN STUFFED CABBAGE
(Töltött Kaposzta)

Serves 6

Preparation 30 Minutes
Cook 1 1/2 Hours

1 large head cabbage
1 cup chopped onions
1 large clove garlic, minced
1 pound lean ground pork or 1/2 pound pork and 1/2 pound beef
1 1/2 cups cooked rice
1 egg, beaten
2 tablespoons sweet Hungarian paprika
Salt and pepper to taste
1/4 pound bacon
2 pounds sauerkraut, washed and drained
1 can (28-ounce) diced tomatoes and juice
3 tablespoons tomato paste
1 cup sour cream

1. In large pot, boil enough water to cover cabbage. Cook until leaves wilt, about 8 to 10 minutes. Pull off large leaves and set aside to dry.
2. Mix onions, garlic, meat, rice, egg, paprika, salt, and pepper.
3. Place 2 tablespoons meat mixture in center of each cabbage leaf. Fold in sides and roll up.

4. Fry bacon until almost done but not crisp. Drain.
5. Mix sauerkraut and bacon and spread half on bottom of large casserole. Place rolled cabbage on top and spread remaining sauerkraut mixture over cabbage rolls.
6. Combine tomatoes, juice, and tomato paste and pour over sauerkraut. Bring to a boil, cover tightly, and reduce heat. Simmer 1 1/2 hours.
7. Remove cabbage rolls and set aside. Add sour cream to sauerkraut mixture in casserole. Mix well.
8. With slotted spoon, remove sauerkraut to serving platter. Place cabbage rolls on top and cover with some sauce. Serve remaining sauce separately.

NOTE:

This is best made several days ahead through Step 7. When ready to serve, reheat and finish.

Sheryl Kuempel
Boulder, Colorado

Serve with an Egri Bikaver (Hungarian red).

PORK AND *HALUSKI* WITH CABBAGE

Serves 4 to 6

Preparation 25 Minutes
Cook 20 Minutes

1 pound fresh side pork, diced
1 medium head cabbage, shredded
1/2 teaspoon seasoned salt
1 recipe *Haluski* (see Index)

1. In 6-quart Dutch oven, sauté pork until transparent but not crisp, about 15 minutes. Do not drain.
2. Add cabbage and salt. Cover and simmer 20 minutes or until cabbage is tender but still crisp. Stir frequently.
3. Add well drained *Haluski*, heat through, and serve.

VARIATION:

Bacon may be substituted for side pork and egg noodles for *Haluski*.

Grace Dryer Dionigi
Arvada, Colorado

Serve with a German *spaetlese.*

ITALIAN TORTE
(*Torta Rustica*)

Serves 6 to 8

Preparation 45 Minutes
Bake 20 Minutes at 400°F

1 package (13 3/4-ounce) hot roll mix
1 1/2 cups chopped onion
1 pound Italian sausage
1 cup chopped fresh parsley
2 zucchini, sliced
1 teaspoon basil
1/2 teaspoon salt
1/2 teaspoon oregano
4 fresh tomatoes, chopped
1 cup sliced fresh mushrooms
8 ounces Mozzarella cheese, shredded

1. Prepare hot roll mix as directed on package; let rise once.
2. Cook sausage and onion 15 minutes over medium heat, drain excess fat.
3. Add parsley, zucchini, basil, salt, oregano, tomatoes, and mushrooms. Simmer 15 minutes.
4. Roll out 2/3 of dough to 1/2-inch thickness to fit 2-quart casserole. Line casserole with dough, allowing 1-inch overhang.
5. Fill with meat mixture and top with cheese.
6. Roll out remaining dough to cover top of casserole. Seal edges securely. Cover edge of casserole with strips of foil to prevent burning.
7. Bake 20 minutes at 400 degrees or until dough is browned.

NOTE:

Frozen bread dough, thawed, may be substituted for packaged roll mix. Freezes well. To bake, allow 15 minutes at room temperature after thawing in refrigerator and add 15 minutes to cooking time.

Kathy Van Arsdale
Denver, Colorado

Serve with a Zinfandel or an Italian Gattinara.

HAM-POTATO STEW

Serves 3 to 4

Preparation 20 Minutes
Cook 15 Minutes

4 cups cubed potatoes
2 cups cubed cooked ham
1 1/2 cups water (from boiling potatoes)
1 cup milk
1/2 teaspoon pepper
3/4 cup shredded Cheddar or American cheese

1. Boil potatoes until nearly done. Drain off water and reserve 1 1/2 cups.
2. Add ham, reserved water, milk, pepper, and cheese to saucepan with potatoes.

3. Cook over low heat until cheese melts and ham is hot (about 15 minutes).

Susan J. Mowry
Boulder, Colorado

Serve with a Vouvray or a California Chenin Blanc.

RED *SCALOPPINE*

Serves 4 to 6

Preparation 45 Minutes
Cook 20 Minutes

1 1/2 pounds veal, cut into 1/4-inch thick slices
1/2 cup flour
1 teaspoon salt
1/8 teaspoon pepper
6 tablespoons butter
2 tablespoons oil
1 large onion, chopped
1/2 pound fresh mushrooms, sliced
1 or 2 cloves garlic, minced
2 tablespoons red wine vinegar
2 tablespoons soy sauce
1 can (8-ounce) tomato sauce
1/3 cup dry sherry or dry white wine
1/2 to 1 cup chicken broth
1 1/2 teaspoons oregano
1/3 cup grated Parmesan cheese
1 cup grated sharp Cheddar cheese

1. Pound veal until very thin. Mix flour with salt and pepper. Dredge veal lightly in seasoned flour.
2. Heat 3 tablespoons butter and the oil in a 12-inch skillet. Brown each piece of meat quickly on each side. Set aside as it browns.
3. Add remaining butter to pan and sauté onion, mushrooms, and garlic for 5 minutes. Stir in vinegar, soy, tomato sauce, sherry, 1/2 cup chicken broth, and oregano.
4. Return meat to skillet, cover, and simmer gently for 15 minutes.
5. Stir in Parmesan and Cheddar cheese just until melted and blended. Serve immediately or cool and refrigerate. Reheat slowly over low heat. Dilute with chicken broth if too thick.

Ellen Denton
Piedmont, California

Serve with a Barola or a Chianti Classico Riserva.

VEAL *SCALOPPINE* MARSALA

Serves 5

Preparation 25 Minutes
Cook 15 Minutes

2 pounds boneless veal, cut into thin, even slices
1/3 cup flour
1 teaspoon salt
1/2 teaspoon pepper
1/2 cup butter or olive oil or 1/4 cup each
1/2 pound fresh mushrooms, sliced
1/2 cup Marsala wine
1 tablespoon lemon juice

1. Dredge veal in flour, salt, and pepper.
2. Brown quickly in butter or oil. Add mushrooms and wine. Cover and simmer for 5 to 10 minutes.
3. Stir in lemon juice and serve immediately.

Marguerite Cateora
Dallas, Texas

Serve with a rich California Chardonnay or a Meursault.

VEAL VELOUTÉ

Serves 6 to 8

Preparation 30 Minutes
Cook 2 Hours

2 pounds veal shoulder, cut into 2-inch cubes
1 onion, halved
1 carrot, quartered
***Bouquet garni* (see Index)**
1 tablespoon salt
1/4 teaspoon white pepper
Water just to cover
3 tablespoons butter
1 cup sliced onions
1/2 pound fresh mushrooms, sliced
2 cups Veloute' Sauce (see Index) made with veal cooking liquid
1 teaspoon lemon juice
1 teaspoon butter
2 teaspoons chopped parsley
Rice or buttered noodles

1. In a large heavy saucepan, place veal, onion, carrot, bouquet garni, salt, pepper, and water to cover. Cover and simmer about 2 hours.
2. Remove meat and set aside. Discard onion and carrot. Reserve liquid.
3. In the same pan, melt butter and saute' onions until transparent, add mushrooms and cook 5 minutes longer. Add to meat.
4. Prepare Veloute' Sauce in same pan, then return meat, onions, and mushrooms to pan with sauce.
5. Just before serving, blend in lemon juice and butter. Garnish with chopped parsley. Serve over rice or buttered noodles.

Esther deOnis
Boulder, Colorado

Serve with a Santenay, Volnay or a light California Pinot Noir.

VEAL MILANESE

Serves 4

Preparation 25 Minutes
Cook 10 Minutes

1 pound veal, cut into 1/4-inch-thick slices
Salt and pepper
1 cup cracker meal
1/8 teaspoon each basil, oregano, rosemary, thyme, and parsley
1 egg, beaten
1 tablespoon butter
1 tablespoon olive oil
2 cloves garlic, crushed
2 lemons, cut in eighths

1. Pound veal until very thin. Season with salt and pepper.
2. Mix cracker meal with basil, oregano, rosemary, thyme, and parsley. Dip veal in egg and then into seasoned cracker meal.
3. In a large frying pan, heat butter and olive oil. Add garlic and veal. Saute' veal until browned on both sides.
4. Remove to a warm serving platter and serve immediately with lemon wedges. Squeeze lemon juice onto hot meat.

Ellen Denton
Piedmont, California

Serve with a California Sauvignon Blanc or a Soave.

VEAL STEW ON RICE

Excellent entree for a low-salt diet.

Serves 6

Preparation 30 Minutes
Bake 1 1/2 Hours at 275°F

2 pounds veal rump, cut into 2-inch cubes
1/4 teaspoon freshly ground pepper
2 tablespoons oil
1/8 teaspoon rosemary, crushed
2 green peppers, chopped
2 medium fresh tomatoes, peeled and cubed
Beef broth as needed
1 1/2 cups cooked rice
2 tablespoons unsalted butter

1. Season veal with pepper and brown in hot oil on all sides in heavy 4-quart casserole or skillet.
2. Add rosemary, green peppers, and tomatoes. Mix well. Cover, reduce heat, and simmer 1 1/2 hours or until veal is tender. Add beef broth as needed to keep meat moist. Serve over buttered rice.

Florence White
Boulder, Colorado

Serve with a Zinfandel or a Merlot.

VEAL SAUTÉ

Serves 12 to 14

Preparation 30 Minutes
Cook 1 1/2 Hours

- **6 pounds veal stew meat, cubed**
- **1/3 cup oil (half vegetable and half light olive oil)**
- **Salt to taste**
- **3/4 teaspoon freshly ground pepper**
- **1/2 pound fresh mushrooms, sliced**
- **2 cloves garlic, minced**
- **2 medium onions, chopped**
- **1/2 cup chopped celery**
- **2 green peppers, cut in strips**
- **2 cans (28-ounce each) Italian-style tomatoes**
- **3/4 cup dry red wine**
- **2 small bay leaves**
- **2 tablespoons cornstarch**
- **3 tablespoons cold water**

1. In large Dutch oven, brown veal in hot oil. Add salt and pepper. Remove meat and set aside.
2. To the same oil, add mushrooms and garlic; saute' until golden. Add onions and celery and cook until onions are limp. Add green pepper and cook 3 minutes.
3. Add tomatoes including juices, wine, bay leaves, and veal; mix thoroughly. Cover and simmer over low heat 1 1/2 hours.
4. When ready to serve, remove bay leaves and correct seasonings. Dissolve cornstarch in cold water, add to sauce, and stir until thickened, about 8 minutes.

NOTE:

Serve with Almond Poppy Seed Noodles (see Index) and Green Beans with Garlic (see Index).

Nancy Cateora
Boulder, Colorado

Serve with a Cotes-du-Rhone or a Spanish Rioja.

CORONATION CHICKEN

Serves 6

Preparation 30 Minutes
Bake 1 Hour at 400°F

- **2 chickens (2 1/2-pounds each)**
- **2 tablespoons butter**
- **1 tablespoon olive oil**
- **1 small onion, chopped**
- **1 tablespoon curry powder**
- **1/2 cup chicken broth**
- **1 tablespoon tomato paste**
- **2 tablespoons chutney**
- **2 tablespoons lemon juice**
- **1 1/4 cups mayonnaise**
- **3 tablespoons cream**
- **2 to 3 cups cold cooked rice**
- **1/2 cup each chopped tomato and green pepper**
- **Oil and vinegar to taste**

1. Rub chicken with butter; roast at 400 degrees for 1 hour. Cool.
2. Heat oil in saucepan and cook onion over low heat 5 minutes. Add curry powder and cook a few minutes to bring out flavor. Add broth, tomato paste, chutney, and lemon juice and stir constantly until boiling. Simmer 5 minutes.
3. Strain sauce into small bowl. When cool, stir in mayonnaise and cream.
4. Combine rice with tomatoes and green pepper and toss with oil and vinegar. Set aside.
5. Debone chicken and cut into chunky pieces. Toss lightly with mayonnaise mixture. Serve with rice-tomato mixture.

Cicely Kane
Boulder, Colorado

Serve with a Chenin Blanc or a Pinot Blanc.

CHINESE CASHEW CHICKEN

Serves 4

Preparation 30 Minutes
Cook 10 Minutes

1 egg white, slightly beaten
1 1/2 tablespoons cornstarch
2 1/2 tablespoons soy sauce
2 whole boned chicken breasts, cubed
1 tablespoon dry sherry
1 1/2 teaspoons vinegar
1 teaspoon sugar
1 cup cooking oil
1 green pepper, cubed or 1 to 2 green chili peppers, minced, 1 sweet red pepper, cubed or 1 dry hot chili, whole
3 green onions, cut in 1-inch pieces
2 quarter-sized slices ginger root
5 ounces cashew nuts, unsalted

1. Mix egg white, 1 tablespoon cornstarch, and 1/2 tablespoon soy sauce. Add chicken cubes and set aside.
2. Mix remaining soy sauce, sherry, vinegar, remaining cornstarch, and sugar and set aside.
3. Heat oil in wok or skillet and fry chicken 3 to 4 minutes. Remove and drain.
4. Pour off all but 2 tablespoons oil and add peppers, green onions, and ginger. Fry about 2 minutes. Add cooked chicken and sauce. Cook until sauce has thickened. Add cashews. Mix and serve.

Sheryl Kuempel
Boulder, Colorado

Serve with Chinese beer or Champagne.

CHICKEN CURRY

Serves 6 to 8

Preparation 20 Minutes
Cook 1 to 1 1/2 Hours

4 teaspoons peanut oil
1 teaspoon cumin
1 teaspoon coriander
1 teaspoon turmeric
1 teaspoon ginger
1/4 to 1/2 teaspoon cayenne
2 to 3 cloves garlic, finely chopped
1 teaspoon salt
2 to 3 medium onions, coarsely chopped
1 chicken, cut up
2 to 3 tomatoes, or 1 can (16-ounce) whole peeled tomatoes
1/2 cup water
8 ounces plain yogurt
Cooked rice

1. In oil, fry all spices including garlic and salt for 1 to 2 minutes. Add chopped onion and saute' for 3 to 4 minutes.
2. Add chicken pieces and brown for approximately 10 minutes, turning occasionally to coat all pieces with oil and spices.
3. Add tomatoes and 1/2 cup water. Cover and simmer at least 1 hour. Stir occasionally and add more water as needed.
4. Remove from heat and skim off chicken fat. Add yogurt and mix well. Bring back to boiling point. Serve immediately over rice.

Chris Busick
Boulder, Colorado

Serve with beer.

CEYLON CHICKEN CURRY

Serves 4

Preparation 15 Minutes
Cook 35 Minutes

2 tablespoons butter or safflower oil
1 cup minced onion
1 to 2 tablespoons minced garlic
1/2 teaspoon saffron
1/4 cup grated coconut
1 tablespoon poppy seeds
1 teaspoon powdered chili
1 1/2 teaspoons coriander powder
1/2 bunch coriander leaves (optional)
1 frying chicken, cut up
2 cups hot water
1/4 cup yogurt
1 cup coconut milk
1 to 2 tablespoons lime juice
1/4 teaspoon cumin powder

1. Heat butter. Fry onion and garlic until clear. Add saffron, coconut, poppy seeds, chili, coriander powder and leaves. Fry about 5 minutes.
2. Add chicken and water. Simmer until chicken is tender, about 25 minutes. Add yogurt and simmer another 5 minutes. Remove from heat.
3. Add coconut milk, lime juice, and cumin. Mix and heat through.

NOTE:

This unusual curry is much milder in spices than most such dishes. If coconut milk is not available, soak 1/4 cup flaked coconut in 1 cup milk, then strain.

Larry Chartrand
Boulder, Colorado

Serve with beer or a medium-dry Chenin Blanc.

CHICKEN GUAVA

Serves 6 to 8

Preparation 15 Minutes
Bake 15 Minutes at 450°F
45 Minutes at 350°F

5 pounds chicken thighs
1 cup guava or apple jelly
1 tablespoon cornstarch
1 cup water
1/4 cup lime juice
2 tablespoons Worcestershire sauce
2 ounces sherry
1 tablespoon chopped ginger root
1 1/2 teaspoons allspice
2 teaspoons salt
1/4 teaspoon pepper
Rice Pepita (see Index)

1. Place thighs in single layer in shallow baking pan.
2. Combine remaining ingredients except Rice Pepita and bring to a boil. Simmer 5 minutes.
3. Pour marinade over chicken. Bake for 15 minutes at 450 degrees. Reduce heat to 350 degrees and continue baking for 45 minutes, basting frequently. Serve with Rice Pepita.

Serve with an Italian Pinot Grigio.

SESAME CHICKEN

Serves 2

Preparation 35 Minutes
Bake 20 Minutes at 350°F

3 chicken breasts, boned
3 eggs, slightly beaten
1 teaspoon salt
1 cup bread crumbs
1 cup sesame seeds
4 tablespoons margarine

1. Cut chicken into strips. Combine eggs and salt. Dip chicken strips in mixture and roll in bread crumbs, dip again in egg, then roll in sesame seeds.
2. Thread each strip onto a wooden skewer and fry in margarine until browned. Bake in 350-degree oven for 20 minutes.

Sheryl Kuempel
Boulder, Colorado

Serve with a California or Washington Sauvignon Blanc.

POLLO CHINOISE

Serves 4 to 6

Preparation 1 1/2 Hours
Cook 15 Minutes

3 tablespoons vegetable oil
2 green onions, diced
1 teaspoon minced ginger root
1/4 teaspoon cayenne pepper
1/4 teaspoon Szechuan chili powder
4 tablespoons soy sauce
2 tablespoons honey
1 clove garlic, crushed
1/4 teaspoon salt
1/4 teaspoon MSG (optional)
1 chicken, baked and cubed
6 ounces frozen snow peas, thawed
1 medium head iceberg lettuce, shredded
10 flour tortillas

1. Heat oil. Add onions, ginger root, cayenne, and chili powder. Saute' until onion is transparent. Add soy sauce, honey, garlic, salt, and MSG. Mix well. Add chicken and peas. Stir.
2. Wrap tortillas in foil and warm in oven, or heat briefly on a griddle.
3. Serve chicken mixture, tortillas, and lettuce separately so each diner may fill his own tortillas.

Deborah Taylor
Boulder, Colorado

Serve with a medium-dry California Gewurtztraminer.

GUINEAN CHICKEN STEW

Serves 4 to 6

Preparation 20 Minutes
Cook 50 to 60 Minutes

2 1/2 pounds chicken pieces
2 teaspoons salt
1/2 teaspoon pepper
3 tablespoons peanut oil
2 cloves garlic, minced
2 medium onions, chopped
6 ounces tomato paste
2 tomatoes, cut up
1/2 teaspoon crushed red pepper
2 cups water
1/2 cup chunk-style peanut butter
10 ounces frozen okra, thawed

1. Rub chicken pieces with 1 teaspoon salt and pepper. Heat oil in large skillet and brown chicken on all sides. Remove and set aside.
2. In same skillet, saute' garlic and onions until golden. Stir in tomato paste, tomatoes, red pepper, remaining salt, and 1 1/2 cups water.
3. Return chicken to pan, bring to a boil, then reduce heat and simmer, covered, for 40 minutes.
4. Blend peanut butter with 1/2 cup water and add with okra to chicken. Stir. Cook 8 to 10 minutes or until chicken and okra are tender.

VARIATION:

Paprika, chili pepper, or cayenne may be used to vary spiciness of recipe.

Susannah Jordon
Jamestown, Colorado

Serve with a California Zinfandel or Petite Sirah.

ITALIAN CHICKEN

Serves 8

Preparation 10 Minutes
Bake 1 1/2 Hours at 325°F

5 pounds chicken pieces
1 teaspoon salt
1/4 teaspoon pepper
1/2 teaspoon garlic powder
1/2 teaspoon onion powder
6 Italian sweet sausages, sliced
2 jars (16-ounce each) Ragu Italian Cooking Sauce (traditional)
Cooked spaghetti

1. Season chicken with spices and place in baking dish. Cover with a layer of sliced sausages. Bake at 325 degrees for 45 minutes.
2. Spread cooking sauce over chicken and bake 45 minutes longer. Serve over spaghetti.

Joy Rousso
Woodland Hills, California

Serve with a Valpolicella or lighter Chianti.

CHICKEN AND BEANS

Serves 4 to 6
Soak Overnight

Preparation 20 Minutes
Cook 3 Hours

1 cup dry small white beans or baby limas
1 large onion, sliced
4 garlic cloves, sliced
1 fryer chicken, cut up
1 1/2 teaspoons salt
1/2 teaspoon pepper
1/2 teaspoon paprika

1. Place beans in a 5- or 6-quart heavy saucepan with 3 quarts water. Soak overnight.
2. Drain and add fresh water to cover beans. Add onion and garlic and cook 1 1/2 hours.
3. Add chicken, salt, pepper, and paprika. Cook 1 to 1 1/2 hours more.

Edith Schiffman
Boulder, Colorado

Serve with a California Chardonnay or Pinot Blanc.

WEST AFRICAN LEMON CHICKEN

Serves 8

Preparation 35 Minutes
Bake 1 Hour at 350°F

2 chickens, cut up
3/4 cup peanut oil
Juice of 5 lemons
3 onions, thinly sliced
1/2 cup white wine vinegar
1 clove garlic
1/2 teaspoon pepper
1 teaspoon salt
1/2 teaspoon thyme
1 bay leaf
1/2 to 1 1/2 teaspoons chopped hot pepper
1 cup water
Hot cooked rice

1. Brown chicken in 1/4 cup hot oil in heavy skillet. Transfer to large casserole.
2. Combine lemon juice, onions, 1/2 cup oil, vinegar, garlic, pepper, salt, thyme, bay leaf, and hot pepper, bring to a boil, add water, and pour over chicken. Cover tightly and bake in 350-degree oven until tender, about 1 hour. Serve on hot rice.

VARIATION:

Fish and lamb may also be prepared in this sauce.

NOTE:

Can be cooked in heavy pan on top of stove. Add sliced pimiento at the last minute for color. May marinate chicken overnight.

Pauline Poehlmann
Boulder, Colorado

Serve with beer or a California Sauvignon Blanc.

HAWAIIAN CHICKEN

Serves 6 to 8

Preparation 30 Minutes
Bake 1 Hour at 350°F

2 chickens, cut up
1 cup flour
1 1/2 teaspoons salt
1/4 pound butter or margarine, melted
1 1/2 cups orange juice
3 tablespoons lemon juice
1 1/2 tablespoons cornstarch
3/4 cup brown sugar
1 1/2 tablespoons soy sauce
2 cups papaya, cubed
Pineapple, banana, water chestnuts to taste

1. Shake chicken pieces in bag with mixture of flour and 1 teaspoon salt.
2. Grease shallow baking dish with part of butter, add chicken pieces in single layer, and drizzle with remaining butter. Bake at 350 degrees for 50 minutes or until chicken is tender.
3. Combine juices, cornstarch, sugar, soy sauce, and 1/2 teaspoon salt in saucepan. Cook and stir until sauce thickens and is clear.

4. Add fruit and pour sauce over chicken. Bake 10 minutes longer.

NOTE:

Delicious served over rice. May be made ahead and frozen, unsauced. Sauce also freezes well without fruit.

Sheryl Kuempel
Boulder, Colorado

Serve with a Chenin Blanc.

INDONESIAN CHICKEN IN LIME

Serves 4

Preparation 25 Minutes
Cook 45 Minutes

1 chicken, cut up
1/4 cup peanut oil
1 tablespoon minced onion
1 clove garlic, minced
1 tablespoon honey
1/4 teaspoon turmeric
1/2 teaspoon each crushed red pepper, ground cumin, and ground coriander
2 tablespoons soy sauce
2 tablespoons lime juice
1 lime, quartered

1. Brown chicken in oil, push to one side and saute' onion and garlic until tender.
2. Add honey, turmeric, pepper, cumin, coriander, and soy sauce. Stir. Simmer 45 minutes or until chicken is tender.
3. Sprinkle with lime juice just before serving. Garnish with lime quarters.

NOTE:

An easy recipe with an unusual flavor, this can be prepared several hours in advance. Reheat but don't overcook. Use chicken wings to serve as an appetizer.

Kathy Van Arsdale
Denver, Colorado

Serve with beer or an off-dry White Riesling.

GREEK CHICKEN *KAPOMA*

Serves 4 to 6

Preparation 45 Minutes
Cook 1 1/2 Hours

3 1/2 to 4 pounds chicken pieces
Juice of 1 lemon
1 teaspoon salt
1/4 teaspoon pepper
3 tablespoons olive oil
3 tablespoons butter
2 cups sliced onions
1/4 cup tomato paste
1 cup tomato sauce
1/2 stick cinnamon
1/2 cup dry wine (red or white)
1 1/2 cups boiling water

1. Wash and dry chicken pieces. Sprinkle with lemon juice, salt, and pepper. Let stand 15 minutes.
2. Heat oil and butter in heavy skillet and brown chicken. Set aside.
3. In same oil, saute' onions until soft but not brown. Add tomato paste, tomato sauce, cinnamon, wine, and boiling water. Cook gently for 10 minutes, stirring to keep sauce smooth.
4. Return chicken to sauce. Cover and simmer 1 1/4 hours.

NOTE:

Serve with linguini, macaroni, potatoes, or rice.

Serve with a California or Australian Chardonnay.

Mary Lymberopoulos
Boulder, Colorado

BATTER FRIED CHICKEN

Serves 6 to 8
Stand 1 Hour

Preparation 25 Minutes
Cook 15 Minutes

2 fryers, 2 1/2 to 3 pounds each
1 teaspoon salt
1 egg, slightly beaten
1/2 cup milk
1 teaspoon celery salt
1/4 teaspoon pepper
1 1/2 cups flour
3 pounds vegetable shortening or 3 cups oil

1. Spread chicken pieces on waxed paper. Sprinkle with 1 teaspoon salt. Let stand about one hour.
2. Combine egg, milk, celery salt, pepper, and remaining salt in shallow bowl. Beat in 2 tablespoons flour until smooth.
3. Dip chicken pieces one at a time into batter, then dredge in remaining flour to lightly coat.
4. Heat oil in large saucepan or deep-fat fryer set at 350 to 360 degrees. Fry chicken 3 to 4 pieces at a time in hot fat, turning with tongs until a rich golden brown on all sides (12 to 15 minutes).
5. Transfer browned chicken to a pan lined with paper towels and place in 250-degree oven to keep warm while frying the rest of the chicken.

Mary Wing
Boulder, Colorado

BREASTS OF CHICKEN PARISIENNE

Serves 6

Preparation 15 Minutes
Cook 30 Minutes

1/2 cup flour
6 chicken breasts, boned
6 tablespoons butter
3 tablespoons hot Marsala wine
1 teaspoon tomato paste
1 cup chicken broth
2 cups sour cream
1 teaspoon salt
1/4 teaspoon pepper
1 tablespoon currant jelly
2 tablespoons freshly grated Parmesan cheese
Dash cayenne pepper
2 tablespoons grated Swiss cheese

1. Set aside 1 1/2 tablespoons flour, dredge chicken breasts in remaining flour. Fry quickly in hot butter.
2. Add wine and continue to cook 1 to 2 minutes. Remove breasts and set aside.
3. Add reserved flour to pan, stir and cook 2 minutes. Add tomato paste and broth and stir constantly until sauce thickens.
4. Stir in sour cream in small amounts. Add salt, pepper, jelly, Parmesan cheese, and cayenne. Return breasts to pan. Cover and simmer for 15 to 30 minutes until tender.
5. Place breasts in baking dish. Pour sauce over top and sprinkle with grated Swiss cheese. Brown under flame.

Peg Pettit
Boulder, Colorado

Serve with a German *kabinett* or a Washington White Riesling.

PARTY-PERFECT CHICKEN

Serves 6 to 8

Preparation 20 Minutes
Bake 1 Hour at 400°F

2 fryer chickens, cut up
6 tablespoons flour
1 1/2 teaspoons salt
1 teaspoon ginger
6 tablespoons margarine, melted
Curry Glaze (see Index)

1. Toss chicken with flour, salt, and ginger to coat well.
2. Dip floured chicken in melted margarine, place in shallow baking pan and bake, uncovered, for 20 minutes at 400 degrees.
3. Spoon 1/2 recipe Curry Glaze over chicken and bake 20 minutes longer.
4. Add remaining glaze and bake until tender.

Anne Dykstra
Boulder, Colorado

Serve with an Alsatian Gewurztraminer or Pinot Gris.

Richard Grausman, U.S. Representative of Le Cordon Bleu de Paris, *has been conducting cooking classes in major cities throughout the United States for over 10 years. Mr. Grausman has earned* Le Cordon Bleu's Grand Diplome *and is the first and only foreign representative the school has ever had.*
We wish to thank Mr. Grausman for sharing his original recipes with us and for his help and advice.

CANARD AU CIDRE

Serves 6

Preparation 1 1/2 Hours
Bake 15 Minutes at 475°F
1 Hour at 425°F

2 5-pound ducks, prepared (trussed for roasting)
Salt and pepper to taste
Wing tips, necks, gizzards and hearts
2 medium onions, quartered
2 large carrots, sliced
2 stalks celery, quartered
2 shallots, cut in half
4 sprigs parsley
1/4 teaspoon thyme
1 bay leaf
6 to 9 apples (Golden Delicious)
1 cup dry white wine
2 cups French apple cider
1 teaspoon *Glace de Viande* or 1/4 teaspoon *Bovril*
1 cup heavy cream
White vinegar
2 tablespoons butter
1 to 2 tablespoons sugar
2 or 3 ounces *Calvados* Brandy

1. Preheat oven to 475 degrees.
2. Season ducks with salt and pepper and poke with a fork. Cut up wing tips, necks, gizzards and hearts and place ducks on top of these parts on their sides in a large roasting pan.
3. Arrange vegetables around ducks. Season with salt, pepper, thyme, and bay leaf.
4. Place in oven and roast 15 minutes at 475 degrees, then reduce heat to 425 degrees and roast 1 hour (or 15 minutes per pound), turning ducks and stirring vegetables mid-way. Turn ducks breast-side up for the last 10 minutes of roasting. Ducks are fully cooked when cavity juices run clear.
5. Place ducks on carving board and allow to stand 10 to 20 minutes before carving.
6. While ducks are roasting, peel, core, and slice apples 1/4-inch thick. Soak apples in white wine for 1/2 hour.
7. In covered saute' pan, poach apples in wine until tender, but not soft (5 to 7 minutes). Pour off liquid and reserve. Set aside apples.
8. When ducks are cooked, pour off all fat, retaining vegetables in pan. Place roasting pan on heat and add cider and liquid from apples. Bring to a boil, then reduce heat. Simmer 5 to 10 minutes, stirring vegetables from time to time.

9. Strain sauce into small saucepan. Reduce liquid to 1 cup and skim off fat. Stir in *Glace de Viande*, add cream and boil to thicken slightly. Sauce should coat back of spoon. Taste sauce, if too sweet, add vinegar (several drops at a time) to taste, beginning with 1/2 teaspoon.
10. Carve ducks. Place on ovenproof platter.
11. When ready to serve, place platter in upper third of 500-degree oven for 3 to 5 minutes to reheat duck.
12. Reheat apples with butter and sugar, and flame with *Calvados*. Arrange apples around duck and serve sauce separately.

NOTE:

This recipe can be done the day ahead through Step 4. Cover and refrigerate pan containing the ducks and vegetables. Increase reheat time to 10 minutes. If French apple cider is not available, use American cider. Serve with *Pommes Gaufrettes* or with wild rice and mushrooms sautéed with salt, pepper, thyme, and parsley.

Richard Grausman
U.S. Representative
Le Cordon Bleu de Paris
New York, New York

Serve with a Puligny-Montrachet.

ALMOND DUCK

Serves 4
Freeze 4 Hours

Preparation 30 Minutes
Cook 2 Hours

1 duckling, 5 pounds
1 tablespoon salt
4 slices fresh ginger root (optional)
1/2 teaspoon Chinese 5-spice
1 bunch Chinese parsley
6 green onions, chopped
2 ounces gin
1 rice bowl water
Dash white pepper
Cornstarch
Oil for frying
1 cup vinegar
1 cup brown sugar
1 cup water
3 tablespoons cornstarch
Catsup for color
Finely chopped almonds, toasted

1. Split back of duck and place on rack in large pot for steaming.
2. Add salt, ginger root, spices, parsley, onions, gin, water, and white pepper to cavity of the duck. Steam 2 hours in lightly covered pot. Debone and press duck flat.
3. Dredge duck in cornstarch until well covered. Freeze for 4 hours.
4. Deep fry in hot oil until a dark golden brown. Cut into serving pieces.
5. Combine vinegar, sugar, water, cornstarch, and catsup. Bring to a boil and pour over duck. Sprinkle with finely chopped almonds.

Serve with Chinese beer or Champagne.

SOUSED TURKEY

Serves 10

Preparation 20 Minutes
Bake 3 1/2 Hours at 400°F

1 turkey, 12 pounds
1/4 cup dry white wine
1/4 cup brandy
1 teaspoon thyme
1 teaspoon basil
Salt and pepper to taste

1. Stuff turkey with your own special dressing. Place in roasting pan.
2. Pour mixture of wine, brandy, thyme, basil, salt, and pepper over turkey. Cover tightly with foil or with tight-fitting lid.
3. Bake 3 hours at 400 degrees. Fold back foil or remove lid and continue baking for 1/2 hour to brown.

Pat C. Harwood
Littleton, Colorado

Serve with a Vouvray or a young California Chardonnay.

CHICKEN LIVERS ALLA ROMA

Serves 1

Preparation 5 Minutes
Cook 14 Minutes

6 to 8 chicken livers
2 tablespoons olive oil
3 tablespoons fresh sage leaves or 2 teaspoons dried sage
Salt and pepper to taste
4 to 6 drops Worcestershire sauce
1/4 to 1/2 cup white wine

1. Saute' chicken livers in olive oil over moderate heat for 3 minutes.
2. Add sage, salt, and pepper. Cook over high heat, stirring, about 10 minutes.
3. Add Worcestershire sauce and wine. Saute' 30 seconds.

Rosemary Jones
San Francisco, California

Serve with a Valpolicella or a young Oregon Pinot Noir.

CHICKEN LIVERS ANNETTE

Serves 3 to 4

Preparation 15 Minutes
Cook 15 Minutes

1/4 pound bacon
1/3 cup flour
Salt and pepper to taste
1 pound chicken livers, halved
1 green pepper, diced
1 cup red wine
1/2 to 1 cup pitted black olives
2 cups cooked rice

1. Fry bacon, drain, reserving 2 tablespoons bacon grease. Crumble bacon and set aside.
2. Season flour with salt and pepper and dredge chicken livers. Saute' in bacon grease for 5 minutes.
3. Add green pepper and saute' for a few minutes. Remove from heat and add wine and olives. Serve over rice.

Serve with a California Cabernet Sauvignon.

SAUTÉED CALVES' LIVER WITH ORANGE

Serves 3 to 4

Preparation 15 Minutes
Cook 7 Minutes

2 tablespoons flour seasoned with chili powder, dry mustard, salt and pepper
6 slices calves' liver
4 tablespoons butter
1 tablespoon oil
4 tablespoons dry red wine
1 teaspoon minced onion
2 cloves garlic, chopped
Pinch each of basil, thyme, tarragon, and parsley
1/4 cup beef broth
1 orange, unpeeled and sliced
Sugar
2 teaspoons oil

1. Dust slices of liver very lightly with seasoned flour.
2. In a large frying pan, melt 2 tablespoons butter, add 1 teaspoon oil to prevent butter from burning. Brown both sides of liver very quickly, 1 to 2 minutes according to preference. Remove from pan and arrange on serving dish and keep warm.
3. Add 2 tablespoons wine and additional 2 tablespoons butter to the frying pan, heat and add chopped onion. Fry for 1 minute. Add garlic and cook 1 minute longer; add herbs and remaining 2 tablespoons red wine and 1/4 cup beef broth. Heat and pour over liver.
4. Sprinkle orange slices with sugar and brown on both sides in 2 teaspoons hot oil. Serve as a garnish.

Peg Pettit
Boulder, Colorado

Serve with a California Zinfandel or an Australian Shiraz.

LIVER WITH BACON AND ONIONS

Serves 3 to 4

Preparation 10 Minutes
Cook 30 Minutes

1/3 pound bacon, diced
1 1/2 cups diced onion
1/2 pound calves' liver, diced
1/3 cup flour
1/4 teaspoon each pepper, celery salt, paprika
1 cup water

1. In a large skillet, fry diced bacon until crisp. Remove and set aside. Pour off half of bacon drippings.
2. Saute' onion in bacon drippings until transparent. Set aside.
3. Dredge liver in flour, shaking off excess flour. Brown in bacon drippings and add pepper, celery salt, paprika, water, bacon, and onion.
4. Cover and simmer 10 minutes or until liver is tender. Add more water, if neccessary, to prevent sticking.

Jean Foss
Boulder, Colorado

Serve with a Petite Sirah or a Syrah.

SWEETBREADS

Serves 4
Soak 2 Hours

Preparation 1 Hour
Bake 45 to 60 Minutes at 325°F

1 1/2 to 2 pounds veal or beef sweetbreads
1 tablespoon vinegar
1 teaspoon salt
1 tablespoon lemon juice
3 tablespoons butter
1/4 cup each minced ham, celery, onion, carrot
1/2 pound mushrooms, chopped (optional)
1 teaspoon chopped fresh parsley
Pinch thyme
1 bay leaf
Salt and pepper to taste
3/4 cup dry white wine
1 cup beef broth
1 tablespoon tomato paste (optional)
Heavy cream to taste

1. Wash sweetbreads in cold water. Soak about 2 hours in water with vinegar. Drain.
2. Place sweetbreads in saucepan and cover with cold water, salt, and lemon juice. Bring to a boil and simmer 5 minutes. Drain well and cool immediately under cold running water. Remove outer membrane and connective tissue.
3. Saute' sweetbreads in butter for about 10 minutes, then transfer to a buttered casserole, large enough to hold one layer.
4. Melt butter and saute' celery, carrot, onion, ham, and mushrooms. Add parsley, thyme, bay leaf, salt, and pepper and spoon over sweetbreads.

5. To frying pan, add wine and broth. Boil until reduced to 3/4 cup. Add tomato paste, if desired, and pour over sweetbreads. Bake at 325 degrees for 35 to 45 minutes or until sweetbreads are tender. Add more broth if needed.
6. Before serving, add cream to taste and adjust seasonings. Remove bay leaf.

Joyce Lind
Eaton, Colorado

Serve with a mature red Bordeaux or California Cabernet Sauvignon.

SAVORY BAKED WILD DUCK OR PHEASANT

Serves 2 to 4

Preparation 20 Minutes
Bake 1 1/2 to 2 Hours at 350°F

1 wild duck or pheasant, quartered
Flour for dredging
6 tablespoons butter
1/4 cup lemon juice
1/2 teaspoon salt
Freshly ground black pepper
1/2 teaspoon leaf thyme
1/4 teaspoon each leaf rosemary, oregano, and basil
1 clove garlic, minced
1 tablespoon chopped onion

1. Dredge duck or pheasant in flour and saute' in 2 tablespoons melted butter in ovenproof casserole until lightly browned.
2. Meanwhile, in a small saucepan, combine lemon juice, 4 tablespoons butter, salt, pepper, thyme, rosemary, oregano, basil, garlic, and onion. Simmer, covered, for 5 to 10 minutes.
3. Pour over browned bird. Cover and bake 1 1/2 to 2 hours at 350 degrees or until tender. Baste 2 or 3 times with sauce.

NOTE:

Serve with Turkish Pilaf, Armenian Pilaf, or Rice Pepita (see Index) and Carrots and Leeks Vichy (see Index).

Serena Dubach
Boulder, Colorado

Serve with a Gevray-Chambertin or a California Pinot Noir.

PHEASANT IN SOUR CREAM-MUSHROOM SAUCE

Serves 6 to 8

Preparation 30 Minutes
Cook 1 Hour

2 pheasant, quartered or 4 to 6 breasts, split
2/3 cup flour seasoned with garlic salt
5 tablespoons butter
1 1/2 cups beef broth
2/3 cup chopped onion
1/4 pound fresh mushrooms, sliced
1 teaspoon Worcestershire sauce
2 tablespoons catsup
2 tablespoons flour
1 cup sour cream
2 tablespoons chopped parsley

1. Lightly coat pheasants in seasoned flour and brown on all sides in 2 tablespoons melted butter adding more butter as needed. Add 1 cup broth and braise slowly about 1 hour or until tender.
2. In another skillet, melt 2 tablespoons butter and saute' onions until transparent, add mushrooms and saute' 3 minutes longer. Stir in Worcestershire sauce, catsup, flour, and remaining 1/2 cup broth. Cook over moderate heat, stirring until sauce is thickened and smooth.
3. Arrange pheasant on serving platter. Add any remaining braising liquid to mushroom sauce along with sour cream. Pour sauce over pheasant and garnish with parsley.

Serena Dubach
Boulder, Colorado

Serve with an Hermitage or Cote Rotie.

VENISON PAPRIKA

Serves 8

Preparation 20 Minutes
Cook 1 3/4 Hours

3 pounds venison cut into 1-inch cubes
1/2 cup flour seasoned with salt and pepper
1/2 cup butter
1 1/2 cups chopped onions
2 cloves garlic, minced
1 teaspoon marjoram
1 to 2 tablespoons sweet Hungarian paprika
1/3 cup dry sherry
1 cup diced tomatoes
1 cup sour cream
Salt and pepper to taste

1. Lightly coat meat with seasoned flour and brown in butter in large skillet.
2. Set meat aside. Saute' onions and garlic for 4 minutes. Add marjoram, paprika, sherry, and tomatoes. Cook, covered, over low heat for 15 minutes.
3. Add browned meat, continue cooking, covered, until meat is tender, 45 minutes to 1 hour.

4. Stir in sour cream and salt and pepper to taste. Serve at once.

NOTE:

1. Serve with noodles or Barley Casserole (see Index).
2. Make this dish ahead, freeze before adding sour cream. Reheat, then add sour cream and thin sauce if necessary with sherry or water.

Serena Dubach
Boulder, Colorado

Serve with a Chateauneuf-du-Pape or an Amarone.

RABBIT, VENISON, OR BEEF BRAISED WITH ONIONS (*Stifatho*)

Serves 6 to 8
Soak 1 Hour
Preparation 30 Minutes
Cook 2 to 3 Hours

2 to 3 pounds rabbit, venison, or beef
1 1/2 teaspoons salt
1/2 cup vinegar
Pepper to taste
Flour for dredging
1/2 cup olive oil
2 1/2 pounds small whole white onions, peeled
2 cloves garlic
2 cups dry red wine
4 cups water
1 tablespoon whole mixed spices tied in cheese-cloth bag
4 bay leaves
1/2 cup tomato sauce
Peel of 1/4 orange

1. Wash rabbit or venison and soak in water with 1 teaspoon salt and 1/2 cup vinegar. Let stand 1 hour. (Omit this step if using beef.)
2. Sprinkle meat with 1/2 teaspoon salt and pepper and dredge in flour. Heat oil in skillet and brown meat. Transfer to heavy kettle or Dutch oven.
3. Lightly brown onions and garlic in skillet, then add to kettle with remaining ingredients. Cover and simmer for 2 to 3 hours until meat is tender.

NOTE:

Serve with noodles and crusty French bread.

Mary Lymberopoulos
Boulder, Colorado

Serve with a California Cabernet or a St. Emilion from Bordeaux.

TROUT WITH WINE AND GRAPES

Serves 6

Preparation 30 Minutes
Cook 20 Minutes

6 trout (8 to 12-ounce each), head and tail removed
Salt and pepper
1 cup flour
1 cup buttermilk
1 cup cornmeal
3 tablespoons each oil and butter
1/2 to 3/4 cup white wine
30 to 35 seedless green grapes, halved
2 tablespoons minced parsley
Thyme
1/2 lemon, juiced
Lemon wedges and parsley sprigs

1. Clean and scale trout. Season inside with salt and pepper. Dip in 3/4 cup flour, salt, and pepper, then in buttermilk, then roll in mixture of cornmeal and remaining 1/4 cup flour.
2. Fry in large pan over medium heat in oil and butter until fish is golden and done. Remove and keep warm.
3. Let oil cool slightly and add wine. Cook, uncovered, until sauce is reduced, about 5 minutes. Add grapes, minced parsley, thyme, and juice of 1/2 lemon. Taste and adjust seasonings (may want a touch of sugar).
4. Add trout to pan and heat through. Place fish on platter, spoon sauce over, and garnish with lemon and parsley.

NOTE:

You may want to skin the fish. This sauce is also good over saute'ed lamb or calves' liver.

Joyce Lind
Eaton, Colorado

Serve with an Alsatian Riesling.

BUTTER STEAMED FISH

Serves 4

Preparation 10 Minutes
Cook 5 to 10 Minutes

1 pound fish filets
1 tablespoon white wine
Salt and pepper to taste
3/4 to 1 teaspoon dill weed
1 lemon, thinly sliced
Paprika
2 tablespoons butter

1. Place fish in 8-inch round baking dish suitable for serving. Pour on wine.
2. Sprinkle with salt, pepper, and dill weed.
3. Cover each filet with 3 slices of lemon, then sprinkle with paprika and dot with butter.

4. Cover dish lightly with foil. Put steamer rack in wok and add 2 inches hot water. Bring to boil. Place baking dish with fish on rack.
5. Steam 5 minutes for 1/2-inch filets. Steam 10 minutes for 1-inch filets. Do not overcook.

NOTE:

Red snapper, sole, whitefish, or turbot work equally well in this recipe.

Rosemary Tedesco
The Cookery
Boulder, Colorado

Serve with a French Muscadet or a Washington Sauvignon Blanc.

SOLE *BONNE FEMME*

Serves 8

Preparation 1 Hour
Bake 15 Minutes at 350°F

1 pound fresh white mushrooms, sliced
1/2 cup chopped onions
2 tablespoons chopped parsley
3 pounds filet of sole
2 tablespoons lemon juice
1/2 teaspoon salt
1/4 teaspoon white pepper
1/2 cup dry vermouth
1 cup chicken broth
1/2 cup butter
2 tablespoons flour
1/2 cup heavy cream
1 egg yolk

1. Place half the mushrooms, onions, and parsley in greased baking pan.
2. Dry fish filets and place in pan. Cover with remaining mushrooms, onions, parsley, lemon juice, salt, and pepper.
3. Pour vermouth and chicken broth over fish and bring to boil on top of stove. Cover pan and bake at 350 degrees for 10 minutes.
4. Drain liquid from baking pan into saucepan and simmer until reduced by one-half.
5. Blend butter with flour and add to fish liquor. Stir constantly.
6. Mix cream with egg yolk and add slowly to sauce, stirring. Do not boil.
7. Be sure fish filets are thoroughly drained then pour on sauce. Brown under broiler, and serve.

Janet Abbott
Albuquerque, New Mexico

Serve with a mature white Graves (Bordeaux) or a Meursault.

BAKED STUFFED SALMON

Serves 8

Preparation 30 Minutes
Bake 1 Hour at 400°F

4 pounds fresh salmon, center section
1 teaspoon salt
Pepper to taste
1 tablespoon minced parsley
1 tablespoon chopped green pepper
2 tablespoons chopped fresh mushrooms
2 tablespoons finely chopped onions
2 tablespoons finely chopped ripe olives
1/4 teaspoon dried basil
1 cup dry bread crumbs
1/2 cup butter, melted
4 slices bacon

1. Sprinkle fish cavity lightly with 1/2 teaspoon salt and pepper.
2. Lightly mix parsley, green pepper, mushrooms, onions, olives, basil, bread crumbs, butter, and remaining salt.
3. Fill cavity with stuffing. Fasten with small skewers or toothpicks.
4. Place in shallow baking dish. Lay bacon strips on fish. Bake 1 hour at 400 degrees.

Nona Jahsman
Palo Alto, California

Serve with an Alsatian Pinot Gris or an Italian Pinot Grigio.

SMELT STUFFED WITH CHEESE

Serves 4 to 6

Preparation 35 Minutes
Cook 5 Minutes

Cheddar cheese (sharp)
1 package (16-ounce) thawed smelt
2 eggs, separated
4 tablespoons flour
1/2 teaspoon salt
Oil for deep frying
2 cups chicken broth
2 tablespoons oil
1/2 medium onion, finely chopped
1 clove garlic, crushed
3 to 4 tablespoons tomato paste
1/4 teaspoon oregano
1/2 teaspoon chili powder
Pepper to taste

1. Cut cheese into 1 1/4 x 1/4-inch strips and fit a piece into cavity of each smelt.
2. Beat egg whites until stiff. Beat egg yolks with 2 tablespoons flour and 1/4 teaspoon salt. If too stiff, add a little water. Fold yolk mixture into whites.
3. Holding smelt by the tail, carefully dip each one into batter.
4. Heat deep oil enough to make a bread cube sizzle and brown in 5 minutes. Drop fish into oil and fry until light, golden brown. Set aside in warm oven.

5. For sauce, blend remaining flour with cold broth and cook until thickened. Heat 2 tablespoons oil and brown onions. Add remaining ingredients and stir into broth. Boil 5 minutes. Pour over smelt.

NOTE:

This dish is rich but very good. Keeping the cheese inside smelt is the hardest part, handle gently and cheese will stay in. Trout or other fish may be prepared in the same way.

T. Paul Maslin
Boulder, Colorado

Serve with a dry Gewurztraminer or a Soave.

CHINESE SWEET AND PUNGENT FISH

Serves 4

Preparation 1 Hour
Fry 8 to 10 Minutes

1 small onion, sliced
1 teaspoon minced ginger root
1/4 teaspoon salt
Dash of pepper
2 1/2 tablespoons soy sauce
1 teaspoon dry sherry
2 pounds whole fish, (rock cod or sea bass), cleaned, head and tail left on, if desired
2 1/2 tablespoons cornstarch
1 clove garlic, minced
2 tablespoons oil
1 small onion, diced
1 carrot, sliced
1/2 green pepper, diced
1/2 cup sugar
1 cup water
1/2 cup vinegar
1 tablespoon catsup
Oil for frying

1. Combine onion, ginger root, salt, pepper, 1/2 tablespoon soy sauce, and sherry. Rub over inside and outside of fish. Let stand 45 minutes, then coat fish lightly with 1 tablespoon cornstarch. Let stand 5 minutes longer.
2. Meanwhile prepare sauce: cook garlic in oil until lightly browned. Add onion, carrot, and green pepper and fry quickly until barely tender.
3. Mix sugar, 1/2 cup water, vinegar, and remaining 2 tablespoons soy sauce and add to vegetables. Heat to almost boiling.
4. Blend remaining 1 1/2 tablespoons cornstarch with remaining 1/2 cup water and add to vegetable sauce. Cook and stir until thickened and clear. Stir in catsup.
5. Fry fish in 375-degree oil until golden. Serve sauce over fish.

Serve with Chinese beer.

BARBECUED FISH FILETS

Serves 4 to 6

Preparation 25 Minutes
Cook 15 Minutes

3 tablespoons butter
3/4 cup diced onion
2 pounds fish filets, fresh or thawed
1 teaspoon salt
1/8 teaspoon pepper
1/2 cup catsup
3 tablespoons lemon juice
1/4 cup water
2 teaspoons sugar
1 teaspoon mustard
2 teaspoons Worcestershire sauce

1. Preheat electric frying pan to 360 degrees. Melt 1 tablespoon butter and add onions. Saute' until golden brown and remove.
2. Add remaining 2 tablespoons butter. Cut filets into 6 serving pieces. Brown lightly, turning carefully.
3. Spread onions over fish. Season with salt and pepper. Combine remaining ingredients and pour over fish. Cover, reduce temperature to 220 degrees, and simmer about 15 minutes or until fish flakes easily.

Sheryl Kuempel
Boulder, Colorado

Serve with a California or Australian Chardonnay.

SWEET AND SOUR FISH

Serves 8

Preparation 15 Minutes
Cook 75 Minutes

1 white fish or salmon (five-pound), cleaned
1 teaspoon salt
1/4 teaspoon pepper
1 quart water
8 ginger snaps, crumbled
1 large sweet onion, sliced thinly
1/2 cup brown sugar
Juice of large lemon
1/2 cup raisins

1. Wash fish and remove head and tail. Slice into 1 1/2-inch portions, leaving bone and skin on. Salt and pepper each piece separately.
2. Combine water, ginger snaps, onion, brown sugar, lemon juice, and raisins. Boil 15 minutes.
3. Place fish carefully in sauce and cook 1 hour over low heat.
4. Remove fish to platter and pour small amount of sauce over fish.

NOTE:

May be served cold. Filets may also be used. Slice into portions and cook in sauce 5 minutes or until fish flakes.

Lois Linsky
Boulder, Colorado

Serve with a Vouvray, Chenin Blanc or a German *spaetlese.*

SHRIMP WITH COCONUT
(*Udang Kelapa*)

Serves 6

Preparation 20 Minutes
Cook 20 Minutes at 400°F

1 large onion, quartered
Juice of 3 fresh lemons
1 cup sweetened coconut
1 small red chili pepper, fried
1/2 teaspoon ground coriander
1 pound cooked shrimp, shelled and deveined

1. Combine onion, lemon juice, coconut, chili pepper, and coriander in blender. Blend at medium speed until onion is pureed.
2. Place shrimp in a small casserole. Pour on blended ingredients. Mix slightly. Cover with aluminum foil. Bake 20 minutes at 400 degrees.

Kathy Van Arsdale
Denver, Colorado

Serve with a Pouilly-Fuissé or a California Chardonnay.

ECUADORIAN *CEBICHE*

Cebiche *is a traditional appetizer throughout South America. This version comes from Quito, Ecuador.*

Serves 12 to 14

Preparation 40 Minutes

4 pounds large shrimp
3 burmuda onions, very thinly sliced
1 1/4 cups fresh lemon juice
Juice of 12 oranges
3 tablespoons sugar
3/4 cup catsup
1 tablespoon olive oil (optional)
Salt to taste
Tabasco to taste
2 tablespoons cold water
Parsley for garnish

1. Cook shrimp for 5 to 8 minutes in boiling salted water. Shell and devein, then refrigerate.
2. Rinse onion slices in cold water and drain. Place in a bowl and cover with boiling water. Immediately add 1 cup lemon juice and marinate for 10 minutes. Drain and discard liquid.
3. Prepare the sauce by combining orange juice, sugar, catsup, oil, salt, Tabasco, 1/4 cup lemon juice, and cold water. Chill until ready to use.
4. Combine shrimp and onions 15 minutes before serving in individual serving dishes. Cover with sauce and garnish with parsley.

NOTE:

Traditionally, popcorn is added to shrimp and sauce as one eats.

Susan Maxwell Campbell
Houston, Texas

Serve with a Sancerre or a California Sauvignon Blanc.

SHRIMP AND RICE

Serves 6

Preparation 30 Minutes
Cook 25 Minutes

1/4 cup oil
1 cup raw rice
1 1/2 pounds raw, peeled shrimp
2 green peppers, sliced
1 onion, sliced
1 tomato, sliced
2 cloves garlic, mined
1/2 cup catsup
Pinch of thyme
2 tablespoons Worcestershire sauce
1 bay leaf
1/2 envelope onion soup mix
1 can (16-ounce) peas

1. Heat oil to very hot. Add rice and stir until puffed and lightly browned (do not let burn).
2. Add cleaned shrimp and continue to stir until shrimp are slightly pink. Reduce heat to medium.
3. Add green peppers, onion, and tomato in layers.
4. Combine garlic, catsup, thyme, Worcestershire sauce, bay leaf, and onion soup mix. Pour over vegetables. Add peas and juice, cover, and cook over low heat until rice is tender, about 25 minutes. Finished dish should be slightly dry. If too much liquid remains, increase heat and uncover the last 10 minutes.

Hattie Cateora
Port Isabel, Texas

Serve with a Vouvray or a white Zinfandel.

SHRIMP CREOLE PORTER

Serves 8

Preparation 1 Hour
Cook 15 Minutes

2 pounds fresh shrimp
1 cup water
1 cup chopped onion
1 clove garlic, minced
1 cup minced celery
1/2 cup chopped carrots
Green pepper to taste
1/4 cup butter
1/2 cup dry Vermouth
1 cup crushed Italian-style tomatoes
1 tablespoon tomato paste
1/8 teaspoon thyme
4 dashes Tabasco
1/2 crumbled bay leaf
2 tablespoons chopped parsley

1. Shell and devein shrimp. Do not cook. Reserve in refrigerator.
2. Wash and boil shells in water. Drain and reserve liquid.
3. Combine onion, garlic, celery, carrots, and green pepper. Saute' in butter until soft and transparent in heavy 2-quart saucepan. Add Vermouth. Simmer to evaporate alcohol.
4. Add liquid from boiled shrimp shells, tomatoes, tomato paste, thyme, Tabasco, and bay leaf. Simmer mixture until thickened and reduced.

5. Ten minutes before serving time, return vegetable mixture to a boil and add prepared shrimp. Cook on low heat only until shrimp are pink. Add parsley.

NOTE:

Recipe may be prepared through Step 4 the day before serving.

Elizabeth Porter
Boulder, Colorado

Serve with a French white Hermitage or a rich California Fumé Blanc.

FINNY-FEATHER

Serves 6 to 8

Preparation 35 Minutes
Cook 50 Minutes

1/4 cup butter
2 chicken breasts, boned and cubed
1/2 pound fresh mushrooms, sliced
6 medium green onions, chopped
2 cups Be'chamel Sauce (see Index)
8 scallops, halved
2 medium lobster tails, cut into 1-inch pieces
16 medium shrimp, shelled and deveined
1/4 pound crab meat
1/4 cup brandy or 1/2 cup dry sherry or Marsala

1. Melt butter in skillet and saute' chicken pieces 10 to 15 minutes. Remove and set aside.
2. Add mushrooms and onions and saute' lightly. Remove.
3. To Be'chamel sauce, add scallops, lobster, and prawns (in that order) about 5 minutes apart. Cook 20 minutes.
4. Add crab meat, cooked chicken, and mushroom-onion mixture. Heat.
5. Just before serving, add brandy, sherry or Marsala.

Bette Heimann
Boulder, Colorado

Serve with a Puligny-Montrachet or a Meursault.

SHRIMP DINO

Serves 6

Preparation 30 Minutes
Bake 7 to 10 Minutes at 400°F

4 bay leaves, crumbled
1/2 cup minced onion
3/4 cup butter
2 tablespoons flour
1 cup milk
1 teaspoon curry powder
1/3 cup dry white wine
1 pound shrimp, peeled and cooked
3/4 cup sliced fresh mushrooms, saute'ed
2 cloves garlic, crushed
1/2 pound Swiss cheese, grated

1. Saute' bay leaves and onion in 1/2 cup butter until golden brown. Strain butter into small saucepan and discard onions and bay leaves.
2. Add flour to strained butter and cook until thick and bubbling. Add milk, stirring until medium thick. Stir in curry powder and wine, and mix well.
3. Line individual shells or 1-quart casserole with shrimp and mushrooms. Cover with sauce and dot with 1/4 cup butter blended with garlic. Cover with cheese and bake 7 to 10 minutes at 400 degrees until cheese starts to brown.

Serve with a Sancerre.

Gwen Shurm
Boulder, Colorado

CLAM-CORN STEW

Serves 6 to 8

Preparation 30 Minutes
Cook 20 to 25 Minutes

1/4 pound bacon
2 medium onions, sliced
1 can (16 1/2-ounce) corn
1 can (10-ounce) baby clams
3 large potatoes, diced
1 or 2 carrots, diced
Salt and pepper to taste
1 tablespoon butter
1 tablespoon flour
1 cup milk

1. Fry bacon in a large skillet. Remove and drain on paper toweling.
2. Saute' onions in 1 tablespoon bacon drippings. Drain on paper towels. Set skillet aside for later use.
3. Drain juices from corn and clams into 3- to 4-quart saucepan. Add onion, potatoes, carrots, salt, and pepper and cook over medium heat 15 minutes.
4. In skillet, melt butter and stir in flour. Cook, stirring, until blended. Slowly add milk and stir until thickened.
5. To potato-carrot mixture add clams and corn. Then stir in flour-milk mixture. Continue stirring over medium heat until smooth. Do not boil.
6. Crumble bacon over stew and serve.

Serve with a Pinot Blanc.

Sue Biter
Boulder, Colorado

SAVORY SAUCES

BARBECUE SAUCE

This recipe has been in the family for 35 years.

Yields 1/2 Gallon

Preparation 30 Minutes
Cook 1 Hour and 10 Minutes

1/2 teaspoon pickling spice
1 cup water
32 ounces catsup
2 cups vinegar
1 cup Worcestershire sauce
1/4 cup dry mustard
1/2 teaspoon salt
1/4 teaspoon freshly ground pepper
1/2 teaspoon paprika
1 tablespoon liquid smoke
3 tablespoons honey
1/2 cup fresh squeezed orange juice
1/2 cup sorghum molasses (unsulphured)
1/2 onion, chopped
1 clove garlic

1. Boil pickling spice in 1 cup of water. Strain and reserve liquid.
2. Add pickling-spice liquid to large kettle with all other ingredients.
3. Boil 40 minutes, reduce heat and simmer 30 minutes more.
4. Cool, strain, and put in bottles or jars (these can be the catsup and vinegar bottles).

NOTE:

Use on cold or hot dishes. Excellent for pork ribs, beef, game, duck, turkey, lunch meat, and as a dash of seasoning. Try this for excellent Bloody Marys as well as a salad dressing. Do not cook in this sauce for any length of time as the tomato burns.

John D. Farr
Breckenridge, Colorado

CECILIA'S MAMA'S BARBECUE SAUCE

Yields 4 1/2 Cups

Preparation 10 Minutes
Cook 30 Minutes

1/4 cup canned taco sauce
1 small bottle (14-ounce) tomato catsup
1 tablespoon Worcestershire sauce
1 tablespoon Heinz 57 or A-1 sauce
1 can (16-ounce) applesauce
1 cup water
2 tablespoons vinegar
Dash cayenne pepper

1. Simmer all ingredients until thick, about 30 minutes.

NOTE:

Use on ribs or chicken.

Anne Dykstra
Boulder, Colorado

BASIC BASTING SAUCE

Yields 4 Cups | Preparation 15 Minutes

1/4 cup olive oil or vegetable oil
3/4 cup chopped onion
1 clove garlic, chopped
1 cup honey
1 cup catsup
1 cup red wine vinegar
1/2 cup Worcestershire sauce
1 tablespoon dry mustard
1 1/2 teaspoons salt
1 teaspoon each leaf oregano, leaf thyme, and black pepper

1. Heat oil in saucepan, add onion and garlic, and cook until tender.
2. Stir in honey, catsup, vinegar, Worcestershire sauce, mustard, salt, oregano, thyme, and pepper. Bring to a boil, stirring constantly. Reduce heat and simmer slowly for 5 minutes.
3. Cool, transfer to covered jars, and store in refrigerator.

NOTE:

Excellent on all meats. Keeps well.

Mrs. Garry G. Gordon
Boulder, Colorado

BARBECUE SAUCE FOR HAM

Yields 2 Cups | Preparation 10 Minutes

Juice of 1 lemon
2 tablespoons flour
1/4 to 1 teaspoon red pepper sauce
1 teaspoon black pepper
1 teaspoon brown sugar
1 teaspoon white sugar
2 teaspoons mustard
2 tablespoons minced onion
Vinegar
1 cup margarine

1. Combine all seasonings in 1-cup measure and fill with enough vinegar to make 1 cup.
2. Melt margarine, add vinegar mixture and cook 5 minutes until slightly thickened.
3. Place ham, with rind trimmed, on covered charcoal grill.
4. Baste with sauce and turn every 20 minutes for 2 1/2 to 3 hours.

NOTE:

As sauce cooks on the grill, it loses some of the spiciness from the red pepper but the flavor remains.

Sara McNice
Boulder, Colorado

HOT PEPPER SEASONING
(*Berberé*)

Yields 1 Cup | Preparation 30 Minutes

2 teaspoons cumin seeds
4 whole cloves
6 cardamom pods
1/2 teaspoon whole black pepper
1/4 teaspoon whole allspice
1 teaspoon whole fenugreek (optional)
1/2 cup dried minced onions
3 dried long red chili peppers
3 to 6 small dried hot chili peppers
1/2 teaspoon ground ginger
1/4 teaspoon turmeric
2 teaspoons salt

1. In a small frying pan, combine cumin, cloves, cardamom, pepper, allspice, and fenugreek. Cook over medium-low heat, stirring until lightly toasted, about 1 minute.
2. Place mixture in a blender or food processor and add onions. Blend until finely ground, turn into a bowl.
3. Prepare peppers by discarding stems and seeds (if desired) from chilies. Break up pods and whirl in blender or food processor until finely ground. You should have about 1/2 cup.
4. Combine ground spices, ground chilies, ginger, turmeric, and salt. Store in a tightly covered container.

NOTE:

Instead of chilies, use 1/3 cup paprika and 1 to 2 teaspoons cayenne pepper. The pepper mixture will be hotter if seeds are left in. Use with *Dabo Kolo* (see Index). Add a small amount to various sauces, dips, cheese balls or baked cheese appetizers.

Susannah Jordan
Jamestown, Colorado

KOREAN MEAT MARINADE

Yields 1 1/2 Cups | Preparation 15 Minutes

1 cup salad oil
1/4 cup sugar
2 tablespoons soy sauce
4 tablespoons finely chopped green onion
2 cloves garlic, minced
1/2 teaspoon salt
1/2 teaspoon pepper
4 tablespoons sesame seeds

1. Combine all ingredients.

NOTE:

Use to marinate any cut of beef. Cut beef into thin strips and cover with marinade. Refrigerate overnight, turning occasionally. Grill meat over hot coals or stir fry with vegetables.

Sue McMillan
Boulder, Colorado

ASIAN STYLE SAUCE FOR BARBECUED STEAK

Yields 3/4 Cup | Preparation 5 Minutes

- **1/2 cup soy sauce**
- **2 jiggers gin or sherry**
- **2 cloves garlic, mashed**
- **2 to 3 slices fresh ginger root**
- **1 tablespoon Worcestershire sauce**
- **4 tablespoons brown sugar**

1. Combine all ingredients. Marinate meat at least 3 hours before barbecuing or broiling, turning occasionally.

NOTE:

Excellent marinade for flank steak. Serve, thinly sliced across the grain, on rice or noodles.

Friends of the Chinatown Library
Los Angeles, California

MARINADE FOR COOKED PORK

Yields 1 Cup | Preparation 30 Minutes

- **1/2 cup white wine vinegar**
- **1/3 cup vegetable oil**
- **3 tablespoons dry red wine**
- **1 small onion, minced**
- **1 teaspoon salt**
- **1 teaspoon dry mustard**
- **1 clove garlic, minced**
- **1/2 teaspoon tarragon**
- **1/2 teaspoon cumin**
- **2 tablespoons capers**

1. Combine vinegar, oil, wine, onion, salt, mustard, garlic, tarragon, cumin, and capers. Mix well. Pour over meat (up to 2 pounds sliced meat).

NOTE:

Arrange cooked, sliced pork in a single layer. Pour on marinade, cover and refrigerate at least 4 hours or overnight. Cooked, thinly sliced beef steak is also delicious in this marinade.

TOMATO-SOY MARINADE

Yields 1 1/2 Cups | Preparation 10 Minutes

- **2/3 cup soy sauce**
- **1/2 cup vinegar**
- **1/4 cup tomato paste**
- **1 teaspoon paprika**
- **3 cloves garlic, crushed**

1. Combine ingredients and pour over meat.

NOTE:

Use on Peppered Beef (see Index). Also delicious with pork or chicken. Allow meat to marinate overnight, refrigerated.

SPICY BEEF KABOB MARINADE

Yields 1 Cup

Preparation 10 Minutes

2 teaspoons salt
1 teaspoon chili powder
1/2 teaspoon each ground thyme, oregano leaves, ground ginger, and pepper
3/4 teaspoon garlic salt
1 bay leaf, crumbled
2 tablespoons minced onion
1 lemon, juiced
2 tablespoons cider vinegar
1/2 cup salad oil

1. Combine seasonings with lemon juice, vinegar, and salad oil.

NOTE:

Marinate 2 pounds boneless sirloin cubes 4 to 5 hours at room temperature or overnight. Alternate with small onions, cherry tomatoes, mushrooms, and green pepper pieces on a skewer and grill.

Joan First
Denver, Colorado

HOT MUSTARD SAUCE

Yields 2 Cups
Stand 2 Hours

Preparation 10 Minutes
Cook 10 to 20 Minutes

1 cup cider vinegar
2 cans (2-ounce each) dry mustard
2 eggs, beaten
1 cup sugar
Pinch of salt

1. Stir vinegar into mustard, cover, and allow to stand for 2 hours or overnight if possible.
2. Blend eggs, sugar, and salt in top of double boiler. Add mustard mixture, stir well, and cook over simmering water until thick, 10 to 20 minutes.
3. Transfer to a jar and store in refrigerator.

Ellen Doenges
Austin, Texas

MUSTARD HORSERADISH SAUCE

Yields 1 Cup

Preparation 10 Minutes
Refrigerate 2 Hours

3 ounces cream cheese
1/2 cup mayonnaise
Salt to taste
2 teaspoons dry mustard
1 1/2 tablespoons prepared horseradish

1. Blend all ingredients until smooth. Refrigerate for several hours or overnight before serving.

SALSA VERDE

Yields 1 Cup

Preparation 20 Minutes

- 2 stalks celery, minced
- 1 large green tomato or 8 Mexican green tomatoes, finely chopped
- 3 Serrano chilies, finely chopped
- 3 cloves garlic, minced
- 2 tablespoons oil
- 2 tablespoons vinegar
- 1/4 cup dry white wine
- 1 tablespoon chopped cilantro

1. Mix all ingredients several hours ahead to blend flavors.

NOTE:

Good with all Mexican food. Also use as a garnish on crisp tortillas spread with cream cheese.

SALSA FRIA

Yields 4 1/2 Cups

Preparation 25 Minutes

- 4 cups tomatoes, freshly peeled or canned Italian plum tomatoes
- 5 tablespoons chopped green chilies
- 2 tablespoons chopped parsley
- 2 cloves garlic, minced
- 2 tablespoons oil
- 4 tablespoons wine vinegar
- 1 teaspoon oregano
- 1/4 teaspoon thyme
- 1 teaspoon dried basil
- Salt and pepper to taste

1. Chop tomatoes and combine remaining ingredients. Chill until ready to serve.

NOTE:

Flavor enhanced if made at least a day ahead of time.

SALSA ROJA

Yields 1 Cup

Preparation 10 Minutes
Cook 30 to 45 Minutes

- 3 fresh, ripe tomatoes, chopped, or 1 can (16-ounce) tomatoes, mashed
- 2 tablespoons diced green chilies (or to taste)
- 1/2 teaspoon salt
- 1 large clove garlic, minced
- 1 1/2 teaspoons cider vinegar
- 1 teaspoon Worcestershire sauce
- Sugar to taste

1. Combine all ingredients in saucepan.
2. Simmer, uncovered, 30 to 45 minutes until sauce has thickened and flavors blended. Serve at room temperature.

MEXICAN HOT SAUCE

Yields 2 1/2 Cups | Preparation 25 Minutes

8 small fresh chili peppers
4 large fresh green peppers
2 garlic cloves
Salt to taste
1 can (16-ounce) solid pack tomatoes

1. Roast or grill peppers until dark on all sides.
2. Put peppers in dampened towel or paper bag to steam 5 minutes and peel.
3. Puree all ingredients in blender. Add additional tomatoes if too hot.

Fela Machado
Avalon, California

BRAZILIAN HOT SAUCE

Yields 2 1/2 Cups | Preparation 10 Minutes

1/2 medium onion, chopped
1 tomato, chopped
1 tablespoon red hot pepper, crushed
1 drop Tabasco
3 tablespoons chopped parsley
1 tablespoon vinegar
1 1/2 cups bean liquid from *Feijoada*

1. Mix all ingredients and heat. Serve warm with *Feijoada* (see Index).

NUỐC MAM SAUCE

Yields 3/4 Cup | Preparation 15 Minutes

2 fresh, ripe red chili peppers (or canned)
2 cloves garlic, chopped
1 lime or lemon
1 tablespoon sugar
1 tablespoon vinegar
1 tablespoon water
4 or more tablespoons Vietnamese fish sauce

1. Split the chilies and remove seeds and membrane. Cut up into small pieces and mash together with garlic.
2. Juice the lime or lemon and add slowly with the sugar, stirring well.
3. Add vinegar, water, and fish sauce. Serve in small bowl.

NOTE:

The Vietnamese add this to almost everything. Where Vietnamese fish sauce is not available, add a little shrimp paste to Chinese fish sauce.

Indo-China Mobile Education Project
Washington, D.C.

HOT PEPPER SAUCE
(Harissa)

Yields 6 Tablespoons

Preparation 5 Minutes

4 tablespoons cayenne pepper
1 to 2 tablespoons ground cumin
1 teaspoon salt
1/2 clove garlic, crushed
Hot water

1. Mix cayenne, cumin, salt, and garlic. Add enough water to make a thick paste.

NOTE:

An accompaniment to *Couscous* (see Index) but delicious on other meat and vegetable dishes or in soups.,

CHINESE HOT SAUCE

Yields 1 1/2 Cups

Preparation 10 Minutes

1 tablespoon cornstarch
1/2 cup water
1/2 cup cider vinegar
1/2 cup sugar
1/4 teaspoon red liquid Chinese pepper or Tabasco sauce
Soy sauce to color

1. In a small saucepan, dissolve cornstarch in water. Add vinegar, sugar, liquid pepper, and soy sauce. Cook until thickened.

NOTE:

Use as a dipping sauce for egg roll or fried wonton.

Judy Brooks
Los Angeles, California

SWEET AND SOUR SAUCE

Yields 2 1/2 Cups

Preparation 25 Minutes

1 cup white vinegar
1/3 cup catsup
1 tablespoon Worcestershire sauce
3/4 cup sugar
1/2 teaspoon salt
1/2 teaspoon cornstarch in 1 teaspoon water
1/4 green pepper, cubed
1/2 sweet red pepper, cubed
1/4 onion, cubed
1/4 cup sliced carrots
1/2 tablespoon peanut oil
1/3 cup pineapple chunks

1. In saucepan, combine vinegar, catsup, Worcestershire sauce, sugar, and salt. Bring to boil. Mix cornstarch with water and stir into sauce. Cook and stir until thick and smooth. Sauce may be cooled and refrigerated up to one month.

2. When ready to serve, saute' green and red peppers, onion, and carrots in oil. Add pineapple. Add to reheated sauce.

NOTE:

Serve over crisp fried chicken, pork, or fish.

Wendy Brooks
Los Angeles, California

CURRY GLAZE

Yields 2 Cups — Preparation 20 Minutes

- **6 slices bacon, finely diced**
- **1 onion, chopped**
- **2 tablespoons flour**
- **1 tablespoon sugar**
- **1 tablespoon curry powder**
- **2 tablespoons applesauce**
- **2 tablespoons flaked coconut**
- **2 tablespoons catsup**
- **2 tablespoons lemon juice**
- **1 can (10 3/4-ounce) beef broth**

1. Fry bacon until crisp and remove from pan, reserving drippings.
2. Add onion, flour, sugar, curry powder, applesauce, coconut, catsup, lemon juice, and broth to bacon drippings.
3. Bring to a boil while stirring. Reduce heat and simmer until thick.

NOTE:

Serve over Party-Perfect Chicken (see Index). Also good over pork roast.

Anne Dykstra
Boulder, Colorado

CRANBERRY GLAZE

Yields 2 Cups — Preparation 35 Minutes

- **2 cups cranberry juice cocktail**
- **1/4 cup honey**
- **1/2 cup white corn syrup**
- **1/4 cup butter**

1. In small saucepan, cook cranberry juice until it is reduced to 1 cup. Add honey, corn syrup, and butter.
2. Use as basting sauce for turkey during last 45 minutes of cooking.

NOTE:

The drippings from a turkey basted with this sauce make marvelous gravy.

Marcia Cutter
Lubbock, Texas

PINEAPPLE SAUCE

Yields 1/2 Cup | Preparation 10 Minutes

4 tablespoons sugar
1 teaspoon cornstarch
4 tablespoons pineapple juice, unsweetened
4 tablespoons white vinegar
Pineapple chunks for garnish

1. Combine sugar, cornstarch, juice, and vinegar in small saucepan. Cook until sauce thickens and clears, about 5 minutes.
2. Garnish with pineapple chunks.

NOTE:

Great for dipping wonton. Good also on Sesame Chicken (see Index).

Judy Brooks
Los Angeles, California

WILD BERRY SAUCE

Yields 4 Cups | Preparation 15 Minutes

6 tablespoons butter
1 orange, unpeeled and sliced
1/4 cup sugar
6 tablespoons sherry
2 cups concentrated beef broth
1 cup canned lingonberries or other wild berries
1/8 teaspoon cayenne pepper
1/8 teaspoon cinnamon

1. Melt butter in frying pan. Saute' orange slices and sugar for 3 minutes.
2. Stir in sherry and broth. Simmer for 5 minutes.
3. Strain sauce into saucepan. Add berries, cayenne, and cinnamon. Simmer 5 minutes longer.

NOTE:

Excellent on roasted duck or chicken.

Sheryl Kuempel
Boulder, Colorado

LEMON SAUCE FOR CHICKEN

Yields 21/2 Cups | Preparation 10 Minutes

2 tablespoons butter
2 tablespoons flour
Salt and pepper to taste
2 cups chicken broth
2 egg yolks, beaten
1 to 2 tablespoons fresh lemon juice

1. Melt butter, add flour and seasonings and cook 3 minutes.

2. Stir chicken broth into flour and butter gradually. Bring to a boil.
3. Remove from heat. Add several tablespoons chicken sauce to beaten yolks and stir. Return egg yolk mixture to pan and blend thoroughly. Stir in lemon juice to taste.
4. Cook, stirring, 3 minutes. Do not boil. Serve over cooked chicken.

BÉCHAMEL SAUCE

Yields 2 Cups

Preparation 10 Minutes

2 tablespoons butter
2 tablespoons flour
1 1/2 cups hot milk
Salt and pepper to taste
1/2 cup heavy cream

1. Over medium heat, melt butter in saucepan. Add flour and with whisk or slotted spoon, mix rapidly, cooking for 2 minutes. Add milk slowly; stir and cook over medium heat until sauce thickens.
2. Stir in salt, pepper, and heavy cream. Keep warm until needed but do not let boil.

Ellie Pollack
Boulder, Colorado

VELOUTÉ SAUCE

Yields 4 1/2 Cups

Preparation 10 Minutes

4 tablespoons butter
4 tablespoons flour
3 cups chicken broth
Salt and pepper to taste
2 egg yolks
1 cup half-and-half

1. Melt butter in saucepan, stir in flour, and cook 2 minutes. Add broth, salt, and pepper. Stir and cook over medium heat for 2 minutes or until thickened. Remove from heat.
2. Mix egg yolks with half-and-half and stir in small amount of hot broth mixture. Then add egg mixture to saucepan. Cook over low heat for 2 minutes.

Juanita Kahler Laumets
Redwood City, California

MORNAY SAUCE

Yields 2 cups

Preparation 10 Minutes

2 cups Béchamel or Velouté sauce
1/4 to 3/4 cup grated Swiss or Parmesan cheese

1. Add cheese to sauce. Stir to melt cheese.

HOLLANDAISE SAUCE

Yields 1 Cup | Preparation 20 Minutes

3/4 cup butter
1/4 teaspoon tarragon leaves
1/4 teaspoon minced parsley
3 egg yolks
1 tablespoon lemon juice
1 teaspoon white wine vinegar

1. Melt butter with tarragon and parsley.
2. Beat yolks until very thick and creamy. Add cooled butter in a trickle, beating constantly.
3. Stir in lemon juice and vinegar. Chill.

NOTE:

This recipe is foolproof and can be made in advance.

James Delamata
Corona del Mar, California

CHEESE SAUCE

Yields 2 Cups | Preparation 15 Minutes

3 tablespoons butter
3 tablespoons flour
1 1/2 cups milk
1/2 cup grated Cheddar cheese
Salt to taste

1. Melt butter in small saucepan. Stir in flour and cook briefly. Add milk slowly, stirring constantly.
2. Add cheese and stir until melted and well blended. Add salt to taste.

NOTE:

Serve with Cabbage Potato Casserole (see Index) or over plain cooked vegetables.

Marsha Paull
Avalon, California

MOM'S WINTER CHILI SAUCE

Yields 3 Pints | Preparation 35 to 40 Minutes

1 can (28-ounce) tomatoes, chopped
2 large onions, chopped
1 tablespoon salt
1 teaspoon pepper
1 cup sugar
1/2 cup vinegar
1/2 teaspoon cinnamon
1/2 teaspoon cloves
1/2 teaspoon allspice

1. Mix all ingredients together in a large saucepan. Bring to boil over moderate heat. Stir constantly. Reduce heat to simmer and cook 1/2 hour or until thick.
2. Let cool and transfer to glass jars. Refrigerate.

NOTE:

Good on meat loaf and as a base for Russian dressing.

Roslyn Pfaff
Boulder, Colorado

SPAGHETTI SAUCE BERGER

Yields 6 Cups

Preparation 25 Minutes

- 3 cans (8-ounce each) tomato sauce
- 1 can (6-ounce) tomato paste
- 1 cup water
- 1 package (1 1/2-ounce) Lawry's spaghetti sauce mix
- 1 large clove garlic
- 1 large onion, diced
- 3/4 pound fresh mushrooms, sliced
- 1/2 cup oil

1. Mix tomato sauce, tomato paste, and water. Add spaghetti sauce mix and stir well. Place over low heat and simmer.
2. Using garlic press, press whole clove into pan while sauce is simmering.
3. Saute' onion and mushrooms in oil until lightly brown. Do not overcook. Add to rest of ingredients (some of oil used for saute'eing may be added, but only a little). Mix well.

Bob Berger
Berkeley, California

EGGPLANT SPAGHETTI SAUCE

Serves 4

Preparation 25 Minutes
Cook 45 Minutes

- 1 onion, chopped
- 1 clove garlic, minced
- 1/2 teaspoon each basil, oregano, cinnamon
- 2 stalks celery, chopped
- 1/2 eggplant, diced
- 1/2 green pepper, chopped
- 1/4 cup olive oil
- 6 to 8 tomatoes, chopped
- 1 can (6-ounce) tomato paste
- 1 cup water
- Parmesan cheese, grated

1. Saute' onion, garlic, spices, celery, eggplant, and green pepper in olive oil.
2. When vegetables are clear and limp, add tomatoes, tomato paste, and water. Stir until smooth. Simmer 45 minutes. Sprinkle with Parmesan cheese.

Ilene Kasper
Boulder, Colorado

BACON SPAGHETTI SAUCE

Serves 4

Preparation 15 Minutes
Cook 30 Minutes

8 bacon slices, cubed
4 tablespoons butter
1 cup sliced mushrooms
2 cups Italian plum tomatoes, drained and chopped
1/4 cup chopped parsley
1/2 cup dry white wine or dry vermouth
Salt and pepper to taste
1/4 teaspoon crushed red pepper
Parmesan cheese

1. Cook bacon, saving 1 tablespoon fat. Add butter to bacon fat and cook mushrooms until wilted. Add remaining ingredients and simmer 30 minutes.

NOTE:

Serve over cooked pasta and sprinkle with Parmesan cheese. Sauce is delicious as a vegetable side dish.

Deborah Taylor
Boulder, Colorado

WHITE CLAM SAUCE FOR SPAGHETTI

Yields 2 1/2 Cups

Preparation 15 Minutes
Cook 15 Minutes

2 jars (7 1/2-ounce each) minced clams
1/3 cup olive oil
1/4 cup butter
4 cloves garlic, minced
2 tablespoons minced parsley
1 1/2 teaspoons salt

1. Drain clams, reserving 3/4 cup liquid. Set aside.
2. In medium skillet, slowly heat olive oil and butter. Saute' garlic until golden, about 5 minutes. Remove from heat.
3. Stir in reserved clam liquid, parsley, and salt; bring to boil. Reduce heat and simmer, uncovered, 10 minutes. Add clams and simmer 3 to 5 minutes.

Joe Corrizo
Purchase, New York

SEAFOOD COCKTAIL SAUCE

Yields 1 Cup

Preparation 5 Minutes

1/2 cup chili sauce
1 1/2 teaspoons horseradish
1/3 cup catsup
1 teaspoon Worcestershire sauce

1. Combine and chill thoroughly.

NOTE:

For sharper sauce, add 1/4 teaspoon salt or 2 tablespoons lemon juice and a dash of pepper. Serve over cooked seafood with finely chopped celery.

Ethel Zager
Avalon, California

TANGY CUCUMBER SAUCE

Yields 3 Cups

Preparation 35 Minutes

4 cucumbers, peeled and chopped
Salt and pepper
1 cup sour cream
Juice of 1/2 lemon
Grated rind of 1 lemon
2 tablespoons caviar
2 tablespoons freshly ground horseradish
1 tablespoon minced onion
1 tablespoon chopped parsley
1 egg yolk, riced

1. Sprinkle cucumbers with salt and let stand 30 minutes.
2. Drain thoroughly and season with pepper, sour cream, and lemon juice. Add grated lemon rind, caviar, horseradish, and minced onion. Top with chopped parsley and riced egg yolk.

VARIATION:

For added elegance, this recipe may be served in a fresh tomato shell, on an artichoke bottom, or as a garnish for cold salmon.

Joyce Thurmer
Boulder, Colorado

CUCUMBER SAUCE

Yields 1 1/2 Cups

Preparation 20 Minutes

1 medium cucumber, unpeeled
1 tablespoon grated onion
1/4 cup mayonnaise
Salt and pepper
1 1/2 tablespoons vinegar
1 tablespoon chopped parsley
1/2 cup sour cream

1. Cut cucumber in half lengthwise and scoop out seeds. Grate and drain.
2. Combine cucumber with remaining ingredients. Blend well and chill.

NOTE:

Serve on Salmon Quiche (see Index) or cold cooked salmon.

Esther deOnis
Boulder, Colorado

BOOT'S DIPPING SAUCE FOR VEGETABLES

Yields 2 Cups

Preparation 10 Minutes

1 cup mayonnaise
1 1/2 tablespoons lemon juice
1/4 teaspoon salt
1/4 teaspoon paprika
1 tablespoon grated onion
1/4 cup chopped parsley
1 tablespoon chopped chives
1/2 teaspoon Worcestershire sauce
1/2 cup sour cream

1. Mix ingredients in order listed and stir.

NOTE:

Delicious with celery, carrot, zucchini, cucumber, and most vegetable strips.

Peg Waldrop
Boulder, Colorado

GARLIC MAYONNAISE

Yields 1 Cup

Preparation 30 Minutes

5 cloves garlic, crushed
1 tablespoon lemon juice or 2 tablespoons vinegar
2 egg yolks
3/4 to 1 cup olive oil
Salt and pepper to taste

1. Mix crushed garlic with 1/2 tablespoon lemon juice or 1 tablespoon vinegar and pinch of salt.
2. Add egg yolks to garlic mixture and beat until slightly thickened. Add olive oil, a drop or two at a time, until mayonnaise is quite thick. Once mayonnaise starts to thicken, add oil a little faster.
3. When mayonnaise is very thick, add remaining lemon juice or vinegar and continue beating in oil. Taste for seasoning and add a little warm water if mayonnaise is too thick.

NOTE:

Garlic mayonnaise, *ali oli* in Spanish or *Aioli* in French, is used as a vegetable dip with raw vegetables or added to vegetable soup for a change of flavor. This recipe takes 10 minutes with food processor or blender.

VEGETABLES • AND • ACCOMPANIMENTS

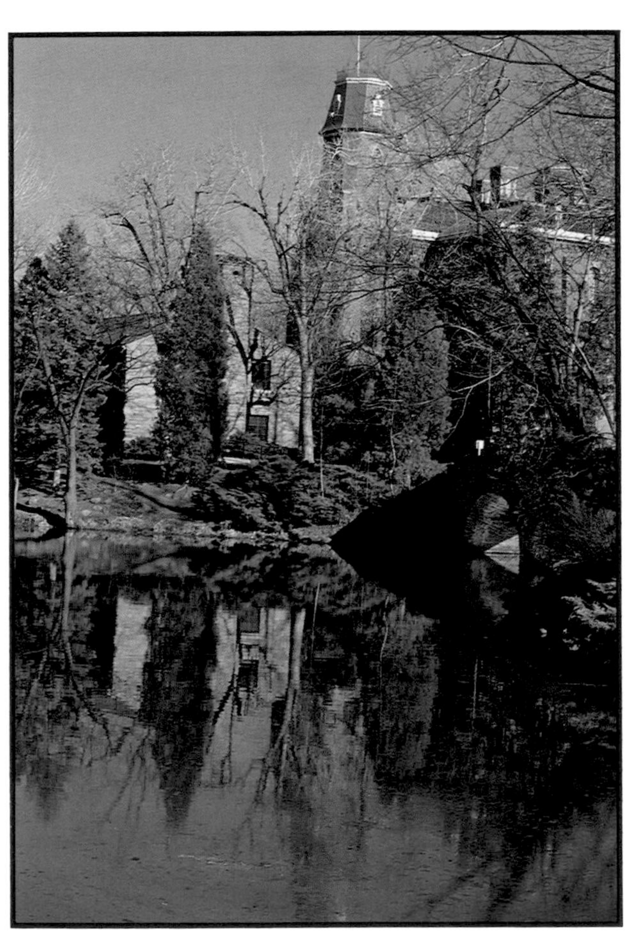

ASPARAGUS *SHUNG TUNG*

Serves 10

Preparation 15 Minutes
Cook 1 1/2 Minutes

1 1/2 pounds asparagus
1 1/2 quarts water
1 1/2 teaspoons salt
1 tablespoon sugar
1 teaspoon Oriental sesame oil

1. Break off tough ends of asparagus. Cut diagonally in 1/4-inch pieces.
2. Add water to wok, or any deep pot, and bring to boil. Add asparagus and cook 1 1/2 minutes. Do *not* overcook.
3. Pour into strainer and immerse in cold water to stop cooking. Change water several times to cool quickly, or refrigerate covered in water. It will keep several days.
4. Prepare dressing by mixing salt, sugar, and oil. Pour over drained asparagus.

VARIATION:

Stir fry asparagus in 1 tablespoon oil with 1/2 pound sliced fresh mushrooms and 4 chopped scallions. Add 1 1/2 teaspoons salt and 1 tablespoon each sugar and Oriental sesame oil. Mix and serve immediately.

Michael Patrone
New York, New York

BAKED ARTICHOKE HEARTS

Serves 6

Preparation 20 Minutes
Bake 20 to 30 Minutes at 375°F

2 eggs
1/2 cup olive oil
3 tablespoons lemon juice
6 whole cloves garlic
2 cans (8 1/2-ounce each) artichoke hearts, drained
1/2 to 1 cup seasoned bread crumbs
1/2 to 1 cup grated Romano cheese

1. Mix eggs, olive oil, lemon juice, and garlic. Cook until thickened, stirring well to prevent curdling. Remove garlic cloves.
2. Add artichokes, mix well, and place in 9 x 9-inch pan. Sprinkle crumbs and cheese on top.
3. Bake at 375 degrees for 20 to 30 minutes. Serve hot.

Nancy Kuempel
Cincinnati, Ohio

MARINATED ARTICHOKES

Serves 6

Preparation 1 Hour
Cook 10 to 15 Minutes

6 artichokes
2 tablespoons lemon juice
6 to 8 garlic cloves, minced
3/4 cup chopped parsley
1/2 cup salad oil
3/4 cup lemon juice
1 teaspoon salt

1. Cut tips off artichoke leaves with sharp knife or scissors. Cook in boiling, salted water with 2 tablespoons lemon juice until just tender. (For microwave: cook artichokes in 1 1/2 cups of water, 2 tablespoons lemon juice, and 1 tablespoon oil in covered casserole. Cook 5 minutes bottom up, 3 minutes right side up.)
2. Remove choke carefully, leaving artichoke intact. Place artichokes in large skillet. Add garlic, parsley, oil, lemon juice, and salt. Try to get some between leaves and down into heart. Cover.
3. Cook over low heat 10 to 15 minutes. (For microwave: place in shallow dish, cook 6 to 8 minutes, turning dish every 2 minutes.)
4. Chill before serving.

Nancy Cateora
Boulder, Colorado

BAKED AVOCADO HALVES

Serves 6

Preparation 20 Minutes
Bake 8 Minutes at 350°F

3 ripe but firm avocados
1 egg white
2 tablespoons mayonnaise
Salt to taste
Pimiento strips
Lettuce leaves to garnish

1. Peel avocados, cut in half lengthwise, and remove seeds. Enlarge cavities with a spoon, place on a lightly greased baking sheet.
2. Beat egg white until stiff, fold in mayonnaise, and add salt. Spoon into cavities.
3. Bake in 350-degree oven for 8 minutes. Slip pan under broiler until sauce is lightly browned. Decorate top with pimiento strips. Serve on lettuce leaves.

Peg Pettit
Boulder, Colorado

GREEN BEANS WITH GARLIC

Serves 4

Preparation 10 Minutes
Cook 8 Minutes

1 pound fresh green beans, trimmed
4 tablespoons butter
1 clove garlic, crushed
Salt and pepper to taste

1. Cook green beans, covered, in a small amount of boiling salted water until barely tender.
2. Melt butter and add garlic. Pour over green beans, add salt and pepper, mix well, and serve.

VARIATION:

Top green beans with 2 tablespoons finely chopped walnuts.

Mark Kuempel
Boulder, Colorado

GREEN BEANS WITH HERB SAUCE

Serves 4 to 6

Preparation 5 Minutes
Cook 15 Minutes

1/2 cup chopped green onion including tops
2 tablespoons butter
1 package (10-ounce) frozen green beans
1 can (28-ounce) Italian tomatoes in puree
Pinch each of thyme and rosemary
1/2 teaspoon salt

1. In large skillet, saute' onion in melted butter about 3 minutes. Add frozen green beans and stir until thawed.
2. Add tomatoes, thyme, rosemary, and salt. Cover and simmer 7 to 10 minutes.

VARIATION:

Alternate layers of the vegetable-tomato mixture with grated mozzarella cheese for a different flavor. Use greased casserole and bake at 350 degrees until cheese is bubbly.

NOTE:

Other suitable vegetables include fresh green beans, zucchini, yellow squash, peas, okra, cauliflower, artichoke hearts, potatoes, cubed eggplant, and leeks (omit onions).

Barbara Ogarrio
Half Moon Bay, California

NAN'S 3-VEGETABLE CASSEROLE

Serves 6 to 8

Preparation 20 Minutes
Bake 20 Minutes at 350°F

1 box (10-ounce) frozen string beans
1 box (10-ounce) frozen lima beans
1 box (10-ounce) frozen peas
1 cup heavy cream, whipped
1 cup mayonnaise
1/2 cup grated Parmesan cheese

1. Cook vegetables until just tender, drain thoroughly.
2. Fold together whipped cream, mayonnaise, and Parmesan cheese.
3. Layer vegetables in 9 x 9-inch baking dish. Pour cream mixture over vegetables.
4. Bake 20 minutes at 350 degrees.

Hattie Bartram
Boulder, Colorado

ITALIAN BEANS AU GRATIN

Serves 6

Preparation 25 Minutes
Bake 25 to 35 Minutes at 350°F

2 packages (10-ounce each) frozen Italian green beans
2 tablespoons butter
2 tablespoons flour
1 teaspoon salt
1/4 teaspoon white pepper
1/4 teaspoon Worcestershire sauce
1 cup half-and-half
2 tablespoons butter
1/2 cup freshly grated Parmesan cheese

1. Cook beans according to package directions and drain.
2. Melt 2 tablespoons butter in saucepan and stir in flour, salt, pepper, and Worcestershire sauce. Cook, stirring constantly, 2 minutes.
3. Add half-and-half and cook until thickened, stirring constantly. Pour over beans.
4. Dot with 2 tablespoons butter, then sprinkle with cheese.
5. Bake in 350-degree oven for 25 to 35 minutes until hot and lightly browned.

Charles Hill
Indianapolis, Indiana

SWEET AND SOUR PICKLED BEETS

Yields 1 1/2 Quarts

Preparation 5 Minutes
Cook 15 Minutes

1 cup sugar
2 tablespoons cornstarch
1 cup white vinegar
24 whole cloves
2 1/2 tablespoons catsup
3 tablespoons olive oil
1 teaspoon vanilla
Pinch of salt
6 cans (8-ounce each) whole beets, quartered (reserve 1 1/2 cups juice)

1. In large saucepan, mix sugar and cornstarch. Add vinegar, cloves, catsup, olive oil, vanilla, and salt. Stir well. Add beets and juice.
2. Cook and stir over medium heat until thick.

NOTE:

This can be served as a hot vegetable over cooked rice, or cold on salads, cottage cheese, or as a relish. Store in refrigerator 2 to 3 weeks. Bring to room temperature before using.

Florence White
Boulder, Colorado

DELUXE BEETS

Serves 4

Preparation 15 to 20 Minutes
Cook 10 Minutes

1 can (16-ounce) spiced beets, diced or sliced
1 can (11-ounce) mandarin oranges
1/4 cup beet juice
Liquid from fruit
1/2 cup brown sugar
3 tablespoons flour
1/4 teaspoon salt
1/2 cup white raisins
2 tablespoons butter or margarine

1. Drain liquid from beets and fruit. Combine 1/4 cup beet liquid and all the fruit syrup.
2. Mix sugar (see Note), flour, and salt. Stir in beet-syrup liquid. Cook over medium heat, stirring constantly. When mixture thickens, add raisins, butter, beets, and fruit. Cook until hot.

VARIATION:

Substitute 1 can (8-ounce) pineapple chunks and the juice for oranges.

NOTE:

For those who prefer less sweet vegetable dishes, start with 1 tablespoon brown sugar and add to taste.

Crede Dever
Boulder, Colorado

BROCCOLI-CHILI BAKE

Serves 8

Preparation 20 Minutes
Bake 45 Minutes at 325°F

- **2 packages (10-ounce each) frozen chopped broccoli**
- **1/4 cup chopped onion**
- **1/4 cup butter**
- **2 tablespoons flour**
- **1/2 cup milk**
- **1 jar (8-ounce) Cheese Whiz**
- **1 can (4-ounce) green chilies, diced**
- **1 can (8-ounce) water chestnuts, sliced**
- **1/4 teaspoon salt**
- **1/8 teaspoon pepper**
- **2 eggs, well beaten**
- **1/2 cup bread crumbs**
- **1 tablespoon butter**

1. Cook broccoli according to package directions and drain.
2. Saute' onion in butter until soft. Blend in flour and milk and cook until thickened. Stir in Cheese Whiz, chilies, water chestnuts, and seasonings. Stir in eggs.
3. Add broccoli and pour into greased 1 1/2-quart casserole. Top with bread crumbs and dot with butter. Bake in 325-degree oven for 45 minutes or until set.

Judy Schatan
Avalon, California

BROCCOLI SUPREME

Serves 6 to 8

Preparation 15 Minutes
Bake 30 to 40 Minutes at 375°F

- **1 egg, slightly beaten**
- **1 package (10-ounce) broccoli spears, partially thawed**
- **1 can (8 1/2-ounce) cream-style corn**
- **1 tablespoon grated onion**
- **1/4 teaspoon salt**
- **Dash pepper**
- **3 tablespoons butter or margarine**
- **1 cup herb stuffing mix**

1. Combine egg, broccoli, corn, onion, salt, and pepper in mixing bowl.
2. In saucepan, melt butter and add stuffing mix. Toss. Stir 3/4 cup buttered stuffing into vegetable mixture.
3. Put mixture in 1-quart casserole and sprinkle with remaining stuffing. Bake, uncovered, 30 to 40 minutes in 375-degree oven.

Ethel Zager
Avalon, California

BRUSSELS SPROUTS AU GRATIN

Serves 4

Preparation 30 Minutes
Broil 5 Minutes

2 cups chicken broth
1 quart fresh Brussels sprouts
1/8 teaspoon nutmeg
Pepper to taste
2 cups Béchamel sauce (see Index), made with cooking liquid
1/2 cup grated Swiss cheese
2 tablespoons dry white wine
1/2 cup dry bread crumbs
Butter

1. Bring broth to boil. Add sprouts, nutmeg, and pepper. Simmer 15 minutes or until done. Drain and keep hot.
2. Make Béchamel sauce. Over medium heat add cheese to sauce, and melt, stirring often. Add wine.
3. Place hot sprouts in a 1 1/2-quart baking dish and cover with sauce. Sprinkle with bread crumbs and dot with butter. Place under broiler until golden brown.

NOTE:

If fresh sprouts are not available, use 2 packages (10-ounce each) frozen Brussels sprouts. Cook as above.

Ellie Pollack
Boulder, Colorado

BRUSSELS SPROUTS WITH SOUR CREAM

Serves 5 to 6

Preparation 20 Minutes
Bake 15 Minutes at 350°F

1 package (10-ounce) frozen Brussels sprouts
1 can (10 3/4-ounce) chicken broth
1/4 cup mayonnaise
1/2 cup sour cream
1/4 cup bread crumbs
3/4 cup freshly grated Parmesan cheese

1. Cook Brussels sprouts in chicken broth until barely tender. Drain.
2. In casserole, combine mayonnaise, sour cream, and sprouts. Top with bread crumbs and thick layer of cheese.
3. Bake about 15 minutes at 350 degrees.

Sue McMillan
Boulder, Colorado

SPICED NAPA CABBAGE

Serves 3 to 6

Preparation 15 Minutes
Cook 5 Minutes

1 pound Napa cabbage
3 tablespoons red wine vinegar
3 tablespoons light brown sugar
1 tablespoon light soy sauce
1 teaspoon Chinese hot oil
2 tablespoons peanut oil
1 quarter-size slice ginger root

1. Slice cabbage leaves into 1-inch pieces.
2. In a small bowl, mix vinegar, sugar, soy sauce, and hot oil. Set aside.
3. Heat a wok or skillet over high heat until a drop of water immediately sizzles into steam. Add peanut oil and ginger root. Stir 30 seconds or until ginger root begins to brown.
4. Add cabbage and stir fry for 2 minutes. Remove pan from heat and stir in sauce mixture. Serve lukewarm.

Barbara Loskutoff
Solano Beach, California

VIETNAMESE STIR-FRIED VEGETABLES (*Com Chay*)

Serves 6

Preparation 30 Minutes
Cook 5 Minutes

8 dried black Chinese mushrooms, soaked 1/2 hour and sliced
2 to 3 cups chopped Chinese cabbage
2 carrots in 1/2-inch slices
4 green onions, sliced
3 to 4 cups fresh bean sprouts
3/4 cup water
2 1/2 tablespoons soy sauce
1 teaspoon Oriental sesame oil
2 teaspoons sugar
1 tablespoon vegetable oil
1 clove garlic, crushed
1/2 teaspoon finely minced ginger root
1 teaspoon cornstarch dissolved in 1 tablespoon water
Cooked rice

1. Have all vegetables prepared for cooking and set aside.
2. In saucepan, mix 1/2 cup water, 1 tablespoon soy sauce, sesame oil, and sugar. Add mushrooms and simmer until liquid is almost absorbed.
3. Heat vegetable oil in wok and briefly fry garlic and ginger. Add cabbage, carrots, onions, and bean sprouts and stir-fry 2 to 3 minutes.

4. Add mushroom mixture and 1/4 cup water. Bring to a boil and add cornstarch dissolved in water. Stir until thickened. Serve over rice.

NOTE:

Substitute or add any vegetable desired including turnips and mustard greens.

Indo-China Mobile Education Project
Washington, D.C.

CRISP RED CABBAGE

Serves 6 to 8

Preparation 25 Minutes
Cook 50 Minutes

2 tablespoons oil
1 head (2 pounds) red cabbage, shredded
2 medium onions, sliced
2 large apples, peeled and chopped
1/4 cup white vinegar
Salt and pepper to taste

1. Heat oil in a 12-inch skillet over medium-high heat. Add cabbage, onions, and apples, stir to coat.
2. Lower heat, add vinegar, salt, and pepper. Stir again. Cover and cook 45 to 50 minutes. Stir occasionally.

Patt Hanson
Boulder, Colorado

CABBAGE-POTATO CASSEROLE

Serves 4

Preparation 25 Minutes
Bake 15 Minutes at 350°F

4 cups shredded cabbage
3 cups sliced potatoes
Boiling salted water
Cheese sauce (see Index)
1/2 cup bread crumbs

1. Cook cabbage and potatoes quickly in salted water until just done. Drain.
2. Put vegetables in casserole and pour on cheese sauce. Top with crumbs.
3. Heat in 350-degree oven for 15 minutes or until bubbly and crumbs are brown.

Marsha Paull
Avalon, California

COPPER PENNIES

Serves 10

Preparation 30 Minutes
Refrigerate 12 Hours

- 2 pounds carrots, peeled and sliced
- Boiling salted water
- 1 medium green pepper, diced
- 1 onion, sliced and separated into rings
- 1/4 to 3/4 cup sugar
- 1/4 cup oil
- 1/2 cup vinegar
- 1 teaspoon mustard
- 1 teaspoon Worcestershire sauce
- Salt and pepper to taste

1. Cook carrots briefly in boiling water. They should still be quite firm. Drain. Combine with peppers and onions.
2. Mix sugar, oil, vinegar, mustard, Worcestershire sauce, salt, and pepper. Pour over vegetables.
3. Mix and refrigerate 12 hours or longer. Stir occasionally.

NOTE:

These make sensational appetizers for large parties. If carrots are not overcooked, they will stay firm in marinade several days.

Betty Dozier
Avalon, California

CARROT CURRY

Serves 4 to 6

Preparation 10 Minutes
Cook 35 Minutes

- 1 1/2 pounds fresh carrots
- 1 cup fresh orange juice
- 1 teaspoon salt
- Water
- 4 tablespoons butter
- 4 to 5 cardamom pods (seeds only)
- 1 teaspoon turmeric
- 1 teaspoon mustard seeds
- 4 whole cloves
- 1 tablespoon cumin seeds
- 1/8 to 1/4 teaspoon cayenne pepper
- 1/2 teaspoon curry powder (optional)
- 2 to 3 tablespoons raisins
- 1 ripe banana, thinly sliced
- 1 1/2 tablespoons cornstarch

1. Slice carrots on slant, 1/4 to 1/2-inch thick. Simmer 5 minutes in orange juice, salt, and water to cover.
2. Heat butter in small skillet, add spices and heat a few minutes. Add to carrots along with raisins and banana.
3. Simmer for 1/2 hour. Thicken with cornstarch, if needed.

Edith Schiffman
Boulder, Colorado

CREAMED CARROTS

Serves 6 to 8

Preparation 15 Minutes
Cook 1 Hour

2 pounds fresh carrots, thinly sliced
Cold water
1 tablespoons sugar
1/2 teaspoon salt
1/4 teaspoon white pepper
4 sprigs parsley
1/2 teaspoon thyme leaves
2 bay leaves
1 large clove garlic
2 tablespoons butter
SAUCE
1 1/2 tablespoons butter
1 1/2 tablespoons flour
1 cup milk
Salt and pepper to taste
Dash nutmeg

1. Put carrot slices in a 3- to 4-quart heavy bottomed pan and just cover with cold water. Add sugar, salt, pepper, parsley, thyme, bay leaves, whole garlic clove, and butter. Cook until all water has been absorbed (about 1 hour).
2. While carrots are cooking, prepare sauce. Melt butter, add flour and cook for several minutes. Slowly add milk, stirring constantly, and cook until thick. Season with salt, pepper, and nutmeg.
3. When carrots are cooked, remove parsley, bay leaves, and garlic clove.
4. Add sauce to carrots and serve.

Camilla Tabaud
Paris, France

CARROTS AND LEEKS VICHEY

Serves 4 to 6

Preparation 20 Minutes
Cook 20 Minutes

10-12 carrots
4 leeks
1/4 cup butter, melted
2 tablespoons cold water
2 teaspoons sugar
1 teaspoon salt
1/2 teaspoon freshly ground pepper
1/4 cup butter, melted (optional)

1. Cut carrots and leeks into very thin slices.
2. In saucepan, melt butter and add water, sugar, salt, pepper, carrots, and leeks.
3. Cover with foil, pressing right down onto carrots and leeks, cover pan with lid.
4. Cook over medium heat, shaking occasionally, about 20 minutes.
5. Transfer carrots and leeks to serving dish and pour on melted butter.

Pat Wright
Boulder, Colorado

CAULIFLOWER IN GARLIC MAYONNAISE
(*Coliflor con Ali-Oli*)

Serves 6

Refrigerate 2 Hours

1 cauliflower, divided into flowerets
Boiling salted water
Garlic Mayonnaise (see Index)
Pitted black olives and 1 tablespoon chopped parsley for garnish

1. Cook the cauliflower in boiling salted water for 8 to 10 minutes or until just tender. Drain and cool.
2. Pile the cauliflower in a bowl and cover with the garlic mayonnaise. Garnish with olives and parsley. Serve cold.

Meraly Gordon
Boulder, Colorado

CAULIFLOWER WITH ALMONDS

Serves 4

Preparation 10 Minutes
Cook 20 Minutes

1 medium cauliflower, divided in flowerets
4 tablespoons butter
1/2 cup sliced almonds
1 clove garlic, minced
1/4 cup grated Parmesan cheese

1. Steam cauliflower for 20 minutes, or microwave 7 to 8 minutes covered.
2. Melt butter and saute' almonds and garlic until almonds are golden.
3. Toss with cooked cauliflower and sprinkle with Parmesan cheese. Serve at once.

FANCY CAULIFLOWER

Serves 8 to 10

Preparation 25 Minutes
Bake 5 Minutes at 375°F

1 whole cauliflower
Boiling salted water
Salt and pepper
2 teaspoons mustard
1/2 cup mayonnaise
3/4 cup grated Cheddar cheese

1. Cook whole cauliflower in boiling salted water until tender or in microwave oven 7 minutes. Place cooked cauliflower in shallow baking dish, add salt and pepper.
2. Combine mustard and mayonnaise and spread over cauliflower. Sprinkle with grated cheese.
3. Bake at 375 degrees for 5 minutes or 1 1/2 to 2 minutes in microwave oven until cheese is melted and bubbling.

Sue Bray
Avalon, California

NUTTY CREAMED CELERY

Serves 4

Preparation 25 Minutes
Bake 15 Minutes at 400°F

3 cups sliced celery, in 1/2-inch pieces
4 tablespoons butter
1 tablespoon flour
3/4 teaspoon salt
1 cup half-and-half or milk
3/4 cup slivered almonds, toasted
1/2 cup bread crumbs

1. Steam celery until tender with as little water as possible in a saucepan with a tight fitting lid. Drain thoroughly.
2. Melt 2 tablespoons butter in another saucepan and stir in flour and salt. Cook briefly, then stir in half-and-half. Continue stirring and cook until thickened.
3. Combine celery and cream sauce and pour into buttered 1-quart casserole.
4. Mix together remaining 2 melted tablespoons butter, almonds, and bread crumbs. Sprinkle over casserole. Bake 15 minutes at 400 degrees.

Kate Michaels
Kansas City, Kansas

COLLARD GREENS AND ORANGES

(Serve with feijoada, *Brazilian black bean stew)*

Serves 12

Preparation 15 Minutes
Cook 10 Minutes

4 slices bacon, chopped
1 to 2 cloves garlic, minced
3 pounds fresh collard greens
Salt and pepper to taste
12 small oranges, rind and pith removed, sliced

1. Fry bacon, add garlic, collard greens, salt, and pepper. Cook, stirring until just cooked and the greens do not taste raw.
2. Prepare one orange per person and place on one side of large platter with collard greens mounded on the other side.

NOTE:

Fresh greens are much better to use, but, if frozen greens are necessary, use 4 packages (10-ounce each). Thaw and squeeze dry.

Sue McMillan
Boulder, Colorado

GRANDMA BRICK'S CORN PUDDING

Serves 8

Preparation 15 Minutes
Bake 45 to 60 Minutes at 400°F

3 eggs
3 tablespoons flour
1/8 to 1/2 cup sugar
1 cup milk
2 cups corn
1/2 teaspoon salt
2 to 4 tablespoons butter or margarine

1. Combine eggs, flour, and sugar and beat well. Add milk, corn, and salt.
2. Melt butter in 1 1/2-quart baking dish and add corn mixture.
3. Bake at 400 degrees for 45 to 60 minutes or until firm.

VARIATION:

Add chopped chilies. Or, if you want a smoother pudding, puree the corn.

Catherine P. Ware
Franklin, Kentucky

FRIED EGGPLANT

Serves 6

Preparation 15 Minutes
Cook 40 Minutes

1 eggplant (about 2 pounds) peeled and thinly sliced
2 cups cracker meal
2 to 3 tablespoons garlic powder
4 teaspoons onion powder
2 teaspoons paprika
1 teaspoon salt
1/2 teaspoon pepper
2 eggs, beaten
1/4 cup milk
Oil for frying

1. Mix cracker meal, garlic powder, onion powder, paprika, salt, and pepper. Taste mixture and correct seasoning.
2. Mix eggs with milk. Dip eggplant slices in egg mixture then in cracker meal.
3. Fry slices in hot oil until golden on both sides. Drain well. Keep warm in low oven. Serve.

VARIATION:

1. Follow the same recipe using zucchini slices or sticks.
2. Both fried eggplant and zucchini make excellent Parmesan. Alternate layers of either vegetable with Parmesan cheese, grated; spaghetti sauce, without meat (see Index); ending with sauce. Top with sliced mozzarella cheese. Bake at 350 degrees for 20 to 30 minutes or until hot and bubbly. This freezes well.

Alan Parry
Tempe, Arizona

PEAS AND ARTICHOKES

Serves 4 to 6

Preparation 15 Minutes
Cook 8 Minutes

1 tablespoon butter
3 green onions, chopped
1 package (10-ounce) frozen peas
1 can (8 1/2-ounce) artichoke hearts, drained
1 1/2 cups shredded lettuce
1/2 teaspoon basil
1/2 teaspoon oregano
Salt and pepper to taste

1. Melt butter and sauté onions in 10-inch skillet.
2. Meanwhile, in small saucepan cook peas 4 minutes. (Use as little water as possible.) Drain and add to onions.
3. Quarter artichoke hearts and add to peas and onions.
4. Stir in lettuce and seasonings. Cover and cook over medium heat 8 minutes.

Nancy Cateora
Boulder, Colorado

SWEET POTATO BALLS

Serves 12

Preparation 1 Hour
Bake 20 Minutes at 350°F

2 pounds sweet potatoes, cooked and mashed
1/4 to 3/4 cup brown sugar
2 to 4 tablespoons melted butter
Salt and pepper to taste
12 large marshmallows
2 cups crushed cereal flakes

1. Combine potatoes, brown sugar to taste, melted butter (in lesser amounts if potatoes are moist), salt, and pepper.
2. Shape into balls around marshmallows. Roll in crushed cereal flakes. It may be necessary to roll lightly in melted butter to get flakes to stick.
3. Place on lightly greased baking sheet. Bake at 350 degrees for 20 minutes.

NOTE:

Take these to a pot-luck supper; they stay warm for 2 hours when covered with foil. Terrific served with ham or turkey. Take care if served directly from the oven, the marshmallows are extremely hot.

Janet Sparkman
Boulder, Colorado

SWEET POTATO BAKE

Serves 8

Preparation 1 Hour
Bake 25 Minutes at 350°F

6 large sweet potatoes
6 tablespoons butter
1/2 cup milk
1/2 teaspoon cinnamon
1/2 teaspoon salt
1/4 teaspoon freshly grated nutmeg
2 tablespoons freshly grated orange rind
1/2 cup chopped pecans

1. Bake sweet potatoes 40 minutes in 400-degree oven or until tender. For microwave, bake 3 potatoes at a time for 12 to 15 minutes turning potatoes every 5 minutes. Either method, potatoes should be very tender.
2. Peel potatoes and mash with butter, milk, cinnamon, salt, nutmeg, and orange rind.
3. Turn into buttered 1 1/2-quart baking dish, sprinkle top with nuts. Bake 25 minutes at 350 degrees.

NOTE:

Leftover mashed sweet potatoes can be used to make Sweet Potato Muffins (see Index).

A Friend of the Library
Miami, Florida

POTATO PANCAKES
(*Latkes*)

Serves 4

Preparation 30 Minutes
Cook 30 Minutes

1 1/2 cups peeled and grated raw potatoes, well drained
1 egg
3 tablespoons grated onion
1/2 teaspoon salt
Pepper to taste
1 tablespoon flour
Oil for shallow frying
Sour cream
Applesauce

1. In a mixing bowl, add drained potatoes, egg, onion, salt, pepper, and flour. Mix well.
2. Heat oil. Drop the potato mixture by the spoonful into the oil. Press to flatten the pancakes. Fry on both sides until golden brown. Drain.
3. Keep pancakes hot until all are fried.
4. Serve with sour cream and applesauce.

Leo Zager
Avalon, California

EGGPLANT STUFFED WITH MUSHROOMS

Serves 4

Preparation 45 Minutes
Bake 40 Minutes at 350°F

1 medium eggplant
1/4 cup butter
4 ounces fresh mushrooms, sliced
3 tablespoons flour
1/4 cup finely chopped onions
1 large clove garlic, crushed
1 teaspoon salt
1/8 teaspoon pepper
1/4 cup half-and-half
2 tablespoons grated Parmesan cheese
2 tablespoons bread crumbs
1/8 teaspoon basil
1/2 teaspoon dried parsley

1. Cut eggplant in half lengthwise. Remove and cube enough eggplant to make 3 cups. Set shells aside.
2. In a 10-inch skillet, melt butter and add eggplant, mushrooms, flour, onion, garlic, salt, and pepper. Cook and stir over medium heat for 10 minutes.
3. Remove pan from heat and add half-and-half. Mix well. Fill eggplant shells.
4. Mix Parmesan cheese, bread crumbs, basil, and parsley. Sprinkle over eggplants.
5. Bake in a 350-degree oven for 40 minutes.

Jennifer Shelt
Boulder, Colorado

VEGETABLES AL FORNO

Serves 8

Preparation 20 Minutes
Bake 45 Minutes at 350°F

1/2 eggplant, peeled and sliced
4 fresh tomatoes, peeled and sliced
2 large onions, sliced
1 zucchini, sliced
1/4 cup olive oil
3/4 pound mozzarella cheese, grated

1. Place a layer of each vegetable in a 9 x 13-inch baking dish. Pour olive oil over all. Top with mozzarella cheese.
2. Bake in 350-degree oven for 45 minutes.

Marguerite Cateora
Dallas, Texas

MARINATED MUSHROOMS

Serves 8 to 10

Preparation 1 Hour
Marinate Overnight

3 pounds raw mushrooms, sliced
1/3 cup olive oil
2 tablespoons lemon juice
2 onions, sliced
2 cloves garlic, crushed
3 bay leaves
1/2 teaspoon each thyme, marjoram, and black pepper
3 cups canned Italian tomatoes, drained (reserve 1/2 cup juice) and chopped
1 cup red wine vinegar
1 teaspoon sugar
Dash hot pepper sauce
Salt to taste
Chopped parsley

1. In a large skillet, saute' mushrooms in 1/3 cup olive oil in two batches until golden. Transfer to a large bowl and toss with lemon juice.
2. In same pan, saute' onions and garlic adding more olive oil as necessary until softened. Add bay leaves, thyme, marjoram, and pepper. Saute' one minute.
3. Stir in tomatoes, juice, vinegar, sugar, and hot pepper sauce and simmer 20 minutes. Add to mushrooms and salt to taste. Cool and cover with plastic wrap. Marinate, chilled, at least 12 hours.
4. Serve at room temperature, sprinkled with parsley.

NOTE:

A food processor is a great help in slicing mushrooms.

The Cookery
Boulder, Colorado

MUSHROOMS AND CREAM

Serves 2

Preparation 10 Minutes
Cook 1 1/2 Hours

1/2 pound large fresh mushrooms, sliced
6 ounces heavy cream

1. Combine mushrooms and cream in 8-inch skillet over low heat.
2. Let simmer uncovered about 1 1/2 hours or until cream is thick and browned. Stir lightly once or twice.

NOTE:

For increased quantities, be sure to use larger-size skillet so cream layer is not too deep. You may also have to increase cooking time.

Nancy Kuempel
Cincinnati, Ohio

MASHED POTATOES PARMESAN

Serves 4

Preparation 60 Minutes
Bake 30 Minutes at 350°F

4 potatoes, peeled
Boiling salted water
1/2 medium onion, chopped
3/4 cup freshly grated Parmesan cheese
3/4 cup mayonnaise
6 tablespoons butter
1/2 to 2/3 cup milk
Salt and pepper to taste

1. Quarter potatoes and cook covered in boiling water until tender. Drain.
2. While potatoes are cooking, mix onions, 1/2 cup cheese, and mayonnaise. Set aside.
3. Mash potatoes (do not use blender or food processor, it makes potatoes very starchy), add 5 tablespoons butter, milk, salt, and pepper and beat.
4. Add mayonnaise-cheese mixture to potatoes. Turn into a 1-quart casserole and top with remaining 1/4 cup Parmesan cheese and 1 tablespoon butter. Bake 30 minutes at 350 degrees or until top is golden brown.

NOTE:

An interesting way to use leftover mashed potatoes.

Sheryl Kuempel
Boulder, Colorado

VEGETABLE PUREES

Most vegetables make tasty purees. Cook vegetables or vegetable combination in water or broth depending on flavor desired. Puree in blender, food processor, or food mill. Add heavy cream, or broth, butter, salt, and white pepper or a Be´chamel Sauce (see Index). Added cooked and pureed rice and/or cooked onion gives a nice flavor. Purees can be served hot or cold. If served hot, heat by baking in a shallow serving dish or in individual molds. If not used right away, refrigerate pureed vegetables. When ready to use, add cream and heat.

To serve puree cold, season with salt and white pepper and bind with a little mayonnaise. This is an excellent use for leftover vegetables.

STUFFED ROMAINE

Serves 4

Preparation 30 Minutes
Cook 20 Minutes

3 onions
4 1/2 tablespoons butter
1 teaspoon vegetable oil
12 mushrooms, coarsely chopped
2 tablespoons dry white wine
1 teaspoon lemon juice
2 teaspoon flour
4 ounces sour cream
4 small heads of romaine
1 cup cooked ham, cut in julienne strips
1 cup chicken broth

1. Finely chop 2 onions. Melt 2 1/2 tablespoons butter, add the oil and fry onion until tender.
2. Add mushrooms, wine, and lemon juice. Cover and simmer 2 minutes. Uncover and cook until liquid is reduced by half.
3. Mix 1 teaspoon flour and sour cream, add to mushrooms and bring just to boiling point. Remove from heat and set aside.
4. Cut romaine in half lengthwise. Parboil upright with stem ends down in salted water for 5 minutes. Drain well, refresh under cold water and drain again.
5. Spread 2 teaspoons filling between leaves of each head, filling only halfway up from base to middle. Fold upper half over stuffed lower half until the two ends meet. Place in baking dish with unfilled sides down.
6. Thinly slice remaining onion lengthwise and fry in 1 tablespoon butter until tender. Add ham, sauté 1 minute.
7. Place ham mixture over stuffed romaine, add chicken broth, cover and simmer 20 minutes.
8. Remove to serving platter, add remaining 1 tablespoon butter and flour to pan juices. Bring to boil and pour over romaine.

André Krohn
Bad Nauheim, West Germany

SAUERKRAUT

1 head of cabbage
1 to 2 tablespoons salt

1. Using food processor, shred cabbage finely. If not using food processor, cabbage should be finely shredded and then pounded to bruise.
2. Place cabbage in large glass or ceramic mixing bowl and mix in salt.
3. Top with a plate that will cover but rests on the cabbage. Weight the plate.
4. Leave at room temperature until cabbage has nice tang, usually about a week. If weather is very warm, it will take less time. Refrigerate to store.

Jean Loeffler
Boulder, Colorado

SPINACH-CHEESE PIE
(Spanakopita)

Serves 10 to 12

Preparation 2 Hours
Bake 15 Minutes at 350°F
1 Hour at 300°F

2 pounds fresh spinach, trimmed and coarsely chopped
2 bunches green onions, including tops, finely chopped
1 bunch fresh parsley, finely chopped
6 eggs, beaten
1/2 pound small curd cottage cheese
1 pound feta cheese crumbled
1 tablespoon dried dill weed
1 1/2 cups olive oil
Salt to taste
1/2 cup uncooked cream of wheat
1/2 pound butter
1 pound *filo* pastry sheets

1. Combine spinach, onions, parsley, beaten eggs, cottage cheese, feta cheese, dill, 1/2 cup olive oil, salt, and cream of wheat.
2. Melt butter with 1 cup olive oil in a small saucepan.
3. Brush a large pan (11 x 15 x 2-inch) with butter-oil mixture.
4. Unfold the *filo* and place under a damp cloth. Brush 8 to 10 sheets of *filo* one at a time with butter-oil mixture and place one layer on the other in the pan.
5. On top of the 8 to 10 sheets layer as follows: spinach mixture, 1 sheet of *filo* (brushing every sheet with butter-oil mixture), the spinach mixture, *filo* again, etc. Continue in this way until all the spinach mixture is used. Top with remaining *filo* sheets, again brushing between each sheet. Sprinkle with water before baking.
6. Bake at 350 degrees for 15 minutes, reduce heat to 300 degrees and continue baking for one hour or until pastry turns a golden brown.

NOTE:

1. For traditional procedure: use 1/2 pound *filo*. Place 8 to 10 sheets *filo*, brushed with butter-oil mixture between each sheet, in a pan. Pour in all of the spinach mixture at once. Top with 8 to 10 sheets of *filo*, brushed between layers.
2. Other fillings such as cheese only may be used.
3. For delicate *floyeras* (flutes) or rolls of spanakopita: brush sheet of *filo* with the butter-oil mixture, cut in thirds, lengthwise. At the bottom of each piece, place a generous tablespoon of the spinach mixture. Fold the long sides, right and left, towards the center approximately 1/2 inch then roll jelly-roll fashion. Place flutes on a baking sheet, seam-side down. Bake at 400 degrees for 15 minutes.
4. Can be kept for 10 days (before or after baking).

Ellen Denton
Piedmont, California

TANGY COLD SPINACH

Serves 8 to 10

Preparation 50 Minutes
Refrigerate 2 Hours

3 hard-cooked eggs
2 packages (10-ounce each) frozen spinach
1 cup mayonnaise
2 teaspoons prepared horseradish
1/2 teaspoon Tabasco
1 1/2 teaspoons vinegar
1/2 teaspoon salt
1 cup shredded sharp Cheddar cheese
1/2 cup chopped onion
1/2 cup chopped celery

1. Chop 2 eggs and slice 1 egg. Thaw and drain spinach.
2. Combine mayonnaise, horseradish, Tabasco, vinegar, and salt.
3. Mix spinach, cheese, onion, celery, and the 2 chopped eggs. Combine with mayonnaise mixture. Garnish with egg slices.
4. Refrigerate several hours before serving.

Gail Madden
Boulder, Colorado

SPINACH-ARTICHOKE BAKE

Serves 6 to 8

Preparation 25 Minutes
Bake 20 Minutes at 325°F

2 packages (10-ounce each) frozen spinach
5 tablespoons butter, melted
1 bunch green onions, minced, including 1/2 inch of tops
3 tablespoons flour
1 cup sour cream or half-and-half
1 teaspoon salt
1/2 teaspoon pepper
Garlic powder to taste
1 package (10-ounce) frozen artichoke hearts, thawed
2/3 cup Hollandaise sauce (see Index)
Nutmeg to taste

1. Cook spinach until just tender. Refresh in cold water to stop the cooking and drain thoroughly.
2. Add onion to melted butter and saute' 3 to 4 minutes over low heat. Stir in flour and cook 2 to 3 minutes.
3. Add sour cream or half-and-half slowly to make a smooth sauce. Stir in spinach, salt, pepper, and garlic powder.
4. Butter a 2-quart casserole. Layer with 1/2 of spinach, then artichokes and remaining spinach. Top with Hollandaise sauce. Dust with nutmeg.
5. Bake at 325 degrees for 15 to 20 minutes.

SPINACH WITH COCONUT MILK AND PEANUT SAUCE
(*Mchicha Wa Nazi*)

Serves 4 to 6

Preparation 30 Minutes
Cook 10 Minutes

2 pounds fresh spinach, well trimmed
1 teaspoon salt
2 tablespoons butter
1 cup finely chopped onion
1/4 teaspoon minced fresh hot chilies
1 cup coconut milk (see Index)
1/2 cup unsalted, roasted peanuts, pureed

1. Cook spinach with salt and water in covered saucepan over moderate heat until tender, about 10 minutes.
2. Drain spinach completely and coarsely chop.
3. Melt butter in a heavy 10-inch skillet and saute' onions and chilies, being careful not to brown.
4. Stir in coconut milk and peanuts and bring to a simmer. Reduce heat to lowest temperature and cook for 2 to 3 minutes with constant stirring.
5. Add spinach and cook until it is heated through. Serve at once in a heated dish.

Susannah Jordan
Jamestown, Colorado

ORANGE-PECAN STUFFED SQUASH

Serves 4 to 6

Preparation 60 Minutes
Bake 10 Minutes at 350°F

3 small acorn squash
1 tablespoon brown sugar
1 tablespoon butter or margarine
1 teaspoon grated orange peel
2 tablespoons orange juice
1/4 teaspoon salt
2 tablespoons chopped pecans

1. Halve squash and remove seeds. Place, cut side down, on greased baking sheet. Bake 30 to 35 minutes at 350 degrees.
2. Scoop out pulp leaving a thin shell. Add brown sugar, butter, orange peel, orange juice, and salt to pulp. Mix until fluffy.
3. Refill shells and sprinkle with pecans. Bake 10 minutes at 350 degrees.

NOTE:

You may prefer 4 heaped shells to 6 less full shells or you may prepare and serve this in a casserole. Either way, the squash can be prepared ahead and heated just before serving.

Dottie Herman
Costa Mesa, California

BUTTERNUT SQUASH SOUFFLÉ

Serves 8

Preparation 30 Minutes
Bake 90 Minutes at 350°F

2 pounds butternut or acorn squash
2 tablespoons water
3 tablespoons butter
4 tablespoons flour
1 cup milk
1/2 teaspoon ground ginger
1 teaspoon ground cinnamon
1/4 teaspoon salt
1 cup sugar
1/2 cup orange juice
4 eggs, separated
3 egg whites

1. Cut squash in thick chunks and remove seeds. Bake covered with water at 350 degrees until tender.
2. Using a food processor, blender, or food mill, puree squash until smooth.
3. Melt butter, add flour and cook briefly. Add milk, stirring, and cook until thickened.
4. Stir in ginger, cinnamon, salt, sugar, orange juice, and squash puree. Cool slightly, then add beaten egg yolks.
5. Beat 7 egg whites until stiff but not dry, and fold into squash mixture.
6. Spoon into 2-quart souffle' dish and place dish in pan filled with water halfway up side of dish.
7. Bake 1 1/2 hours at 350 degrees. Test for doneness as for a cake. The souffle' will stay fluffy 30 minutes.

Sara McNice
Boulder, Colorado

SPINACH STUFFED SQUASH

Serves 8

Preparation 30 Minutes
Bake 15 Minutes at 350°F

4 yellow summer squash
Boiling salted water
3/4 cup butter or margarine
Salt and pepper to taste
1/2 cup grated Parmesan cheese
2 packages (10-ounce each) frozen chopped spinach
1/2 cup chopped onion
1 teaspoon salt
1 cup sour cream
2 teaspoons red wine vinegar
1/2 cup bread crumbs

1. Cook whole squash in boiling salted water 10 to 12 minutes or until tender. Cut in halves lengthwise and scoop out seeds. Brush squash halves with 2 tablespoons melted butter. Sprinkle with salt, pepper, and 1/4 cup Parmesan cheese.
2. Cook spinach according to package directions and drain thoroughly.

3. Saute' onion in 1/2 cup butter until tender, add spinach, salt, sour cream, and vinegar. Blend well.
4. Fill squash with stuffing mixture. Sprinkle with remaining 1/4 cup Parmesan cheese and bread crumbs. Dot with 2 tablespoons butter and bake at 350 degrees for 15 minutes.

Sara McNice
Boulder, Colorado

CHEESE STUFFED ZUCCHINI

Serves 6

Preparation 25 Minutes
Bake 15 to 20 Minutes at 350°F

6 zucchini, about 6 inches long
2 eggs
1 cup shredded sharp Cheddar cheese
1/2 cup cottage cheese, drained
2 tablespoons chopped onion
1/4 cup chopped parsley
1/2 teaspoon salt
1/4 teaspoon freshly ground pepper

1. Partially cook whole zucchini in microwave oven about 3 minutes each.
2. Cut in half lengthwise and scrape out seeds. Turn upside down to drain.
3. Mix eggs, cheese, cottage cheese, onion, parsley, salt, and pepper.
4. Lightly salt inside of prepared zucchini shells and fill with cheese mixture.
5. Place in buttered baking dish and bake 15 to 20 minutes at 350 degrees. If top is not browned, increase heat to 400 degrees for 5 minutes.

NOTE:

If not using microwave oven, parboil zucchini in salted water about 10 minutes. Proceed as above.

Mary Gerlitz-Garnett
Boulder, Colorado

EMALLEES ZUCCHINI CASSEROLE

Serves 6 to 8

Preparation 30 Minutes
Bake 30 Minutes at 350°F

2 pounds zucchini, sliced
Dash of salt
3 tablespoons water
1 1/2 cups dried bread crumbs
4 egg yolks, lightly beaten
1/2 cup finely chopped onion
2 tablespoons butter
4 egg whites, beaten to stiff peaks
Salt and pepper to taste
1/2 cup grated sharp Cheddar cheese

1. Cook zucchini, covered, in salt and water until tender. Drain and mash.
2. Add bread crumbs and egg yolks.
3. Saute' onion in butter until golden. Add squash mixture. Fold in beaten egg whites. Season to taste.
4. Pour into 2-quart casserole. Sprinkle top with cheese and bake at 350 degrees for 30 minutes.

Mary Lymberopoulos
Boulder, Colorado

CRUNCHY SQUASH

Serves 6 to 8
Stand 1 to 2 Hours

Preparation 30 Minutes
Bake 30 Minutes at 350°F

1 can (8-ounce) water chestnuts, quartered
1/4 cup Worcestershire sauce
1 medium onion, sliced
2 tablespoons butter
2 medium zucchini, cubed
2 medium yellow squash, cubed
1 egg, beaten
1 1/2 cups grated Cheddar cheese

1. Cover water chestnuts with Worcestershire sauce and let stand 1 to 2 hours. Stir occasionally.
2. Saute' onion in butter until limp. Add squash and cook briefly over medium heat (about 5 minutes).
3. Pour squash-onion mixture into 2 1/2- to 3-quart casserole. Stir in beaten egg, cheese, and water chestnuts including what remains of the Worcestershire sauce.
4. Bake, uncovered, 30 minutes at 350 degrees.

Marguerite Cateora
Dallas, Texas

BROILED TOMATOES

Serves 6

Preparation 15 Minutes
Bake 10 Minutes at 425°F

3 large tomatoes, halved
3/4 cup bread crumbs
2 tablespoons butter, melted
1 large clove garlic, crushed
1/2 teaspoon dried basil
1/2 teaspoon dried parsley
1/4 teaspoon dried tarragon
Salt and pepper to taste

1. Turn tomato halves over to drain for a few minutes.
2. Mix bread crumbs, butter, garlic, basil, parsley, tarragon, salt, and pepper.
3. Place 2 tablespoons bread crumb mixture on each tomato half and put in shallow, ovenproof serving dish or on baking sheet.
4. Bake for 10 minutes at 425 degrees or until tops are brown. You may want to broil for a few minutes to brown.

Jay Marks
Houston, Texas

SCALLOPED TURNIPS AND APPLES

Serves 6

Preparation 20 Minutes
Bake 30 Minutes at 350°F

4 cups sliced turnips, cooked
2 cups sliced raw apples
1/4 cup brown sugar
1 teaspoon salt
1/4 cup butter
1/4 cup bread crumbs

1. In greased 1 1/2-quart casserole, layer 2 cups turnips and 1 cup sliced apples. Sprinkle with 2 tablespoons brown sugar, 1/2 teaspoon salt and dot with 2 tablespoons butter. Repeat layers.
2. Cover and bake 20 minutes at 350 degrees.
3. Uncover, sprinkle with bread crumbs. Bake another 10 minutes or until apples are tender and crumbs lightly browned.

Charlotte Coffin
Cherry Hills, New Jersey

JAPANESE STYLE BOILED VEGETABLE DINNER

Serves 4 to 6

Preparation 1 Hour 15 Minutes
Cook 20 Minutes

2 cups sliced carrots
3 1/2 cups fresh cauliflower flowerets
4 cups fresh broccoli flowerets
1 1/2 cups sliced onion
2 cups thinly sliced zucchini
12 green onions cut in 1 1/2-inch lengths
2 cups thinly sliced green pepper
14 ounces tofu cut in 3/4-inch cubes
4 cups fresh spinach leaves
4 cups cooked rice
***O-Mizu-Take* Sauce (see below)**

1. Have all vegetables prepared for cooking and the sauce made before you actually start the cooking. Vegetables should be cut in small enough pieces so that they cook quickly.
2. In a large pot, bring to boil 3 inches of water. Add one vegetable at a time, carrots, cauliflower, broccoli, onion, zucchini, green onions, green pepper in order given. Stir briefly between additions and allow water to return to a boil.
3. Scatter tofu cubes on top of vegetables, then add spinach leaves loosely on top of tofu. Cook 1 minute longer.
4. Remove vegetables with a slotted spoon and serve over rice with *O-Mizu-Take* Sauce.

NOTE:

The goal is to have all vegetables reach the "just cooked" stage at the same time. With practice, you can do it by timing each item. Any vegetable may be substituted or used in addition to above recipe, i.e., mushrooms, green beans, asparagus, etc. The broth makes a lovely soup with a little soy sauce and *O-Mizu-Take* Sauce stirred in. The leftovers can be reheated as soup or stew. Chicken or beef, thinly sliced, can be substituted for tofu. Meat should be added with the onions.

O-MIZU-TAKE SAUCE

Yields 3 1/2 Cups

Preparation 15 Minutes

4 tablespoons sesame paste
2 tablespoons honey or sugar
3 cups mayonnaise
6 tablespoons soy sauce
3 tablespoons sherry
1 tablespoon catsup
1/8 teaspoon ground pepper
1/2 teaspoon mashed garlic
1 teaspoon finely minced fresh ginger root

1. Mix sesame paste and honey thoroughly.
2. Add three 1/2 cup portions mayonnaise to honey mixture. Blend well after each addition.
3. Add remaining mayonnaise, soy sauce, sherry, catsup, pepper, garlic, and ginger root. Mix well.

NOTE:

Sauce keeps for weeks in refrigerator. It is good on leftovers or as a dip for raw vegetables.

John Stevens
Boulder, Colorado

VEGETABLE SPECIAL

Serves 6

Preparation 30 Minutes
Bake 10 to 15 Minutes at 375°F

2 tablespoons oil
1 onion, sliced
1 zucchini, sliced
1 yellow squash, sliced
1 cup cut green beans
1 green pepper, cubed
1 can (16-ounce) whole peeled tomatoes with juice
1/4 teaspoon each of thyme, marjoram, sage, summer savory, and pepper
1/2 teaspoon salt
5 to 6 slices Monterey Jack cheese

1. Heat oil in large, deep skillet. Fry onions, zucchini, squash, green beans, and green pepper until just done. Do not over cook.
2. Add tomatoes, break into pieces in pan. Add 1/2 cup tomato juice. Add thyme, marjoram, sage, summer savory, pepper, and salt. Mix well. Cover and cook 5 minutes.
3. Pour in casserole. Cover with slices of cheese. Bake at 375 degrees until brown, about 10 to 15 minutes. Serve immediately.

Arleen Garfinkle Claussner
Boulder, Colorado

VARIATION:

Substitute 2 cups diced fresh tomato for canned tomato. Add 1/2 pound bacon, fried, drained and crumbled, and 1 cup slivered almonds on top of cheese. One small eggplant, diced, may be substituted for green beans.

Catherine Ware
Franklin, Kentucky

BUBBY'S CRANBERRY SAUCE

Serves 12 to 16

Preparation 30 Minutes
Cook 25 Minutes

1 package (12-ounce) fresh cranberries
Water
Sugar
3 large tart green apples, peeled and cut into eighths

1. Mix cranberries and 1/2 cup less water than stated on package. Cook cranberries until skins pop.
2. Remove from heat and put cranberries and their liquid through food mill or heavy duty sieve to remove all skins.
3. Return sieved cranberries and juice to saucepan. Add sugar to taste. Cook over low heat, uncovered, stirring with wooden spoon until sugar has dissolved.
4. Add apples to sauce and cook until apples are just tender. Refrigerate until serving time.

NOTE:

Serve as side dish to a Thanksgiving turkey. Excellent also with ham or chicken and on cold turkey sandwiches. Can be made several days ahead.

Ethel Zager
Avalon, California

CUCUMBER AND YOGURT

Serves 4 to 6

Preparation 10 Minutes
Stand 1 Hour

2 medium cucumbers, pared, thinly sliced or grated
2 teaspoons salt
10 ounces plain yogurt
1/2 teaspoon sugar
1/4 teaspoon cumin
1/2 cup onion, finely chopped

1. Sprinkle 1 teaspoon of the salt over cucumbers. Let stand 1 hour, then drain thoroughly.
2. Whisk yogurt, remaining teaspoon of salt, sugar, and cumin until smooth. Stir in cucumbers and onion.

VARIATION:

Instead of cumin, or in addition to it, use dry mustard. Or, use mustard seeds fried in a little oil (cover, they will pop).

HAPPY'S APPLE SKILLET

Serves 6 to 8

Preparation 15 Minutes
Cook 25 Minutes

1/2 cup butter
6 medium apples, cored and cut into eighths
1 teaspoon grated fresh orange peel
1 cup brown sugar
1/2 cup orange juice concentrate
2 tablespoons rum (optional)

1. Melt butter in large skillet, add apple slices, orange peel, brown sugar, and juice. Stir to coat apple slices.
2. Bring to a gentle simmer and cook over low heat, uncovered, 20 to 25 minutes or until apples are tender and sauce thick. Stir occasionally, turning apple slices over.
3. Stir in rum and serve hot.

NOTE:

An unusual and tasty side dish for turkey, pork, ham, or chicken.

Hattie Cateora
Port Isabel, Texas

CURRIED FRUIT

An exciting side dish to serve with ham or poultry.

Serves 8

Preparation 20 Minutes
Bake 1 Hour at 325°F

7 cups cut fresh fruit (use a variety)
1/3 cup butter or margarine, melted
3/4 cup brown sugar
1 to 4 teaspoons curry powder

1. Place fruit in a 2-quart casserole.
2. Mix butter, brown sugar, and curry powder and pour over fruit.
3. Bake, covered, for 1 hour at 325 degrees.

NOTE:

1. Peaches, pears, apricots, pineapple, bananas, and cantaloupe are particularly good in this dish.
2. If using canned fruit, use 4 cans (16-ounce each) drained and 1 jar (6-ounce) maraschino cherries.
3. For 2 servings, use 1 jar (29-ounce) fruit for salad or an equivalent amount of fresh fruit and 2 tablespoons butter, 1/4 cup brown sugar, and 1/2 teaspoon curry powder (or to taste).

Jean T. Williams
Boulder, Colorado

VINEGAR ONIONS

Raw onion haters love this one.

Serves 6 to 8

Preparation 10 Minutes
Cook 5 Minutes

2 onions, sliced paper thin
Salted water
1 to 2 small fresh, hot green chilies, sliced into strips
1/2 carrot, sliced paper thin
1/8 teaspoon cumin seeds
1/8 teaspoon oregano
Pinch basil
1 bay leaf
2 cloves garlic, halved
1 cup white vinegar
1 cup water

1. Soak onions in salted water for 10 minutes. Drain and discard liquid.
2. In a saucepan, combine drained onions, chilies, carrots, cumin, oregano, basil, bay leaf, garlic, vinegar, and water. Bring to a boil, remove from heat, and let cool.

NOTE:

An excellent side dish for barbecued meats, chicken or Mexican food.

Sheryl Kuempel
Boulder, Colorado

TOMATO PUDDING

Serves 4 to 6

Preparation 10 Minutes
Bake 25 Minutes at 350°F

1/2 cup butter or margarine
2 cups soft white bread cubes
1 can (10 1/2-ounce) tomato puree
1/4 cup water
2/3 cup brown sugar
1/2 teaspoon each salt and pepper

1. Melt butter and pour over bread cubes.
2. Heat together tomato puree, water, sugar, salt, and pepper until sugar has dissolved. Pour over bread cubes and mix.
3. Bake for 25 minutes in a 2-quart casserole at 350 degrees.

Kathy Bickel
Boulder, Colorado

RICE, BEANS,
•
AND
•
PASTA

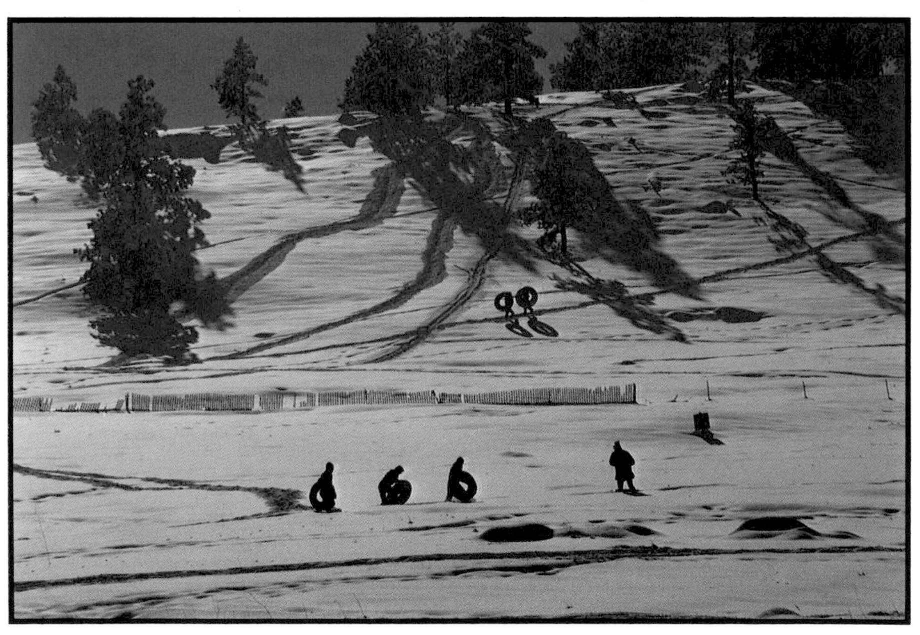

BRAZILIAN RICE

Serves 12 to 14

Preparation 20 Minutes
Cook 20 Minutes

1 large onion, chopped
2 tablespoons bacon grease
2 cups raw rice
3 tomatoes, chopped
4 cups boiling water

1. Brown onion in bacon grease. Add rice and brown lightly.
2. Stir in chopped tomato and add boiling water. Cover and cook 20 minutes without lifting lid.

NOTE:

Serve with *Feijoada* (see Index).

Sue McMillan
Boulder, Colorado

YELLOW RICE

Serves 4 to 6

Preparation 5 Minutes
Cook 30 Minutes

2 1/2 cups water
1 cup rice
2 to 4 tablespoons brown sugar
1 teaspoon salt
1 cinnamon stick
1 teaspoon turmeric
1/2 cup raisins
2 tablespoons butter or margarine

1. Bring water to boiling and add rice, brown sugar, salt, cinnamon stick, turmeric, raisins, and butter. Cover and return to a boil. Reduce heat and simmer for 30 minutes or until rice is tender.

NOTE:

To be served with *Bobotie* (see Index).

Susie Quick
Longmont, Colorado

RICE PEPITA

Serves 6 to 8

Preparation 10 Minutes
Cook 20 Minutes

1 cup raw white rice
2 cups beef broth
1/2 cup pumpkin seeds, salted

1. Cook rice in broth until tender.
2. Toss cooked rice with pumpkin seeds.

Georgia Barnum
Scottsdale, Arizona

TURKISH PILAF
(*Iç Piläv*)

Serves 8

Preparation 5 Minutes
Cook 30 Minutes

2 cups raw long grain rice
1 cup finely chopped onion
1/4 cup pine nuts
4 tablespoons butter
4 cups boiling water
4 bouillon cubes, chicken or beef
Salt and pepper to taste

1. Saute' rice, onion, and pine nuts in butter until lightly brown.
2. Add boiling water, bouillon cubes, salt, and pepper. Stir to dissolve cubes.
3. Cook, uncovered, over medium heat until water is absorbed and rice is tender.

NOTE:

Can be prepared ahead. Rice dishes reheat best in a microwave oven. For a truely Turkish dish, try to find pine nuts at a specialty store. Pine nuts and pinon nuts *are* different in flavor.

Rosyln Pfaff
Boulder, Colorado

VARIATION:

Increase onion to 2 cups, dissolve pinch of saffron in chicken broth and add 2 tablespoons currants, 2 teaspoons sugar, and a cinnamon stick to above recipe.

ARMENIAN PILAF

Serves 6

Preparation 15 Minutes
Cook 30 Minutes

4 bouillon cubes (beef or chicken)
2 3/4 cups hot water
2 vermicelli coils
1/2 cup butter
1 cup raw rice, long grain

1. Dissolve bouillon cubes in water in a 2-quart saucepan and set aside.
2. Crumble vermicelli and brown in butter. Add vermicelli and rice to bouillon. Cover and simmer 30 minutes, stirring once.

VARIATION:

Before serving add chopped, cooked chicken or beef and mushrooms.

Elizabeth James Luckow
Nederland, Colorado

CHILI-CHEESE RICE

Serves 6

Preparation 25 Minutes
Bake 1 Hour at 350°F

2 cups raw rice, long grain
4 cups boiling water
2 large bell peppers, chopped
2 large onions, chopped
1/3 cup oil
1 teaspoon salt
8 ounces Cheddar cheese, shredded
1 tablespoon chili powder

1. Add rice to boiling water, cover, and cook 20 minutes or until water is absorbed.
2. Saute' peppers and onions in oil.
3. In baking dish, mix cooked rice, peppers, onions, salt, cheese, and chili powder.
4. Bake at 350 degrees for 1 hour.

Betty Berger
Los Angeles, California

VARIATION:

Add 1 pound cooked and drained hamburger to this dish before baking for an easy main dish.

INDONESIAN RICE

Serves 8 to 10

Preparation 20 Minutes
Cook 30 Minutes

2 cups raw rice
4 cups boiling water
1 cup sliced or shredded carrots
1 cup julienned celery
1 cup French-style green beans, fresh or canned
1 cup sliced onion
1/2 cup butter
1 teaspoon salt
1/2 cup sliced almonds
1/2 cup raisins
1/4 teaspoon each thyme, marjoram, basil, and dried parsley

1. Add rice to boiling water, cover, and cook until water is absorbed.
2. Cook carrots, celery, green beans, and onions until tender. Drain and mix with cooked rice.
3. Add butter, salt, almonds, raisins, thyme, marjoram, basil, and parsley. Mix well and serve.

Kathy Van Arsdale
Denver, Colorado

ORIENTAL FRIED RICE

Serves 4

Preparation 15 Minutes
Cook 5 Minutes

2 slices bacon
3 eggs, beaten
3 cups cooked rice (at least 1 day old)
1 1/2 cups chopped and cooked pork, shrimp, chicken, or ham
1/2 pound fresh bean sprouts, chopped
1/2 cup mushrooms, sliced
2 tablespoons soy sauce
Salt and pepper to taste
Cayenne or crushed red pepper to taste
1 clove garlic, crushed
2 green onions, chopped
Fresh cilantro, chopped

1. In a large skillet, brown bacon and remove from pan and crumble. Fry eggs, cut into thin strips, and remove.
2. Add rice to skillet and stir. Add choice of meat, bean sprouts, mushrooms, soy sauce, salt, pepper, cayenne or crushed pepper, garlic, reserved bacon, and egg slices. Mix well.
3. Cook 5 minutes and mix in onions. Serve topped with cilantro (see Index).

Indo-China Mobile
Education Project
Washington, D.C.

NUT AND RICE LOAF WITH CUMBERLAND SAUCE

Serves 4 to 6

Preparation 25 Minutes
Bake 35 Minutes at 375°F

1 cup mixed nuts, chopped
1 cup soft whole wheat bread crumbs
1 cup cooked rice
1 cup finely chopped onions
1/4 teaspoon sage
1/4 teaspoon thyme
1 teaspoon salt
1/8 teaspoon pepper
6 tablespoons butter, melted
1 orange
Boiling water
2 tablespoons red currant jelly
Cayenne to taste
1/8 teaspoon dry mustard

1. In a medium-sized bowl, mix nuts and bread crumbs. Add rice, onions, sage, thyme, salt, pepper, and 2 tablespoons melted butter.
2. Blend well and add just enough water to make mixture stick together. Shape into a loaf. Place in buttered dish and bake at 375 degrees for 35 minutes, basting twice with remaining 4 tablespoons melted butter.
3. Remove colored skin from orange with potato peeler and cut into slivers. Cover with boiling water and let stand 5 minutes. Drain.

4. Mix peel with juice of orange, jelly, cayenne, and mustard in a saucepan. Stir and bring to a boil.
5. Serve loaf with sauce.

Barbara Patterson
Newark, New Jersey

RICE WITH SEAFOOD
(*Arroz con Mariscos*)

Serves 4 to 6

Preparation 25 Minutes
Cook 35 Minutes

4 tablespoons olive oil
1 clove garlic, mashed
1 large onion, diced
2 tomatoes, skinned and coarsely chopped
1 cup water
2 teaspoons salt
Dash each pepper and saffron
1 cup long-grained rice
1 cup clam juice
1/2 cup fresh green peas
12 raw clams with their liquid, shelled
1/4 pound cooked lobster meat

1. Heat 3 tablespoons olive oil in skillet. Add garlic and onion and saute' until onion is transparent but not brown.
2. Add tomatoes and simmer until soft. Add water, salt, pepper, and saffron, simmer 15 minutes more.
3. Wash rice with cold water and shake off all water. Saute' in small skillet in remaining oil until grains are coated with oil.
4. Add clam juice to onion-tomato mixture. Add peas and bring to rolling boil.
5. Add clams and bring to boil again. Add rice and lobster. Boil for 10 minutes. Lift mixture gently with fork to keep it from sticking to bottom.
6. Cover and simmer for 10 minutes more. Turn off heat and let stand for 10 minutes. Serve hot.

VARIATION:

Chicken, shrimp, and crab may also be used in place of or in addition to clams and lobster.

Esther deOnis
Boulder, Colorado

Serve with a 1979 or 1980 Charles F. Shaw Napa Gamay.

RICE WITH CHEESE
(*Arroz con Queso*)

Serves 6

Preparation 35 Minutes
Bake 45 Minutes at 350°F

1 cup raw rice
16 ounces Monterey Jack cheese
2 cups sour cream
1 can (3 1/2-ounce) diced chili peppers

1. Cook rice until tender and fluffy. While rice is simmering, slice cheese into 1/4-inch slices.
2. Layer by placing 1/2 cup cooked rice in bottom of casserole dish, then place half of cheese slices on top, followed by 1 cup sour cream spread over cheese. Sprinkle 1/2 can chilies on sour cream. Repeat layers. Cover casserole.
3. Bake at 350 degrees for 45 minutes.

Linda Gleason
Lafayette, Colorado

RICE-VEGETABLE-SAUSAGE STUFFING FOR TURKEY

Serves 4 to 6

Preparation 30 Minutes

2 cups raw rice
1 green pepper, chopped
1 large onion, chopped
2 cups chopped mushrooms
Butter
1 pound bulk sausage
3 cups very thinly sliced carrots
Salt
2 cups chopped celery

1. Cook the rice and set aside to cool.
2. Fry green pepper, onion, and mushrooms in butter over medium heat until tender.
3. Add sausage, mashing down into the vegetables with a fork until it is cooked and separated into small chunks. Set aside to cool. Drain.
4. In a second frying pan, fry carrots briefly in butter. Salt lightly.
5. In a large pan, mix the carrots and celery together. Add the rice and mix all thoroughly. Add the sausage mixture and again mix thoroughly.
6. If the stuffing has been refrigerated overnight, it should be placed, covered, in a 300-degree oven for 10 to 15 minutes to take off the chill. Otherwise, the time required to roast the turkey is lengthened.

NOTE:

This makes enough to stuff a 13- to 14-pound turkey and provide a surplus. The extra stuffing should be baked in foil the final hour of the turkey's roasting time. This also can be used as a delicious casserole. Follow preparation instructions and bake 25 minutes at 325 degrees.

Ellsworth Mason
Boulder, Colorado

RICE AND HAM ALMONDINE

Serves 24

Preparation 1 Hour
Bake 25 Minutes at 375°F

16 cups cooked rice
4 cups sour cream
1 pound Swiss cheese, shredded
1 1/2 cups sliced almonds, toasted
2 cups milk
1 cup chopped parsley
5 cups cubed, cooked ham
3 tablespoons onion powder
2 tablespoons marjoram
1 1/2 tablespoons salt
2 teaspoons paprika

1. Combine, in a large mixing bowl, rice, sour cream, 3 cups cheese, 1 cup almonds, milk, parsley, ham, onion powder, marjoram, salt, and paprika.
2. Transfer to 1 very large or 2 smaller baking dishes. Sprinkle top with remaining cheese and almonds.
3. Cover and bake for 15 minutes at 375 degrees. Uncover and bake 10 minutes longer or until hot throughout. Adjust baking time for smaller pans.

Gloria Hitchcock
Boulder, Colorado

CRANBERRY BAKED BEANS

Serves 8

Preparation 30 Minutes
Bake 8 Hours at 250°F

1 1/2 cups dry beans (your choice)
2 cups cranberry juice cocktail
2 cups water
1/3 cup chopped onion
2 tablespoons molasses
1 teaspoon dry mustard
1/8 teaspoon ginger
1/4 cup catsup
2 tablespoons vinegar
1/4 pound salt pork, sliced
Salt to taste

1. Rinse beans, place in pot with cranberry juice and water and bring to boil. Remove from heat and let stand one hour.
2. Return to heat, continue cooking until tender, and then drain, reserving liquid.
3. Mix onion, molasses, mustard, ginger, catsup, and vinegar. Add to beans and mix well.
4. Layer by pouring half the bean mixture into a casserole, then add half of sliced pork, the remaining bean mixture, and top with remaining pork. Pour 1/2 cup bean liquid over all.
5. Bake at 250 degrees for 8 hours. If beans get dry, add remaining bean liquid or cranberry juice cocktail. Salt to taste.

Marcia Cutter
Lubbock, Texas

TWO-BEAN BEEF BAKE

Serves 8

Preparation 30 Minutes
Bake 30 Minutes at 350°F

1 package (10-ounce) frozen lima beans
1 pound ground beef
1/2 cup chopped celery
1/2 cup chopped green pepper
1/2 cup chopped onion
1 cup water
1 can (6-ounce) tomato paste
2 cans (16-ounce each) pork and beans
1 tablespoon chili powder
1/2 teaspoon salt
Tortilla chips

1. Cook lima beans until almost tender; drain.
2. Cook and stir ground beef 5 to 6 minutes. Add celery, green pepper, and onion and continue cooking until well browned.
3. Add water, lima beans, tomato paste, pork and beans, chili powder, and salt. Pour into a 2-quart casserole and bake 30 minutes at 350 degrees.
4. Garnish with tortilla chips.

Ruth Cannon
Lubbock, Texas

BAKED LIMAS WITH SAUSAGE

Serves 6
Soak Overnight

Preparation 1 1/4 Hours
Bake 5 to 6 Hours at 275°F

16 ounces dry lima beans
Pinch of baking soda (optional)
1/2 pound bulk pork sausage
1 large green pepper
1 teaspoon salt
2 teaspoons sugar
4 1/2 tablespoons brown sugar
1 can (10 1/2-ounce) tomato soup
1 1/2 cups tomato juice

1. Cover beans with cold water and soak overnight.
2. Drain beans. Cover again with cold water. Simmer until tender, about 1 hour, or cook in pressure cooker 15 minutes. A pinch of soda may be added to the water.
3. Place cooked beans in a casserole or bean pot. Add uncooked sausage, green pepper, salt, and sugars.
4. Heat the tomato soup with the tomato juice and pour over beans. Cover and bake 5 to 6 hours at 275 degrees.

Helen Wasley
Boulder, Colorado

4-NAME BEAN BAKE

Serves 15

Preparation 15 Minutes
Bake 30 Minutes at 350°F

1 can (29-ounce) baked beans
1 can (15-ounce) kidney beans, drained
1 can (15-ounce) lima beans, drained, or 1 package (10-ounce) frozen limas, cooked and drained
1 can (15-ounce) cut green beans, drained
1/2 cup chopped onion
1/2 cup brown sugar
1/2 cup catsup
1 tablespoon Worcestershire sauce

1. Mix beans with onion, sugar, catsup, and Worcestershire sauce.
2. Pour into large casserole and bake at 350 degrees for 30 minutes.

Eleanor Taylor
Boulder, Colorado

VARIATION:

1. Combine 15-ounce cans of red beans, butter beans, kidney beans, and lima beans with a 28-ounce can of pork and beans. Add 1/2 pound cubed bacon browned with onion, 2 cloves garlic, minced, and 1/4 teaspoon dry mustard. Increase catsup to 1/3 cup and brown sugar to 3/4 cup. Bake as above.

Lillian Neldner
Aurora, Colorado

2. For a sweet and sour dish, use 15-ounce cans of lima beans, kidney beans, baked beans, and 2 cans butter beans, all drained, with 8 strips bacon (fried, crumbled, and drained), 4 medium onions (chopped and saute'ed in bacon drippings), 1/2 teaspoon garlic salt, 1/2 cup vinegar, 1/2 to 1 cup brown sugar, 1 teaspoon dry mustard, and 1 teaspoon salt. Combine drained beans and seasonings, top with crumbled bacon and bake as above.

Vallie Burke
Avalon, California

3. To any of above combinations, add 2 to 3 tablespoons barbecue sauce, 1 can (4-ounce) chopped chilies, drained, and/or wax beans or garbanzo beans.

Elaine Fowler
Boulder, Colorado

FEIJOADA

Serves 12 to 16
Soak Overnight

Preparation 1 Hour
Cook 4 Hours

4 1/2 pounds black turtle beans, soaked overnight
1 bay leaf
2 pounds chuck roast
2 pounds fresh pork
2 smoked pig knuckles
Salt and pepper to taste
1 1/2 pounds Polish sausage (6 to 7 pieces)
1 1/2 pounds smoked link sausage
Lean pork sausage links (1 per person)
1 pound ham
6 slices bacon, cut into 1-inch squares
3 medium onions, chopped
3 cloves garlic, chopped
2 tomatoes, peeled and chopped

1. In a very large kettle, combine soaked beans, bay leaf, chuck roast, fresh pork, pig knuckles, salt, and pepper in water to cover. Simmer 1 1/2 hours.
2. Add Polish sausage, link sausages, and ham and cook 1 hour more.
3. When meat is tender but not breaking apart, remove and set aside. Continue to cook beans until tender.
4. In a 10-inch skillet, fry bacon pieces until crisp. Add onion and garlic and fry until onion is soft. Add tomatoes and fry until mushy.
5. Remove 2 cups of beans, including some juice, from cooking pot and puree in a blender, food processor, or food mill. Add pureed beans to bacon-onion mixture and fry, stirring, for 3 minutes. Taste and correct seasoning. Stir bean-bacon mixture back into large bean pot.
6. Break cooled meats into serving-sized chunks, trimming off all fat. Slice sausages into 1-inch pieces except lean pork links. Leave those whole. Return all meat to beans and simmer 15 minutes.

NOTE:

This is better made at least a day ahead. When cold, remove all congealed fat. Reheat to serve. Serve with Collard Greens and Orange Slices (see Index), Brazilian Rice (see Index), Mandioc (see Index), and Brazilian Hot Sauce (see Index).

Sue McMillan
Boulder, Colorado

REFRIED BEANS

Serves 6 to 8

Preparation 10 Minutes
Cook 4 Hours

2 cups dry pinto beans
2 heaping tablespoons vegetable shortening
Salt to taste

1. Place beans in pot, add cold water to 3 inches above beans.
2. Bring to boil, then lower heat to simmer. Check after 1 hour, adding more water if necessary. Continue cooking 2 hours longer.
3. Add vegetable shortening, boil 20 minutes, then add salt to taste. Mash beans and stir.
4. Let boil until broth is thick, about 15 minutes.

Lucille Machado
Avalon, California

HALUSKI

Serves 4 to 6

Preparation 15 Minutes
Cook 10 Minutes

4 quarts boiling water
3 cups flour
2 eggs
Pinch of salt
3/4 cup cold water

1. While waiting for water to boil, combine flour, eggs, salt, and cold water. Mixture should be thick and sticky (the stickier the dough, the more tender the dumpling).
2. Place dough on a dinner plate. Spread small amount to edge of plate. With a large metal spoon, "chop" small pieces of dough off the plate into boiling water. Dip spoon into boiling water to prevent sticking as you chop. Continue until all dough is in water.
3. Lower heat and cook until tender, 5 to 10 minutes. Drain and rinse in cold water. Drain again.

Grace Dryer Dionigi
Arvada, Colorado

NOODLES WITH CABBAGE

Serves 6

Preparation 10 Minutes
Cook 30 Minutes

16 ounces wide noodles
1 large onion, chopped
6 tablespoons butter
1 small cabbage, shredded
Salt and pepper to taste
2 tablespoons poppy seeds
1/4 cup sour cream
2 tablespoons grated Parmesan cheese

1. Cook noodles in boiling salted water until tender but not soft. Drain.
2. Using large skillet, saute′ onion in 4 tablespoons butter until golden. Add cabbage and cook over low heat until tender.
3. Stir in noodles with remaining 2 tablespoons butter and add salt, pepper, poppy seeds, sour cream, and cheese. Mix. Cover and heat.

Ilene Kasper
Boulder, Colorado

FRESH EGG PASTA
(*Pasta Fresca all'Uovo*)

Yields 1 1/2 Pounds — Preparation 1 1/2 Hours

3 cups flour
4 large eggs, lightly beaten
1/2 teaspoon salt
2 to 4 tablespoons water

1. Make a well in the center of the flour. Add the eggs and salt, mixing into the flour gradually. Add enough water to make a soft dough.
2. Knead the dough by hand 10 to 20 minutes, until smooth, or use pasta machine following machine instructions.
3. Divide the dough into several balls. Wrap each ball in waxed paper or cover with a slightly damp towel. Let rest 20 to 30 minutes at room temperature.
4. Working with one ball at a time, roll out on a floured surface 1/4 to 1/8 inch thick depending on the pasta to be made.
5. Cut dough into desired shapes and sizes (see note). Let rest and dry 15 minutes to 1 hour. Cook in 4 to 8 quarts of boiling water until *al dente*. Remember, fresh pasta cooks much faster than commercial dried pasta. Watch carefully.

NOTE:

1. Directions for cutting noodles by hand.
   Long noodles such as fettucine: roll up dough jelly-roll style and cut into strips to desired width (1/4-inch for fettucine). Unfold strips and let dry about 1 hour covered.
   Cannelloni: roll 1/8-inch thick or less and cut into 4-inch squares. Dry 1 hour covered.
   Lasagne: roll 1/8-inch thick and cut dough into strips 2 inches wide, 4 to 6 inches long. Dry 1 hour covered.
2. For cutting pasta with pasta machine, follow instructions.
3. Pasta dough can be made very quickly in a food processor. Add flour and salt to bowl with steel blade. Mix briefly to blend. With machine running, add the eggs and process until mixture resembles coarse meal. Add enough water and continue processing until dough forms a ball. Remove and knead by hand or with pasta machine. Cut as mentioned above.

VARIATION:

Use semolina, wheat, or soy flour. Make colored noodles by using vegetable purees. (12 ounce raw spinach, cooked and well drained, for green noodles; beets, cooked, for pink noodles.)

CHOW MEIN FRIED NOODLES

Serves 6 to 8

Preparation 10 Minutes
Cook 8 Minutes

4 to 5 quarts boiling water
1/2 pound Chinese egg noodles, fettuccini, or linguini
1 tablespoon salt
1 tablespoon soy sauce
2 teaspoons Oriental sesame oil
5 tablespoons peanut or vegetable oil

1. Add noodles and salt to boiling water and stir. Let boil 8 to 10 minutes until *al dente*. Drain.
2. Place noodles in bowl. Add soy sauce, sesame oil, and 1 tablespoon peanut oil. Toss.
3. In wok or skillet, heat 1 tablespoon peanut oil. Spread 1/2 to 1/3 of noodles in pan like a large pancake and brown well. Turn and brown other side using additional oil if necessary. Remove to warm platter. Repeat for second batch. Noodles should be crisp outside and tender inside.
4. Before serving, cut noodle cakes into smaller serving-sized pieces.

Rosemary Tedesco
Boulder, Colorado

FETTUCINI WITH AVOCADOS AND HAM

Serves 6

Preparation 40 Minutes
Cook 7 Minutes

8 ounces fettucini, homemade or packaged
1/2 cup butter
1 teaspoon flour
1 cup heavy cream
3 avocados (chop 2, slice 1 for garnish)
4 ounces Prosciutto ham, shredded
4 ounces grated Parmesan cheese
Freshly ground pepper

1. Boil pasta in salted water until *al dente*. Drain well.
2. Melt butter in saucepan. Add flour and stir. Cook 2 minutes.
3. Add cream and cook 5 minutes, stirring constantly.
4. Place pasta on warm platter. Pour on sauce, add chopped avocado, 3/4 of ham, 3/4 cup Parmesan cheese, and pepper. Toss thoroughly.
5. Arrange sliced avocado and remaining ham on top. Serve immediately with grated Parmesan cheese.

Audrey Benedict
Ward, Colorado

FETTUCINI WITH SHRIMP

Serves 4

Preparation 20 Minutes
Cook 5 Minutes

8 ounces fine egg noodles
8 ounces small shrimp, shelled and deveined
1/2 cup butter
Freshly ground pepper
3 ounces grated Parmesan cheese

1. Cook noodles *al dente* according to package directions, about 5 to 8 minutes. Drain.
2. Saute' shrimp in butter until shrimp is pink, about 5 minutes. Add pepper to taste.
3. Toss noodles, shrimp with butter and cheese. Serve hot.

Carol Powell
Denver, Colorado

NEW ORLEANS SPAGHETTI

Serves 6

Preparation 45 Minutes
Cook 15 Minutes

1 pound frozen shrimp, peeled and deveined
1/2 pound thin spaghetti
1/4 cup margarine or oil
1/4 pound fresh mushrooms, sliced
1/4 cup diced green onions
3 tablespoons flour
1 teaspoon salt
1/4 teaspoon paprika
1 cup milk
1 cup half-and-half
1/2 cup shredded Swiss cheese
2 tablespoons dry sherry
2 tablespoons diced pimiento
2 tablespoons grated Parmesan cheese

1. Thaw shrimp. Cook spaghetti *al dente,* drain and turn into 2-quart baking dish. Keep warm.
2. Heat margarine in skillet and add mushrooms and onions. Cook until tender. Then add shrimp and cook until shrimp turns pink.
3. Stir in flour, salt, and paprika. Add milk and half-and-half and cook, stirring constantly, until sauce thickens.
4. Add Swiss cheese, sherry, and pimiento. Heat to just below boiling point.
5. Spoon shrimp mixture over spaghetti, sprinkle on Parmesan cheese, and broil 4 minutes or until hot, bubbly, and cheese is slightly browned.

NOTE:

Two packages (6-ounce each) frozen crabmeat, thawed, or 2 cans (7 1/2-ounce each) crabmeat may be substituted for shrimp. Drain and remove any shell or cartilage, flake or cut into small pieces. Add to sauce last, stirring in carefully.

Mitzi Baier
Boulder, Colorado

GREEN LASAGNE

Serves 10

Preparation 30 Minutes
Bake 1 Hour at 350°F

1 cup chopped onions
1 tablespoon olive oil
8 ounces mushrooms, chopped
1 can (6-ounce) tomato paste
1 1/2 cups water
1 1/2 teaspoons salt
1 teaspoon sugar
1/2 teaspoon basil
1/8 teaspoon pepper
1 teaspoon oregano
8 ounces lasagne noodles
16 ounces mozzarella cheese, sliced
1 package (10-ounce) frozen, chopped spinach, thawed and drained
16 ounces ricotta cheese
1/2 cup (or more) grated Parmesan cheese

1. Saute' onions in oil until transparent. Add mushrooms and saute' another 5 minutes.
2. Add tomato paste, water, salt, sugar, basil, pepper, and oregano and simmer 1 hour.
3. Cook lasagne noodles following package directions.
4. Butter a 9 x 15-inch baking dish. Make layers in the following order: 1/3 sauce, 1/3 noodles, all the mozzarella cheese; 1/2 spinach, 1/3 noodles, 1/3 sauce, all the ricotta cheese; 1/2 spinach, 1/3 noodles, 1/3 sauce, and top with Parmesan cheese.
5. Bake at 350 degrees for 1 hour. Cut into squares and serve.

VARIATION:

One pound ground beef, browned and drained, may be substituted for chopped spinach.

Ethel Zager
Avalon, California

LASAGNE WITH MUSHROOMS

Serves 6

Preparation 45 Minutes
Bake 45 Minutes at 325°F

4 tablespoons butter
1 pound mushrooms, sliced
1 teaspoon lemon juice
1/4 cup flour
1 teaspoon salt
1/8 teaspoon cayenne pepper
2 cups milk
1/3 cup minced parsley
8 ounces lasagne noodles, cooked and drained
1 pound cottage cheese
3/4 pound mozzarella cheese, sliced
1/2 cup grated Parmesan cheese

1. Melt butter. Add mushrooms and lemon juice. Saute', stirring 6 minutes until wilted.
2. Blend in flour, salt, and cayenne. Gradually add milk. Bring to boil, stirring. Add parsley.
3. Spread 1/2 cup sauce in 9 x 13-inch pan. Layer noodles, cottage cheese, mozzarella cheese, mushroom mixture, and Parmesan cheese. Repeat.
4. Bake at 325 degrees for 45 minutes. Let stand 20 minutes before serving.

Delia Taylor
Boulder, Colorado

MOCK LASAGNE

Serves 6

Preparation 30 Minutes
Bake 1 Hour at 350°F

2 packages (1 1/2-ounce each) spaghetti sauce mix
1 can (12-ounce) tomato paste
3 1/2 cups water
2 tablespoons butter
1 pound rigatoni
12 ounces ricotta cheese
1/4 cup grated Parmesan cheese
6 ounces mozzarella cheese, grated
1/4 cup dried parsley
2 eggs, beaten

1. Prepare spaghetti sauce mix with tomato paste, water, and butter as directed on package.
2. Cook rigatoni *al dente*; drain.
3. Add cheeses and parsley to eggs. Add cooked rigatoni and sauce. Mix well and pour into a large casserole.
4. Bake at 350 degrees for 1 hour.

NOTE:

Add 1 1/2 pounds ground beef, cooked and drained, for a non-vegetarian dish.

CANNELLONI

Serves 6 to 8

Preparation 1 1/2 Hours
Bake 15 Minutes at 425°F

2 tablespoons minced shallots or green onion
1 tablespoon olive oil
5 tomatoes, peeled, seeded, and diced
1/2 cup chicken broth
1 1/2 teaspoons dry basil
1 teaspoon salt
4 tablespoons butter
1 large onion, chopped
1 clove garlic, minced
3/4 pound boned chicken, ground or minced
1/2 pound boneless veal, ground or minced
8 ounces ricotta cheese
4 ounces Parmesan cheese, grated
3 egg yolks
Pinch of nutmeg
1 package (10-ounce) chopped spinach, thawed and well drained
1 recipe Fresh Egg Pasta (see Index) or 8 ounces manicotti shells
2 cups Mornay Sauce (see Index)
1/2 cup grated Teleme or Monterey Jack cheese

1. Saute' shallots in olive oil until soft. Stir in tomatoes, broth, basil, and 1/4 teaspoon salt. Simmer, uncovered, 40 minutes.
2. While tomato sauce is simmering, melt butter in large skillet. Add onions and garlic and cook until onion is clear. Add meats, then cheeses. Stir to mix thoroughly. Remove from heat.
3. Add egg yolks and stir in quickly. Add 3/4 teaspoon salt and the nutmeg.
4. Fold in spinach and correct seasonings.
5. Prepare egg noodle dough, roll as thin as possible, and cut into 4-inch squares. Cook squares, several at a time, in a large quantity of boiling water for 8 to 10 minutes or until tender. Remove pasta with a slotted spoon and spread on damp towels and cover until ready to fill.
6. Fill prepared pasta squares and roll or fill manicotti shells with meat filling. Place in buttered baking dish in one layer.
7. Cover with Mornay Sauce and top with tomato sauce from Step 1. Sprinkle with grated cheese. Bake 10 to 15 minutes at 425 degrees.

Ellen Denton
Piedmont, California

PIQUANT MACARONI

Serves 8

Preparation 20 Minutes
Bake 30 Minutes at 350°F

3 1/2 cups elbow macaroni
2 quarts boiling salted water
12 green onions, chopped
4 tablespoons butter
1 can (16-ounce) stewed tomatoes
2/3 cup canned red chili sauce
Salt and pepper to taste
1 can (3-ounce) black olives, chopped
6 ounces Cheddar cheese, grated

1. Cook macaroni in salted boiling water until tender. Drain.
2. Saute' green onions lightly in 2 tablespoons butter. Remove from heat.
3. Add tomatoes, chili sauce, salt, pepper, olives, and macaroni. Mix thoroughly.
4. Place half the tomato-macaroni mixture in buttered casserole, sprinkle with half the Cheddar cheese. Add remaining tomato-macaroni mixture and rest of cheese. Dot with 2 tablespoons butter.
5. Bake at 350 degrees for 30 minutes.

Irene Mills
Los Angeles, California

TAGLIARINI

Serves 2 to 10

Preparation 15 Minutes
Cook 1 Hour

1 pound lean ground beef
1 medium onion, diced
1 can (28-ounce) peeled tomatoes
1 can (15-ounce) cream style corn
1/2 cup green olives
1/4 cup olive juice
1 teaspoon garlic powder
1/4 teaspoon salt
1/4 teaspoon pepper
1/2 teaspoon crushed hot dried pepper (optional)
12 ounces small noodles
1 pound Colby Longhorn cheese, grated (optional)
Parmesan cheese, grated
Dash of hot pepper juice (optional)

1. Brown meat and onions; drain grease.
2. Add tomatoes, corn, olives, olive juice, garlic powder, salt, pepper, and dried pepper. Simmer 35 to 45 minutes, stirring frequently.
3. Boil noodles, drain, and add to meat mixture. Simmer 15 minutes.
4. Just before serving, add grated cheese and mix well. Top each serving with grated Parmesan and hot pepper juice, if desired.

VARIATION:

Pork may be substituted for or added to ground beef for additional flavor.

Cynthia Dionigi Cinquanta
Arvada, Colorado

MACARONI AND BEEF CASSEROLE
(*Pastichio*)

Serves 20

Preparation 1 1/2 Hours
Bake 1 1/4 Hours at 350°F

1 pound macaroni
1 1/2 cups butter
2 cups grated Parmesan cheese
14 eggs
2 large onions, chopped
3 pounds lean ground beef
1 can (8-ounce) tomato sauce
1 1/2 teaspoons nutmeg
1 teaspoon cinnamon
5 teaspoons salt
1/2 teaspoon pepper
6 tablespoons flour
8 cups milk

1. Cook macaroni according to package directions, about 15 minutes. Rinse with cold water and drain thoroughly.
2. Combine 1/2 cup melted butter, 1/2 cup Parmesan cheese, and 3 beaten eggs. Stir into well-drained macaroni and set aside.
3. In large skillet, saute' onions and meat in 1/4 cup butter, add tomato sauce, 1 teaspoon nutmeg, cinnamon, 3 teaspoons salt, pepper, and 1/2 cup Parmesan cheese and simmer about 10 minutes, stirring constantly.
4. In 18 x 12 x 3-inch pan, layer half of macaroni, then the meat mixture evenly and top with remaining macaroni.
5. Melt 3/4 cup butter, add flour gradually, stirring constantly, and saute' for a few minutes until flour dissolves and mixture bubbles. Add milk slowly, stirring constantly, and bring to low boil. Cook until sauce thickens.
6. Add 2 teaspoons salt and cool. Add remaining 11 eggs one or two at a time, beating well after each addition.
7. Slowly pour white sauce over macaroni-meat mixture, shaking pan to let it seep through.
8. Sprinkle with remaining 1 cup Parmesan cheese and nutmeg. Bake in preheated 350-degree oven for about 1 hour and 15 minutes until custard becomes firm and puffed. Cover with foil loosely if browning too fast.

NOTE:

Best made a day ahead and reheated. Recipe may be cut in half for a 13 x 9-inch pan.

Electra Falliers
Denver, Colorado

SICILIAN CASSEROLE

Serves 6

Preparation 30 Minutes
Bake 30 to 40 Minutes at 325°F

6 ounces noodles, cooked and drained
1 pound ground meat
1/2 cup chopped onion
1/2 cup chopped green pepper
1 can (6-ounce) tomato paste
3/4 cup water
1 teaspoon salt
1/4 teaspoon pepper
1/4 cup milk
8 ounces cream cheese
1 teaspoon garlic salt
3/4 cup Parmesan cheese

1. Brown meat and add onion, green pepper, and tomato paste. Stir in water, salt, and pepper and simmer 1/2 hour.
2. Heat together milk, cream cheese, garlic salt, and 1/4 cup of Parmesan cheese in a saucepan. Stir until smooth. Add to cooked noodles and mix well.
3. In a 9 x 9 x 2-inch pan, alternate layers of meat and noodle mixtures, ending with noodles. Sprinkle with remaining Parmesan cheese and bake at 325 degrees for 30 to 40 minutes.

Betty Dozier
Avalon, California

NOODLE PUDDING

Serves 8 to 10

Preparation 15 Minutes
Bake 1 Hour at 350°F

8 ounces wide noodles
2 tablespoons butter
4 ounces American cheese, diced
1 1/2 pounds cottage cheese
1/2 cup sugar
3 eggs, well beaten
1 cup sour cream
1/4 teaspoon salt
1 teaspoon vanilla extract
1 can (8-ounce) crushed pineapple (optional)
1/2 cup raisins (optional)
1/2 cup corn flake crumbs

1. Cook noodles as directed on package and drain well. To the hot noodles, add butter, cheese, cottage cheese, sugar, eggs, sour cream, salt, vanilla, pineapple, and raisins, if desired, and mix thoroughly.
2. Place in large casserole and top with corn flake crumbs. Bake at 350 degrees for 1 hour.

NOTE:

May be served hot or cold, as a main dish or as a dessert.

Ellie Pollack
Boulder, Colorado

COMPANY GRITS

Serves 10 to 12

Preparation 30 Minutes
Bake 1 Hour at 300°F

2 teaspoons salt
3/4 cup butter
6 cups boiling water
1 1/2 cups quick grits
4 eggs, beaten well
16 ounces processed cheese, cubed
1 1/2 cups grated sharp Cheddar cheese
1/2 cup slivered almonds

1. Add salt and butter to boiling water. When butter melts, add grits and cook until thick.
2. Add eggs and processed cheese to grits mixture. Cook until thick, stirring occasionally.
3. Pour into 3-quart buttered casserole. Top with grated Cheddar cheese and almonds. Bake for 1 hour at 300 degrees.

NOTE:

This is excellent with ham for a buffet.

Janet Desgalier
Boulder, Colorado

VARIATION:

Sprinkle casserole with 1/2 to 3/4 teaspoon crushed red pepper before baking.

Jackie Valenga
Denver, Colorado

MANDIOC

Serves 12 to 14

Cook 15 Minutes

1 box (13-ounce) Mandioc or instant farina
3 tablespoons butter
1/4 teaspoon garlic salt

1. Brown Mandioc or farina in butter until golden. Sprinkle with garlic salt.

NOTE:

Meat from *Feijoada* (see Index) is dipped in this browned cereal.

Sue McMillan
Boulder, Colorado

COUSCOUS

Serves 6 to 8

Preparation 1 Hour
Cook 40 to 60 Minutes

1 pound *couscous* (cracked wheat)
4 1/2 cups water
6 tablespoons butter, melted
1 teaspoon salt
Pinch turmeric
4 tablespoons vegetable oil
1 onion, quartered
1 tablespoon paprika
1 teaspoon black pepper
1 cinnamon stick, broken
3 bay leaves
Large pinch saffron or turmeric
Salt to taste
1 bunch parsley, tied
1 to 1 1/2 pounds meat (see Note 2)
1/2 head cabbage, shredded
2 carrots, quartered
2 turnips, quartered
1 sweet potato, peeled and quartered
2 small zucchini, quartered
1 bell pepper, cut into 8 strips
1 cup cooked fresh or canned chick peas
***Harissa* (hot pepper sauce) (see Index)**

1. In a large bowl, mix *couscous* with 1 1/2 cups water, 4 tablespoons melted butter, salt, and turmeric. Let stand about 1 hour, mixing it with your hands occasionally to break up lumps.
2. In the lower part of *couscous* cooker (see Note 1), heat 2 tablespoons oil and add onion. Saute' for 5 minutes, then add paprika, pepper, cinnamon stick, bay leaves, saffron or turmeric, and salt. Mix and cook several minutes.
3. To the spices, add remaining 3 cups water, parsley bundle, desired meat, and remaining 2 tablespoons oil. Bring to a boil.
4. Place the steamer or colander on top of the *couscous* cooker or kettle. Add the *couscous* to the steamer by rubbing it through your hands to break up any lumps. Cover and cook 20 minutes. Stir the *couscous*.
5. To the meat, add cabbage, carrots, turnips, and sweet potato. Replace the steamer, cover, and continue cooking and steaming 15 to 20 minutes.
6. Next, add to meat mixture the zucchini, bell pepper, and chick peas. Add remaining melted butter to the *couscous*, stir again, cover, and cook/steam 15 to 20 minutes more.
7. To serve, spread the *couscous* on a platter and arrange the vegetables and meat on top. Add a little broth to moisten. Serve the remaining broth and *Harissa* separately.

NOTE:

1. A *couscous* cooker (called a *couscoussiere*: a two-part steaming pot that resembles a large double boiler, the holes in the bottom of the top part let the *couscous* steam) is best to use when making this dish. However, a colander lined with cheese cloth tightly fitted into a large kettle will do as well.
2. Any vegetable may be used in this dish. Use whatever combination suits the diners. Add them in order of how quickly they cook. Use chicken, beef, or lamb, or any combination of these cut into serving-sized pieces. *Couscous* may also be prepared without meat.

Rafih Benjelloun
Mataam Fez
Denver, Colorado

BARLEY CASSEROLE

Serves 10

Preparation 20 Minutes
Bake 2 Hours at 275°F

1 1/2 cups barley
2 medium onions, chopped
1/2 cup butter or margarine
3 cans (1 3/4-ounce each) clear chicken broth
1/4 pound fresh mushrooms or 1 can (4-ounce) mushrooms, drained
1 jar (4-ounce) chopped pimientos

1. Brown barley and onions in melted butter.
2. Put in casserole and add chicken broth, mushrooms, and pimiento.
3. Bake at 275 degrees for 2 hours.

VARIATION:

Add 1/4 cup sliced almonds and/or 1 can (5-ounce) water chestnuts, drained and sliced.

NOTE:

A satisfying substitute for potatoes or rice. It is particularly good with roast beef. Recipe may be prepared through Step 2 and refrigerated overnight but increase baking time.

Carlen Penfold
Boulder, Colorado

POSOLE WITH PORK

Serves 12 to 16

Preparation 3 to 4 Hours
Cook 3 Hours

1 pound dry *posole*, washed and sorted
6 cups cold water (or more as needed)
5 medium yellow onions, peeled and coarsely chopped
4 large garlic cloves, peeled and crushed
3 to 4 tablespoons oil
3 pounds boned pork shoulder, cut into 1-inch cubes
2 teaspoons crumbled leaf oregano
1 teaspoon crumbled leaf thyme
2 teaspoons (or more) salt
1/8 teaspoon freshly ground black pepper
3 tablespoons cider vinegar
1 2/3 cups chicken broth (should be very rich in flavor; if not add dry bouillon)
1 can (10-ounce) whole, mild, roasted and peeled green chilies, drained and cut into long thin strips
1 to 3 canned Jalapeño peppers, minced

1. Place *posole* and water in a large, heavy kettle. Bring to a simmer. Cover and cook slowly until puffed and almost tender (about 3 to 4 hours).
2. When *posole* is almost done, stir-fry onions and garlic in 2 tablespoons oil in a large, heavy skillet over moderate heat until lightly browned (about 10 minutes). Drain on paper towels.
3. Add another tablespoon of oil to skillet. Brown pork cubes, adding more oil as needed. Drain browned cubes on paper towels.
4. Add the onion, garlic, and pork to kettle of *posole*. Then add oregano, thyme, salt, pepper, vinegar, and broth. Stir. Cover and simmer slowly for 2 hours.
5. Add the chilies. Re-cover and simmer about 1 hour longer or until pork and *posole* are both tender. *Taste for salt.*

NOTE:

1. Serve as a soup-stew in large soup plates. May be made ahead. *Posole* is white corn or hominy and may be found in the Mexican food section at most large supermarkets. You may soak the *posole* overnight and reduce the cooking time in Step 1.
2. *Salsa Roja* (see Index) may be served with this. Also, bowls of sliced radishes, shredded lettuce, finely chopped onion, and wedges of lime may be served as side dishes.

Serena Dubach
Boulder, Colorado

BREADS, ROLLS,
•
AND
•
COFFEE CAKES

QUICK HOMEMADE BREAD

Yields 1 Loaf

Preparation 2 1/2 Hours
Bake 45 Minutes at 350°F

1 1/4 cups lukewarm water
1 package dry yeast
1 egg
2 tablespoons sugar
2 tablespoons melted shortening
3/4 teaspoon salt
3 cups flour

1. Mix water, yeast, egg, sugar, shortening, salt, and flour. Let rise in bowl until doubled in bulk, about 1 1/2 hours.
2. Stir down and pour into greased 1 1/2-quart bread pan. Let rise, uncovered, until doubled, about 1 hour.
3. Bake at 350 degrees for approximately 45 minutes.

Nancy Goodwin
New Iberia, Louisiana

HERB BREAD

Yields 1 Loaf

Preparation 2 Hours
Bake 45 to 50 Minutes at 350°F

1 package dry yeast
1 1/4 cups warm water
3 tablespoons butter, softened
2 tablespoons sugar
2 teaspoons salt
1 tablespoon caraway seed (optional)
1 teaspoon nutmeg
1 teaspoon dry sage
1 teaspoon dry basil
3 cups flour, sifted

1. In mixing bowl, dissolve yeast in warm water. Add 2 tablespoons butter, sugar, salt, all herbs, and 1 1/2 cups flour. Beat 2 minutes at medium speed. Scrape sides of bowl frequently.
2. Add remaining 1 1/2 cups flour and stir until smooth. Scrape batter from sides of bowl. Cover with damp towel and let rise in warm place until doubled.
3. Stir batter 25 strokes, then spread evenly in greased 9 x 5 x 3-inch pan. Lightly flour top of dough and let rise again until batter is 1 inch from top of pan.
4. Bake at 350 degrees 45 to 50 minutes or until golden brown. Remove immediately from pan and place on cooling rack.
5. Melt remaining 1 tablespoon butter and brush top. Cool before cutting.

NOTE:

Wrap cut bread in foil and freeze. Reheat before serving. Makes excellent sandwiches.

Pat Wright
Boulder, Colorado

BEER BREAD

Yields 1 Loaf

Preparation 10 Minutes
Bake 55 Minutes at 350°F

3 cups flour
1/3 cup sugar
4 teaspoons baking powder
1 teaspoon salt
12 ounces beer, room temperature
2 tablespoons butter

1. Mix flour, sugar, baking powder, salt, and beer with a fork until moistened.
2. Pour into greased 9 x 5 x 3-inch loaf pan and bake 55 minutes at 350 degrees.
3. Brush top with butter. Cool before slicing.

Ellen Gille
Boulder, Colorado

GERMAN DARK RYE BREAD

Yields 2 Loaves

Preparation 2 Hours
Bake 30 Minutes at 400°F

3 cups all-purpose flour
2 packages dry yeast
1/4 cup cocoa powder
1 tablespoon caraway seeds
2 cups water
1/3 cup molasses
2 tablespoons butter or oil
1 tablespoon sugar
1 tablespoon salt
3 1/2 to 4 cups rye flour

1. In large bowl, combine all-purpose flour, yeast, cocoa powder, and caraway seeds and blend well.
2. In saucepan, combine water, molasses, butter, sugar, and salt; heat until warm. Stir to melt butter and add to dry ingredients. Beat at low speed for 1/2 minute, scraping sides of bowl constantly. Beat 3 minutes at high speed.
3. By hand, stir in enough rye flour to make soft dough, turn on floured surface, and knead until smooth, about 5 minutes. Cover, let rest 20 minutes, then punch down.
4. Divide dough in half and shape into round loaves. Place on greased baking sheet or two 8-inch pie plates and brush tops with butter. Slash with sharp knife and let rise until double in bulk, 45 to 60 minutes.
5. Bake at 400 degrees 25 to 30 minutes or until loaf sounds hollow when tapped. Remove from pans, cool on wire racks.

Suzanne Taylor
Boulder, Colorado

DILL BREAD

Yields 1 Loaf

Preparation 2 Hours
Bake 40 to 50 Minutes at 350°F

1 package dry yeast
1/4 cup warm water
1 cup cottage cheese, lukewarm
2 tablespoons sugar
1 tablespoon onion flakes, toasted
1 tablespoon butter
2 teaspoons dill seed
1 1/2 teaspoons dill weed
1 teaspoon salt
1/4 teaspoon baking soda
1 egg
2 1/4 to 2 1/2 cups flour

1. Dissolve yeast in warm water.
2. Combine cottage cheese, sugar, onion, butter, dill seed, dill weed, salt, baking soda, and egg. Mix with yeast mixture.
3. Add 1 cup flour. Continue adding flour a little at a time, mixing well. Dough should be stiff. Cover and let rise until doubled in bulk.
4. Punch down dough and turn into well-greased bread pan or 2-quart casserole. Let rise 30 to 40 minutes.
5. Bake 40 to 50 minutes at 350 degrees. Brush top with melted butter after baking. Remove from pan while warm.

Margaret Felkley
Avalon, California

NORTH FARM HOUSE BREAD

Yields 2 Loaves

Preparation 40 Minutes
Bake 1 Hour at 400°F

1 package dry yeast
2 1/2 cups lukewarm water
4 cups whole wheat flour
1 teaspoon brown sugar
1 teaspoon salt
1/4 to 1/2 cup each, wheat germ, bran, soy flour (optional)

1. Dissolve yeast in 1 cup water. Let stand 5 to 10 minutes.
2. In large bowl, combine flour, sugar, salt, and optional ingredients. Add yeast mixture. Mix by hand.
3. Add remaining 1 1/2 cups water or just enough to make dough a wet, sticky mixture.
4. Pour into two 1 1/2-quart greased and floured bread pans. Put in a warm place for 10 to 15 minutes.
5. Bake at 400 degrees for 1 hour.

NOTE:

Do not knead or let dough rise.

Larry Chartrand
Boulder, Colorado

READY-WHEN-YOU-ARE FRENCH BREAD

Yields 2 Loaves
Refrigerate 2 to 24 Hours

Preparation 1 1/4 Hours
Bake 15 Minutes at 450°F
20 Minutes at 250°F

2 packages yeast
2 1/4 cups warm water
2 tablespoons sugar
1 tablespoon salt
3 tablespoons salad oil
6 to 7 cups unsifted flour
1 to 2 tablespoons corn meal
Salad oil
1 egg white
1 tablespoon water

1. Stir yeast into warm water and add sugar, salt, and oil. Add 2 cups flour and beat until smooth.
2. Work in more flour and turn onto board. Knead 8 to 10 minutes.
3. Cover with plastic wrap, then a towel and let stand on board 20 minutes.
4. Divide dough in half and roll into 10 x 15-inch rectangle.
5. Beginning at 15-inch side, roll up tightly and seal edges by pinching together.
6. Grease large cookie sheet, sprinkle corn meal where bread will be placed and place loaves on sheet. Brush with oil. With sharp knife, make 6 to 7 diagonal cuts on top of each loaf.
7. Place plastic wrap loosely over loaves, refrigerate 2 to 24 hours.
8. Remove loaves, uncover, and let stand 1 to 2 hours at room temperature. Puncture any gas bubbles with greased toothpick.
9. Bake 15 minutes at 450 degrees on middle rack. Reduce heat to 250 degrees and continue baking 15 to 20 minutes.
10. Remove from oven, brush on egg white mixed with cold water, and return to oven. Bake 5 minutes longer at 450 degrees.

Margaret Felkley
Avalon, California

BILLIE'S OATMEAL BREAD

Yields 2 Loaves

Preparation 2 1/2 Hours
Bake 15 Minutes at 375°F
40 Minutes at 325°F

2 cups old-fashioned oats
1/2 cup packed brown sugar
2 teaspoons salt
1 tablespoon shortening
1 cup boiling water
1 cup lukewarm milk
1/2 cup lukewarm water
1 package yeast
1/2 teaspoon sugar
4 1/2 to 5 cups flour

1. In a large bowl, combine oats, brown sugar, salt, shortening, and boiling water. Cover with a cloth and let rest 1 hour. Add warm milk and mix well.

2. Dissolve yeast and sugar in lukewarm water and add to oatmeal mixture.
3. Add enough flour to make dough easy to handle. Turn out and knead 10 minutes.
4. Return to greased bowl, cover, and let rise in warm place until doubled, about 1 hour. Punch down and let rest 15 minutes.
5. Divide dough into two loaves, place in well-greased pans and let rise again.
6. Bake 15 minutes at 375 degrees, reduce heat to 325 degrees and bake 40 minutes or until bottom sounds hollow when tapped.

VARIATION:

Up to 1/2 the total amount of flour can be substituted with specialty flours other than white. Use 1/2 cup molasses or scant 1/2 cup honey instead of brown sugar.

NOTE:

Make 3 dozen cloverleaf or crescent rolls instead of 2 loaves of bread. Bake for 15 minutes at 375 degrees and 15 minutes at 325 degrees.

Susan Maxwell Campbell
Houston, Texas

WHITE BREAD

Yields 2 Loaves

Preparation 3 Hours
Bake 25 Minutes at 425°F

3 tablespoons sugar
1 tablespoon salt
3 tablespoons shortening
1 package yeast
1/3 cup powdered milk
2 1/4 cups warm water
5 to 6 cups sifted flour

1. Mix sugar, salt, shortening, yeast, and powdered milk. Add water and mix well.
2. Beat in 1 cup flour at a time until dough can be kneaded. Dough should not stick to hands. Knead 10 minutes.
3. Place dough in greased bowl, cover, and let rise until double, about 1 hour.
4. Punch down. Shape into 2 loaves and put into greased 8 x 4 x 2-inch loaf pans. Let rise 1/2 hour. Bake 25 minutes at 425 degrees.

NOTE:

Dough will make 3 dozen rolls. Follow procedures for bread, shape into rolls, and bake 15 minutes at 425 degrees.

Marion Long Roth
Arvada, Colorado

FOOD PROCESSOR CHALLAH

For large capacity food processor

Yields 2 Loaves

Preparation 2 Hours
Bake 40 Minutes at 375°F

5 1/2 cups unbleached flour (not bread flour)
1 package dry yeast
1 1/4 cups lukewarm water
3 tablespoons sugar or honey
1 teaspoon salt
3 eggs
1/4 cup vegetable oil
Poppy seeds or sesame seeds (optional)

1. With plastic blade in place, add flour to processor bowl.
2. Mix yeast with 1/2 cup water, then stir in sugar or honey. Set aside.
3. Add salt, 2 eggs, remaining water, and oil to flour; then add yeast mixture and process 90 seconds after ball has formed.
4. Place dough in greased bowl, cover and let rise in warm place until it triples in volume.
5. Divide dough in half and divide each half into 5 pieces. Briefly knead each piece, then roll into ropes 6 to 8 inches long.
6. Braid the five ropes together being careful to pinch ends together. Put on greased baking sheet, cover, and let rise in warm place 30 minutes.
7. Brush bread with remaining egg, lightly beaten, and sprinkle with poppy seeds or sesame seeds if desired. Bake 30 to 40 minutes at 375 degrees or until bread is golden brown.

Cecile Lazar
Boulder, Colorado

SYRIAN POCKET BREAD

Yields 7 Loaves

Preparation 2 Hours
Bake 6 Minutes at 475°F

1 cup warm water
1 package yeast
3 to 4 cups flour
2 tablespoons sugar
1 tablespoon salt
1 tablespoon oil

1. Dissolve yeast in warm water. Add 3 cups flour and mix. Add sugar, salt, and additional flour to make dough stiff enough to knead.
2. Knead vigorously about 15 minutes. Let rise (oil top if it looks dry), covered, for one hour.
3. Punch down. Divide dough into 7 pieces about 3/4 cup each. Knead each piece again and roll into circles about 7 inches in diameter and 1/4-inch thick.
4. Place dough directly on oven rack and bake 6 minutes at 475 degrees or until lightly browned. Cool on wire rack.

SWEDISH RYE BREAD

Fast rise method

Yields 5 Loaves

Preparation 3 1/2 Hours
Bake 1 Hour at 350°F

4 cups water
6 tablespoons margarine
3 to 4 tablespoons caraway seeds
1 cup brown sugar
1 cup light molasses
3 tablespoons salt
2 cups warm water
1 tablespoon sugar
4 tablespoons yeast
12 to 13 cups unbleached white flour
4 cups sifted rye flour
1 egg yolk, or 1 egg white
1 tablespoon water
Poppy seeds or sesame seeds

1. Boil 4 cups water, margarine, caraway seeds, brown sugar, light molasses, and salt for 5 minutes. Let cool to 105 to 115 degrees.
2. Mix together in 1-quart warm bowl 2 cups warm water and sugar. Sprinkle with yeast (yes, 4 tablespoons yeast). When yeast mixture has doubled in volume, stir in 1 cup unbleached white flour.
3. Place sifted rye flour in a large prewarmed mixing bowl. Add the cooled water-molasses mixture and beat well. Add yeast mixture and beat again. Add remaining white flour, mix and let stand 10 minutes.
4. Set oven at 105 to 115 degrees. Knead dough 10 minutes and turn into warm, greased mixing bowl. Cover and let rise to double in bulk, about 45 minutes.
5. Punch down hard. Let rise to double again, about 35 minutes.
6. Punch down once more and shape into loaves; place in greased baking pans and let double again, about 30 minutes.
7. Brush tops of loaves with well-mixed egg yolk and water, or egg white and water. If desired, sprinkle with poppy or sesame seeds. Bake loaves 50 to 60 minutes at 350 degrees.
8. Remove from oven, let stand 5 minutes in pans, then turn out on wire racks to cool.

NOTES:

Dough is stiffer than most and can't be over-kneaded; it must also be punched down hard to expel air bubbles. Rye flour is best bought in bulk from a health-food store. Grated dried orange peel and/or cardamom can be added to give a more Scandinavian flavor. It is excellent just out of the oven and keeps well when frozen, after it has cooled.

Martin Ball
Denver, Colorado

REFRIGERATOR ROLLS

Yields 3 to 4 Dozen
Refrigerate Overnight

Preparation 40 Minutes
Bake 12 to 15 Minutes at 400°F

2 cups water
1/2 cup butter
1 teaspoon salt
1 package dry yeast
2 eggs
1/2 cup sugar
5 1/2 to 6 cups flour

1. Bring 1 cup water to boil, remove from heat. Add butter and salt. Set aside to cool.
2. In a large bowl, mix remaining 1 cup water, lukewarm, and yeast and let dissolve. Add eggs and sugar and mix. Add water-butter mixture when cool. Mix well.
3. Beat in flour one-third at a time (dough will be sticky).
4. Cover tightly and refrigerate. Air briefly after several hours. Refrigerate a day or more.
5. Two hours before baking, shape desired amount of dough into any shape and place on a baking sheet or in baking pans. Cover rolls with a towel and let rise until double.
6. Bake 12 to 15 minutes at 400 degrees.

NOTE:

Dough is better if handled as little as possible. It can be kept in refrigerator as long as two weeks.

Kathleen Lewis
Boulder, Colorado

SPECIAL YEAST DINNER ROLLS

Yields 4 to 5 Dozen

Preparation 5 Hours
Bake 15 Minutes at 350°F

1/3 cup yellow corn meal
1/2 cup sugar
1 teaspoon salt
1/2 cup butter
2 cups milk
1 package yeast
1/4 cup lukewarm water
2 eggs, beaten
4 to 6 cups flour, all-purpose or bread flour

1. Put corn meal, sugar, salt, butter, and milk in the top of a double boiler. Cook until thick, stirring frequently. It will be like cream of wheat or mush. Cool to lukewarm, about 105 to 115 degrees. (Cooling can take up to 45 minutes. Be sure to test temperature.)
2. Dissolve yeast in water, beat eggs, and add both to lukewarm mixture. Beat thoroughly. Cover and let rise in a warm place about 2 hours.
3. Stir in approximately 4 cups flour to form a soft ball. Turn out on floured board and knead about ten minutes. The dough tends to be soft, so add more flour as you work it to keep it from sticking to board and hands. (Use another cup of flour before kneading if

dough seems to be too sticky to handle easily.) Place kneaded dough in greased bowl, grease exposed surface, cover with damp cloth, and let rise until doubled, about 1 hour. Punch down and turn out on floured board and shape as desired.

4. For crescent rolls: divide dough into 4 equal balls. Roll into circles about 1/4-inch thick. Brush with melted butter. Using a pizza cutter, cut dough like a pie into 12 to 16 wedges depending upon the size rolls you wish. Roll wedge tightly from wide end to point. Place on greased baking sheet point side down and bend roll into a crescent shape. Let rise 1 hour, until double.
5. Bake 15 minutes at 350 degrees or until lightly browned.,

NOTE:

Rolls can be frozen, but are better when eaten fresh from the oven. This dough may be too sticky for pan rolls. For successful yeast breads, measure water temperature with a thermometer. To dissolve dry granular yeast, the water should be 105 to 115 degrees. It should be lower for compressed yeast.

Priscilla Peale
Santa Barbara, California

HEARTY CORN FRITTERS

Serves 6

Preparation 10 Minutes
Fry 5 Minutes

1 1/4 cups sifted flour
1/2 cup yellow corn meal
3 teaspoons baking powder
1 teaspoon salt
2 teaspoons sugar
1 can (12-ounce) whole kernel corn
2 eggs
2 tablespoons vegetable oil
1 cup yellow cream-style corn
Oil for frying

1. Sift together flour, corn meal, baking powder, salt, and sugar. Set aside.
2. Drain whole kernel corn, reserving 1/2 cup liquid.
3. Combine corn liquid, eggs, and salad oil. Beat until well blended. Stir in cream-style corn.
4. Gradually stir in dry ingredients and drained corn.
5. Heat 2 inches of oil to 365 degrees and fry batter by the tablespoonful, 5 to 6 at a time, about 5 minutes, turning once. Drain. Keep fried fritters warm in oven while cooking others.

Crede Dever
Boulder, Colorado

CHEESY ONION BURGER BUNS

Yields 20 Buns

Preparation 2 Hours
Bake 15 to 20 Minutes at 400°F

5 3/4 to 6 3/4 cups unsifted flour
3 tablespoons sugar
1 1/2 teaspoons salt
2 packages dry yeast
2 tablespoons margarine, softened
2 cups very hot tap water
1 1/2 cups grated sharp Cheddar cheese
1/4 cup finely chopped onion
Margarine

1. In a large bowl, thoroughly mix 2 cups flour, sugar, salt, and dry yeast. Add softened margarine.
2. Gradually add tap water to dry ingredients and beat 2 minutes at medium speed. Scrape bowl.
3. Add 1 cup flour, or enough flour to make a thick batter. Beat at high speed 2 minutes. Scrape bowl, and stir in cheese, onion, and enough additional flour to make a soft dough.
4. Turn out on lightly floured board; knead until smooth and elastic, 8 to 10 minutes. Place in greased bowl, turning to grease top. Cover and let rise in warm place until doubled in bulk, about 1 hour.
5. Punch dough down; turn out on lightly floured board. Divide dough into 20 pieces. Form each piece into a smooth ball.
6. Place balls 2 inches apart on greased baking sheets. Cover and let rise in a warm place until doubled in bulk, about 45 minutes.
7. Bake 15 to 20 minutes at 400 degrees or until done. Remove from oven, place on wire racks and brush with margarine.

NOTE:

To make cocktail-size buns, form dough into balls about size of walnuts.

Helen Wasley
Boulder, Colorado

MEXICAN BREAD (*Sopaipillas*)

Yields 2 1/2 Dozen

Preparation 10 Minutes
Fry 1 Minute

3/4 teaspoon salt
1 teaspoon baking powder
4 to 4 1/2 cups flour
2 eggs
1 cup milk
Oil for frying

1. Sift salt, baking powder, and 4 cups flour together. Beat eggs and milk and add to dry ingredients. Add as much additional flour as will be absorbed.
2. Roll out as thin as possible and cut into squares.
3. Heat oil to 375 degrees, add one piece of dough, press dough down

lightly. When it starts to puff up, turn *sopaipilla* over. Cook a few seconds, until golden, remove, and drain.

NOTE:

These *sopaipillas*, from Old Town, Albuquerque, were originally used as a bread for any part of the meal. Now, they generally are served with honey for dessert.

Susan Maxwell Campbell
Houston, Texas

ZOAR BATTER BREAD

Serves 4

Preparation 5 Minutes
Bake 30 Minutes at 350°F

2 eggs
1 cup milk
1/2 cup corn meal
1 teaspoon salt
1 tablespoon baking powder
1 tablespoon butter or margarine

1. Beat eggs and milk together until frothy. Add corn meal, salt, and baking powder. Beat thoroughly so that corn meal is suspended in liquid.
2. Melt butter in a 8-inch square pan, add batter and bake 30 minutes at 350 degrees. The bread will be a golden brown on top and center will peak when done.
3. Serve at once with plenty of butter.

NOTE:

This is almost a cornbread souffle' but can be eaten with fingers.

Ellen Gille
Boulder, Colorado

SCONES

Yields 16

Preparation 10 Minutes
Cook 5 to 10 Minutes

1 3/4 cups flour
1/2 teaspoon baking soda
1/2 teaspoon cream of tartar
3 tablespoons sugar
2 eggs, beaten
1 cup sour milk or buttermilk

1. Sift together flour, baking soda, and cream of tartar. Add sugar.
2. Mix with eggs and milk to make a fairly thick batter.
3. Place spoonsful of mixture, on hot greased griddle. Keep at a steady medium heat and turn scones when bubbles break. Cook until golden brown.

NOTE:

An electric frying pan works well at 350 degrees to keep a steady heat for frying the scones.

BUTTERMILK BISCUITS

Yields 1 1/2 Dozen

Preparation 20 Minutes
Bake 10 to 15 Minutes at 425°F

2 cups flour, unsifted
1 teaspoon salt
1/2 teaspoon baking soda
7 tablespoons butter or margarine
1 cup buttermilk

1. Sift flour, add salt and soda and sift again.
2. Add 4 tablespoons butter, cut in small pieces, and work into flour by hand until blended. Add buttermilk and blend.
3. Roll dough to 1/2-inch thickness, cut with 2-inch round cookie cutter. Place on greased cookie sheet, touching one another.
4. Melt 3 tablespoons butter and brush biscuits. Bake at 425 degrees for 10 to 15 minutes.

NOTE:

Do not use electric mixer to blend ingredients.

Nancy Blue Riley
Denver, Colorado

CINNAMON FLAKE BISCUITS

Yields 1 Dozen

Preparation 30 Minutes
Bake 12 Minutes at 425°F

2 cups flour
1/2 teaspoon salt
4 teaspoons baking powder
1/2 teaspoon cream of tartar
3 tablespoons sugar
1/2 cup shortening
2/3 cup milk
1/4 cup melted butter
1/4 cup sugar
1 tablespoon cinnamon

1. Sift dry ingredients into bowl. Cut in shortening until mixture resembles coarse crumbs. Add milk all at once and stir until dough follows fork around bowl.
2. Turn onto a floured board and knead gently 1 minute. Roll dough 1/4-inch thick. Brush with melted butter and sprinkle with sugar and cinnamon.
3. Cut into 2-inch strips. Stack strips 5 high and cut off 2-inch pieces. Place, cut side down, in greased muffin pan. Bake in 425-degree oven for 12 minutes.

Kathleen Reese
Salt Lake City, Utah

GROUNDNUT MUFFINS

Yields 8 Muffins

Preparation 25 Minutes
Bake 12 to 15 Minutes at 425°F

1/2 cup butter or margarine
1/4 cup sugar
2 eggs
1 cup sifted all-purpose flour
1/2 teaspoon baking powder
1/4 teaspoon salt
1/2 cup plus 2 tablespoons chopped, salted peanuts

1. Mix butter and sugar, beat until creamy. Add eggs, one at a time, beating after each addition. Continue beating until light and fluffy.
2. Sift flour with baking powder and salt, fold into butter mixture, then stir in 1/2 cup peanuts.
3. Divide the mixture into greased muffin tins. Sprinkle with 2 tablespoons chopped peanuts.
4. Bake 12 to 15 minutes at 425 degrees or until golden brown.

NOTE:

Can be made early in the day.

Susannah Jordan
Jamestown, Colorado

ORANGE MUFFINS

Yields 1 Dozen

Preparation 20 Minutes
Bake 15 to 20 Minutes at 400°F

1 3/4 cups flour
2 1/2 teaspoons baking powder
2 tablespoons sugar
3/4 teaspoon salt
3 tablespoons grated orange peel
1 egg, well beaten
3/4 cup milk
1/3 cup salad oil
12 sugar cubes
1/2 cup orange juice

1. Mix flour, baking powder, sugar, salt, and orange peel. Make a well in center.
2. Combine egg, milk, and salad oil. Add all at once to well in dry ingredients. Mix only until dry ingredients are moistened.
3. Fill muffin cups 1/2 to 2/3 full. Dip sugar cubes in orange juice until soaked. Place one cube on top of each muffin. Bake 15 to 20 minutes at 400 degrees. Serve warm.

Corinne Effinger
Boulder, Colorado

BLUEBERRY BRAN MUFFINS

Yields 2 Dozen

Preparation 10 Minutes
Bake 15 to 20 Minutes at 425°F

2 cups bran
1 1/2 cups whole wheat flour
1 1/2 teaspoons salt
1/2 cup brown sugar
1 teaspoon baking soda
1 1/2 cups blueberry yogurt
2 eggs
1/2 cup vegetable oil

1. Mix bran, flour, salt, sugar, and baking soda. Add yogurt, eggs, and oil. Mix only long enough to moisten dry ingredients.
2. Place in muffin tins and bake 15 to 20 minutes at 425 degrees.

Carrie Ann Thoms
Denver, Colorado

SWEET POTATO MUFFINS

Yields 3 Dozen

Preparation 30 Minutes
Bake 25 Minutes at 400°F

1/2 cup butter
1 cup plus 2 tablespoons sugar
2 large eggs
1 1/2 cups mashed sweet potatoes
1 1/2 cups flour
2 teaspoons baking powder
1/8 to 1/4 teaspoon salt
1 teaspoon cinnamon
1/2 teaspoon nutmeg
1 cup milk
1 cup chopped nuts
1 cup raisins or currants, soaked and drained

1. Cream butter and sugar, add eggs and beat well. Blend in sweet potatoes.
2. Combine flour, baking powder, salt, cinnamon, and nutmeg and add alternately with milk. Mix briefly.
3. Fold in nuts and raisins or currants and fill greased muffin tins 2/3 full. Bake 25 minutes at 400 degrees.

NOTE:

A great way to use leftover Sweet Potato Bake (see Index). Canned, drained sweet potatoes may also be used. Muffins freeze well.

Nancy Cateora
Boulder, Colorado

HEAVENLY PECAN ROLLS

Yields 3 Dozen

Preparation 2 Hours
Bake 20 to 25 Minutes at 350°F

1 package yeast
1 tablespoon sugar
1/2 cup warm water
1 cup hot milk (not boiling)
1/2 cup butter
1/2 cup sugar
3/4 teaspoon salt
3 eggs, beaten
4 to 5 1/2 cups flour

FILLING
1/2 cup butter, melted
1 cup brown sugar
4 teaspoons cinnamon

PAN GOO
3/4 cup butter or margarine
1 1/2 cups brown sugar
3/4 cup dark corn syrup
1 cup chopped pecans

1. Mix yeast with sugar and water and set aside.
2. Pour milk over butter, sugar, and salt in a large bowl and allow butter to melt.
3. Add eggs to butter mixture and beat well. Add half of flour and beat until very smooth. Add yeast mixture and remaining flour. Stir well. Dough will be sticky. Do not knead.
4. Let dough rise, covered. Punch down and let rise again (the more times it rises, the less sticky it becomes).
5. In saucepan, combine butter, brown sugar, and corn syrup. Heat, stirring, until sugar dissolves. Divide Pan Goo into four round cake pans or the equivalent. Sprinkle nuts in each pan.
6. Divide dough into quarters and roll or pat each into a 6 x 9-inch rectangle 1/4-inch thick. Spread each rectangle with 2 tablespoons butter. Combine cinnamon and sugar and sprinkle evenly over each quarter.
7. Roll dough from long side, jelly-roll fashion, cut each into 9 slices and arrange in prepared pans.
8. Allow to rise until doubled in bulk (covered in the refrigerator overnight makes them ready for breakfast).
9. Bake 20 to 25 minutes at 350 degrees, then cool 5 minutes. Invert on plate or waxed paper.

NOTE:

This dough can be used for dinner rolls. Butter the dough, roll, cut, and continue as above eliminating the sugar, cinnamon and Pan Goo.

Peg English
Costa Mesa, California

GLAZED APPLE CRESCENTS

Yields 16 Rolls

Preparation 20 Minutes
Bake 25 to 30 Minutes at 375°F

1 cup peeled, finely chopped apple
1/3 cup chopped nuts
1/4 cup sugar
1 teaspoon flour
1 teaspoon cinnamon
2 cans (8-ounce each) refrigerated crescent rolls
2 tablespoons butter or margarine, melted
1/2 cup firmly packed brown sugar
1/2 cup dairy sour cream
1/4 cup butter or margarine
1/4 cup chopped nuts

1. Combine apple, nuts, sugar, flour, and cinnamon.
2. Separate crescent dough into triangles and brush each with melted butter.
3. Spoon rounded tablespoon of apple mixture on wide end of each triangle and roll up to opposite point.
4. Arrange rolls, point-side down, in rows on ungreased 12 x 8-inch pan.
5. Bake 25 to 30 minutes at 375 degrees or until golden brown.
6. Make a glaze by combining brown sugar, sour cream, and butter and bring to a boil. Boil 3 minutes, stirring occasionally. Pour over rolls and sprinkle with chopped nuts. Serve warm or cool.

NOTE:

Refrigerate leftovers.

Trev Lewis
Denver, Colorado

MAPLE SWEET ROLLS

Yields 1 1/2 to 2 Dozen

Preparation 1 Hour
Bake 15 to 20 Minutes at 375°F

1 package yeast
1/4 cup warm water
1/3 cup butter
3/4 cup scalded milk
1/3 cup sugar
2 teaspoons salt
2 eggs, beaten
4 1/2 cups sifted flour
FILLING
1/3 cup butter or margarine
1 1/2 cups powdered sugar
2 teaspoons maple flavoring
1/4 cup finely chopped nuts
Evaporated milk
ICING
1 cup powdered sugar
1 1/2 to 2 tablespoons evaporated milk
1 tablespoon soft butter
1/2 teaspoon vanilla

1. Dissolve yeast in warm water. Combine butter and milk. Stir until butter melts, cool to lukewarm, and add yeast mixture.
2. Combine sugar, salt, and eggs. Add yeast-milk mixture and stir in flour. Knead until smooth. Let rise until double in bulk.
3. Roll out in rectangle 1/4-inch thick (3 times as long as wide). Let rest.
4. Mix butter, powdered sugar, and maple flavoring until creamy and light. Add nuts. Cut dough in half and spread all the filling on one half. Cover with other half. Cut in 1-inch strips and roll to form a spiral. Brush with evaporated milk.
5. Place on greased baking sheet and let rise until double in bulk. Bake 15 to 20 minutes at 375 degrees.
6. Make the icing by mixing powdered sugar, milk, butter, and vanilla. Frost rolls while still warm.

Leah Call
Bountiful, Utah

CINNAMON ROLLS

Yields 2 Dozen

Preparation 65 Minutes
Bake 20 Minutes at 375°F

2 cups warm water
1/3 cup sugar
6 1/2 to 7 cups flour
1 tablespoon salt
2 packages yeast
2 eggs
1/3 cup shortening

Melted butter
Cinnamon and sugar
CARAMEL TOPPING
2 cups brown sugar
2/3 cup butter
2/3 cup heavy cream

1. Mix water, sugar, 2 cups flour, salt, and yeast. Beat for 2 minutes at high speed. Add eggs, shortening, and beat again for 1 minute.
2. Add 4 1/2 cups flour and stir well. (Add slightly more flour if needed for smooth dough.) Knead about 5 minutes; place in greased bowl. Set in warm place approximately 40 minutes.
3. Combine brown sugar, butter, and heavy cream in small saucepan. Heat over low heat until blended but do not boil.
4. Pour topping into two 9 x 13-inch baking pans, spreading evenly.
5. Divide dough in half and roll each piece in a rectangle about 3/8-inch thick. Spread with melted butter and sprinkle with cininamon and sugar. Roll dough from long side as for jelly roll. Cut each roll into 12 slices. Arrange rolls on top of carmel topping. Bake immediately for 20 minutes at 375 degrees.

NOTE:

These rolls do not need to rise after being sliced and placed on carmel topping.

Mikki Matheson
Boulder, Colorado

BUTTERSCOTCH CRESCENTS

Yields 3 Dozen

Preparation 3 Hours
Bake 15 Minutes at 375°F

1 package yeast
1/4 cup warm water
1 box (3 1/8-ounce) butterscotch pudding
1 1/2 cups evaporated milk
1/2 cup butter
2 eggs, beaten
2 teaspoons salt
4 1/2 to 5 cups flour

FILLING
1/4 cup butter, melted
2/3 cup grated coconut
2/3 cup packed brown sugar
1/3 cup chopped pecans
2 tablespoons flour

1. Soften yeast in warm water. Set aside.
2. Mix pudding with evaporated milk. Cook and stir over medium heat until it starts to thicken. Remove from heat and add butter. Cool to lukewarm.
3. Blend in eggs, salt, and softened yeast. Gradually add flour to form a stiff dough and beat well. Cover and let rise in warm place until doubled, about 1 1/2 hours.
4. Divide dough into thirds. Roll each third into a 15-inch circle. Cut into 12 wedges.
5. For the filling, combine melted butter, coconut, brown sugar, nuts, and flour. Place a teaspoonful on dough wedge and roll from wide end. Place point side down on greased cookie sheet and curve to make crescent shape. Let rise one hour and bake 15 minutes at 375 degrees.

NOTE:

Freezes well.

Marta Janssen
Portland, Oregon

SPUDNUTS

Yields 5 to 6 Dozen

Preparation 2 1/2 Hours
Fry 3 to 5 Minutes

1 cup hot, mashed potatoes
3 tablespoons shortening
3 egg yolks, beaten
3 egg whites, beaten
5 cups flour
1 teaspoon salt
4 tablespoons sugar
1/2 teaspoon nutmeg
1/2 teaspoon cinnamon
2 fresh yeast cakes
1/2 cup warm water
1 1/2 cups milk
1 pound powdered sugar
1 1/3 cups boiling water (approximately)
1 teaspoon vanilla extract
Oil for frying

1. Mix potatoes, shortening, and egg yolks. Fold in stiffly beaten egg whites.
2. Sift flour with salt, 2 tablespoons sugar, nutmeg, and cinnamon.

3. Dissolve yeast cakes in warm water with 2 tablespoons sugar. Mix with milk.
4. Add flour mixture to potato mixture alternately with yeast-milk mixture; beat until smooth. Let rise 1 hour.
5. Roll dough out on a floured surface to 1/2-inch thickness. Cut with a doughnut cutter, and let rise until double, about 45 minutes to 1 hour.
6. Meanwhile, mix powdered sugar, water, and vanilla. Glaze should be the consistency of a medium white sauce.
7. Deep fry at 375 degrees or fry in 2 inches of oil in an electric skillet (375 degrees) turning spudnuts once. Drain on brown paper.
8. Place spudnuts on a rack over a pan to catch drippings, and glaze while still warm.

NOTE:

The cut, uncooked spudnuts can be frozen. Thaw 4 to 5 hours before frying. Cut glaze recipe down if you are not planning to fry all spudnuts at once.

Bertha Blonquist
Salt Lake City, Utah

NORWEGIAN KRINGLAR

This cream puff on a pastry base makes any breakfast festive.

Serves 9 to 12

Preparation 1 Hour
Bake 45 Minutes at 375°F

2 cups flour
1 cup butter
1 cup plus 1 tablespoon water
3 eggs
1/2 teaspoon almond extract

FROSTING
1 cup powdered sugar
1 tablespoon milk
1 tablespoon butter
1 teaspoon almond extract

1. Mix 1 cup flour, 1/2 cup butter, and 1 tablespoon water (dough is very soft). Divide dough into 3 pieces. Gently pushing with fingers, pat each piece into a strip 3 inches wide and 7 to 8 inches long onto a cookie sheet.
2. In a saucepan, heat 1 cup water and remaining 1/2 cup butter to boiling point. Remove from heat and add remaining 1 cup flour. Stir vigorously until mixture forms a ball.
3. Beat in eggs all at one time and continue beating until smooth. Add almond extract.
4. Spread the mixture directly on top of each pastry strip. Bake at 375 degrees for 45 minutes.
5. Meanwhile, make frosting by mixing powdered sugar, milk, butter, and almond extract until smooth. Frost while still slightly warm.

Janet Rutland
Blacksburg, Virginia

MELT-IN-YOUR-MOUTH COFFEE CAKE

Serves 16 to 20 | Preparation 30 Minutes
Refrigerate Overnight | Bake 50 to 60 Minutes at 350°F

1/4 cup milk, lukewarm
1 package yeast
3/4 cup plus 2 tablespoons sugar
1 cup butter, softened
3 eggs, separated
2 1/2 cups flour, sifted
2 teaspoons cinnamon
3/4 cup chopped nuts
1/2 cup shredded coconut

1. Combine milk, yeast, and 2 tablespoons sugar. Set aside to dissolve.
2. Mix butter, egg yolks, and flour. Add yeast mixture. Mix well.
3. Wrap dough in waxed paper and refrigerate overnight or at least several hours.
4. Remove dough from refrigerator and let warm while making filling. Beat egg whites and remaining 3/4 cup sugar. Set aside. Mix cinnamon, nuts, and coconut. Set aside.
5. Divide dough in half. Roll each half into a rectangle about 1/4-inch thick. Spread with half the egg white mixture and sprinkle with half the cinnamon mixture. Roll up, jelly-roll fashion, and place on a baking sheet. Repeat procedure with remaining dough. Place on same baking sheet.
6. Bake 50 to 60 minutes at 350 degrees. Since this coffee cake tends to brown before it is done, check at 40 to 45 minutes. If already light brown, cover lightly with aluminum foil and continue baking until cakes are done in center. Slice while still warm.

NOTE:

The coffee cake is slightly crumbly on the outside and moist on the inside. Slices keep well in an airtight container. Whole baked coffee cakes can be frozen for months. The reciple doubles easily.

Ethel Zager
Avalon, California

WORLD WAR II COFFEE CAKE

Serves 8 to 12 | Preparation 1 1/2 Hours
Refrigerate Overnight | Bake 35 to 40 Minutes at 375°F

1 package dry yeast
3 tablespoons sugar
1 cup warm milk
1/2 cup shortening
1/2 teaspoon salt
1 egg and 1 egg yolk (reserve the white)
3 to 3 1/2 cups flour
Sugar
Cinnamon
Raisins
Nuts, chopped

1. Mix yeast, 1 tablespoon sugar, and 1/2 cup milk. Let rise a few minutes.

2. Meanwhile, in large bowl, combine shortening, remaining 1/2 cup milk, 2 tablespoons sugar, salt, egg, egg yolk, and flour. Add yeast mixture and stir.
3. Store, covered, in refrigerator overnight.
4. In the morning, roll yeast dough out in a long, narrow rectangle. Brush with reserved egg white. Sprinkle to taste with sugar, cinnamon, raisins, and chopped nuts.
5. Roll, lengthwise, jelly-roll fashion, and arrange in a greased tube pan. Let rise in a warm place about 1 hour. Bake at 375 degrees 35 to 40 minutes or until browned.

Pat Harwood
Littleton, Colorado

CHOCOLATE CHIP COFFEE CAKE

Serves 15 to 20

Preparation 15 Minutes
Bake 45 to 60 Minutes at 350°F

1/2 cup butter
1 1/4 cups sugar
2 eggs
2 teaspoons vanilla extract
1 teaspoon baking powder
1 teaspoon salt
1 teaspoon baking soda
1 cup sour cream
2 cups sifted flour
1/3 cup brown sugar
1 teaspoon cinnamon
1 cup chopped nuts
12 ounces chocolate chips

1. Cream butter and 1 cup sugar until smooth. Add eggs, vanilla, baking powder, salt, baking soda, and sour cream. Mix thoroughly.
2. Add flour and mix until smooth.
3. Combine 1/4 cup sugar, brown sugar, cinnamon, nuts, and chocolate chips in separate bowl. Sprinkle some of the topping on the bottom of greased and floured tube pan. Alternate layers of batter and topping, ending with topping.
4. Bake in 350-degree oven for 45 to 60 minutes.

Lila Linsky
Los Angeles, California

NUTMEG COFFEE CAKE

Serves 12 to 15

Preparation 20 Minutes
Bake 40 Minutes at 350°F

- **3 cups sifted flour**
- **2 1/4 cups firmly packed brown sugar**
- **3/4 cup butter or margarine**
- **1 cup sour cream**
- **1 1/2 teaspoons baking soda**
- **2 eggs**
- **1 teaspoon nutmeg**
- **3/4 cup chopped pecans**

1. Blend flour, brown sugar, and butter with a pastry blender until crumbly. Set aside 3/4 cup of this mixture.
2. Combine sour cream, soda, eggs, and nutmeg and add to crumb mixture. Mix well.
3. Pour batter into a greased and floured 9 x 13-inch pan and sprinkle nuts and reserved crumb mixture over top. Bake at 350 degrees for 40 minutes or until done.

Mikki Matheson
Boulder, Colorado

NORWEGIAN CHRISTMAS BREAD

Yields 3 Loaves
Rise Overnight

Preparation 3 Hours
Bake 45 to 50 Minutes at 350°F

- **2 packages yeast**
- **1/2 cup lukewarm water**
- **2 cups scalded milk**
- **1 cup sugar**
- **2 teaspoons salt**
- **1 cup melted butter**
- **8 cups flour**
- **1 teaspoon ground cardamom**
- **1 cup raisins**
- **1/2 cup chopped citron**
- **1/2 cup candied cherries**
- **1/2 cup chopped almonds**
- **Vanilla Glaze** **(see Index)**

1. Mix yeast in lukewarm water.
2. In large bowl, combine milk, sugar, salt, and butter. Cool to lukewarm and add yeast-water mixture.
3. Add half the flour. Beat well. Let double in greased bowl covered with plastic wrap.
4. Add remaining flour, cardamom, raisins, citron, cherries, and almonds. Mix with spoon. Knead in bowl.
5. Let rise, covered, overnight at room temperature.
6. Knead and form into 3 loaves. Place in greased loaf pans. Let rise, not quite double. Bake 45 to 50 minutes at 350 degrees.

Thelma Schwarz
Denver, Colorado

HOBO BREAD

Yields 3 Loaves
Refrigerate Overnight

Preparation 15 Minutes
Bake 1 Hour 10 Minutes at 350°F

2 cups raisins
2 tablespoons butter
2 teaspoons baking soda
2 cups boiling water
4 cups flour
2 cups sugar
1 teaspoon cinnamon
1/2 teaspoon salt
2 eggs
1 cup chopped pecans

1. Combine raisins, butter, soda, and water. Stir to mix thoroughly. Cool and refrigerate overnight.
2. When ready to bake, mix flour, sugar, cinnamon, and salt. Add eggs, pecans, and raisin mixture. Mix thoroughly.
3. Divide dough among 3 1-pound coffee cans that have been greased and floured. Bake 1 hour 10 minutes at 350 degrees.

Ellen Doenges
Austin, Texas

DENVER PANCAKES

Serves 4

Preparation 15 Minutes
Cook 7 Minutes

2 eggs
3/4 cup buttermilk
1 cup flour
1 tablespoon sugar
1 teaspoon baking powder
1/4 teaspoon baking soda
1/4 teaspoon salt
1 apple, peeled, and grated
2 tablespoons oil

1. Beat eggs and buttermilk. Add flour, sugar, baking powder, soda, and salt. Beat well.
2. Stir in grated apple and oil.
3. Cook on hot griddle. Turn once.

Josephine Cateora
Golden, Colorado

PERFECTION PANCAKES

Serves 2 to 4

Preparation 5 Minutes
Cook 3 Minutes

1/2 cup pancake mix
1/2 cup corn muffin mix
2 eggs, slightly beaten
3/4 cup milk

1. Combine pancake mix, muffin mix, eggs, and milk. Stir until smooth.
2. Bake on hot griddle, turning once.

Grace Baker
San Gabriel, California

CRISPY WAFFLES

Serves 2 to 4

Preparation 10 Minutes
Cook 8 Minutes

2 eggs, separated
1 cup flour
2 teaspoons baking powder
1/4 teaspoon salt
3/4 cup milk
3 tablespoons butter, melted

1. Beat egg whites stiff but not dry. Set aside.
2. Combine flour, baking powder, salt, egg yolks, and milk. Blend well.
3. Stir in butter then fold in egg whites.
4. Bake in pre-heated waffle iron until golden brown. Yields two 9-inch waffles.

VARIATION:

Add 1/2 cup melted chocolate chips to above batter before folding in egg whites. To freeze, slightly underbake, remove from iron and cool on wire rack. Wrap well and freeze. Toast frozen waffles lightly.

Hank Cateora
Boulder, Colorado

OVERNIGHT YEAST WAFFLES

Yields 12 Waffles
Stand Overnight

Preparation 10 Minutes
Cook 8 Minutes

2 1/3 cups lukewarm water
1 package dry yeast
3/4 cup powdered milk
1/4 cup oil or margarine, melted
1 teaspoon salt
3 cups flour
1/2 teaspoon baking soda
2 eggs or 4 egg whites

1. Dissolve yeast in warm water, add powdered milk, oil, salt, and flour. Mix until smooth (batter will be thin).
2. Cover and let stand overnight at room temperature.
3. The following morning, add baking soda and eggs. Beat well.
4. Bake in hot waffle iron.

NOTE:

Batter does not freeze or store well. Freeze cooked waffles, reheat in toaster without thawing.

Marcia Cutter
Lubbock, Texas

QUICK BREADS • AND • CAKES

BANANA-CRANBERRY NUT BREAD

Yields 1 Loaf

Preparation 25 Minutes
Bake 45 to 60 Minutes at 350°F

2 cups fresh cranberries
1 cup sugar
3/4 cup water
1/3 cup shortening
2/3 cup sugar
2 eggs
1 3/4 cups sifted flour
1/2 teaspoon salt
2 teaspoons baking powder
1/4 teaspoon baking soda
1/2 cup chopped walnuts
1 cup mashed bananas
GLAZE (optional)
1 1/4 cups sugar
1/4 cup water

1. Combine cranberries, sugar, and water. Boil 5 to 10 minutes until berries pop. Drain and measure to make 1 cup berries.
2. Cream shortening and sugar. Add eggs one at a time. Beat well.
3. Sift flour, salt, baking powder, and soda. Add alternately with bananas and nuts. Fold in cranberries.
4. Bake in 9 1/2 x 5 1/2-inch loaf pan at 350 degrees for 45 to 60 minutes. A double recipe makes 5 small loaf pans (bake 45 minutes).
5. If glaze is desired, boil sugar and water 2 minutes until slightly syrupy. Spread on hot bread and decorate with walnuts.

Dorothy Lewis
Boulder, Colorado

LEMON BREAD

Yields 1 Loaf

Preparation 15 Minutes
Bake 50 to 55 Minutes at 375°F

1/2 cup shortening
1 1/2 cups sugar
2 eggs slightly beaten
1 2/3 cups flour
1 teaspoon baking powder
1/2 teaspoon salt
1/2 cup milk
1/2 cup finely chopped nuts
Grated peel of 1 lemon
Juice of 1 lemon

1. Cream shortening and 1 cup sugar. Mix in eggs.
2. Blend flour, baking powder, and salt. Add to batter alternately with milk. Fold in nuts and lemon peel.
3. Pour batter into well-greased 9 x 5-inch loaf pan. Bake at 375 degrees for 50 to 55 minutes.
4. Meanwhile, mix lemon juice with 1/2 cup sugar for topping. Pour over loaf immediately after it is removed from oven. Cool in pan 10 minutes; remove from pan and cool completely before slicing.

June DeFore
Boulder, Colorado

PINEAPPLE BREAD

Yields 1 Loaf

Preparation 30 Minutes
Bake 1 to 1 1/2 Hours at 300°F

2 1/4 cups flour
3/4 cup sugar
3 teaspoons baking powder
3/4 teaspoon salt
1 egg, lightly beaten
1/3 cup margarine, softened
1 cup crushed pineapple, drained
1 cup chopped dates
1 cup chopped walnuts

1. Combine flour, sugar, baking powder, and salt.
2. Mix together egg, margarine, pineapple, dates, and nuts. Combine with dry ingredients.
3. Pour batter into greased and lightly floured 9 x 5-inch loaf pan. Bake at 300 degrees for 1 to 1 1/2 hours or until done.

Paul R. Flippen
Boulder, Colorado

POPPY SEED BREAD

Yields 1 Loaf

Preparation 10 Minutes
Bake 1 Hour at 375°F

2 eggs
1 cup vegetable oil
1 cup evaporated milk
1 cup sugar (some honey may be substituted)
2 cups flour
2 teaspoons baking powder
1/4 teaspoon salt
1 teaspoon vanilla extract
1/4 cup poppy seeds

1. Combine eggs, oil, milk, and sugar. Beat well.
2. Add flour, baking powder, and salt and beat again. Stir in vanilla and poppy seeds.
3. Bake in greased 9 x 5-inch loaf pan 1 hour in 375-degree oven.

Arvilla Fey
Lyons, Colorado

CARROT CAKE

Serves 16

Preparation 15 Minutes
Bake 1 Hour at 300°F

2 cups sugar
1 1/2 cups vegetable oil
4 eggs
2 cups sifted flour
2 teaspoons baking soda
2 teaspoons cinnamon
1 teaspoon salt
3 heaping cups grated carrots
1 cup chopped nuts
Cream Cheese Frosting (see Index)

1. Cream sugar, oil, and eggs.

2. Sift flour, soda, cinnamon, and salt and add to creamed mixture. Add carrots and nuts and mix well.
3. Bake in a 9 x 13-inch baking pan for 1 hour at 300 degrees. Cool and frost with Cream Cheese Frosting.

VARIATION:

Add raisins or chopped dates. Use soy flour or blend of soy and unbleached wheat or white flour.

Nancy Putney
Boulder, Colorado

JOURNEY CAKE

Keeps so well, you can take it along on your next journey.

Serves 12

Preparation 5 Minutes
Bake 35 Minutes at 375°F

1 1/2 cups sugar
3/4 cup margarine
1 teaspoon baking soda
1 teaspoon cinnamon
1 teaspoon cloves
4 1/2 cups flour
1 3/4 cups apple cider

1. Blend sugar and margarine. Combine baking soda, cinnamon, and cloves with flour and add alternately to sugar mixture with cider.
2. Pour into 9 x 13-inch pan and bake at 375 degrees for 35 minutes.

Sue Tennison
Tucson, Arizona

APPLESAUCE CAKE

Serves 12 to 16

Preparation 15 Minutes
Bake 1 Hour 10 Minutes at 350°F

2/3 cup shortening
3/4 cup sugar
1 cup raisins
1/2 cup chopped nuts (optional)
10 to 20 dates, chopped (optional)
2 cups flour
1 teaspoon cinnamon
1/2 teaspoon cloves
1/2 teaspoon nutmeg
1/4 teaspoon salt
1 can (16-ounce) applesauce
2 teaspoons baking soda

1. Melt shortening. Cool slightly and add sugar, raisins, nuts, and dates. Stir well.
2. Add flour sifted with cinnamon, cloves, nutmeg, and salt. Stir.
3. Combine applesauce and soda and add to other ingredients. Stir well.
4. Bake in greased and floured tube pan or 9 x 13-inch pan about 1 hour 10 minutes in 350-degree oven.

Royce A. Miller
Arvada, Colorado

GREEK YOGURT CAKE

Serves 24 or More

Preparation 20 Minutes
Bake 45 to 60 Minutes at 350°F

1 cup butter or margarine
1 3/4 cups sugar
1 teaspoon vanilla or almond extract or lemon juice and rind
4 large eggs
3 cups flour
2 teaspoons baking powder
1/2 teaspoon salt
1 cup yogurt
1 cup candied fruit, nuts or raisins

1. Thoroughly cream butter and sugar. Add vanilla and eggs, one at a time, beating well after each addition.
2. Sift flour with baking powder and salt and add alternately with yogurt. Stir in fruit, nuts or raisins and mix until just coated with butter.
3. Pour into a greased and floured bundt pan or in 3 loaf pans similarly treated and bake at 350 dgreees for 45 to 60 minutes.

Ruth Yearns
Boulder, Colorado

FRENCH ORANGE CAKE

Serves 9 to 12

Preparation 35 Minutes
Bake 20 to 25 Minutes at 350°F

1 teaspoon soda
1/4 cup hot water
1/2 cup chopped dates
1 1/2 cups sugar
1/2 cup butter
1 egg
Grated rind of 1 orange
2 cups sifted flour
1 teaspoon baking powder
1 cup milk
1/2 cup finely chopped pecans
Juice of one orange
Heavy cream, whipped

1. Dissolve soda in hot water and pour over dates. Let stand for 5 to 6 minutes. Drain.
2. Cream 1 cup sugar and butter together. Add egg and orange rind and mix.
3. Sift flour and baking powder together. Add to creamed mixture alternately with milk, a little at a time, mixing thoroughly with each addition. Add dates and nuts.
4. Pour into greased 9- to 10-inch square pan. Bake at 350 degrees for 20 to 25 minutes.
5. Mix 1/2 cup sugar and orange juice and pour over cake as soon as it comes out of oven.
6. Cut in squares and serve with whipped cream.

Grace Baker
San Gabriel, California

BLACK BOTTOM CUPCAKES

Yields 18 to 20 Cupcakes

Preparation 20 Minutes
Bake 30 to 35 Minutes at 350°F

8 ounces cream cheese
1 egg
1 1/3 cups sugar
1/8 plus 1/2 teaspoon salt
6 ounces chocolate chips
1 1/2 cups flour
1/4 cup cocoa
1 teaspoon baking soda
1 cup water
1/3 cup vegetable oil
1 tablespoon vinegar
1 teaspoon vanilla extract

1. Combine cream cheese, egg, 1/3 cup sugar, and 1/8 teaspoon salt. Beat well. Stir in chocolate chips and set aside.
2. Combine flour, cocoa, baking soda, 1 cup sugar, and 1/2 teaspoon salt. Add water, oil, vinegar, and vanilla. Beat well.
3. Line muffin tin with paper liners. Fill 1/3 full with chocolate batter. Add a teaspoonful of cream cheese mixture on top.
4. Bake in 350-degree oven for 30 to 35 minutes. Cool overnight and, if desired, frost with Chocolate Velvet Creme (see Index).

Karen Dickey
Boulder, Colorado

GREAT-GRANDMOTHER'S PEANUT BUTTER CUPCAKES

Yields 24 Cupcakes

Preparation 20 Minutes
Bake 18 to 20 Minutes at 400°F

1 1/2 cups packed brown sugar
1/3 cup butter
1/2 cup peanut butter
2 eggs
2 cups unsifted flour
2 1/2 teaspoons baking powder
Pinch of salt
3/4 cup milk

1. Cream brown sugar, butter, and peanut butter. Add eggs and beat.
2. Sift flour, baking powder, and salt and add to batter. Mix thoroughly.
3. Add milk to batter and beat. Pour into greased cupcake pans. Bake 18 to 20 minutes at 400 degrees.

NOTE:

These cupcakes always fall in the middle, but if recipe is changed to prevent this, they are not as good and chewy.

Terri Evans
Boulder, Colorado

BUTTER TORTE

Serves 12

Preparation 40 Minutes
Bake 25 Minutes at 350°F

2 cups sugar
1/2 cup butter
1/2 cup shortening
5 eggs, separated
2 cups unsifted flour
1 teaspoon baking soda
1 cup buttermilk
1 teaspoon vanilla extract
1 cup finely chopped walnuts
1 cup coconut
Cream Cheese Frosting (see Index)

1. Cream sugar, butter, and shortening until smooth. Add egg yolks and beat well.
2. Sift flour and baking soda 3 times and add alternately with buttermilk to creamed mixture. Add vanilla, nuts, and coconut. Mix.
3. Beat egg whites to stiff peaks and fold into batter.
4. Pour batter into 3 greased 9-inch cake pans. Bake 25 minutes at 350 degrees. Cool and frost with Cream Cheese Frosting.

NOTE:

Frosted cake freezes well. Let thaw, uncovered, for 6 hours before serving.

Min DeSalvo
Boulder, Colorado

GATEAU AU CHOCOLAT

Serves 8 to 10

Preparation 25 Minutes
Bake 35 Minutes at 350°F

5 eggs
7 ounces semi-sweet chocolate
7 tablespoons unsalted butter
1/2 cup milk
1/2 cup sugar
1/3 cup plus 3 tablespoons flour
1 teaspoon vanilla
***Ganache* (see Index)**

1. Butter and flour two 8-inch cake pans.
2. Separate eggs and set aside.
3. Combine chocolate, butter, milk and 1/4 cup sugar in a saucepan over medium-low heat. When butter is melted, stir until chocolate is smooth and remove from heat.
4. Sift flour and stir into chocolate mixture. Add egg yolks and vanilla and stir thoroughly. Transfer to a large mixing bowl.
5. Beat egg whites to soft peaks and add the remaining 1/4 cup sugar and beat until very stiff.
6. Fold egg whites into chocolate mixture and pour into prepared pans. Tap pans firmly on counter and bake 30 to 35 minutes in a 350-degree oven.

7. When cakes are done (batter will rise in pan, fall a little and come away from side of pan), unmold onto cake rack. Cover with inverted cake pans and allow to cool.
8. Trim layers and frost with *Ganache*. Spread icing between layers of cake and over top. Spread evenly, allowing excess to run down sides of cake. Refrigerate.
9. Allow cake to stand at room temperature for 1/2 hour before serving.

VARIATION:

Decrease vanilla to 1/2 teaspoon and add zest of 1 orange and 1 ounce Grand Marnier or Cointreau. Freezes well.

Richard Grausman
U.S. Representative
Le Cordon Bleu de Paris
New York, New York

VERSATILE POUND CAKE

Yields 2 Loaves

Preparation 25 Minutes
Bake 1 Hour at 325°F

1 1/2 cups butter or margarine
3 1/2 cups powdered sugar
6 eggs, extra large
1 teaspoon vanilla extract
1 teaspoon lemon extract
3 1/2 cups flour
Zest of 2 lemons (optional)
Lemon Glaze (see Index)

1. Beat butter and powdered sugar until fluffy. Add eggs one at a time, beating well after each addition.
2. Add vanilla and lemon extracts. Mix well, add flour and beat well. Stir in zest.
3. Pour into greased 10-inch tube pan or two 9 x 5-inch loaf pans. Bake 1 hour in 325-degree oven until golden. Cool in pan 5 minutes, then remove. Cover with Lemon Glaze while still hot.

NOTE:

Cake can be served plain without glaze.

VARIATION:

Omit glaze, slice cake into 3 layers, and sprinkle each cut surface with 1 to 2 tablespoons sherry. Spread a layer of ice cream (pistachio, coffee, chocolate) about 1 inch thick on bottom and center slice. Restack and add top layer. Wrap well in foil and freeze until ready to use. Slice as needed. Keeps 6 to 8 weeks in freezer.

Deborah Cateora
Boulder, Colorado

ENGLISH TEA CAKE

Serves 20

Preparation 15 Minutes
Bake 1 Hour 45 Minutes at 300°F

1 1/4 cups butter
1 1/2 cups sugar
4 eggs
3 tablespoons brandy
2 3/4 cups flour
2 cups currants

1. Beat butter until light and fluffy. Continue beating while slowly adding sugar. Add eggs one at a time, beating after each addition. Add brandy and mix well.
2. Fold in flour, then currants. Pour into greased and floured bundt pan or 13-inch loaf pan.
3. Bake 1 hour 45 minutes in 300-degree oven until golden. Turn out after cooling slightly.
4. Sprinkle with powdered sugar. Cut into very thin slices.

NOTE:

This cake keeps well and freezes well.

Delores Thurnauer
Boulder, Colorado

CUSTARD TEA CAKE

Serves 12 to 14
Chill 2 Hours

Preparation 40 Minutes
Bake 60 to 65 Minutes at 325°F

4 egg yolks
1 1/4 cups sugar
1 tablespoon cold water
2 tablespoons lemon juice
1 cup sifted flour
8 egg whites
1/2 teaspoon cream of tartar
1/4 teaspoon salt

CUSTARD
2 envelopes unflavored gelatin
1/2 cup cold water
3 cups milk, scalded
1 1/2 cups sugar
1 teaspoon salt
3 tablespoons flour
8 egg yolks
4 teaspoons vanilla extract
2 cups heavy cream, whipped

1. Beat egg yolks until thick. Gradually beat in 1/4 cup sugar. Combine water and lemon juice and beat in alternately with flour.
2. In large bowl, beat egg whites, cream of tartar, and salt until stiff. Gradually beat in 1 cup sugar.
3. Gently fold the yolk mixture into the egg whites. Pour into ungreased tube pan and bake 60 to 65 minutes in 325-degree oven. Remove from pan and cool completely. Cut into 3 layers.
4. Soften gelatin in cold water and stir in scalded milk.
5. Mix sugar, salt, and flour. Add to milk mixture.

6. Beat egg yolks, add a little milk mixture, stir, and blend all back into milk. Boil one minute.
7. Cover with waxed paper and cool 1 hour. (Do not let custard get too firm.)
8. Fold in vanilla and whipped cream. Spread over each layer, then on the sides and top. Refrigerate at least 2 hours before serving.

Ethel Zager
Avalon, California

NUT TORTE

Serves 10 to 12

Preparation 20 Minutes
Bake 1 Hour at 350°F

1 pound nuts, toasted
1 1/2 cups sugar
1/4 cup white bread crumbs, dried
10 eggs, separated
1 teaspoon vanilla extract
Chocolate Velvet Creme (see Index)
Whipped cream

1. In a food processor or blender, pulverize nuts with 1/2 cup sugar until they resemble fine meal. (Watch closely for the fine meal stage so that nuts do not turn to paste.) Add bread crumbs, blend briefly. Set aside.
2. Beat egg yolks until creamy and slowly add 1 cup sugar. Continue beating until thick and lemon colored. Add vanilla.
3. Beat egg whites until stiff peaks form. Fold a small amount into egg yolk mixture. Set aside.
4. Fold nuts into egg yolk mixture 1 cup at a time, then fold in remaining egg whites.
5. Pour into greased and floured 10-inch springform pan or two 10-inch cake pans. Bake at 350 degrees for 1 hour. Let cool 20 minutes and remove from pan.
6. If baked in springform, cut into 4 layers; if baked in cake pans, cut each into 2 layers. Spread Chocolate Velvet Creme between layers. Frost top and sides with Chocolate Velvet Creme or whipped cream.

NOTE:

1. Any kind of nut may be used in this cake. Pecans or hazelnuts are especially good.
2. Make bread crumbs from fresh bread and dry for 5 minutes at 250 degrees.
3. Use any available pan size for baking but carefully watch baking time.
4. Freezes well frosted or unfrosted.

Ellen Denton
Piedmont, California

GRAHAM CRACKER CAKE

Serves 12

Preparation 20 Minutes
Bake 35 Minutes at 350°F

1 cup milk
2 1/4 cups graham cracker crumbs
1/2 cup butter
1 cup sugar
3 eggs, separated
1 1/2 teaspoons baking powder
1 cup chopped nuts
1/2 cup coconut
1 teaspoon vanilla extract
Broiled Topping (see Index)

1. Pour milk over graham cracker crumbs. Let stand until moist.
2. Cream butter, sugar, and egg yolks. Stir in graham cracker mixture. Add baking powder, nuts, and coconut. Mix until smooth.
3. Beat egg whites until stiff and fold into batter. Add vanilla and mix.
4. Pour into greased and floured 9 x 13-inch pan. Bake at 350 degrees for 35 minutes. While cake is still hot, spread on Broiled Topping and broil 2 to 3 minutes.

Charles Taggart
Columbus, Ohio

VARIATION:

Add 3/4 cup raisins, 1/2 teaspoon nutmeg, and 1 teaspoon cinnamon for a nice spice cake.

SPICY SOUTHERN GINGERBREAD

Serves 10 to 12

Preparation 25 Minutes
Bake 40 Minutes at 350°F

2 eggs
3/4 cup molasses
3/4 cup brown sugar
3/4 cup oil
2 1/2 cups flour
1 1/2 teaspoons cinnamon
1/2 teaspoon cloves
2 teaspoons ginger
1/2 teaspoon baking powder
2 teaspoons baking soda
1 cup boiling water

1. Add eggs to molasses, sugar, and oil.
2. Sift flour with cinnamon, cloves, ginger, baking powder, and baking soda and add to molasses mixture. Gradually add boiling water, stirring constantly.
3. Pour into greased and floured 9 x 13-inch pan and bake at 350 degrees for 40 minutes.

NOTE:

Serve with sweetened whipped cream or Hot Golden Sauce (see Index). Keeps well in freezer 3 to 4 months. Be sure to wrap it well.

VARIATION:

Use 3/4 cup honey or 1/2 cup sucrose instead of brown sugar, 2/3 cup safflower oil in place of regular oil, wheat flour (or stoneground whole wheat) in place of white flour and double the spices.

Dr. Evelyn Finnell Chandler
Denver, Colorado

CASSAVA CAKE

Serves 16

Preparation 30 Minutes
Bake 40 Minutes at 400°F

3/4 cup grated raw cassava or minute tapioca
2 cups milk
6 tablespoons butter
1 cup sugar
1 egg, beaten
3/4 cup grated coconut
1/2 cup flour
2 1/2 teaspoons baking powder
Dash of salt
1 teaspoon vanilla extract

1. Mix cassava or tapioca with milk and let stand 5 minutes. Stir frequently.
2. Cream butter, sugar, and eggs. Mix in tapioca and coconut and stir thoroughly.
3. Sift flour, baking powder, and salt. Add to batter, stir, then stir in vanilla.
4. Pour batter into 2 greased and floured 8-inch-square pans. Bake 40 minutes at 400 degrees. Serve warm or cold.

Susannah Jordan
Jamestown, Colorado

CHERRY CAKE

Serves 9

Preparation 30 Minutes
Bake 40 Minutes at 350°F

1/2 cup shortening
1 cup sugar
1 egg
1 1/2 cups sifted flour
1 teaspoon baking soda
1/8 teaspoon salt
1 cup sour milk
1 jar (4-ounce) maraschino cherries with juice, chopped
1/2 cup chopped English walnuts
1 ounce semi-sweet chocolate, melted

1. Cream shortening and sugar. Add egg and beat well. Set aside.
2. Sift flour with baking soda and salt.
3. Add sour milk to sugar mixture alternately with sifted ingredients. Stir in cherries and the juice, walnuts, and chocolate.
4. Pour into greased 9-inch square pan and bake at 350 degrees for 35 to 40 minutes.

CANDIED FRUIT CAKE

Serves 30 to 40

Preparation 50 Minutes
Bake 1 1/2 Hours at 275°F

24 ounces dates
1 pound candied pineapple
2 cups sifted flour
2 teaspoons baking powder
1/2 teaspoon salt
4 eggs
1 cup sugar
1 pound candied cherries
7 cups pecan halves

1. Cut dates and pineapple into coarse pieces and set aside.
2. Sift 1 3/4 cups flour, baking powder, and salt.
3. Beat eggs and gradually add sugar and sifted ingredients.
4. Combine fruits and nuts with remaining flour and add to batter in a very large mixing bowl.
5. Pack into a 9-inch tube pan that has been greased and lined with greased paper. Bake in preheated 275-degree oven for 1 1/2 hours. Makes 5 pounds.

NOTE:

May be baked in 2 greased and lined 9 x 5-inch loaf pans. Reduce baking time to 1 hour and 15 minutes.

VARIATION:

Add 1 cup raisins and 2 teaspoons vanilla extract. May also substitute 3 cups brazil nuts for 3 cups pecan halves.

Denise Austin
Austin, Texas

GOLDEN FRUIT CAKE

Yields 2 Loaves

Preparation 2 Hours
Bake 1 1/2 Hours at 275°F
1 Hour at 300°F

1 cup butter
1 1/2 cups sugar
4 eggs
1 teaspoon vanilla extract
Grated peel of 1 lemon
Grated peel of 1 orange
2 1/2 cups flour
1 teaspoon baking powder
2 1/2 cups each of diced prunes, figs, apricots, golden raisins, peaches and walnuts
Rum for soaking cakes

1. Cream butter, add sugar gradually. Beat in eggs one at a time. Add vanilla, lemon and orange peel, flour, and baking powder. Beat until smooth.
2. Mix diced fruit and nuts together. Fold into batter.
3. Grease two 9 x 5-inch loaf pans and line with greased paper. Spoon mixture in and press to eliminate air spaces. Smooth top. Cover pans lightly with greased foil.

4. Bake in 275-degree oven for 1 1/2 hours. Remove foil, increase temperature to 300 degrees and bake one hour longer. Cool in pans 15 minutes before removing.
5. Soak with rum, cover well, and store.

NOTE:

Freezes well. May also use 3 of the smaller loaf pans and adjust baking time to 1 hour at 275 degrees and 45 minutes at 300 degrees.

VANILLA GLAZE

Frosts 1 Layer | Preparation 5 Minutes

1 cup powdered sugar
1/2 teaspoon vanilla extract
1 to 2 tablespoons milk

1. Combine powdered sugar and vanilla. Add milk until of spreading consistency.

NOTE:

Use on Norwegian Christmas Bread (see Index).

LEMON GLAZE

Yields 1/2 Cup | Preparation 5 Minutes

1 cup powdered sugar
Juice of 2 lemons

1. Combine sugar and lemon juice. Stir until smooth. Spoon over hot cake or rolls.

NUTTY COCOA FROSTING

Frosts 1 Sheet Cake | Preparation 10 Minutes

1/2 cup butter or margarine
4 teaspoons cocoa
6 tablespoons milk
3 to 4 cups powdered sugar
1 teaspoon vanilla extract
1 cup chopped pecans or walnuts

1. Combine butter, cocoa, and milk in saucepan and bring to a boil. Remove from heat.
2. Add sugar and vanilla. Beat until thick and stir in nuts.

Okla Barbiero
Denver, Colorado

CHOCOLATE ICING
(Ganache)

Yields 2/3 Cup

Preparation 10 Minutes

6 ounces semi-sweet chocolate
1/2 cup heavy cream
2 tablespoons Cointreau, Grand Marnier, cognac, rum, or Kahlua (optional)

1. Combine chocolate and cream in small saucepan over low heat. Stir until smooth and remove from heat.
2. When chocolate mixture is cool to the touch, it thickens and is ready for use. Add liqueur desired. Stir.

Richard Grausman
U.S. Representative
Le Cordon Bleu de Paris
New York, New York

CHOCOLATE VELVET CREME

Frosts 4 Layers

Preparation 15 Minutes

6 ounces semi-sweet chocolate, melted and cooled
1 cup butter, softened
1 egg yolk
1/2 teaspoon vanilla extract
2 teaspoons brandy or cognac
1 teaspoon instant coffee crystals (optional)

1. Mix all ingredients and beat until creamy. Chill frosting until it is of an easy spreading consistency.

NOTE:

Use plastic blade if using a food processor. Use on Nut Torte (see Index).

Ellen Denton
Piedmont, California

CHOCOLATE-BUTTER CREME FROSTING

Frosts Three 9-inch Layers

Preparation 10 Minutes

3 1/2 cups powdered sugar
2 tablespoons cocoa or to taste
1/3 cup butter
1 teaspoon vanilla extract
1/4 cup milk, warmed

1. Combine ingredients and mix until smooth. Add a few more drops of milk if mixture is too thick to spread easily.

Claramay Trainor
Golden, Colorado

ORANGE-BUTTER CREME FROSTING

Frosts 9 x 13-inch Cake

Preparation 10 Minutes

3 cups powdered sugar
3 tablespoons orange juice concentrate
1 1/2 tablespoons orange rind
1/3 cup butter, softened

1. Blend all ingredients until smooth.

NOTE:

Use on Orange Poppy Seed Cake or Applesauce Cake (see Index).

Sue McMillan
Boulder, Colorado

BROILED TOPPING

Frosts 9 x 13-inch Cake

Preparation 10 Minutes

1 cup brown sugar
1 cup coconut
1/2 cup chopped nuts
1/2 cup evaporated milk
4 teaspoons butter

1. Mix ingredients and cook over medium heat until it just comes to a boil.
2. Spread on hot or cooled cake and place under broiler until browned. Watch carefully to prevent burning.

Ruth Yearns
Boulder, Colorado

BROWN SUGAR FROSTING

Frosts Two 9-inch Layers

Preparation 25 Minutes

1 1/2 cups brown sugar
1/2 cup water
2 egg whites
Pinch of salt
1/8 teaspoon cream of tartar
1 teaspoon vanilla extract

1. Mix brown sugar and water, stir over low heat until sugar has dissolved. Cook without stirring until syrup reaches the soft-crack stage.
2. While syrup is boiling, mix egg whites, salt, and cream of tartar. Beat until they form stiff peaks. Add syrup slowly, beating all the time. Add vanilla and continue beating until thick enough to spread.

NOTE:

Use on any spice cake, chocolate cake, or zucchini cake.

Francis Whaley
Omaha, Nebraska

TEA ROOM WHITE FROSTING

Frosts 3 Layers

Preparation 30 Minutes

1 1/2 cups sugar
1/2 cup water
1 1/2 teaspoons vinegar
1/4 teaspoon salt
3 egg whites
1 teaspoon vanilla extract

1. Mix sugar, water, vinegar, and salt; cook and stir over low heat until sugar dissolves, then cook without stirring until syrup reaches the soft-crack stage.
2. Meanwhile, beat egg whites to form stiff peaks. Add syrup gradually, beating continuously. When all the syrup has been added, add vanilla.
3. Continue beating until mixture forms soft peaks.

Crede Dever
Boulder, Colorado

CREAM CHEESE FROSTING

Frosts Two 9-inch Layers

Preparation 15 Minutes

8 ounces cream cheese
1/2 cup butter or margarine
3 1/2 cups powdered sugar
1 to 2 teaspoons vanilla extract
4 to 5 tablespoons milk

1. Cream together cream cheese and butter. Add powdered sugar, vanilla, and enough milk to make an easy spreading consistency.

VARIATION:

1. Orange Cream Cheese Frosting: substitute orange juice concentrate for milk and add 2 tablespoons grated orange rind. Use 1/2 recipe for Orange Poppy Seed Cake (see Index).
2. Lemon Cream Cheese Frosting: substitute fresh lemon juice for milk and add grated rind of 1 lemon.

NOTE:

Butter may be omitted in any of the above frostings for a lighter frosting.

COOKIES • AND • CANDIES

SCOTCH SHORTBREAD

Yields 16 Cookies

Preparation 15 Minutes
Bake 30 Minutes at 300°F

1 cup butter, softened
1/2 cup sugar
2 cups flour

1. Cream butter and sugar until light. Add flour and mix well.
2. Knead dough with hands until smooth. Do not overwork.
3. Divide dough in half and press evenly into two 9-inch cake pans. Prick with a fork and bake at 300 to 325 degrees for 20 to 35 minutes. Cut each pan into 8 wedges immediately.

NOTE:

Do not substitute margarine. Watch baking time closely, cookies should be barely brown. They burn very quickly. Dough can be rolled to 1/4-inch thickness and cut into desired shapes.

Patt Hanson
Boulder, Colorado

SPICE COOKIES

Keeps for weeks in an airtight container or until family finds them.

Yields 5 Dozen

Preparation 30 Minutes
Bake 15 Minutes at 300°F

3/4 cup butter or margarine
1 cup brown sugar
1/2 cup dark molasses
2 eggs, beaten
3 cups flour
1/2 teaspoon baking soda
1 teaspoon ginger
1/2 teaspoon each cloves, cinnamon, chili powder
1/4 teaspoon salt
1/4 cup water (if needed for soft dough)
Sugar (optional)

1. Cream butter or margarine and sugar. Add molasses and eggs; blend well.
2. Sift together flour, soda, ginger, cloves, cinnamon, chili powder, and salt. Add to creamed mixture and blend well. If dough is too stiff, gradually add water to make workable dough.
3. Form into small balls, flatten (the thinner the better), and place on well-greased cookie sheet. Sprinkle with sugar.
4. Bake at 300 degrees for 15 minutes; remove to rack while warm.

NOTE:

If cookie press is used, be sure batter is very smooth. Use a bar disc to make long strips, bake and cut diagonally.

Hazel W. Olmsted
Boulder, Colorado

PFEFFERNUSSE

Yields 14 Dozen
Refrigerate Overnight

Preparation 45 Minutes
Bake 10 Minutes at 350°F

1 1/2 cups butter or margarine
1 1/2 cups sugar
1/2 cup molasses
1/4 cup brandy
8 drops anise oil
1 teaspoon vanilla extract
5 1/4 cups flour
1 teaspoon baking powder
1/2 teaspoon baking soda
2 teaspoons cinnamon
1/2 teaspoon cloves
1/2 teaspoon black pepper
Powdered sugar

1. Cream butter and gradually beat in sugar. Add molasses, brandy, anise oil, and vanilla.
2. Mix flour with baking powder, soda, cinnamon, cloves, and pepper. Add to butter mixture and mix well.
3. Press dough into waxed paper lined 7 x 12-inch pan. Cover and refrigerate overnight or up to 3 days.
4. Invert pan on board and remove paper. Cut into 8 bars, 1 1/2 inches wide. Slice bars into 1/4-inch wide slices.
5. Put on buttered cookie sheet and bake about 10 minutes at 350 degrees.
6. Remove from pan and dredge in powdered sugar while still hot. Store in airtight container.

NOTE:

Freeze well after they are baked and rolled in sugar. May be made at least 6 weeks ahead. Cookies keep well for over 2 months.

Nancy Cateora
Boulder, Colorado

PECAN OATMEAL THINS

A delicious mistake, the result of reading a recipe without my glasses. The results are better than the original recipe.

Yields 5 Dozen

Preparation 15 to 20 Minutes
Bake 8 to 10 Minutes at 350°F

1 1/2 cups margarine
1/2 cup sugar
1 cup packed brown sugar
1/4 cup water
1 teaspoon vanilla extract
1 cup flour
3 cups quick-cooking oats
1 teaspoon salt
1/2 teaspoon baking soda
8 ounces pecans, finely chopped

1. Beat margarine, both sugars, water, and vanilla until creamy.
2. Add flour, oats, salt, and baking soda. Mix well.

3. Add nuts and drop by rounded teaspoonsful onto ungreased cookie sheet allowing for spreading. Bake at 350 degrees for 8 to 10 minutes until very lightly browned. Remove from pan while still warm.

NOTE:

Bake 6 to 7 minutes if teflon cookie sheet is used.

Helen Goldman
Boulder, Colorado

STANDARD COOKIES

Yields 4 Dozen

Preparation 15 Minutes
Bake 10 Minutes at 325°F

1/2 cup shortening
1/2 cup brown sugar
1/2 cup white sugar
2 eggs
1/2 cup sour milk
1/2 teaspoon baking soda
1/2 teaspoon salt
1 teaspoon vanilla extract
2 cups flour
1 cup chopped nuts

1. Cream shortening and sugars. Add eggs and mix well.
2. Add sour milk, soda, salt, and vanilla, mix well. Add flour and blend thoroughly. Add nuts. (Dough should be very stiff if you want a cake-like cookie. Keep adding flour until dough is so stiff it is hard to stir. Exact amount varies.)
3. Drop by teaspoonful on ungreased cookie sheet or roll into balls and place on sheet. Bake at 325 degrees for approximately 10 minutes. (Can be tested with toothpick until exact time is determined.)

VARIATION:

1. Raisins, chocolate chips, candied fruits, dates, or figs may be substituted for nuts, or in combination with nuts. Nuts or candied fruit can be used for decoration before baking to make appropriate for special seasons.
2. For chocolate cookies, add 2 squares chocolate or 1/2 cup cocoa and frost with Chocolate-Butter Creme Frosting (see Index) while cookies are still warm.
3. For lemon cookies, substitute lemon flavoring for vanilla, and frost with Lemon Cream Cheese Frosting (see Index).
4. For spice cookies, add 1/2 cup applesauce; keeps fresh for a long time.

Mary Ormsbee
Boulder, Colorado

MOM'S COOKIES

Yields 5 Dozen

Preparation 20 Minutes
Bake 15 Minutes at 350°F

2 eggs, separated
1 teaspoon vanilla extract
1 1/4 cups sugar
2 tablespoons ice water
10 tablespoons melted shortening, cooled
3 1/2 cups flour, sifted
2 teaspoons baking powder
Pinch of salt
1 tablespoon cinnamon

1. Beat egg yolks, add vanilla, 1 cup sugar, ice water, then add slightly beaten egg whites and melted shortening.
2. Mix flour, baking powder, and salt, and gradually add to creamed mixture. Mix well. Knead dough by hand 10 minutes or for 5 minutes with a dough hook. Add additional flour if dough is too soft to handle.
3. Roll out on floured board to 1/8-inch thickness. Cut with cookie cutter. Combine remaining 1/4 cup sugar and cinnamon and sprinkle on cookies.
4. Bake at 350 degrees for 15 minutes or until golden brown. Remove pan and let cool.

NOTE:

Use a diamond cookie cutter for very little waste. Keeps well for weeks in tightly covered cookie jar.

Sadye Peckman
Los Angeles, California

OATMEAL COOKIES

A national prize-winning recipe that pleased many a soldier during World War I and II and continues to please their children and grandchildren.

Yields 6 to 7 Dozen

Preparation 25 Minutes
Bake 15 Minutes at 325°F

1 cup shortening
2 cups sugar (or little less, to taste)
1 egg
3 cups flour
3 teaspoons baking powder
1 cup sour milk
2 teaspoons vanilla extract or 1 teaspoon cinnamon plus 1 teaspoon nutmeg
1 cup raisins
3 cups oats, coarsely ground

1. Cream shortening; add sugar, then egg. Beat well.
2. Sift flour and baking powder and add alternately to creamed mixture with milk.

3. Add vanilla or spices and raisins, then ground oats. Mixture should be rather soft. Drop by teaspoonful on greased cookie sheets.
4. Bake at 325 degrees about 15 minutes for soft cookies or a few minutes longer for crisper ones. Let cool.

NOTE:

A food processor or blender can be used to grind oats.

Ethel R. Zeigler
Boulder, Colorado

PEANUT BUTTER COOKIES

Yields 3 Dozen

Preparation 15 Minutes
Bake 15 Minutes at 350°F

1 cup butter
1 cup sugar
1 cup packed brown sugar
2 eggs, well beaten
1 teaspoon vanilla extract
1/2 teaspoon salt
1 cup chunky peanut butter
2 cups flour
1 teaspoon baking soda

1. Cream butter, add sugars, eggs, vanilla, salt, and peanut butter.
2. Stir in flour and soda and mix well.
3. Form into walnut-sized balls, place on greased cookie sheet, and press down with floured fork.
4. Bake at 350 degrees for 15 minutes.

Phyllis Cateora
Boulder, Colorado

POTATO CHIP COOKIES

Yields 4 to 5 Dozen

Preparation 10 Minutes
Bake 10 Minutes at 350°F

1 cup packed brown sugar
1 cup white sugar
1/2 cup shortening
1/2 cup margarine
2 eggs, beaten
2 cups flour
1 teaspoon baking soda
1/4 teaspoon salt
2 cups crushed potato chips
1 cup chopped nuts

1. Cream sugars, shortening, and margarine. Add eggs, flour, soda, and salt. Mix well.
2. Blend in potato chips and nuts.
3. Roll dough into balls the size of walnuts. Place on ungreased cookie sheets and flatten.
4. Bake 10 minutes at 350 degrees.

Shirley Brown
Boulder, Colorado

MEXICAN MERINGUES

Yields 6 Dozen

Preparation 15 Minutes
Bake 20 to 25 Minutes at 250°F

5 egg whites
3 cups brown sugar
1 1/4 cups flour
2 teaspoons baking powder
1 teaspoon vanilla extract
3 cups whole pecans

1. Beat egg whites and brown sugar on highest speed for 5 minutes.
2. Fold in flour, baking powder, and vanilla, then stir in pecans.
3. Drop from teaspoon onto well-greased cookie sheet. Bake 20 to 25 minutes at 250 degrees. Cookies will be shiny and creamy white. Do not let them get brown.

NOTE:

Cookies keep well and may be frozen.

Margery Long
Boulder, Colorado

DATE ROCKS

Yields 2 1/2 Dozen

Preparation 35 Minutes
Bake 25 to 30 Minutes at 350°F

3 eggs
1 cup sugar
1 teaspoon vanilla extract
1 cup flour
2 teaspoons baking powder
Dash of salt
1 cup coarsely chopped walnuts
1 cup coarsely chopped dates
Powdered sugar

1. Separate eggs; beat whites to stiff peaks.
2. Cream egg yolks, sugar, and vanilla.
3. By hand fold in flour, baking powder, salt, nuts, and dates. Batter should be very, very stiff.
4. Fold in egg whites and spread evenly in greased 8 x 8-inch pan. Press firmly.
5. Bake for 25 to 30 minutes at 350 degrees. Cut, while warm, into 1-inch squares. In a small plastic bag, shake cookies a few at a time in a small amount of powdered sugar.

NOTE:

Recipe doubles very well. Bake double batch in 9 x 13-inch greased pan approximately 45 minutes. This recipe does *not* contain shortening.

Clara Inlow
Avalon, California

STANDING-OVATION COOKIES

So named because my husband received a standing ovation when he took these to a meeting.

Yields 3 Dozen

Preparation 30 Minutes
Bake 20 Minutes at 375°F

8 ounces cream cheese, softened
1 cup butter (not margarine)
2 cups flour
12 ounces jam or jelly
1/2 cup sugar
1 tablespoon cinnamon
Powdered sugar

1. Mix cream cheese and butter with flour.
2. Divide dough in half and roll each into 1/8-inch thick square between sheets of waxed paper.
3. Cut each large square into 1 1/2-inch squares and dot each with jam or sprinkle with sugar and cinnamon mixed.
4. Fold opposite corners to center and overlap tips. Carefully lift each cookie onto ungreased baking sheet. Bake 20 minutes at 375 degrees.
5. Sprinkle liberally with powdered sugar.

Peg English
Costa Mesa, California

FUDGE MELTAWAYS
(unbaked cookies)

Yields 4 Dozen

Preparation 45 Minutes

3/4 cup butter or margarine
2 1/2 ounces unsweetened baking chocolate
1/4 cup sugar
2 cups graham cracker crumbs
1 cup coconut
1/2 cup chopped nuts
2 teaspoons vanilla extract
1 egg, beaten
2 cups powdered sugar
1 tablespoon milk or half-and-half

1. In large saucepan, melt 1/2 cup butter and 1 ounce chocolate. Stir in granulated sugar, graham cracker crumbs, coconut, nuts, 1 teaspoon vanilla, and egg.
2. Press into 9 x 11-inch pan and chill while preparing next layer.
3. Cream remaining 1/4 cup butter with powdered sugar, 1 teaspoon vanilla, and milk. Spread smoothly over chilled bottom layer.
4. Melt remaining 1 1/2 ounces chocolate, cool slightly and drizzle over second layer. Refrigerate until firm. Cut into small squares.

Priscilla Peale
Santa Barbara, California

RAGGEDY ANN COOKIES

Yields 5 Dozen

Preparation 15 Minutes
Bake 10 to 12 Minutes at 350°F

1 cup butter or margarine
1 cup packed brown sugar
1 egg
1 teaspoon maple flavoring
2 1/4 cups flour
1/2 teaspoon salt
1/2 teaspoon baking powder
1/2 teaspoon cinnamon
1 cup shredded coconut
1 cup finely chopped nuts (optional)

1. Cream butter, brown sugar, egg, and flavoring until fluffy.
2. Add flour, baking powder, salt, and cinnamon. Mix well. Stir in coconut and nuts, if desired.
3. Drop by teaspoonsful 2 inches apart on greased cookie sheet. Butter bottom of a glass, dip into granulated sugar, and press cookie flat.
4. Bake at 350 degrees 10 to 12 minutes. Cool on rack.

Becky Spiliotis
Orlando, Florida

ENGLISH TOFFEE BARS

Yields 2 Dozen

Preparation 40 Minutes
Bake 35 to 40 Minutes at 300°F

1 cup butter
1 cup sugar
1 egg, separated
2 cups flour
1/2 cup ground pecans
1 teaspoon vanilla extract
1/2 cup ground vanilla wafers

1. Cream butter and sugar and add egg yolk. Mix well.
2. Add flour, pecans, and vanilla. Mix to form stiff batter.
3. Press into 10 x 15-inch greased baking pan. Spread with beaten egg white and sprinkle with vanilla wafers. Press into dough.
4. Bake at 300 degrees for 35 to 40 minutes. Cool 10 minutes and cut in squares.

NOTE:

Stores well in plastic bag in refrigerator for several days.

Katherine Morton
Denver, Colorado

VARIATION:

1. Omit vanilla and add 4 teaspoons cinnamon and 1 teaspoon nutmeg to batter. After pressing dough in pan, brush top with unbeaten egg white. Sprinkle on 1 cup chopped nuts and press into dough. Bake as above. Cut while still hot.

2. Add 1/4 teaspoon salt to batter. Bake as above omitting egg white and crumb-nut topping. When cookies are removed from oven, place 3 to 4 bars (1 3/4 ounces each) milk chocolate, broken, on top and let stand until soft. Spread evenly to cover and sprinkle with 1/2 cup chopped nuts. Cut while warm.

Joanne Steele
Boulder, Colorado

BROWN SUGAR BROWNIES

Yields 3 Dozen

Preparation 15 Minutes
Bake 20 to 30 Minutes at 325°F

1 pound brown sugar
1/2 cup butter or margarine
2 eggs
1/4 cup water
1 teaspoon vanilla extract
2 1/4 cups flour
1/4 teaspoon salt
1/2 teaspoon baking powder
1/2 cup chopped nuts (optional)

1. Cream sugar and butter and add eggs, water, and vanilla. Beat well.
2. Sift flour, salt, and baking powder. Add to creamed mixture then fold in nuts.
3. Spread in well-greased 10 x 15-inch jelly roll pan. Bake at 325 degrees for 20 to 30 minutes until edges are light brown. Cut into squares while still warm.

Hazel W. Olmsted
Boulder, Colorado

GRASMERE GINGERBREAD BARS

Yields 2 Dozen

Preparation 10 to 15 Minutes
Bake 10 to 12 Minutes at 350°F

1/2 cup butter
1 cup flour
1/3 cup brown sugar, sifted
1/4 teaspoon baking powder
1/2 teaspoon powdered ginger
1/8 teaspoon salt
3 tablespoons chopped candied ginger
Powdered sugar

1. Cream butter and flour.
2. Sift sugar, baking powder, powdered ginger, and salt. Stir in candied ginger.
3. Combine with creamed mixture. (Mix with hands if necessary.)
4. Press into 8 x 8-inch baking pan to 1/8-inch thickness. Bake for 10 to 12 minutes at 350 degrees.
5. Cut into bars while hot and dust with powdered sugar. Cool in pan.

Dorothea Eldridge
Shawnee-Mission, Kansas

RAISIN SQUARES
(Fly Cemetery)

Yields 3 Dozen

Preparation 45 Minutes
Bake 30 to 40 Minutes at 400°F

1 recipe Val's Pie Crust (see Index)
1 1/2 pounds raisins
Water to cover
1 1/2 teaspoons cornstarch
Powdered sugar (optional)

1. In medium saucepan, just cover raisins with water. Bring to a boil and simmer gently 5 minutes.
2. Mix cornstarch with enough water to form a paste. Stir into raisins and cook just until clear. Remove from heat and cool.
3. Roll out half the pie crust dough to fit a 10 x 15-inch jelly-roll pan. Spread raisins to within 1 1/2 inches of crust edge. Roll out remaining dough and cover raisins. Press edges together. Slash top in several places to vent.
4. Bake 30 to 40 minutes at 400 degrees. Cut into 2-inch squares while still warm. Top with powdered sugar if desired.

NOTE:

This recipe does not contain sugar. Without the powdered sugar topping it is an excellent recipe for sugar restricted diets.

Peg Fulton
Boulder, Colorado

VARIATION:

Add 1/2 lemon, thinly sliced, to raisins before they are cooked. Remove slices before spreading on dough. One and one-half cups chopped nuts can also be added to cooked raisins. Other dried fruits can be used in combination with raisins for a delightful variety.

ST. ALBAN'S LEMON SQUARES

Yields 2 Dozen

Preparation 20 Minutes
Bake 45 Minutes at 350°F

2 cups plus 6 tablespoons flour
1 cup butter
1/2 cup powdered sugar
Pinch of salt
4 eggs
1 1/2 cups granulated sugar
2 1/2 tablespoons lemon rind
1/2 cup plus 1 tablespoon lemon juice

1. Mix 2 cups flour, butter, powdered sugar, and salt thoroughly. Press into 9 x 13-inch baking dish and bake 20 minutes at 350 degrees. Do not overcook.
2. Beat eggs with granulated sugar and 6 tablespoons flour, add lemon rind and juice and pour over hot baked crust.

3. Return to oven and continue baking for 25 minutes. Cut when cool.

NOTE:

Food processor instructions: mix 2 cups flour, butter, powdered sugar, and salt in bowl fitted with metal blade. Process 5 to 7 seconds. Proceed as above. Process remaining ingredients 10 seconds.

Suzanne Taylor
Boulder, Colorado

TASTY TEA BARS

Yields 4 Dozen

Preparation 20 Minutes
Bake 20 to 25 Minutes at 350°F

1 cup butter or margarine
2 cups brown sugar
1/2 teaspoon salt
2 teaspoons baking powder
4 cups quick-cooking oats

1. In saucepan, combine butter and sugar and cook, stirring until butter melts.
2. Stir in salt and baking powder. Add oats and mix well. Pour into 9 x 13-inch baking pan. Bake 20 to 25 minutes at 350 degrees. Cut while warm.

Brad Goeldner
Boulder, Colorado

CHRISTMAS CAKE COOKIES

Yields 12 Dozen

Preparation 30 Minutes
Bake 10 Minutes at 400°F

2 1/2 cups flour
1 teaspoon salt
1 teaspoon cinnamon
1 cup butter, softened
1 1/2 cups sugar
2 eggs
2 pounds dates, chopped
1/2 pound candied cherries, quartered
1/2 pound candied pineapple, slivered
1/2 pound almonds, chopped
1/2 pound Brazil nuts, chopped
1/3 to 1/2 cup bourbon

1. Sift flour, salt, and cinnamon. Set aside.
2. Beat butter until creamy, add sugar and mix. Beat in eggs then flour mixture.
3. Stir in fruit, nuts, and bourbon.
4. Drop batter by teaspoonsful onto cookie sheet. Bake at 400 degrees for 10 minutes. Be careful not to overbake.

Sara McNice
Boulder, Colorado

LAYERED FUDGE BARS

Yields 3 Dozen

Preparation 20 Minutes
Bake 25 Minutes at 350°F

1 cup shortening
2 cups brown sugar
2 eggs
3 teaspoons vanilla extract
1 1/2 cups flour
1 teaspoon baking soda
1 1/2 teaspoons salt
4 cups quick-cooking oats
2 cups chopped nuts
2 tablespoons butter
12 ounces chocolate chips
1 can (14-ounce) condensed milk

1. Cream shortening until fluffy; add sugar and beat thoroughly. Add eggs and 1 teaspoon vanilla; beat well.
2. Sift flour, baking soda, and 1 teaspoon salt. Add to mixture and mix well.
3. Stir in oats and 1 cup nuts. Set aside one cup dough.
4. Press remaining dough into greased 9 x 13-inch pan.
5. In saucepan, melt butter and chips, then add 1/2 teaspoon salt and milk. Stir but do not cook. Add remaining 1 cup nuts and 2 teaspoons vanilla.
6. Spread mixture over dough in pan. Crumble the 1 cup reserved dough over chocolate and bake at 350 degrees for 25 minutes or until golden brown. Cool before cutting.

Millie Anderson
Boulder, Colorado

IOWA BROWNIES

Yields 3 Dozen

Preparation 20 Minutes
Bake 25 Minutes at 350°F

1 cup butter or margarine
2 1/2 cups sugar
1 can (16-ounce) chocolate syrup
4 eggs
1 cup flour
1 cup chopped nuts (optional)
1/3 cup evaporated milk
1/2 cup chocolate chips

1. Cream 1/2 cup butter and 1 cup sugar until fluffy. Add chocolate syrup and eggs, one at a time, beating well after each addition.
2. Add flour gradually, blend well and add nuts.
3. Pour into greased 10 x 15-inch jelly-roll pan. Bake at 350 degrees for 25 minutes. *Do not overbake.*
4. In saucepan, combine remaining 1/2 cup butter, 1 1/2 cups sugar, and milk. Bring to boil and boil 1 minute. Add chocolate chips and beat until melted. Frost brownies.

Cicely Kane
Boulder, Colorado

GERMAN BAR COOKIES
(*Duelscher Geback*)

Yields 1 1/2 Dozen

Preparation 25 Minutes
Bake 1 Hour at 325°F

1 cup butter or margarine
1 cup sugar
2 eggs yolks
2 cups flour
1 cup chopped nuts
1/2 cup strawberry jam

1. Cream butter or margarine until soft. Gradually add sugar, creaming until light and fluffy.
2. Add egg yolks and blend well. Add flour gradually and mix thoroughly.
3. Fold in nuts and spoon 1/2 mixture into greased 8 x 8-inch pan. Pat evenly to edges.
4. Spread jam over top. Pat remaining dough somewhat flat and lay over jam. Edges need not meet; dough will spread some while baking.
5. Bake 1 hour at 325 degrees.

NOTE:

Vary the jam for a variety of flavors to suit your tastes.

Mildred Barrick
Boulder, Colorado

OATMEAL CARAMEL BARS

Yields 2 Dozen
Chill 2 Hours

Preparation 30 Minutes
Bake 30 Minutes at 350°F

32 caramel candy squares
5 tablespoons heavy cream
1 cup flour
1 cup quick oats
3/4 cup brown sugar
1/2 teaspoon baking soda
1/4 teaspoon salt
3/4 cup butter, melted
12 ounces chocolate chips
1/2 cup chopped pecans

1. In top of double boiler, melt caramels in cream.
2. Meanwhile, combine flour, oats, brown sugar, baking soda, salt, and butter. Press 3/4 of mixture into a well-greased 11x7-inch baking pan and bake 10 minutes at 350 degrees.
3. Sprinkle chocolate chips and pecans over baked crumb mixture and pour caramel mixture over the top.
4. Sprinkle with remaining crumbs and bake for 20 minutes at 350 degrees. Chill 2 hours before cutting into small bars.

Mikki Matheson
Boulder, Colorado

ALMOND ROCA

Yields 1 1/2 Pounds | Preparation 20 Minutes

1 cup finely chopped almonds, toasted
1 chocolate candy bar (16-ounce), chopped
1 cup butter
1 cup brown sugar

1. Sprinkle 1/2 cup almonds evenly on bottom of buttered 8 x 8-inch pan. Add half the candy bar pieces.
2. Cook butter and sugar 12 minutes from time pan is placed on medium-high heat, stirring constantly.
3. Pour evenly over candy bar and nuts. Then sprinkle on remaining candy bar pieces, and top with remaining nuts. Refrigerate.

NOTE:

Try any type of toasted nuts to suit your taste.

Becky Spiliotis
Orlando, Florida

CHOCOLATE MINTS

Yields 8 Dozen | Preparation 10 Minutes
Bake 20 Minutes at 150°F

4 ounces unsweetened chocolate
8 ounces semi-sweet chocolate chips
24 ounces vanilla almond bark
1 teaspoon peppermint extract

1. Preheat oven to 200 degrees and combine chocolate, chocolate chips, almond bark, and extract in 9 x 13-inch pan.
2. Place pan in oven and reduce heat to 150 degrees. Bake 20 minutes. Remove, stir to mix well, and drop by the half teaspoonful on waxed paper. Cool to set.

Mikki Matheson
Boulder, Colorado

CAROB FUDGE

Yields 1 Pound | Preparation 15 Minutes

1/2 cup honey
1/2 cup peanut butter
1/2 cup carob powder
1/2 cup shelled sunflower seeds
1/4 cup chopped nuts
1/4 cup sesame seeds, toasted
1/4 cup unsweetened flaked coconut
1/4 cup raisins

1. In large saucepan, heat honey and peanut butter, stirring constantly, just until smooth.
2. Remove from heat and stir in carob powder. Mix well.

3. Add sunflower seeds, nuts, sesame seeds, coconut, and raisins.
4. Press into 8-inch-square pan. Store in refrigerator.

Mitzi Baier
Boulder, Colorado

PEANUT HONEYCOMB

Yields 2 Pounds — Preparation 30 Minutes

2 tablespoons butter
2 cups sugar
1/2 cup light corn syrup
1/2 cup water
2 cups raw Spanish peanuts
2 teaspoons baking soda

1. Butter a large baking sheet. Set aside.
2. Combine sugar, syrup, and water in heavy-bottomed pan. Cook over medium heat until mixture boils.
3. Add peanuts and continue cooking until syrup turns brown and peanuts look roasted. Watch carefully as syrup begins to brown. Stir gently from sides and bottom of pan to prevent burning.
4. Remove candy from heat, stir in soda, and quickly pour onto cookie sheet. Do not spread or pull. Let cool completely before breaking into pieces.

Tom Branigan
Arlington, Virginia

BARCLAY LOAF

Yields 1 Large Loaf — Preparation 1 1/2 Hours

4 cups sugar
2 cups heavy cream
1 cup dark corn syrup
2 teaspoons vanilla extract
Pinch of salt
Chopped nuts
Candied fruit
2 1/2 tablespoons cocoa

1. Combine sugar, cream, and corn syrup in large pan and bring to a boil over medium heat. Remove and reserve 5 tablespoons sugar mixture and keep warm. Cook remaining mixture to soft ball stage.
2. Add vanilla and salt and cool slightly. Beat with mixer until mixture begins to thicken.
3. Finish beating by hand, adding desired amount of nuts and fruits, until mixture begins to firm up. Pour into well-buttered 9 x 5-inch loaf pan.
4. Mix cocoa with the reserved syrup and continue to keep warm. When loaf can be removed from pan, place on rack and pour on warm coating.

Verle Plumb
Boulder, Colorado

DIVINITY

Yields 4 Dozen — Preparation 40 Minutes

- 2 1/2 cups sugar
- 3/4 cup light corn syrup
- 1/4 cup hot water
- 2 eggs whites
- Pinch of salt
- 1 teaspoon vanilla extract
- 1 cup chopped nuts

1. Over medium heat, cook sugar, corn syrup, and hot water to soft-crack stage. Do not stir.
2. While syrup cooks, beat egg whites and salt to stiff peaks.
3. When syrup reaches soft-crack stage, slowly pour half of it over stiff whites while continuing to beat at low speed.
4. Return remaining syrup to heat and continue cooking until hard-ball stage. Meanwhile, continue beating egg white-syrup mixture at low speed.
5. When remaining syrup is ready, slowly add to egg whites while continuing to beat. Add vanilla.
6. Increase beating speed to high and beat until mixture begins to cool slightly or to lose its gloss. Quickly fold in nuts and drop by the spoonful onto waxed paper.

VARIATION:

Drained and dried maraschino cherries may be added with or instead of nuts.

Grace Baker
San Gabriel, California

PEANUT BUTTER SQUARES

Yields 4 Dozen — Preparation 30 Minutes

- 1 cup crunchy peanut butter
- 1 cup margarine
- 2 cups powdered sugar
- 2 cups graham cracker crumbs
- 1 tablespoon creamy peanut butter
- 1 cup semi-sweet chocolate chips

1. Combine crunchy peanut butter and margarine in saucepan and melt over medium heat.
2. Add sugar and graham cracker crumbs. Mix thoroughly.
3. Press into 9 x 13-inch pan and refrigerate while making icing.
4. In a small saucepan, melt creamy peanut butter and chocolate chips and stir until smooth.
5. While still warm, spread over peanut butter-crumb mixture. Return to refrigerator until set.

Jackie Moorhead
Denver, Colorado

DESSERTS
•
AND
•
DESSERT SAUCES

VANILLA ICE CREAM

Yields 3 Quarts
Chill 1 Hour

Preparation 30 Minutes
Freeze 45 to 55 Minutes

2 1/2 cups sugar
Pinch of salt
2 tablespoons flour
4 eggs, beaten
4 cups milk
2 to 3 tablespoons vanilla extract
4 cups heavy cream
Half-and-half, approximately 1 1/2 cups

1. Mix sugar, salt, and flour
2. Combine eggs and milk in 3-quart saucepan and beat in sugar-flour mixture. Cook over medium heat, stirring constantly, until scalded but *not* boiling. Cool to room temperature and refrigerate until chilled.
3. Pour into container of large ice cream maker and stir in vanilla, heavy cream, and enough additional half-and-half to bring quantity to recommended level.
4. Freeze according to directions for your ice cream maker.

VARIATION:

For mint chocolate chip ice cream, decrease vanilla to 1 tablespoon, add 2 teaspoons peppermint extract and 4 ounces coarsely shaved semi-sweet or milk chocolate. For plain chocolate chip, omit peppermint extract. For chocolate ice cream, add 4 ounces unsweetened baking chocolate, melted, to custard mixture. Taste for sweetness and add additional sugar if necessary. Cook, stirring, just to melt additional sugar. Proceed as above.

Patt Hanson
Boulder, Colorado

LEMON SHERBET

Serves 10 to 12

Preparation 5 Minutes
Freeze 2 to 3 Hours

1 quart heavy cream, *or* 1 pint each heavy cream and half-and-half
1 1/2 cups sugar
1/2 cup fresh lemon juice
Grated lemon rind

1. Put all ingredients in mixer. Beat until thickened and pour in aluminum bread pan.
2. Freeze until mixture is half frozen. Return to mixer and beat until mushy. Return to pan and freeze until firm.

Harriet P. Steven
Eau Claire, Wisconsin

FRUIT ICE

Serves 10
Chill 1 Hour

Preparation 30 Minutes
Freeze 1 1/2 to 2 Hours

3 cups fruit puree
2 1/2 cups sugar
2 cups water
1 to 3 lemons

1. Prepare fruit puree and chill.
2. Boil sugar and water until clear and syrupy. Chill.
3. Blend syrup and chilled fruit puree, adding lemon juice to taste. Pour into ice cream freezer and freeze according to manufacturer's directions or pour into a container and freeze, stirring every 45 minutes to 1 hour until slushy.

NOTE:

Ices are best when slushy. For later use, pack in tight-sealing freezer containers and freeze. Keeps very well for several weeks. Let stand at room temperature about 20 minutes before serving.

VARIATION:

Fruit ices may be made of most fruits. Fruit should be ripe and fresh. Adjust sweetness by adding lemon juice to taste. Strawberries, pineapple, apricots, peaches, sweet cherries, lemons, and oranges all give delightful results.

FROZEN STRAWBERRY DESSERT

Serves 12 to 14
Freeze 6 Hours

Preparation 20 Minutes
Bake 20 Minutes at 350°F

1 cup flour
1/4 cup brown sugar
1/2 cup nuts, chopped
1/2 cup butter, melted
1 package (10-ounce) frozen strawberries, partially thawed
2 egg whites
2/3 cup sugar
2 tablespoons lemon juice
1 cup heavy cream, whipped

1. Combine flour, brown sugar, nuts, and butter in 9 x 13-inch baking pan. Stir to mix well. Bake at 350 degrees for 20 minutes. Stir with a fork once during baking. Cool completely.
2. In large bowl of electric mixer, combine strawberries, egg whites, sugar, and lemon juice. Beat until creamy and stiff peaks form, 15 minutes or longer. Fold in whipped cream.
3. Remove 1/3 of crumbs from baking dish and set aside. Spread remaining crumbs evenly and pour in strawberry mixture. Top with reserved crumbs. Freeze 6 hours.

VARIATION:

Use raspberries instead of strawberries. Keeps well frozen up to 1 week if well wrapped. For a lighter dessert, omit heavy cream.

Patt Hanson
Boulder, Colorado

CRANBERRY REFRIGERATOR CAKE

Serves 9 to 12

Preparation 20 Minutes
Chill Overnight

2 cups fresh cranberries, chopped
1 large banana, diced
2/3 cup sugar
2 cups crushed vanilla wafers
1/2 cup butter or margarine
1 cup powdered sugar
2 eggs
1/2 cup chopped nuts
1 cup heavy cream

1. Mix cranberries, banana, and sugar. Set aside.
2. Spread 1 cup cookie crumbs in bottom of 8 x 8-inch pan.
3. Cream butter and powdered sugar, then add eggs. Beat well and spread over crumbs.
4. Spread cranberry-banana mixture over creamed mixture and sprinkle on chopped nuts.
5. Whip cream until it peaks and spread on top. Add remaining cookie crumbs and chill at least 4 hours or overnight before serving.

Lillian Case
Boulder, Colorado

DOTTIE'S PUMPKIN PLEASER DESSERT

Serves 16 to 20
Refrigerate Overnight

Preparation 20 Minutes
Bake 50 to 60 Minutes at 350°F

1 can (30-ounce) pumpkin pie mix
1 can (13-ounce) evaporated milk
4 eggs, lightly beaten
1 box yellow cake mix
1/2 cup butter or margarine, melted
1/2 to 1 cup chopped nuts

1. Combine pumpkin, milk, and eggs. Mix well and pour into greased and floured 9 x 13-inch baking pan.
2. Sprinkle cake mix evenly over pumpkin, then drizzle butter evenly over cake mix. Sprinkle on nuts.
3. Bake 50 to 60 minutes at 350 degrees. Chill overnight.

NOTE:

This cake does not freeze well.

A Friend of the Library
Boulder, Colorado

CHOCOLATE MINT FREEZE

Serves 10 to 12
Soak Overnight

Preparation 20 Minutes
Freeze 3 Hours

1 package (10-ounce) after-dinner mints (not chocolate coated)
2 cups heavy cream
1 package (8 1/2-ounce) plain chocolate wafers, crushed
4 tablespoons butter or margarine, melted
1 cup finely chopped walnuts or pecans

1. Dissolve mints in cream overnight.
2. Combine wafer crumbs and butter. Reserve 1/2 cup and press remaining on bottom of 9 x 13-inch pan.
3. Whip cream and mints to stiff peaks and fold in nuts. Spread over cookie layer and sprinkle reserved crumbs on top.
4. Freeze several hours. Serve frozen.

NOTE:

Keeps several days in freezer if well covered.

Mary Gerlitz-Garnett
Boulder, Colorado

ANGEL FOOD MOLD

Serves 8 to 10

Preparation 1 Hour
Chill 2 1/2 Hours

1 1/2 envelopes gelatin
2 1/2 cups milk
2 egg yolks
1 cup sugar
1 teaspoon vanilla extract
2 beaten egg whites
2 1/2 cups heavy cream
1 12-ounce angel food loaf cake or 1/2 homemade, diced
Strawberry halves

1. Soak gelatin in 1/2 cup cold milk. Beat egg yolks and add 2 cups milk and sugar, cooking in double boiler until mixture lightly coats spoon. Stir in softened gelatin until dissolved. Chill.
2. Into chilled gelatin mixture, add vanilla and fold in egg whites and 1 1/2 cups heavy cream whipped quite stiff. Fold in bits of angel cake and pour mixture in mold, chilling until set.
3. Unmold and frost with remaining 1 cup heavy cream beaten stiff and sweetened to taste. Decorate with strawberry halves.

NOTE:

Mold may be made a day ahead of serving. Frost and decorate several hours before serving.

Ellie Scott
Dallas, Texas

CHOCOLATE-TOFFEE ANGEL CAKE

Serves 8 to 12

Preparation 30 Minutes
Refrigerate 2 Hours

2 cups heavy cream
1 can (5 1/2-ounce) chocolate syrup
1/2 teaspoon vanilla extract
12-ounce angel food loaf cake
1 pound English toffee or Almond Brickle Chips and grated chocolate

1. Whip cream until it starts to thicken, then gradually add chocolate syrup and vanilla, beating until thick.
2. Cut cake into four lengthwise layers. Spread each layer with some chocolate cream, saving about half to cover top and sides.
3. Break toffee into small pieces and sprinkle over each layer, reserving some for top.
4. Place layers on top of each other and frost with remaining chocolate cream. Sprinkle top of cake with reserved toffee. Refrigerate at least 2 hours.

Marcia Rothstein
Beverly Hills, California

10-MINUTE CHOCOLATE MOUSSE

Serves 6

Preparation 10 Minutes

3/4 cup sugar
1/3 cup water
4 ounces unsweetened chocolate
4 egg yolks
2 tablespoons cognac (optional)
2 egg whites
1/2 cup heavy cream, whipped

1. Combine sugar and water and bring to boil. Boil until clear and syrupy.
2. Melt chocolate over hot water.
3. Scrape melted chocolate into food processor container with steel blade in place. Add hot syrup to chocolate with machine running.
4. Add egg yolks one at a time, then cognac. Turn off machine and cool mixture to room temperature.
5. Whip egg whites until stiff but not dry. Fold egg whites and whipped cream into chocolate mixture. Pour into serving dishes and chill.

VARIATION:

Add 1 tablespoon instant expresso coffee to water for syrup. Proceed as above.

Nancy Cateora
Boulder, Colorado

MOTHER'S CHOCOLATE BREAD PUDDING

Serves 12

Preparation 25 Minutes
Bake 1 Hour at 300°F

4 cups milk
2 ounces unsweetened baking chocolate
2/3 cup sugar
1/4 teaspoon salt
2 cups stale bread pieces
2 eggs
1 teaspoon vanilla extract

1. Heat milk, chocolate, sugar, salt, and bread in double boiler until scalding.
2. Beat eggs in greased baking dish. Pour a little of scalded mixture over eggs and stir. Pour in remainder and stir in vanilla.
3. Bake 1 hour in 300-degree oven. Cool completely before serving.

Anne H. Riley
Boulder, Colorado

HEAVENLY CHOCOLATE TORTE

Serves 10 to 12
Refrigerate Overnight

Preparation 45 Minutes
Bake 35 to 45 Minutes at 300°F

4 extra-large egg whites (room temperature)
1/2 teaspoon almond extract
1/4 teaspoon salt
1 3/4 cups packed brown sugar
3/4 cup finely chopped pecans
6 ounces semi-sweet chocolate chips
8 ounces cream cheese
1 tablespoon milk
1 teaspoon vanilla extract
Dash of salt
1 cup heavy cream, whipped

1. Beat egg whites with almond extract and salt until soft mounds form. Gradually beat in 1 cup sugar. Continue beating until stiff peaks form. Fold in nuts.
2. Spread on four 8-inch brown paper circles, ungreased.
3. Carefully put on cookie sheets and bake at 300 degrees for 35 minutes or until firm and not sticky when touched with dry finger. Cool completely.
4. Melt chocolate and cool. Beat cream cheese with milk and vanilla until smooth. Gradually add remaining sugar and salt.
5. Fold cooled chocolate into cream cheese mixture, add vanilla, then carefully fold in whipped cream. Spread filling between layers of meringue, on top and sides. Refrigerate overnight.

NOTE:

This is very rich so serve small pieces. Keeps well several days in refrigerator.

Nancy Cateora
Boulder, Colorado

PAVLOVA

Serves 6

Preparation 20 Minutes
Bake 1 1/2 Hours at 300°F

4 extra-large egg whites
1 cup sugar
1 tablespoon baking powder
1 teaspoon vanilla extract
2 teaspoons vinegar
1 tablespoon water
1 cup heavy cream
1/4 cup powdered sugar
Sliced fruit

1. Beat egg whites until stiff and frothy; add sugar gradually and beat until sugar has dissolved. Fold in baking powder, vanilla, vinegar, and water.
2. Line cookie sheet with brown paper (a paper sack will do). Mark with a 9-inch circle and wet paper with a bit of water. Mound meringue in circle.
3. Bake at 300 degrees for 30 minutes. Turn off heat and leave in oven at least 1 hour. Cool completely.
4. Whip cream and beat in powdered sugar. Spread on meringue and top with sliced, drained fresh fruit. Slice as you would a pie.

NOTE:

Kiwis are the traditional fruit to serve on Pavlova in Australia and New Zealand.

Helen Wasley
Boulder, Colorado

COLD CHESTNUT SOUFFLÉ

Serves 12 to 14

Preparation 20 Minutes
Chill 2 Hours

4 eggs plus 4 yolks
1/2 cup sugar
2 tablespoons gelatin
5 to 8 tablespoons rum
1 cup sweetened chestnut puree
1 cup heavy cream, whipped
Additional heavy cream for garnish (optional)

1. Combine eggs, egg yolks, and sugar. Beat well.
2. Soften gelatin in rum and dissolve over hot water. Add to egg mixture.
3. Add chestnut puree and mix well. Then fold in whipped cream.
4. Tie a 4-inch band of double waxed paper around 1-quart souffle' dish to make standing collar. Fill with souffle' mixture and chill until set.

Ellen Becker
Avalon, California

SWEDISH CHEESE CAKE
(*Ost Kaka*)

Serves 10 to 12

Preparation 15 Minutes
Bake 45 Minutes at 325°F
15 Minutes at 350°F

4 eggs
2/3 cup sugar
2 cups heavy cream, or half-and-half
Pinch of salt
1/2 teaspoon almond extract
24 ounces cottage cheese, dry curd if possible
Tart fruit topping

1. Beat eggs. Add all ingredients except fruit topping and mix well.
2. Pour into buttered, shallow, 1 1/2-quart baking dish and set in pan of water in oven.
3. Bake 45 minutes at 325 degrees; increase temperature to 350 degrees and bake 15 minutes more until brown and knife inserted in center comes out clean. Serve with tart fruit topping, such as canned lingonberries.

Ellen Boles
Boulder, Colorado

CARAMEL PUDDING

This is an old Welsh recipe from my great-grandmother who came to Central City in 1860.

Serves 6 to 8

Preparation 20 Minutes
Bake 1 Hour at 350°F

1 cup brown sugar, packed
2 cups water
1/4 cup butter or margarine
1 cup flour
1/2 cup sugar
3/4 teaspoon nutmeg
3/4 teaspoon cinnamon
1 teaspoon baking powder
1/2 cup milk
1/2 cup nuts
1/2 cup raisins

1. Melt sugar, water, and butter in saucepan. Pour into 9 x 12-inch pan.
2. Mix flour, sugar, nutmeg, cinnamon, baking powder, milk, nuts, and raisins together; drop by spoonfuls into the syrup.
3. Bake in 350-degree oven 1 hour or until brown.

VARIATION:

1/2 teaspoon pumpkin pie spice may be substituted for nutmeg and cinnamon.

Wilhelmina Jachem Barton
Lakewood, Colorado

FLAN AU CAFÉ

Serves 10

Preparation 30 Minutes
Bake 30 Minutes at 350°F

2 cups sugar
1/2 cup hot water
5 cups milk
6 teaspoons instant coffee
7 egg whites
1/3 cup sugar
1/3 cup brown sugar
2 tablespoons brandy
Whipped cream
Toasted almonds, shaved

1. Melt sugar in pan over direct heat until golden brown. Be careful not to let it burn. Add hot water and stir until syrup is smooth. Put 2 teaspoons in each of 10 custard cups.
2. Stir instant coffee into milk. Beat egg whites with both sugars and blend in brandy and milk. Pour over caramel in custard cups.
3. Put custard cups in pan of hot water, and bake 30 minutes at 350 degrees. Unmold onto serving dishes while still warm. Garnish with a dollop of whipped cream and almonds.

Ellen Denton
Piedmont, California

CLAFOUTI AUX FRAMBOISES

Serves 6 to 8

Preparation 15 Minutes
Bake 45 Minutes at 400°F

1 egg yolk
1 whole egg
3/4 cup plus 2 tablespoons flour
3/4 cup milk
1 1/2 tablespoons kirsch
6 tablespoons butter, softened
1/2 cup sugar
1 3/4 cups fresh raspberries

1. Combine egg yolk, whole egg, flour, milk, kirsch, butter, and 6 tablespoons of sugar in electric blender. Process at high speed until smooth.
2. Generously butter 9-inch porcelain or earthenware pie plate or quiche pan. Pour half the batter into pie plate, coating bottom evenly.
3. Scatter raspberries over batter and sprinkle with remaining 2 tablespoons sugar. Pour remaining batter over raspberries.
4. Bake in preheated oven (400 degrees) until *clafouti* puffs up and lightly browns, about 45 minutes.
5. This will sink as it cools. Best eaten while still warm, but can be served cold or reheated.

Bruce Healy
Boulder, Colorado

PRUNE CRUNCH

Serves 9

Preparation 20 Minutes
Bake 30 Minutes at 375°F

1 1/2 cups cooked prunes, pitted and chopped
3 tablespoons sugar
2 tablespoons lemon juice
1 teaspoon cinnamon
1 1/2 cups rolled oats, quick or regular
1/2 cup flour
1 cup brown sugar
1/2 cup butter, melted

1. Combine prunes, sugar, lemon juice, and cinnamon. Set aside.
2. Combine oats, flour, brown sugar, and butter. Press 1/2 into bottom of 8 x 8-inch pan. Cover with filling and top with remaining crunch mix. Press lightly.
3. Bake at 375 degrees for 30 minutes.

NOTE:

Any dried fruit could be used.

BAKLAVA

Warning! This may prove to be addictive!

Yields 3 1/2 Dozen

Preparation 1 Hour
Bake 30 Minutes at 350°F
45 to 60 Minutes at 300°F

1 pound unsalted butter
1 pound *filo* pastry leaves
1 1/2 pounds walnuts, finely crushed
1 pound almonds, finely crushed
1 tablespoon cinnamon
1 teaspoon nutmeg
1 teaspoon ground cloves
2 cups sugar

SYRUP

2 1/2 cups sugar
3/4 cup water
1 stick cinnamon
2 tablespoons lemon juice
1 1/2 cups honey

1. Melt butter and clarify. Using a pastry brush, butter a 9 x 13-inch baking pan. Lay in one *filo* leaf and brush with butter. Add 4 more leaves, brushing each with butter as it is placed on top.
2. Combine nuts, cinnamon, nutmeg, cloves, and 2 cups sugar. Spread 1/4 of mixture evenly over layered *filo* leaves.
3. Add 3 more buttered *filo* sheets on top of nuts and spread with another 1/4 of nut mixture. Repeat this step for two more layers, remembering to butter every *filo* leaf as it is put in.
4. Add all remaining *filo* leaves, brushing each with butter. Pour any remaining butter over last *filo* leaf.
5. Using a sharp knife, cut through top layers to form small diamond-shaped pieces. Bake for 30 minutes at 350 degrees, then reduce temperature to 300 degrees and bake 45 to 60 minutes.

6. Combine 2 1/2 cups sugar, water, cinnamon stick, and lemon juice and simmer 10 to 15 minutes. Add honey and simmer 5 minutes. Cool to room temperature.
7. Remove *Baklava* from oven and pour cooled syrup on the hot *Baklava*. Cut pieces through to bottom and refrigerate.

NOTE:

If *Baklava* has been cooled, use hot syrup. You may substitute 2 to 2 1/2 cups honey for syrup; pour on hot *Baklava.*

Harvey M.J. Ames, Jr.
Boulder, Colorado

LEMON CRISP

Serves 8

Preparation 20 Minutes
Bake 40 Minutes at 350°F

6 tablespoons butter
3/4 cup brown sugar
1 cup sifted flour
1/2 teaspoon soda
1/2 teaspoon salt
1/2 cup flaked coconut
3/4 cup finely crushed saltines or Hi-Ho's
3/4 cup granulated sugar
2 tablespoons cornstarch
1/4 teaspoon salt
1 cup hot water
2 egg yolks, beaten
1/2 teaspoon grated lemon peel
1/2 cup lemon juice
Whipped cream

1. Cream butter and brown sugar. Stir in flour, soda, salt, coconut, and cracker crumbs.
2. Press half mixture into 8 x 8 x 2-inch pan. Bake at 350 degrees for 10 minutes.
3. Meanwhile, in saucepan, combine sugar, cornstarch, and salt; gradually stir in hot water. Cook and stir until mixture is thick and boiling; boil 2 minutes.
4. Remove from heat; stir small amount of hot mixture into egg yolks. Return to remaining mixture in pan. Bring to boil, stirring constantly. Remove from heat. Gradually stir in lemon peel and juice.
5. Pour over baked crumb crust; top with reserved crumbs. Bake at 350 degrees for 30 minutes, or until crumbs are lightly browned. Top with whipped cream.

Esther deOnis
Boulder, Colorado

ABRAHAM'S FAVORITE APPLE PIE

Serves 6 to 8

Preparation 20 Minutes
Bake 1 Hour at 350°F

6 tablespoons margarine
3/4 cup sugar
3 eggs, separated
1 1/2 cups applesauce
1 1/2 teaspoons vanilla extract
9-inch pie crust, unbaked (see Index)

1. Cream margarine and sugar, add egg yolks, and beat.
2. Add vanilla and applesauce, stir well. Beat egg whites until stiff and fold into applesauce mixture.
3. Pour into pie crust and bake 1 hour in 350-degree oven.

Crede Dever
Boulder, Colorado

INDIANA APPLE PIE

Serves 8 to 10

Preparation 40 Minutes
Bake 40 Minutes at 375°F

1/2 to 3/4 cup sugar
1/2 cup brown sugar
1 teaspoon cinnamon
1 recipe Reliable Pie Crust (see Index)
3 tablespoons butter
2 cups shredded Cheddar cheese
3 tablespoons cold water
2 pounds tart apples, peeled, cored, and sliced
1 tablespoon flour
1/2 teaspoon nutmeg
1/4 teaspoon mace
1/2 cup coarsely chopped pecans

1. Mix sugars and cinnamon with 1/2 pie crust dough, cut in butter and set aside for topping.
2. Mix 1 cup cheese with remaining pie dough, add water, and toss lightly. Roll out to fit 9-inch pie pan. Flute edges.
3. Spoon apples into lined pie pan. Mix flour, nutmeg, mace, and nuts and sprinkle over apples.
4. Spread 1/2 of reserved topping mixture evenly over pie. Sprinkle on remaining cheese, then add rest of topping mixture.
5. Bake at 375 degrees for 40 minutes or until top is golden and apples are tender.

SUGARLESS APPLE PIE

Serves 6 to 8

Preparation 20 Minutes
Bake 45 Minutes at 350°F

1 can (12-ounce) frozen apple juice concentrate
3 tablespoons cornstarch
1 teaspoon cinnamon
Pinch salt
7 large apples, peeled and sliced
Pastry for 2-crust pie

1. Combine juice, cornstarch, cinnamon, and salt. Heat in saucepan until thickened.
2. Add sliced apples and simmer until apples are tender. Be very careful not to burn.
3. Pour into unbaked pie shell and cover with top crust. Bake in 350-degree oven for 45 minutes.

Southern Hills Junior High School
Boulder, Colorado

MRS. JOLLY'S BUTTERMILK PIE

Serves 8

Preparation 20 Minutes
Bake 50 Minutes at 350°F

9-inch pie crust, unbaked (see Index)
1/2 cup butter
1 1/2 cups sugar
3 rounded tablespoons flour
3 eggs, beaten
1 cup buttermilk
1 teaspoon vanilla extract
1/4 to 1/2 teaspoon nutmeg

1. Cream butter and sugar. Add flour and beaten eggs; beat well.
2. Stir in buttermilk and vanilla. Pour into unbaked pie shell. Sprinkle nutmeg on top. Bake at 350 degrees for 50 minutes. Cool before serving.

Evelyn Butler
Mathes, Texas

BERKELEY FUDGE PIE

Serves 8

Preparation 25 Minutes
Bake 30 Minutes at 350°F

1/2 cup butter
3 ounces unsweetened chocolate
4 eggs
3 tablespoons white corn syrup
1 1/2 cups sugar
1/4 teaspoon salt
1 teaspoon vanilla extract
9-inch pie crust, unbaked (see Index)
Whipped cream

1. In top of double boiler or over low heat, melt butter and chocolate.
2. In mixing bowl, beat eggs until light and add corn syrup, sugar, salt, and vanilla.
3. Add slightly cooled chocolate mixture. Mix thoroughly and pour into 9-inch unbaked pie shell.
4. Bake at 350 degrees for 30 minutes or until top is crusty and filling is set but still somewhat soft inside. Do not overbake. Pie should shake like custard. Serve with whipped cream.

Jackie Moorhead
Boulder, Colorado

CHOCOLATE FUDGE PIE

Serves 8

Preparation 10 Minutes
Bake 20 Minutes at 375°F

1/4 cup flour
1 cup sugar
6 tablespoons cocoa
Pinch salt
2 eggs, beaten
1/2 cup mayonnaise
1 tablespoon each vanilla, almond extracts

1. Mix flour, sugar, cocoa, and salt together. Combine beaten eggs with mayonnaise and mix with flour-sugar mixture. Add vanilla and almond extracts, blending well.
2. Pour into buttered 8-inch pie pan and bake at 375 degrees for 20 minutes. Cool slightly. Serve topped with ice cream, Hot Fudge Sauce (see Index), or whipped cream if desired.

Kathleen O'Donnell Caldwell
Denver, Colorado

OHIO LEMON PIE

Serves 8
Stand 2 Hours

Preparation 20 Minutes
Bake 15 Minutes at 450°F
20 Minutes at 375°F

2 large lemons
2 cups sugar
4 eggs, well beaten
1 recipe Reliable Pie Crust (see Index)

1. Slice the lemons as thin as paper, rind and all. Add sugar and mix well. Let stand for 2 hours or longer, stirring occasionally.
2. Add eggs to lemons and mix well. Turn into pastry lined 9-inch pie pan, arranging lemon slices evenly.
3. Cover with top crust, crimp edges and cut slits to permit steam to escape. Sprinkle with 1/2 teaspoon sugar.
4. Bake 15 minutes at 450 degrees. Reduce heat to 375 degrees and bake 20 minutes, or until knife inserted near edge comes out clean. Cool before serving.

Bonita Nelson
Tempe, Arizona

FLORIDA LIME PIE

Serves 6 to 8

Preparation 45 Minutes

10-inch pie crust, baked (see Index)
1 1/4 cups sugar
3/4 cup fresh lime juice
1 tablespoon grated lime rind
5 eggs, separated
1 envelope unflavored gelatin
2 tablespoons cold water
1 1/2 cups heavy cream
Lime slices for garnish

1. Mix sugar, lime juice and rind, and egg yolks in medium saucepan. Cook, stirring constantly, over medium heat until mixture coats spoon.
2. Soften gelatin in 2 tablespoons cold water. Stir into lime mixture until dissolved. Pour into large bowl and cool completely.
3. Beat egg whites until stiff and fold into lime mixture. Beat 1 1/4 cups cream until stiff and fold into lime mixture. Spoon into pie shell.
4. Chill about 4 hours, until firm. Garnish with remaining 1/4 cup cream, whipped, and lime slices.

A Friend of the Library
St. Petersburg, Florida

MISTY PIE

Serves 8
Refrigerate 3 Hours

Preparation 20 Minutes
Bake 25 to 30 Minutes at 350°F

3 egg whites
1 cup sugar
1 teaspoon vanilla extract
1 teaspoon baking powder
20 finely crushed Ritz crackers
3/4 cup chopped pecans
Whipped cream to taste
Grated chocolate

1. Beat egg whites until stiff. Gradually beat in sugar. Fold in vanilla, baking powder, crackers, and nuts.
2. Pour into greased 9-inch pie pan. Bake at 350 degrees for 25 to 30 minutes.
3. Cool and refrigerate 3 hours.
4. Top with sweetened whipped cream and grated chocolate.

Gail Madden
Boulder, Colorado

PERFECTION PECAN PIE

Serves 6 to 8

Preparation 20 Minutes
Bake 35 to 45 Minutes at 375°F

9-inch pie crust, unbaked (see Index)
8 ounces cream cheese
1/2 cup sugar
4 eggs
1/4 teaspoon salt
1 1/2 teaspoons vanilla extract
1 cup pecans
1 cup corn syrup

1. Beat cream cheese with 1/4 cup sugar, 1 egg, salt, and 1 teaspoon vanilla until thick. Spoon into pie shell and cover with pecans.
2. Beat 3 eggs until just blended and add 1/4 cup sugar, corn syrup, and 1/2 teaspoon vanilla. Blend well. Pour over cheese and pecans.
3. Bake at 375 degrees for 35 to 45 minutes or until set.

Esther deOnis
Boulder, Colorado

FRENCH SILK

Serves 6 to 8

Preparation 25 Minutes
Refrigerate 2 Hours

9-inch pie crust, baked (see Index)
3/4 cup butter
1 1/8 cups sugar
3 ounces unsweetened chocolate
3 eggs

1. Cream butter and sugar until fluffy.
2. Melt chocolate and blend into butter-sugar mixture. Add eggs, one at a time, beating 5 minutes after each egg.
3. Pour into cooled, baked pie shell. Chill 2 hours before serving.

Patt Hanson
Boulder, Colorado

RHUBARB PIE

Serves 6

Preparation 15 Minutes
Bake 15 Minutes at 400°F
35 Minutes at 350°F

8-inch double pie crust, unbaked (see Index)
4 cups rhubarb, cut in 1-inch pieces
1 1/3 cups sugar
6 tablespoons flour
1 egg, beaten
3 tablespoons butter

1. Combine rhubarb, sugar, flour, and egg. Stir to mix well.
2. Pour into pie crust and dot with butter. Cover with top crust. Crimp edges and make slits in top.
3. Bake 15 minutes at 400 degrees, reduce heat to 350 degrees and bake 35 minutes more.

NOTE:

If using frozen rhubarb, mix with other ingredients without thawing.

Maxine Marshall
Boulder, Colorado

STRAWBERRY PIE (sugarless)

Serves 8

Preparation 20 Minutes

2 1/2 cups mashed strawberries
1 cup frozen apple juice concentrate
1/4 cup water
3 tablespoons cornstarch
1/8 teaspoon salt
1 tablespoon lemon juice
1 teaspoon margarine
3 cups whole strawberries
10-inch baked Whole Wheat Pie Crust (see Index)
Whipped cream

1. In a saucepan, bring mashed strawberries and apple juice to boil. Mix water, cornstarch, and salt thoroughly.

2. Add cornstarch mixture slowly to mashed berries and stir until mixture is thick and clear. Add lemon juice and margarine.
3. Pour mixture over whole strawberries in baked pie shell. Chill. Garnish with whipped cream.

Southern Hills Junior High School
Boulder, Colorado

BAKEWELL TART

Serves 6 to 8

Preparation 30 Minutes
Bake 40 Minutes at 350°F

1 recipe Short Pastry, (see Index)
Black currant jam
1/2 cup butter or margarine
9 tablespoons sugar
1 egg
1/4 to 1/2 teaspoon almond extract
2 egg yolks
2 to 4 ounces almonds, ground

1. Line pie pan with pastry and spread on a layer of jam.
2. Cream butter and sugar, add almond extract, then egg and egg yolks, one at a time. Beat well. Stir in almonds.
3. Spread over jam layer and bake at 350 degrees for 40 minutes.

NOTE:

Black currant jam is available in specialty grocery departments.

VARIATION:

Substitute strawberry jam or raspberry jam for black currant jam.

Marylou Siegfried Williams
Wallingford, Connecticut

VINEGAR PIE

Serves 10 to 12

Preparation 15 Minutes
Bake 45 to 50 Minutes at 350°F

1 recipe Reliable Pie Crust (see Index)
2 cups sugar
5 tablespoons flour
2 cups water
3/4 cup cider vinegar
1/2 cup margarine
1/2 cup raisins

1. Mix sugar, flour, water, vinegar, margarine, and raisins. (If desired, use additional margarine and raisins.) Pour into 8 x 11-inch pan.
2. Cut strips of pie crust and push down into mixture. The last strips will be on top of the mixture.
3. Bake 45 to 50 minutes in 350-degree oven.

Denise Austin
Austin, Texas

PEACHES WITH SOUR CREAM AND STRAWBERRIES

Serves 8

Preparation 15 Minutes

8 ripe peaches
Brandy
Lemon juice
2 cups sour cream
1 pint hulled strawberries
Superfine granulated sugar
2 tablespoons Grand Marnier, rum, or brandy
Macaroon crumbs

1. Skin peaches; halve and pit them. Sprinkle with brandy and lemon juice. Chill well.
2. Fold sour cream into strawberries, add sugar (not too much) and Grand Marnier.
3. To serve, arrange peach halves in large bowl, or in individual champagne glasses. Spoon strawberry cream mixture over top and sprinkle with finely crushed macaroon crumbs.

The Cookery
Boulder, Colorado

PEARS CONTINENTAL

Serves 12

Preparation 25 Minutes
Chill 4 to 5 Hours

1 egg
2 tablespoons butter, melted
2 cups powdered sugar
2 cans (29-ounce each) Bartlett pears, drained
12 teaspoons cocoa
1 cup heavy cream, whipped
1 teaspoon vanilla extract
Shaved semi-sweet chocolate

1. On morning before pears are to be served, beat egg, add butter and sugar, and blend well. Refrigerate until serving time.
2. Fill drained pear half with 1 teaspoon cocoa, close with second pear half and hold together with toothpicks. Cover and refrigerate until serving time.
3. To serve, fold whipped cream and vanilla into sugar-egg mixture and pour over pears. Garnish with shaved chocolate.

Janet Desgalier
Boulder, Colorado

HOT GOLDEN SAUCE

Yields 2 1/2 Cups

Preparation 10 Minutes
Cook 20 Minutes

1 cup sugar
4 tablespoons flour
1/2 teaspoon salt
1 1/2 cups boiling water
3 tablespoons grated raw carrot
2 tablespoons lemon juice
2 tablespoons orange juice
4 tablespoons butter

1. Mix sugar, flour, and salt together in top of double boiler.
2. Add boiling water, stirring constantly until mixture is thick.
3. Add carrot, lemon and orange juices, and butter. Place over hot water.
4. Cook about 20 minutes, stirring occasionally.

NOTE:

Tasty warm topping for plain cakes and puddings.

Crede Dever
Boulder, Colorado

LEMON WHIPPED CREAM SAUCE

Yields 3 1/2 Cups
Chill 1 1/2 Hours

Preparation 30 Minutes
Cook 20 Minutes

1 cup sugar
1/2 cup lemon juice
2 teaspoons grated lemon peel
3 eggs
1 cup heavy cream

1. Put sugar, lemon juice, and lemon peel in top of double boiler and place over direct heat. Heat, stirring, until sugar dissolves.
2. Beat eggs with a fork until blended. Stir a little of the hot sugar mixture into the beaten eggs, then add all to the remaining hot sugar mixture. Return to the top of the double boiler.
3. Place over simmering water and cook, stirring constantly, until thickened. Remove from heat and cool by placing in a pan of ice water, or refrigerate.
4. Whip cream until almost stiff and fold into the chilled lemon custard. Cover and chill until serving time.

NOTE:

Excellent topping for strawberries, other berries, or peaches. Also good served over pound cake or gingerbread. May be made a day in advance of serving.

Marge DeFries
Boulder, Colorado

GRANDMOTHER'S SAUCE

Serves 12 to 15

Preparation 15 Minutes

1 egg
1 cup sugar
1/4 cup sherry, brandy or 1 teaspoon vanilla
1/4 cup butter, melted
1 cup heavy cream, whipped

1. Beat egg and add sugar gradually. Add sherry, brandy or vanilla and melted butter. Beat to blend thoroughly.
2. Fold in whipped cream.

NOTE:

No substitutes! (i.e., margarine, dessert topping) this is not low-calorie. May be used as an all-around topping from gingerbread to Christmas pudding.

Betsy Aspinwall
Boulder, Colorado

HARRIETT'S HOT FUDGE SAUCE

Yields 2 Cups

Preparation 10 Minutes

2 ounces unsweetened baking chocolate
2 tablespoons light corn syrup
1 cup sugar
1/3 cup milk
Pinch of salt
1/2 teaspoon vanilla extract
2 tablespoons butter

1. Combine chocolate, corn syrup, sugar, and milk in a small saucepan and bring to a boil over medium heat.
2. Cook, stirring for 4 minutes after chocolate melts. Remove from heat and add salt, vanilla, and butter. Beat until smooth.

Val Havlick
Boulder, Colorado

COCOA SYRUP

Yields 2 Cups

Cook 3 Minutes

1 cup cocoa
1 1/2 cups sugar
1 cup hot water
Dash of salt
2 teaspoons vanilla extract

1. Mix cocoa, sugar, and salt. Add hot water and bring to boil, stirring constantly.
2. Boil 3 minutes; remove from heat and add vanilla. Immediately pour into pint jar. Cool and refrigerate.
3. Serve over ice cream or use to make chocolate milk.

Marion Long Roth
Arvada, Colorado

HOT FUDGE SAUCE

Yields 4 Cups

Cook 15 Minutes

1/2 cup butter
4 ounces unsweetened chocolate
2 3/4 cups sugar
Scant 1/2 teaspoon salt
1 can (13-ounce) evaporated milk

1. In a double boiler, melt chocolate and butter. Gradually add sugar and salt. Mixture is very dry.
2. Slowly add milk, stirring constantly until well mixed and smooth.
3. Pour into jar and cool. Store in refrigerator.
4. Heat before serving over ice cream, cake or brownies.

NOTE:

Divide sauce into 4 small jars for more convenient reheating or for gift giving.

VARIATION:

Mix 1 teaspoon instant coffee with 1 tablespoon hot water. Add to sauce along with milk.

Agatha Matheson
Boulder, Colorado

NECTARINE-CHERRY SAUCE

Serves 6

Cook 20 Minutes

1/2 cup currant jelly
2 tablespoons cornstarch
1 cup orange soda
2 to 3 fresh nectarines thinly sliced
1 cup fresh bing cherries, pitted or canned dark sweet cherries
4 thin lemon slices, quartered
1 tablespoon lemon juice
6 drops red food coloring
2 tablespoons *Chartreuse* or high-proof brandy (optional)

1. Mix currant jelly and cornstarch until smooth. Stir in orange soda and cook, stirring, until thickened.
2. Add nectarines, cherries, lemon slices, lemon juice, and food coloring. Heat through.
3. Set liqueur aflame, pour over hot fruit sauce, stir.
4. Serve over ice cream or sherbet (lemon is especially good).

NOTE:

Fresh or frozen peaches can also be used.

Ronald Leslie
San Diego, California

SHORT PASTRY

Yields One 9-inch Crust | Preparation 15 Minutes

1/4 cup butter or margarine
1 tablespoon sugar
1 egg yolk
1 cup flour

1. Cream butter and sugar. Add egg yolk and mix well.
2. Add flour and mix until the consistency of corn meal.
3. Place in 9-inch pie pan and press down firmly and evenly with hands. Press dough up sides. Fill with fruit filling and bake.

NOTE:

An especially good crust for Italian plum pie. Pit and quarter 1 1/2 pounds of plums. Arrange skin side down in crust and sprinkle on 1/2 cup sugar and 1/4 cup slivered almonds. Bake 5 to 10 minutes at 450 degrees, then reduce heat to 350 degrees for 45 minutes.

Helen Scherer
Boulder, Colorado

SWEET OIL CRUST

Yields One 9-inch Crust | Preparation 10 Minutes
Bake 20 Minutes at 400°F

1/2 cup corn oil
2 tablespoons cold milk
1 1/2 cups flour
2 tablespoons sugar

1. Measure oil and milk into bowl. Stir.
2. Add flour and sugar and mix only until flour is moistened enough to hold mixture together. Shape into ball.
3. Pat into 9-inch pie plate. Prick bottom and sides with fork and bake at 400 degrees for 20 minutes or until light golden color. Cool thoroughly before filling.

NOTE:

Freezes well, unbaked. Do not thaw before baking.

Imelda Hermes
Boulder, Colorado

PARMESAN PIE CRUST

Yields One 12-inch Crust | Preparation 15 Minutes

1 1/2 cups flour
1/3 cup grated Parmesan cheese
1/2 cup butter
4 to 5 tablespoons water

1. Mix flour and cheese and cut in butter. Add water until mixture forms a ball.
2. For prebaked crust, bake 10 to 12 minutes at 400 degrees.

NOTE:

Enough for two 8-inch crusts or one 12-inch quiche crust. Especially good for quiches and homemade meat pies.

VARIATION:

Substitute 1/2 cup grated sharp Cheddar for Parmesan cheese.

Verle Plumb
Boulder, Colorado

VAL'S PIE CRUST

Yields 6 Crusts

Preparation 15 Minutes

2 cups shortening
4 cups flour
1 teaspoon baking powder
1 teaspoon salt
1 egg, beaten
2 tablespoons vinegar
Water

1. Blend shortening, flour, baking powder, and salt.
2. Add egg to 1 cup measuring cup, add vinegar, and fill with cold water to the 3/4 cup level.
3. Sprinkle over flour mixture and toss with fork. Divide into 6 portions.

NOTE:

Use now or wrap in waxed paper and freeze. Thaw before using. This crust has a tendency to slip down the sides of pie tin if baked unfilled. Best used with pies or quiches baked in the crust.

Val Havlick
Boulder, Colorado

WHOLE WHEAT PIE CRUST

Yields One 8-inch Crust

Preparation 15 Minutes
Chill 30 Minutes

1 cup whole wheat flour
1/4 teaspoon salt
1/2 cup butter
1/4 to 1/2 cup ice water

1. Place flour and salt in bowl and cut in butter.
2. Add ice water one tablespoon at a time. Dough should be somewhat sticky. Roll into a ball, cover, and chill 30 minutes.
3. Roll out to 1/8-inch thickness and put in pie pan. Chill again if to be used for a prebaked crust.

NOTE:

Especially good for quiches. Try fillings using vegetables or seafoods.

Ilene Kasper
Boulder, Colorado

NEVER-FAIL PIE CRUST

Yields Two 8-inch Crusts
Or One 12-inch Crust

Preparation 20 Minutes

1 1/2 cups flour
Dash of salt
3/4 cup shortening
6 tablespoons milk

1. Combine flour, salt, and shortening in bowl and cut with pastry blender or two knives until coarsely blended.
2. Stir in milk until absorbed. Divide in half. Knead each half on a lightly floured board just until it holds its shape. Roll out.

Maxine Marshall
Boulder, Colorado

COCONUT PIE CRUST

Yields One 9-inch Crust

Preparation 10 Minutes
Bake 12 to 15 Minutes at 350°F

1 cup shredded coconut
2 tablespoons flour
2 tablespoons melted butter

1. Mix coconut, flour, and butter.
2. Press into 9-inch pie pan and bake at 350 degrees for 12 to 15 minutes.

Marilyn Peltzer
Boulder, Colorado

RELIABLE PIE CRUST

Yields Two 9- to 10-inch Crusts

Preparation 20 Minutes

1/3 cup cold milk
1 tablespoon vinegar
2 cups flour
1 teaspoon salt
1 cup vegetable shortening

1. Mix milk and vinegar and set aside.
2. Mix flour and salt and cut in shortening using a pastry blender or 2 table knives. Mixture should resemble coarse corn meal.
3. Add milk mixture slowly stirring with fork until dough holds together.
4. On well-floured pastry board, pat dough with floured rolling pin until particles stick together and roll without cracking. Divide in half.
5. Roll each half from center out toward edge to 1/8-inch thickness and 1 1/2 inches larger than pan. Fit into pie pan, crimping edges, and fill as desired.

NOTE:

1. Working with pastry too much toughens it. Stir and shape lightly.
2. For baked pie shell, prick bottom and sides with a fork and bake at 375 degrees for 8 to 10 minutes.

Carol Reese
Boulder, Colorado

BEVERAGES

HOLLYBERRY PUNCH

Yields 2 3/4 Quarts

Preparation 10 Minutes

1 can (6-ounce) frozen lemonade
1 can (6-ounce) frozen orange juice
5 cups water
2/3 cup grenadine
1 quart ginger ale

1. Mix lemonade, orange juice, water, and grenadine in 4-quart punch bowl.
2. Add ginger ale and ice when ready to serve.

Peg English
Costa Mesa, California

STRAWBERRY PUNCH

Serves 20 to 25

Preparation 10 Minutes

5 cans (6-ounce each) frozen lemonade
2 1/2 quarts water
3 boxes (10-ounce each) frozen strawberries
1 quart ginger ale

1. Mix lemonade, water, and strawberries in a 4-quart punch bowl. Stir to melt strawberries.
2. When ready to serve, add ice and ginger ale. Mix gently.

Karen Hickey
Boulder, Colorado

VARIATION:

For a drier punch, use club soda in place of ginger ale.

CITRUS SPARKLER

Yields 2 1/4 Quarts

Preparation 10 Minutes

1 can (12-ounce) frozen orange juice
3 3/4 cups cold water
4 tablespoons rum or rum flavoring
2 tablespoons lime juice
1 quart lemon-lime soda
2 limes, sliced
Ice cubes

1. About 10 minutes before serving combine orange juice, water, rum or rum flavoring, and lime juice in a punch bowl. Stir well.
2. Add lemon-lime soda and lime slices. Stir.
3. Serve over ice cubes in cups or glasses.

Carol Forney
Huntington Beach, California

ORANGE SPICED TEA

Yields 2 1/3 Quarts — Preparation 25 Minutes

5-inch strip of orange peel
3-inch strip of lemon or lime peel
1 cinnamon stick
8 whole cloves
2 quarts water
4 tea bags
1 can (6-ounce) orange juice concentrate
Juice of 2 lemons or 2 large limes
1/2 cup sugar

1. Add orange and lemon peel, cinnamon stick, and cloves to water. Bring to a boil and remove from heat.
2. Add tea bags and let steep for 20 minutes.
3. Remove tea bags, peels, and spices. Add orange juice concentrate, lemon juice, and sugar. Mix well.
4. Serve hot or cold over ice.

Beth Ascione
Raleigh, North Carolina

RUSSIAN SPICED TEA

A very light and refreshing drink

Yields 2 Quarts — Preparation 20 Minutes

2 quarts water
1 cup sugar
8 whole cloves
8 whole allspice
2 tea bags
1/4 cup lemon juice
1/2 cup orange juice

1. Boil water and add sugar and spices tied in a little bag. Boil for 10 minutes.
2. Off heat, add tea and let steep until desired color and strength is reached. Cool. Add juices. Serve cold.

NOTE:

To make a spice bag, remove the staples from 2 tea bags. Transfer the tea from one bag to another. To the empty bag, add the spices and restaple both bags.

Catherine P. Ware
Franklin, Kentucky

HOT SPICED PUNCH

Yields 2 1/2 Quarts

Preparation 20 Minutes

1 quart apple cider
1 quart cranberry juice
1/2 cup brown sugar
1 3-inch stick cinnamon
6 whole cloves
4 whole allspice
2 cups tea, brewed

1. Combine cider, cranberry juice, sugar, cinnamon, cloves, allspice, and tea. Heat. Serve warm.

Priscilla Peale
Santa Barbara, California

ORCHATA

A delightful Nicaraguan drink

Yields 3 Cups

Soak Overnight
Preparation 5 Minutes

1/4 cup uncooked rice, covered with water and soaked overnight
1/4 cup sugar
3 cups milk
1 tablespoon cocoa
1/8 teaspoon cinnamon
1/8 teaspoon vanilla extract
Pinch allspice

1. Drain rice and discard soaking liquid. To a blender or food processor, add rice, sugar, milk, cocoa, cinnamon, vanilla, and allspice. Blend for 2 minutes.
2. Strain liquid. Serve over ice cubes.

Maria Elena Brooks
San Francisco, California

MOCHA MINT PUNCH

Serves 20 to 25

Preparation 20 Minutes

4 quarts strong coffee, chilled
1 cup sugar
1 tray ice cubes
1/2 teaspoon peppermint extract
1/2 gallon chocolate ice cream
2 cups heavy cream, whipped

1. Pour coffee into 8-quart punch bowl. Add sugar and ice cubes and stir well.
2. Add peppermint extract and ice cream in scoops.
3. Float dollops of whipped cream on top.

Ellen Doenges
Austin, Texas

COSMOPOLITAN COFFEES

Serves 1

Preparation 5 Minutes

VIENNESE
1 teaspoon sugar
Whipped Cream
Freshly ground nutmeg
BRAZILIAN
2 tablespoon cocoa
Cinnamon stick
Whipped cream
ITALIAN
1 teaspoon sugar
Freshly ground nutmeg
Shaved chocolate

For each, start with one cup hot coffee.
Viennese: add sugar, top with whipped cream, and sprinkle with nutmeg.
Brazilian: add cocoa, stir with cinnamon stick, and top with whipped cream.
Italian: add sugar, sprinkle with nutmeg, and top with shaved chocolate.

NOTE:

In each case, a bit of brandy or cognac is very tasty.

Lane Denton
Piedmont, California

APPLE CIDER PUNCH

Yields 1 3/4 Quarts

Preparation 5 Minutes
Cook 30 Minutes

1 quart apple cider
2 tablespoons brown sugar
1 teaspoon allspice
1 teaspoon whole cloves
1 bottle (.75-liter) Sauterne

1. Simmer apple cider with brown sugar, allspice, and cloves for 1/2 hour.
2. Add Sauterne and heat. Serve hot.

Ann P. Cavender
Lakewood, Colorado

CRANBERRY-WINE PUNCH

Yields 1 1/2 Quarts

Preparation 10 Minutes

2 cups cranberry juice
3/4 cup frozen cranberry juice concentrate
2 cups white wine
12 ounces club soda

1. Chill ingredients and mix just before serving.
2. Serve over ice cubes in glasses or use a block of ice in a punch bowl.

Susan Coe
Minneapolis, Minnesota

WINE COOLER

Yields 2 3/4 Quarts

Preparation 10 Minutes
Freeze 4 to 6 Hours

1 can (12-ounce) frozen grapefruit juice
3 liters chablis
1 can (12-ounce) frozen lemonade

1. Mix grapefruit juice and lemonade with wine. Stir to mix thoroughly.
2. Freeze in wide mouth containers.
3. Remove from freezer 1/2 to 1 hour before serving, depending on temperature.
4. Serve partially thawed.

NOTE:

Can be frozen at least a month.

Delores Wong
Los Angeles, California

ORANGE SANGRIA

Serves 6 to 8

Preparation 15 Minutes
Marinate 2 Hours

1/4 to 1/2 cup honey
1/2 cup hot water
Juice of 1 lemon
1 cup fresh orange juice
1 orange, peeled and sectioned
1 peach or wedge of cantaloupe, chopped
1 bottle (.75-liter) dry red wine
1 orange, sliced
1/2 cup brandy or Triple Sec
Club soda, chilled
Ice cubes

1. Mix honey in hot water, then add lemon juice, orange juice, orange sections, peach or cantaloupe, wine, orange slices, and brandy or Triple Sec.
2. Marinate at least 2 hours.
3. To serve, pour amount of sangria desired into a glass, add club soda and ice to taste.

Serena Dubach
Boulder, Colorado

CHAMPAGNE PUNCH

Yields 4 Quarts

Preparation 15 Minutes

1/2 cup lemon juice
1/2 cup water
1 cup sugar
3 ounces brandy
3 ounces Triple Sec or curaçao
3 ounces maraschino cherry juice
Block of ice
1 quart club soda
3 bottles champagne, chilled

1. Combine lemon juice, water, sugar, brandy, Triple Sec, and cherry juice. Stir until sugar is dissolved. This can be done ahead and refrigerated.
2. Put block of ice in 6-quart punch bowl, add above mix, club soda, and champagne.

Marcia Cutter
Lubbock, Texas

WEDDING PUNCH

Yields 10 Quarts

Preparation 15 Minutes
Refrigerate 2 Hours

2 cans (47-ounce each) pineapple juice
4 cans (6-ounce each) frozen orange juice
3 cans (6-ounce each) frozen lemonade
1 can (6-ounce) limeade
4 bottles champagne, chilled
2 liters white wine
Orange and lime slices

1. Combine pineapple juice, orange juice, lemonade, and limeade. Do not dilute. Refrigerate.
2. When ready to serve, add champagne and wine to fruit mixture in 12-quart punch bowl. Add small block of ice, or an ice ring. Decorate with orange and lime slices.

NOTE:

Freeze some of fruit mixture in ice trays. Add to punch to keep chilled during party. Rum or vodka may be added to taste. For a non-alcoholic punch, substitute 4 quarts ginger ale and 2 quarts club soda for champagne and wine.

Janet Sparkman
Boulder, Colorado

ARTILLERY PUNCH

Yields 5 Quarts

Preparation 15 Minutes
Refrigerate 48 Hours

4 cups strong tea
2 cups orange juice
1 cup lemon juice
1 bottle (.75-liter) dry red wine
2 cups gold rum
2 cups rye whiskey
1 cup gin
1 cup brandy
1 1/2 ounces Benedictine (optional)
1/2 cup sugar
Block of ice
1 bottle champagne, chilled
Lemon slices to garnish

1. Mix tea, orange juice, lemon juice, wine, rum, whiskey, gin, brandy, Benedictine, and sugar. Let stand in cool place or refrigerate 48 hours.
2. Place block of ice in 8-quart punch bowl with punch just before serving. Pour champagne over ice and garnish with lemon slices.

Lee Dalk
Boulder, Colorado

BOSTON FISH-HOUSE PUNCH

Yields 51/2 Quarts

Preparation 10 Minutes

1 cup lime juice
1 cup pineapple juice
6 cups light rum
4 cups brandy
2 cups peach brandy
3 bottles champagne, chilled
Block of ice

1. In 8-quart punch bowl, mix lime juice and pineapple juice, then add other ingredients. Add block of ice to chill.

NOTE:

Can be diluted with 1 1/2 quarts of club soda.

Morris Massey
New Orleans, Louisiana

THE LONGHORN

Yields 3 Quarts

Preparation 10 Minutes

4 cups vodka
1 cup peach brandy
1 quart club soda
1 bottle champagne, chilled
Block of ice

1. Combine vodka, brandy, club soda, and champagne. Pour over block of ice in punch bowl or over ice cubes in punch cups.

NOTE:

A very light tasting but potent punch.

Ron Patton
Storres, Connecticut

TRADITIONAL EGGNOG

Yields 2 1/2 Quarts

Preparation 30 Minutes

1 dozen eggs
1 1/2 cups sugar
1 cup light rum
1 cup brandy
2 cups milk
2 cups heavy cream, whipped
Freshly grated nutmeg

1. Beat eggs until thick and light. Gradually add sugar while beating.
2. Add rum, brandy, and milk, beating after each addition.
3. Just before serving fold in whipped cream and grate nutmeg on top.

NOTE:

If you prefer a thinner mixture, you may add more milk. This would also dilute the liquor if it seems too strong.

Joan Mason
Boulder, Colorado

EGGNOG

Yields 4 Quarts

Preparation 1 Hour
Stand Overnight

2 cups bourbon
1 cup rum
1/2 cup brandy
2 cups sugar
1 dozen eggs
2 quarts vanilla ice cream, melted
Nutmeg

1. Pour liquor over sugar the night before use.
2. Shortly before serving, separate eggs. Beat yolks until light and add liquor mix *very, very slowly*. Then carefully fold in ice cream.
3. Beat egg whites and fold into egg yolk mixture. Pour into punch bowl and sprinkle with nutmeg.

NOTE:

The amount of liquor can be scaled down depending on taste. French vanilla ice cream can be used for richer mixture.

Paul R. Flippen
Boulder, Colorado

JAMS, JELLIES,
•
MARMALADES, PICKLES,
•
AND CHUTNEYS

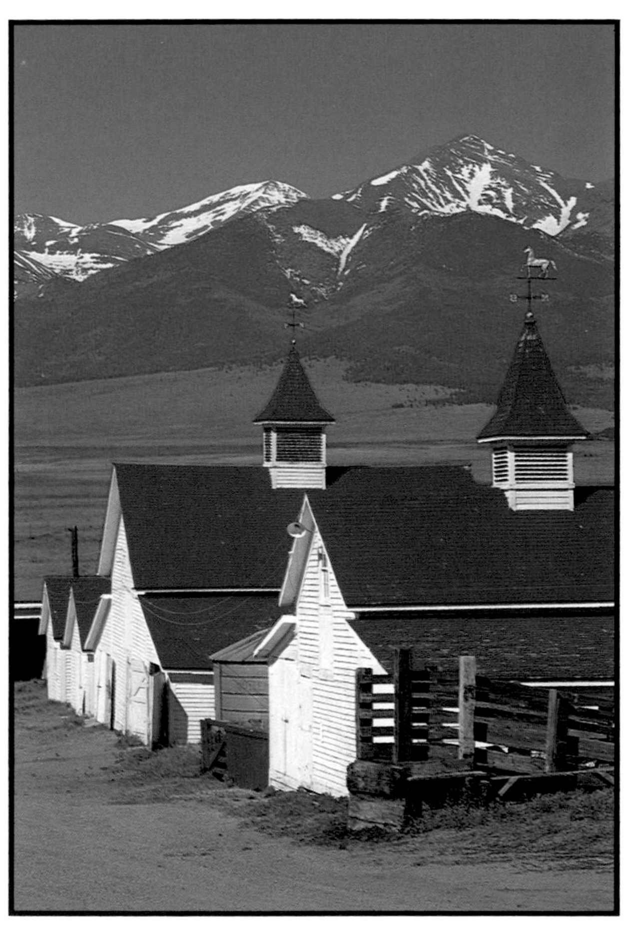

CATALINA FIG-BRANDY JAM

Yields 5 to 6 Pints

Preparation 30 Minutes
Cook 50 Minutes

10 cups figs, cut in small pieces
3/4 cup water
9 cups sugar
1/4 cup lemon juice
1/4 to 1/2 cup lemon rind, grated
1 1/4 cups chopped walnuts
1 package (1 3/4-ounce) powdered pectin
1/4 to 1/2 cup brandy, or 2 to 3 tablespoons brandy flavoring

1. Measure figs, water, sugar, and lemon juice into a large kettle. Cook over low heat, stirring occasionally. Boil slowly for 40 minutes.
2. Add lemon rind and walnuts. Stir in pectin and boil 5 minutes. Skim. Stir in brandy. Pour into sterilized jars, leaving 1/4 inch head room. Cover at once with lids.

Margaret Felkley
Avalon, California

MILLIE'S JAMS AND JELLIES

AMBROSIAL PEACH JAM

Yields 8 Pints
Stand Overnight

Preparation 55 Minutes
Cook 25 Minutes

8 peaches
3 large oranges
1 lemon
2 medium cantaloupes
1 can (8-ounce) crushed pineapple
Sugar

1. Peel and pit peaches. Peel and remove membrane and seeds from oranges and lemon. Peel and seed cantaloupes.
2. Using a food processor, blender or food grinder, coarsely puree peaches, oranges, lemon, cantaloupes, and pineapple. Add 3/4 cup sugar for each cup of fruit. Let stand overnight in a non-metal container.
3. Next day cook gently until mixture thickens and slips off spoon in one sheet. Stir frequently. Pour into hot sterile glasses and seal.

NOTE:

Sliced almonds and well-drained maraschino cherries may be added just before pouring into glasses.

PEAR-RASPBERRY JAM

Yields 10 Medium Glasses

Preparation 45 Minutes
Cook 10 Minutes

2 pounds fully ripe pears
1 package (10-ounce) frozen raspberries, thawed
1/4 cup lemon juice
6 cups sugar
3 ounces liquid pectin
Parafin

1. Peel, core, and grind pears. Put raspberries in 1-quart measure and add ground pears to equal 4 cups. Place in large pan and add lemon juice.
2. Mix in sugar, bring to full boil, and boil hard 1 minute, stirring constantly. Remove from heat and stir in pectin. Skim foam and stir occasionally for 5 minutes.
3. Ladle into glasses and seal at once with 1/8-inch hot parafin.

APRICOT-CHERRY JAM

Yields 7 Cups

Preparation 45 Minutes
Cook 20 Minutes

1 1/2 pounds apricots, pitted but not peeled
1 1/2 pounds sour cherries, stemmed and pitted
5 1/2 cups sugar
1 box (1 3/4-ounce) powdered pectin
3/4 teaspoon almond extract
Parafin (optional)

1. Finely grind or puree apricots and finely chop cherries. Combine and measure 4 1/2 cups, including juice, into large kettle.
2. Measure sugar and set aside. Mix pectin with fruit, and stir until it comes to hard boil. Immediately add sugar, bring to full boil, and boil hard 1 minute, stirring constantly.
3. Stir and skim foam alternately for 5 minutes. Add extract and stir. Ladle into sterilized glasses. Seal with 1/8-inch layer hot paraffin or jar lids.

CHERRY-RASPBERRY FREEZER JAM

Yields 7 Medium Jars

Preparation 40 Minutes
Cook 5 Minutes

1 1/2 pints raspberries or blackberries
1 1/2 pounds fully ripe sour cherries
5 1/4 cups sugar
3/4 cup water
1 box (1 3/4-ounce) powdered pectin

1. Crush raspberries. Pit and grind cherries. Measure 1 1/2 cups each into bowl. Stir in sugar and set aside.
2. Mix water and pectin in saucepan. Boil 1 minute, stirring constantly. Stir into fruits and continue stirring 3 minutes.
3. Ladle into jars. Cover at once with tight lids. When jam is set, store in freezer.

PARADISE PEARS

Yields 9 Medium Glasses

Preparation 40 Minutes
Cook 20 Minutes

1 orange
1 lemon
2 pounds ripe pears
1/4 cup chopped maraschino cherries
1 can (8 1/2-ounce) crushed pineapple
5 cups sugar
1 box (1 3/4-ounce) powdered pectin
Parafin (optional)

1. Peel, seed, and chop orange and lemon. Peel, core, and grind pears. Combine fruits, including cherries, and pineapple and measure 4 1/2 cups into large kettle.
2. Have measured sugar ready. Add pectin to fruit and bring to hard boil, stirring constantly. Add sugar, bring to a rolling boil, and boil 1 minute, stirring constantly.
3. Remove from heat, skim, and stir 5 minutes. Ladle into hot glasses and cover with 1/8-inch hot parafin or jar lids.

GRAPE-PLUM DUO

Yields 9 Cups

Preparation 45 Minutes
Cook 25 Minutes

3 1/2 pounds plums
3 pounds Concord grapes
1 cup water
8 1/2 cups sugar
1 box (1 3/4-ounce) powdered pectin
Parafin (optional)

1. Pit unpeeled plums and crush with grapes. Add water, bring to boil, and simmer 10 minutes.
2. Pour into jelly bag and squeeze out juice. Measure 6 1/2 cups into large kettle. Measure sugar and set aside.
3. Add pectin to fruit juice and stir until it comes to a hard boil. Immediately add sugar and bring to rolling boil. Boil hard 1 minute, stirring constantly.
4. Remove from heat, skim foam, and quickly pour into glass jars. Cover at once with 1/8-inch hot parafin or jar lids.

CHERRY-BLUEBERRY TWO-SOME

Yields 5 1/2 Cups

Preparation 40 Minutes
Cook 15 Minutes

1 1/2 pounds sour cherries
1 pint blueberries
4 cups sugar
1 box (1 3/4-ounce) powdered pectin
Parafin (optional)

1. Stem, pit, and grind cherries. Crush blueberries. Combine and measure 3 1/2 cups into large pan. Measure sugar and set aside.
2. Mix pectin with fruit and bring to hard boil, stirring constantly. Stir in sugar and boil 1 minute. Remove from heat, skim, and stir 5 minutes to prevent fruit floating to the top.
3. Ladle into glasses and cover at once with 1/8-inch hot parafin or jar lids.

Millie Anderson
Boulder, Colorado

STRAWBERRY PRESERVES

Yields 2 Cups
Stand Overnight

Preparation 15 Minutes
Cook 15 Minutes

4 cups strawberries
4 cups sugar

1. Add 1 cup sugar to strawberries and dissolve over low heat, then boil 1 minute. Add 2 cups more sugar, dissolve, and boil 1 minute. Cool.
2. Add 1 cup sugar, dissolve, and boil 3 minutes. Let stand overnight. The following day boil 1 minute. Ladle into sterilized jars and seal or freeze.

Bev Beeler
Arvada, Colorado

MILDRED NORVEL'S ORANGE MARMALADE

Yields 2 Cups
Stand 48 Hours

Preparation 5 Minutes
Cook 1 Hour

1 cup sliced orange, including peel
3 cups water
Juice of 1/2 lemon
Sugar

1. Combine orange slices, water, and lemon juice and let stand at room temperature overnight. Next day cook until tender, then let stand another day.
2. Measure 1 cup sugar to each cup of orange mixture. Cook 20 minutes or until mixture sheets from side of spoon. Seal in jars.

Crede Dever
Boulder, Colorado

GOLD HILL RHUBARB MARMALADE

Yields 12 Pints

Preparation 2 Days
Bake 4 to 5 Hours at 300°F

6 quarts rhubarb, diced
12 cups sugar
6 oranges, unpeeled
1 cup raisins
1 cup walnuts
Parafin

1. Place rhubarb and sugar in large earthen crock and let stand overnight. In the morning, grind the oranges and add to rhubarb.
2. Bake the mixture at 300 degrees all day or until golden and of desired thickness. Add raisins and walnuts mid-way in the cooking. Pour into hot sterilized jars and seal with parafin.

Antoinette F. Stepanek
Boulder, Colorado

VARIATION:

Omit oranges, raisins, and walnuts. Add 3 lemons, quartered and thinly sliced, and 9 tablespoons ground ginger or 5 1/2 tablespoons preserved ginger to rhubarb with sugar. Let stand overnight and simmer next day, uncovered, 45 to 60 minutes.

Peg Fulton
Boulder, Colorado

PEPPER JELLY

Yields 6 Cups

Preparation 1 Hour
Cook 20 Minutes

6 1/2 cups sugar
1 1/2 cups vinegar
1 1/2 cups finely chopped green peppers
1/2 cup finely chopped jalapeño pepper
1 bottle (6-ounce) Certo
Parafin

1. In a 5-quart kettle, combine sugar and vinegar over low heat. Add peppers. Bring to boil over high heat, stirring constantly.
2. Boil hard for 5 minutes, add Certo, stir, and skim.
3. Allow to cool for 8 minutes to prevent peppers from floating. Put into hot sterilized jars, leaving 1/2 inch head room. Seal with parafin.

NOTE:

Use half red sweet pepper for a more colorful jelly. Wear rubber gloves when seeding and chopping the jalapeño and do not rub your eyes! For a less hot jelly, reduce jalapeño and increase the green pepper.

Mary V. Terry
Dallas, Texas

MRS. HEISE'S CARROT-CUCUMBER RELISH

Yields 2 1/2 Pints
Stand 3 Hours

Preparation 30 Minutes
Cook 20 Minutes

3 1/2 cups coarsely ground cucumbers, unpared
1 1/2 cups coarsely ground carrots
1 cup coarsely ground onions
2 tablespoons salt
2 1/2 cups sugar
1 1/2 cups vinegar
1 1/2 teaspoons each celery seed and mustard seed

1. Combine cucumber, carrots, and onions; stir in salt. Let stand 3 hours; drain.
2. Combine sugar, vinegar, celery and mustard seeds and bring to a boil. Add vegetables and simmer, uncovered, 20 minutes.
3. Seal at once in sterilized jars. Chill before serving.

Nan V. Rickey
Evergreen, Colorado

QUICK PICKLES

Yields 3 to 4 Pints
Stand 2 Hours

Preparation 1 1/4 Hours
Refrigerate 4 Days

3 to 4 pounds cucumbers
1 medium onion
1 medium green pepper
1 tablespoon pickling salt
1 cup vinegar
2 cups sugar
1 teaspoon celery salt

1. Slice cucumbers, onions, and green peppers very thin and mix in large bowl with pickling salt. Let stand 2 hours. Drain well.
2. Mix vinegar, sugar, and celery salt, and pour over vegetables. Cover and refrigerate 4 days. Fill jars, cover, and refrigerate.

Millie Anderson
Boulder, Colorado

DILL PICKLES

Yields 6 Quarts

Preparation 45 Minutes
Cook 20 Minutes

36 cucumbers
Dill weed
Garlic cloves
14 cups water
2 cups vinegar
3/4 cup pickling salt

1. Sterilize six 1-quart jars. Put a sprig of dill and 1 or 2 garlic cloves in each. Fill with cucumbers.
2. Boil water, vinegar, and salt for 5 minutes. Pour into jars to 1/2 inch from top. Process 15 minutes in boiling water bath.

June Krantz
Boulder, Colorado

AUNT DOROTHY'S SWEET PICKLES

Yields 10 Pints
Soak 7 Days

Preparation 21/2 Hours
Cook 30 Minutes

7 pounds cucumbers
11/2 cups pickling salt
Water
7 cups vinegar
1 heaping teaspoon alum
3 pounds sugar
4 tablespoons whole allspice
16 sticks cinnamon (1-ounce)
2 tablespoons celery seed
21/2 tablespoons whole cloves

1. Put cucumbers in a large crock. Combine salt and 1 gallon water, pour over cucumbers and soak, covered with weighted lid, for 3 days. Drain. Soak 3 more days in 1 gallon clear water, changing water daily, using weighted lid to cover each time.
2. On 7th day, drain completely, cut up cucumbers and put in non-aluminum pot. Combine 1 cup vinegar, alum, and 1 gallon water and pour over cucumbers. Heat thoroughly, remove from stove, and let stand 2 hours. Drain well. Pack in sterilized jars.
3. Make syrup by combining sugar and 6 cups vinegar. Tie spices in cheesecloth bag, add to sugar mixture, and boil for 10 minutes. Remove spice bag and pour hot syrup over cucumbers. Seal and process in hot water bath for 10 minutes.

Susannah Jordan
Jamestown, Colorado

APPLE CHUTNEY

Yields 4 Cups

Preparation 20 Minutes
Cook 1 to 1 1/4 Hours

8 cups unpeeled apple, chopped
2 1/4 cups brown sugar
1 1/3 cups cider vinegar
1 clove garlic, minced (optional)
1 large onion, chopped
1 red or green pepper, chopped
2 cups raisins, or 1 cup raisins and 1 cup chopped prunes
1 teaspoon salt
1 teaspoon ginger
1 tablespoon mustard seed
1/8 teaspoon cayenne or paprika

1. Combine chopped apple, sugar, vinegar, garlic, onion, and chopped pepper in a heavy kettle. Cook gently until fairly thick, about 30 to 45 minutes.
2. Add raisins, salt, ginger, mustard seeds, and cayenne or paprika. Continue to cook for 30 minutes.

Louise Allenson
Detroit, Michigan

TOMATO CHUTNEY

Yields 2 Cups

Preparation 20 Minutes
Cook 30 to 40 Minutes

1 tablespoon shortening
1 whole dried red chili pepper, crumbled
1/2 teaspoon cumin seeds
1/4 teaspoon mustard seeds
1/4 teaspoon nutmeg
4 medium tomatoes, peeled and sliced 1/8-inch thick
1/3 cup raisins
1/2 cup sugar
1 lemon, quartered

1. Melt shortening in pan and add chili pepper, mustard, cumin seeds, and nutmeg.
2. When seeds start to jump, add tomatoes, raisins, and sugar.
3. Place lemon on top and simmer, stirring frequently, until thickened, about 30 minutes. Chill.

Neva Downing
Rifle, Colorado

SANDWICHES • AND • SNACKS

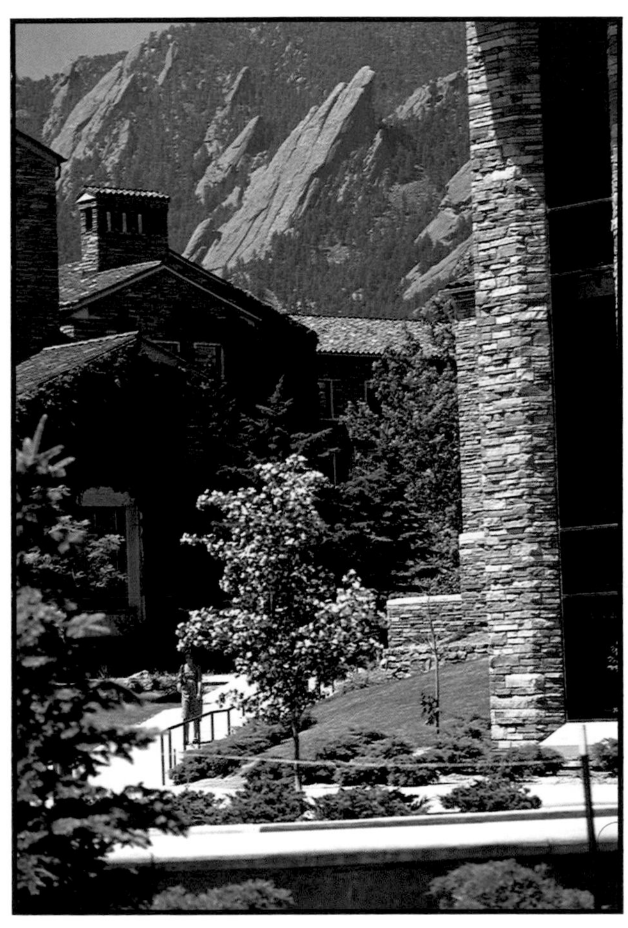

AMALIA'S PRUNE SANDWICHES

Yields 21 Sandwiches

Preparation 30 Minutes
Cook 50 Minutes

2 pounds prunes
8 teaspoons honey
2 teaspoons lemon juice
Firm white or wheat bread, sliced
Softened butter
Mayonnaise
Lettuce

1. Boil prunes in water to cover until soft, add honey and lemon juice and cook 20 minutes longer. Drain and pit.
2. Butter one side of bread slice, taking care to cover the entire surface. Spread layer of prunes on buttered bread and add a little mayonnaise.
3. Cover mayonnaise with small pieces of lettuce. Top with second slice of bread.
4. Cut sandwich in center at slight angle so there are no points of bread to break off.

NOTE:

Butter and lettuce are very important to keep prunes from soaking through bread.

Lillie Malork
Vallejo, California

DATE-NUT TRIANGLES

Yields 40 Sandwiches

Preparation 15 Minutes
Chill 2 Hours

3 ounces cream cheese
1 teaspoon grated orange rind
2 teaspoons orange juice
1 can (8-ounce) date-nut roll

1. Blend cream cheese, orange rind, and orange juice until soft enough to spread.
2. Halve date-nut lengthwise and spread one side with half of cheese mixture. Put back together to form roll.
3. Halve again, lengthwise, at right angles to first cut and spread with rest of cheese mixture. Put back together and wrap tightly.
4. Chill at least 2 hours or overnight.
5. When ready to serve, slice roll crosswise into 10 rounds. Lay each flat and cut into quarters cutting through bread and not filling.

POTTED CHICKEN

A 75-year-old Nova Scotia recipe

Yields 4 1/2 Cups

Preparation 30 Minutes
Bake 1 to 1 1/2 Hours at 350°F

3 cups cooked chicken, skinned and boned
1 cup ham
7 tablespoons butter, melted
1/8 teaspoon cayenne pepper
1/8 teaspoon grated nutmeg
2 teaspoons salt

1. Chop or grind chicken and ham and pound into a paste or puree mixture in a food processor or blender. Add 4 tablespoons butter, pepper, nutmeg, and salt and mix well.
2. Pack mixture solidly in small stone pots or bowls. Cover and bake 1 to 1 1/2 hours at 350 degrees. Remove from oven and cool completely.
3. When meat is cold, pour a thin layer of melted butter on top and store tightly covered in refrigerator.

NOTE:

Keeps 2 weeks in refrigerator if butter seal is renewed after each use. Can be frozen.

Elizabeth Porter
Boulder, Colorado

MINCED CHICKEN SANDWICH

Serves 4

Preparation 10 Minutes

1 cup minced cooked chicken
1/4 cup finely chopped peanuts
1/4 cup chopped celery
1/3 cup mayonnaise

1. Mix ingredients together and chill until served. Serve on German Dark Rye Bread (see Index).

NOTE:

Tuna, crab, or ham may be substituted for chicken.

Crede Dever
Boulder, Colorado

BOMBAY TOAST

Yields 3 1/2 Cups

Preparation 1 Hour

1 cup mayonnaise
2 to 3 teaspoons curry powder
1 cup cooked macaroni in 1/2-inch lengths
3/4 cup chopped cooked chicken
1/4 cup chopped cooked giblets
Pumpernickel or rye bread, Westphaelan variety, thinly sliced
3 hard-cooked eggs, sliced
Smoked salmon to garnish (optional)

1. Mix mayonnaise with curry powder. Set aside to let flavors develop. Add macaroni, chicken, and giblets. Mix well.
2. Pile high on a small slice of bread. Decorate with egg slices and top with a strip of smoked salmon.

Sheryl Kuempel
Boulder, Colorado

PARSLEY-CHEESE FILLING

Yields 1 Cup

Preparation 5 Minutes

3/4 cup bleu cheese spread
3/4 cup finely chopped radishes
3/4 cup finely chopped fresh parsley

1. Combine bleu cheese spread, radishes, and parsley in a small bowl. Mix well. Spread on French bread or pita toast.

Elizabeth Haverly
Portland, Oregon

DANISH CRAB SANDWICH

Yields 1 1/2 Cups

Preparation 10 Minutes

1 can (6 1/2-ounce) crab
1/2 cup chopped cooked asparagus, fresh or canned
1/2 cup mayonnaise
Salt and white pepper to taste
French bread
Lettuce
Diced tomato

1. Mix crab, asparagus, mayonnaise, salt, and pepper.
2. Pile crab mixture on slices of French bread lined with lettuce. Serve open-face decorated with bits of tomato.

Sheryl Kuempel
Boulder, Colorado

SALMON BRAZIL

Serves 4

Preparation 30 Minutes
Broil 7 Minutes

1 can (16-ounce) salmon
1 cup grated Cheddar cheese
1/2 cup mayonnaise
1 tablespoon minced onion
1 can (4 1/2-ounce) black olives, chopped
1 teaspoon mustard
Paprika
4 hamburger buns or English muffins

1. Remove bone and skin from salmon and flake. Reserve liquid.
2. Combine salmon and salmon liquid, cheese, mayonnaise, onion, olives, and mustard.
3. Spread on split hamburger buns or muffin halves. Place on cookie sheet, sprinkle with paprika and broil 7 minutes, 3 inches from heat, or until lightly browned.

Sue McMillan
Boulder, Colorado

HAM SANDWICHES

Serves 12 to 14

Preparation 20 Minutes
Bake 15 Minutes at 350°F

1 pound ham
1 pound Cheddar cheese, sharp preferred
1 small onion
1 small green pepper
2 ribs celery
1 cup tomato sauce
1/4 cup melted butter
12 to 14 individual Brown and Serve French rolls

1. Grind ham, cheese, onion, pepper, and celery, or coarsely puree in food processor. Mix with tomato sauce and melted butter.
2. Scoop out center of rolls, leaving bottoms and sides intact. Fill with ham mixture, mounding on top.
3. Bake on a cookie sheet at 350 degrees for 15 minutes or until rolls and top of filling are brown.

NOTE:

May be cooked, wrapped individually, and frozen for later use. Reheat 2 1/2 minutes in microwave oven or 15 to 20 minutes at 350 degrees.

Sara McNice
Boulder, Colorado

HOT ASPARAGUS SANDWICH

Serves 6

Preparation 15 Minutes
Cook 10 Minutes

6 ounces cream cheese, softened
1 can (8-ounce) asparagus tips, drained
2 tablespoons fresh lemon juice
2 hard-cooked eggs, diced
1/2 teaspoon salt
12 slices bread
Butter, as needed
Parmesan cheese

1. Mix cream cheese, asparagus, lemon juice, eggs, and salt. Spread on six slices of bread. Top with remaining slices.
2. Spread softened butter on outside of sandwiches and grill slowly until heated through and lightly browned.
3. Sprinkle one or both sides of sandwich with Parmesan cheese while it is hot.

NOTE:

An electric frying pan gives a good constant temperature for grilling, or bake the sandwich in a 350-degree oven. Cut into small pieces and use as an hors d'oeuvre. Delicious served with a cup of soup or small salad for luncheon or late-night supper.

Dr. Frank J. Cozzetto
Denver, Colorado

FRENCH-BREAD SANDWICH

Serves 5 to 6

Preparation 10 Minutes
Bake 10 Minutes at 350°F

1/2 pound sharp cheese, grated
1/2 pound boiled ham
2 hard-cooked eggs
1 can (4-ounce) pimientos, drained
1 medium onion
1 can (4 1/2-ounce) chopped ripe olives, drained
1/2 to 1 cup mayonnaise
French bread

1. Grind cheese, ham, eggs, pimientos, onion, and olives.
2. Just before serving, stir in mayonnaise, spread on French bread, wrap in foil, and bake at 350 degrees for 10 minutes or until hot.

Bunny Wanner
Boulder, Colorado

MONTE CRISTO SANDWICH

Serves 6

Preparation 45 Minutes
Fry 7 Minutes at 375°F

18 slices bread
Butter or margarine, as needed
6 slices each ham, turkey or chicken, and Swiss cheese
3 eggs
6 tablespoons milk
Dash salt
Oil for frying
Pineapple slices
Raspberry jam or currant jelly

1. For each sandwich, butter 1 slice bread and cover with slice of ham. Top with slice of turkey and cover with second slice of buttered bread.
2. Butter top side of second bread slice and cover with Swiss cheese. Close sandwich with third slice of buttered bread, buttered side down.
3. Trim crusts and cut sandwiches in halves and fasten with wooden picks.
4. Beat eggs with milk and salt. Dip sandwiches in egg mixture and fry in deep fat heated to 375 degrees until golden brown. Or saute' in butter until brown on both sides.
5. Remove picks and serve with pineapple slices and raspberry jam or currant jelly.

Jordan March
Playa del Rey, California

ORIENTAL HOT TURNOVERS

Serves 4

Preparation 45 Minutes
Bake 10 Minutes at 375°F

1/2 pound ground beef
1 envelope dried onion-mushroom soup mix
1/2 cup diced water chestnuts
1 cup bean sprouts
2 tablespoons chopped onion
2 packages refrigerated crescent rolls

1. Saute' beef lightly. Add soup mix, water chestnuts, bean sprouts, and onion. Cool mixture.
2. Separate each package of rolls into 4 squares and press perforations together. Place 1/8 of filling on each, foid over and crimp edges.
3. Bake in a 375-degree oven for 10 to 15 minutes or until golden brown. Serve immediately.

Patricia Walton
Boulder, Colorado

PITA À LA SUZANNE

Serves 4 to 6

Preparation 30 Minutes
Cook 25 Minutes

2 teaspoons butter
1/2 medium onion, coarsely chopped
1/2 pound cooked ham, cut in julienne strips
12 ounces French-style green beans, cooked
1/2 pound mushrooms, whole or chopped
1/2 cup white wine
1 small bay leaf, crushed
1/8 teaspoon rosemary
1/8 teaspoon thyme
3/4 pound Monterey Jack cheese
1/2 cup milk
4 to 6 pita loaves

1. Melt butter in a large frying pan and saute' onion over low heat 3 to 5 minutes. Add ham, beans, mushrooms, wine, bay leaf, rosemary, and thyme. Simmer about 5 minutes.
2. Grate 1/2 pound cheese and slice remaining 1/4 pound. Add milk and grated cheese to ham mixture and stir until cheese melts and mixture thickens.
3. Split one edge of pita loaves and fill pouches with mixture. Place a slice of cheese on top of filling and broil until cheese melts, about 2 to 3 minutes. Serve hot.

NOTE:

Especially good with shredded lettuce topped with asparagus tips and salad dressing. Also good garnished with ripe olives and cherry tomatoes. Great use for leftovers, anything goes.

Richard W. Thompson
Aurora, Colorado

CALIFORNIA PIZZA

Serves 6 to 12

Preparation 30 Minutes
Broil 5 Minutes

3/4 pound sharp Cheddar cheese, grated
1/3 cup oil
1 can (6-ounce) olives, chopped
4 green onions, chopped
5 hot chili peppers chopped
1 clove garlic, mashed
1/2 teaspoon salt
4 to 6 French rolls, thinly sliced

1. Mix all ingredients together except French rolls. Spread on roll slices.
2. Place on cookie sheets and broil until cheese melts.

NOTE:

Pizzas can be frozen before broiling. Broil directly from the freezer.

Sonia K. Plisco
Golden, Colorado

DELICIOUS SNACKS

Preparation 30 Minutes
Bake 20 Minutes at 350°F

Bacon
Cream of mushroom soup, undiluted
Half slices of bread without crusts

1. Partially fry amount of bacon desired, cut slices in thirds or halves.
2. Spread undiluted cream of mushroom soup on bread.
3. Place bread slice over strip of bacon (trimmed to fit, if desired), roll up and fasten with toothpick. Bacon will be on the outside of the bread roll.
4. Place rolls on rack of broiling pan and bake for 20 minutes at 350 degrees.

Ann Herbert
Wheat Ridge, Colorado

SESAME-CHEESE ROLLS

Yields 4 Dozen

Preparation 30 Minutes
Bake 6 to 7 Minutes at 375°F

8 ounces cream cheese
1/2 **cup butter, softened**
1/4 **cup sesame seeds, lightly toasted**
2 to 3 ounces Cheddar cheese, grated
2 packages refrigerated crescent rolls

1. Blend cream cheese and butter, add sesame seeds and Cheddar cheese. Mix well.
2. Separate each package of crescent roll dough into 4 rectangles; firmly press perforations to seal. Spread cheese-butter mixture and roll lengthwise jelly-roll fashion. Cut each roll into 6 pieces.
3. Bake on greased cookie sheet 6 to 7 minutes at 375 degrees.

VARIATION:

1. Spread sour cream and onion salt on dough; or use sour cream, cooked bacon, and seasoned salt.
2. Turn these into breakfast rolls by spreading lemon butter, orange butter, or cinnamon butter on dough as above.

Sue McMillan
Boulder, Colorado

CHEESE PUFFS

Serves 8 to 10
Freeze

Preparation 40 Minutes
Bake 10 Minutes at 400°F

1 pound loaf unsliced white bread
1/4 cup each grated Swiss cheese, sharp Cheddar cheese, mozzarella cheese
3 ounces cream cheese
8 tablespoons butter
1/2 teaspoon dry mustard
1/8 teaspoon cayenne pepper
Salt to taste
2 egg whites

1. Trim crust from all sides of loaf, cut into 1-inch cubes.
2. Combine cheeses and butter in saucepan and stir over moderate heat until blended. Remove from heat and add mustard, cayenne pepper, and salt.
3. Beat egg whites until stiff, fold into cheese mixture.
4. With long fork, spear cube of bread and swirl into cheese until well coated. Place side by side, but not touching, on baking sheet.
5. Freeze.
6. Preheat oven to 400 degrees and bake on ungreased sheet until brown and golden, approximately 10 minutes.

NOTE:

Delicious with soup or salad.

Anne Turner
Boulder, Colorado

CHEESE CRISPS

Preparation 5 Minutes
Cook 2 Minutes

Monterey Jack or Cheddar cheese, grated
Flour or corn tortillas
Alfalfa or mung bean sprouts

1. Place grated cheese on flat tortilla.
2. Broil 2 minutes or until cheese is melted. Remove and sprinkle with sprouts. Roll up and eat while hot.

NOTE:

A few drops of *Salsa Verde* (see Index) give this snack a little extra zip.

Myhra Hill
Boulder, Colorado

CHEESE SQUARES

Yields 5 Dozen

Preparation 45 Minutes
Bake 15 Minutes at 425°F

1 pound American cheese at room temperature
1 pound butter at room temperature
1 1/2 to 2 1/2 pounds white sandwich bread

1. Cream cheese and butter together in a mixer.
2. Remove crusts from bread slices. Frost bread with cheese mixture. Make stack of 3 slices.
3. Cut each stack into four sections. Frost the cut sides with cheese mixture.
4. Insert toothpick in center of each stack. Bake on cookie sheets for 15 minutes at 425 degrees. Serve hot!

Shirley M. Moore
Carlsbad, New Mexico

VARIATION:

Use 1 pound Cheddar cheese, 1 pound butter, 1 tablespoon Worcestershire sauce, and 1 teaspoon salt. Grate or shred cheese. Blend all ingredients. Proceed as above. Bake at 350 degrees for 12 to 15 minutes. Serve hot!

NOTE:

Serve with a summer salad. May be frozen for several months and then baked.

Marian A. Wightman
Lincoln, Nebraska

CHEESE APPETIZERS

Yields 5 Dozen
Refrigerate 1 Hour

Preparation 15 Minutes
Bake 12 Minutes at 400°F

1 jar (5-ounce) Old English cheese
1 2/3 cups flour
13 tablespoons butter
Dash cayenne pepper

1. Mix cheese, flour, butter, and pepper thoroughly. Form into 2 long rolls. Chill at least one hour.
2. Cut into thin slices and bake on cookie sheet.
3. Bake at 400 degrees for 12 minutes or until light brown. Serve hot.

NOTE:

These may be frozen before slicing. Thaw slightly before slicing.

Rue Megrew
Boulder, Colorado

SWISS CHEESE ROUNDS

Serves 20 to 25

Preparation 30 Minutes

1 pound Swiss cheese, grated
2 teaspoons onion flakes or onion put through a garlic press
1/2 teaspoon paprika
2 tablespoons white wine or sherry
1/3 cup salad dressing or mayonnaise
1 teaspoon dried parsley
1 loaf party rye bread

1. Combine cheese, onion, paprika, wine, mayonnaise, and parsley.
2. Spread on bread slices, place on cookie sheet, and put under broiler until bubbly and light brown.

NOTE:

Cheese mixture may be made ahead and stored in refrigerator.

Suzanne Taylor
Boulder, Colorado

PECAN CHEESE BITES

Yields 5 Dozen

Preparation 20 Minutes
Bake 25 Minutes at 350°F

8 ounces sharp Cheddar cheese, grated
1 cup margarine, softened
2 1/2 cups flour, sifted
1 cup chopped pecans
1 teaspoon salt
1/2 to 1 teaspoon cayenne pepper

1. Mix all ingredients and shape into walnut-sized balls.
2. Place on a cookie sheet. Bake at 350 degrees for 25 minutes.

NOTE:

May be frozen until needed. Reheat and serve immediately. This recipe can be prepared in the food processor. Add flour last and process until just mixed in.

Mary V. Terry
Dallas, Texas

HA' PENNIES

Yields 5 Dozen
Refrigerate 2 Hours

Preparation 10 Minutes
Bake 10 Minutes at 375°F

8 ounces sharp Cheddar cheese, shredded
1/2 cup butter or margarine, softened
1 cup flour
3 tablespoons dry onion soup mix (crumbled)

1. Combine cheese, butter, flour, and soup mix and knead into smooth ball. Divide dough in half and shape into two long rolls. Refrigerate at least two hours.
2. Heat oven to 375 degrees. Cut roll into 1/4-inch slices and bake on ungreased baking sheet until golden brown (10 to 12 minutes). Serve hot.

NOTE:

These freeze well before baking. Thaw slightly before slicing.

Barbara Cotter
Avalon, California

PARMESAN BREAD STICK BATONS

Yields 3 Dozen

Preparation 40 Minutes
Bake 15 to 20 Minutes at 350°F

1 loaf day-old unsliced white bread
1 cup grated Parmesan cheese
1/2 teaspoon garlic powder
1 cup butter or margarine, softened

1. Remove crust from bread with very sharp knife. Cut loaf lengthwise into 5/8-inch slices and cut into sticks.
2. Blend cheese, garlic powder, and butter, and spread on all sides of bread sticks.
3. Place sticks, separated, on a baking sheet and bake at 350 degrees for 15 to 20 minutes, turning frequently the last 10 minutes until all sides are golden brown.
4. Cool. Store in airtight wrap.

VARIATION:

1. Divide butter into 4 bowls, 1/4 cup butter in each. Season as follows, then bake as directed above.
   For Parmesan sticks, add 1/4 cup grated Parmesan cheese and 1/8 teaspoon garlic powder.
   For onion flavor, add 2 teaspoons instant minced onion, 1/4 teaspoon minced parsley, and 1/8 teaspoon dill weed.
   For sesame or caraway sticks, add 2 tablespoons sesame seed or 1 teaspoon caraway seed, 1/2 teaspoon minced onion, and 1/8 teaspoon paprika.
   For herb-flavored sticks, add 1/2 teaspoon dried herb seasoning mix.

2. Use canned buttermilk refrigerator biscuits in place of bread. Cut biscuits into halves or fourths and coat on all sides with any of the butter mixtures. Bake as above.

Angela Coe
Savannah, Georgia

HERB BUTTER BREAD

Serves 3 to 4

Preparation 10 Minutes
Heat 20 Minutes at 350°

1/2 cup butter
1 clove garlic, chopped
3 large sprigs parsley, chopped
1/2 teaspoon tarragon
1/2 teaspoon chives
1 loaf French bread

1. Blend butter, garlic, parsley, tarragon, and chives. Butter should be room temperature if processor or blender are not being used.
2. Cut a loaf of French bread (either in individual slices or in half lengthwise) or sour dough rolls and spread with herb butter. Wrap bread or rolls in foil and heat for 20 minutes at 350 degrees.

Pat Wright
Boulder, Colorado

AFRICAN CRUNCHY APPETIZER BITS (*Dabo Kolo*)

Yields 4 Cups

Preparation 50 Minutes
Bake 25 Minutes at 350°F

2 cups flour
2 to 2 1/2 tablespoons Hot Pepper Seasoning (see Index)
1 tablespoon sugar
1 1/2 teaspoons salt
1/4 cup oil
1/3 to 2/3 cup water

1. Mix flour, Hot Pepper Seasoning, sugar, and salt. Add oil and enough water to form a stiff dough.
2. Turn out on unfloured board; knead until smooth, about 5 minutes. Cover and let rest about 30 minutes.
3. Roll pieces of dough (keep remaining dough covered) into strands about 1/4-inch in diameter. Cut into 1/2-inch-long pieces.
4. Place on baking sheets and sprinkle with salt.
5. Bake in a 350-degree oven for 25 minutes or until lightly browned. Stir several times. Cool. Store in an airtight container.

Susannah Jordan
Jamestown, Colorado

RYE BREAD STICKS WITH CARAWAY SEEDS

Yields 2 Dozen

Preparation 1 Hour 45 Minutes
Bake 15 to 20 Minutes at 400°F

1 1/4 cups warm water
1 package dry yeast
3 tablespoons sugar
1/2 teaspoon salt
4 tablespoons caraway seeds
5 tablespoons butter, softened
2 cups unsifted rye flour
1 1/2 to 2 1/2 cups unsifted white flour

1. Measure warm water into large warm bowl, sprinkle in yeast, stir until dissolved. Add sugar, salt, 1 tablespoon caraway seeds, and 3 tablespoons butter.
2. Stir in rye flour and beat until smooth. Add enough white flour to make a stiff dough.
3. Turn out on lightly floured board and knead until smooth and elastic, 8 to 10 minutes.
4. Place in greased bowl, turning to grease top; cover and let rise in warm place until doubled in bulk, about 1 hour.
5. Punch dough down; divide in half. Cut each half into 12 pieces. Roll each piece into a rope 6 inches long.
6. Place on greased baking sheet 2 inches apart. Cover; let rise in warm place until doubled in bulk, about 30 minutes.
7. Melt remaining 2 tablespoons butter, brush dough lightly, and sprinkle with caraway seeds.
8. Bake at 400 degrees for 15 to 20 minutes or until done. Cool on wire racks.

Helen Wasley
Boulder, Colorado

ONION SHORTCAKE

Serves 8

Preparation 25 Minutes
Bake 20 to 30 Minutes at 425°F

1 large sweet onion, sliced
1/4 cup butter or margarine
1 1/2 cups corn muffin mix
1 egg, beaten
1/3 cup milk
1 cup cream-style corn
2 to 10 drops hot pepper sauce
1 cup sour cream
1/4 teaspoon salt
1/2 teaspoon dill weed (optional)
1 cup shredded sharp Cheddar cheese

1. Cook onion in butter until tender. Set aside.
2. Combine muffin mix, egg, milk, corn, and hot pepper sauce. Turn into greased 8 x 8-inch pan.

3. Add sour cream, salt, dill weed, and 1/2 cup Cheddar cheese to cooked onion. Spread over batter and sprinkle remaining cheese on top.
4. Bake 20 to 30 minutes at 425 degrees. Serve warm.

Lillian Reardon
Princeton, New Jersey

CARMEL CORN

Yields 6 Quarts

Preparation 20 Minutes
Bake 1 Hour at 250°F

6 quarts popped white popcorn
2 cups brown sugar
1/2 teaspoon salt
1/2 cup light corn syrup
1 cup margarine
1/2 teaspoon baking soda
1 teaspoon vanilla extract

1. Spread popped corn in large roaster pan.
2. Combine sugar, salt, corn syrup, and margarine and boil 5 minutes. Remove from heat and stir in soda and vanilla.
3. Pour over popcorn and mix well.
4. Bake 1 hour at 250 degrees. Stir gently but thoroughly every 15 minutes. Remove from oven and stir until slightly cool to prevent large clumps.
5. Store in airtight container when completely cool.

VARIATION:

3 cups cashews, pecans, or unsalted peanuts may be added to the popcorn before syrup.

Nancy Cowee
Denver, Colorado

HONEY-BUTTER POPCORN BALLS

Yields 1 1/2 Dozen

Preparation 45 Minutes

1/3 cup honey
1/4 cup light molasses
1/4 cup light corn syrup
1/2 cup butter
2/3 cup sugar
1 1/2 quarts popped white popcorn
1 cup chopped cashews

1. Cook honey, molasses, corn syrup, butter, and sugar to soft-crack stage. Stir occasionally. Do not overcook.
2. Remove from heat and pour over popcorn and nuts. Allow to cool slightly.
3. Butter hands and mold into balls. Finish cooling on a buttered dish.

Lenore Martinez
Boulder, Colorado

GRANOLA

Yields 6 Cups

Preparation 10 Minutes
Bake 30 Minutes at 300°F

3 cups rolled oats
1/2 cup sesame seeds, toasted
1 cup unsweetened coconut
1/2 cup wheat germ
1/2 cup shelled sunflower seeds
1/4 teaspoon sea salt
1/2 cup oil
1/2 cup honey
1 tablespoon cinnamon
1/2 teaspoon vanilla extract
Raisins, dates, toasted almonds, to taste

1. Mix oats, sesame seeds, coconut, wheat germ, sunflower seeds, and salt in a large bowl.
2. Beat together oil, honey, cinnamon, and vanilla. Mix with oats mixture. Spread on a large, flat pan.
3. Toast at 300 degrees for 1/2 hour, stirring frequently. Cool.
4. Add desired amounts of raisins, dates, and almonds.

Inez Bowman
Santa Ana, California

GRANOLA WITH A DIFFERENCE

Yields 9 to 10 Cups

Preparation 10 Minutes
Bake 45 Minutes at 275°F

3 cups rolled oats
1 cup wheat flakes
1 cup rye flakes
1 cup soy flakes
1 cup bran
1 cup wheat germ
1/2 to 1 cup shelled sunflower seeds
1 teaspoon salt
1/2 cup coconut flakes,
1/2 cup walnuts,
1/4 cup sesame seeds,
brown sugar (optional)
1/2 cup vegetable oil
3/4 cup honey
1/4 cup molasses

1. In large bowl, mix oats, wheat, rye and soy flakes, bran, wheat germ, sunflower seeds, salt, and optional ingredients, if desired.
2. Pour oil over oats mixture and mix thoroughly. Add honey and molasses and mix again.
3. Spread the granola on a baking sheet with sides (11 x 14 x 1/2-inch). Bake 45 minutes at 275 degrees, mixing granola several times during baking.
4. Cool and store in airtight containers.

Martin Ball
Denver, Colorado

OUT • OF THE • PANTRY

We would all like to be able to serve an interesting meal without a special trip to the grocery. This section is designed to help you make that a possibility. The recipes use ingredients found on most pantry, refrigerator, or freezer shelves, and are generally quick and easy to prepare. We have listed here ingredients to keep on hand (in addition to the basic standards) to make these recipes work for you when you need a great meal but not a great deal of work. The list is also a handy reference to use when you want to be sure your kitchen is well stocked, a sure way to make all your meal-planning easier.

PANTRY

Baking chocolate
Beans
Bisquick
Cake mixes, yellow, pound
Chocolate chips
Cocoa
Coconut
Cornmeal
Corn muffin mix
Crackers
Gelatin, flavored, unflavored
Nuts, a variety
Jam, jelly
Olive oil
Pasta
Rice
Minute rice
Raisins
Peanut butter

CANNED GOODS

Artichokes, hearts and marinated
Blackeyed peas
Corn, creamed and whole kernel
Evaporated milk
Fish, clams, crab, salmon, shrimp, tuna
Green beans
Green chilies, whole, chopped
Kidney beans
Mushrooms
Peas
Pimientos
Sauerkraut
Tomatoes, paste, sauce, whole
Olives, green, black
Pickles
Refried beans
Soups, cream of celery, chicken, and mushroom
Taco sauce
Wax beans

REFRIGERATOR

Bacon
Cabbage
Celery
Cheeses
American, Cheddar, cream, Monterey Jack, Old English, Parmesan, Swiss
Crescent rolls
Ginger root
Green onion
Green pepper
Parsley
Sour cream

SPICES

Allspice
Basil
Bay leaves
Cayenne pepper
Cinnamon
Cloves
Cumin
Curry powder
Dill weed, seed
Dry mustard
Marjoram
Poppy seed
Oregano
Soy sauce
Tabasco sauce
Thyme
Turmeric
Worcestershire sauce

FREEZER

Chicken
Chicken breast
Fish filets
Ground round
Hamburger
Ice cream
Juice concentrates
Party breads
Pork chops
Pound cake
Shrimp
Steak
Vegetables, corn, green beans, mixed, peas, spinach

PERISHABLES

Avocado
Corn chips
Garlic
Onions
Lemons

APRICOT-MUSTARD SPREAD

Serves 10 to 12

Preparation 5 Minutes

Apricot jam
Stone-ground mustard
8 ounces cream cheese
Crackers

1. Mix equal portions of apricot jam and mustard, then adjust to taste. Store in refrigerator.
2. Serve crackers and cream cheese accompanied by jam-mustard mixture in bowl with small spoon.

Helen B. Wasley
Boulder, Colorado

ARTICHOKE PUFFS

Serves 6 to 8

Preparation 15 Minutes

1 loaf firm white sandwich bread
1/2 cup grated Parmesan cheese
1 cup mayonnaise
1 can (10-ounce) artichoke hearts

1. Toast one side of all bread slices. Cut each slice into one or two rounds or cut off crusts and quarter.
2. Mix together cheese and mayonnaise. Cut each artichoke heart into 2 or 3 slices. Place 1 or 2 slices on each round of bread (toasted side). Put 1 tablespoon mayonnaise mixture on top.
3. Bake at 400 degrees for 5 minutes, then broil until golden brown.

NOTE:

These freeze well.

Joan Anbuhl Bloom
Boulder, Colorado

CHILI CON QUESO DIP

Serves 8

Preparation 5 Minutes
Cook 15 Minutes

1 can (7-ounce) green chili sauce
1 can (4-ounce) green chilies, diced
8 ounces Old English cheese, diced (use processed cheese only)
Corn chips

1. Combine chili sauce, chilies, and cheese in a double boiler or chafing dish. Stir until cheese has melted.
2. Serve warm with large-size corn chips.

Barbara Breternitz
Boulder, Colorado

CHILI-CHEESE DIP

Serves 8 to 10

Preparation 20 Minutes
Bake 20 Minutes at 350°F

3/4 to 1 pound Monterey Jack cheese, cubed
1 can (4-ounce) green chilies, chopped
1 can (6-ounce) black olives, chopped
Tortilla chips

1. Place the cheese in an oven-proof baking dish. Put some of the chilies and olives on top of the cheese. Repeat the layers three times.
2. Bake at 350 degrees for 20 minutes or until mixture is melted. Serve with tortilla chips.

Pat Wright
Boulder, Colorado

HOPE'S DIP

Yields 4 Cups

Preparation 15 Minutes
Bake 30 Minutes at 350°F

1 pound lean ground beef
1 can (10 1/2-ounce) bean dip
1 can (4-ounce) chopped green chilies
1 can (4-ounce) taco sauce
1 cup grated American cheese
Corn or tortilla chips

1. Brown ground beef and drain. Add bean dip, green chilies, taco sauce, and cheese.
2. Put in small casserole and heat in 350-degree oven about 30 minutes. Additional cheese may be sprinkled on top.
3. To serve, transfer to chafing dish and serve warm with chips.

Mary Kelly Miller
Littleton, Colorado

SHRIMP DIP

Yields 2 1/2 Cups

Preparation 15 Minutes

8 ounces cream cheese
1/3 cup heavy cream
2 tablespoons lemon juice
1/4 teaspoon Worcestershire sauce
1 tablespoon onion flakes
3/4 cup cooked shrimp or 1 can (4 1/2-ounce) shrimp, drained
Catsup for color

1. Soften cream cheese and add cream, lemon juice, onion flakes, and Worcestershire sauce. Mix until smooth.
2. Fold in shrimp and a little catsup for color. Serve as a dip with assorted crackers.

Rose Arno
Avalon, California

BAKED CHEESE SOUP
(*Kasesuppe*)

This is an elegant choice for a soup course, even though it can be made with leftover ham, bits of cheese, yesterday's roll, and yesterday's liquid from cooked vegetables.

Serves 1 to 2

Preparation 10 Minutes
Bake 10 to 15 Minutes at 400°F

1 cup beef or chicken broth (liquid from cooked vegetables may be used with a bit of garlic, some parsley, or chives)
3/4 ounces ham, cubed (1/4-inch)
1/2 cup hard roll or French bread, cubed (1/2-inch)
1 to 1 1/2 ounces cheese (Monterey Jack or similar cheese, but not Swiss) cubed (1/2 to 1 inch)

1. Heat stock.
2. Place ham cubes in a fireproof dish or dishes, add the hot liquid, the bread cubes, and top with cheese.
3. Place in 400-degree oven 10 to 15 minutes or until cheese is golden brown. Serve.

Gertrude K. Phelps
Boulder, Colorado

CALIFORNIA BOUILLABAISSE

Serves 6

Preparation 15 Minutes
Cook 1 Hour

1 cup chopped onion
1/2 cup chopped green pepper
1 clove garlic, minced
2 tablespoons oil
1 can (16-ounce) whole tomatoes, chopped
1/4 cup rice (uncooked)
2 cans (8-ounce each) tomato sauce
1 bay leaf
1 teaspoon salt
Dash cayenne pepper
1 quart hot water
1 can (6 1/2-ounce) crab meat, drained
1 can (4 1/2-ounce) shrimp, drained
1 can (7 1/2-ounce) minced clams, drained
Dash of Tabasco (optional)

1. Cook onion, green pepper, and garlic in oil until tender but not brown.
2. Add tomatoes, including juice, rice, tomato sauce, bay leaf, salt, cayenne, and water. Bring to a boil.
3. Cover, reduce heat, and simmer for 45 minutes.
4. Add crabmeat, shrimp, and clams. Simmer 15 minutes longer. Add Tabasco if desired.

Suzi Kazanjian
Eldorado Springs, Colorado

FRESH TOMATO SOUP

Serves 6 to 8

Preparation 10 Minutes
Cook 25 minutes

1/4 cup butter
1 onion, chopped
1 can (6-ounce) tomato paste
3 fresh tomatoes, chopped
2 cans (10 3/4-ounce each) chicken broth
Salt and pepper to taste
Sour cream for topping

1. In a soup kettle, melt butter and saute' onion.
2. When onion is limp, add tomato paste and stir.
3. Add the tomatoes and cook 2 to 3 minutes.
4. Add chicken broth and simmer for 5 minutes. Salt and pepper to taste.
5. Just before serving, top each portion with a big spoonful of sour cream.

Pat Wright
Boulder, Colorado

MACARONI BEAN SALAD

Serves 12 to 15

Preparation 1 Hour
Refrigerate 12 Hours

1 can (15-ounce) kidney beans, drained
1 cup vinegar
1 package (16-ounce) macaroni
1 package (10-ounce) frozen peas, uncooked
1 can (15-ounce) diced carrots, drained
1 can (15-ounce) French-style green beans, drained
1/2 green pepper, cut into strips
1 medium onion, chopped
1 jar (4-ounce) pimientos, drained
2 cups chopped celery
1 cup sugar
2 cups salad dressing or mayonnaise
1 cup heavy cream or evaporated milk
1 tablespoon dry mustard

1. Soak kidney beans in vinegar for 1 hour. Rinse with water and drain.
2. Meanwhile, cook macaroni according to package directions and rinse with cold water. Drain.
3. In a 3-quart bowl, mix kidney beans, macaroni, peas, drained vegetables, and chopped vegetables.
4. To make dressing, whip sugar with salad dressing or mayonnaise, heavy cream or milk, and mustard.
5. Add dressing to salad, mixing well. Chill for at least 12 hours.

ARTICHOKE SALAD

Serves 6

Preparation 35 Minutes
Refrigerate Overnight

1 cup long grain rice
2 cups chicken broth
2 green onions, chopped
2 jars (6-ounce each) marinated artichoke hearts, drained and liquid reserved
15 stuffed green olives, sliced
1/2 green pepper, finely chopped
1 stalk celery, chopped
1/2 cup mayonnaise
1/2 teaspoon curry powder
Oil from artichokes

1. Cook rice as directed on package using chicken broth and cool.
2. Add onions, artichokes, olives, green pepper and celery.
3. Mix mayonnaise, curry powder, and artichoke oil to taste. Toss with rice mixture and chill.

NOTE:

Salad is better if it sits all day or overnight.

Sue Bray
Avalon, California

COLD PEA SALAD

Serves 4 to 6

Preparation 15 Minutes

1 package (10-ounce) baby peas, frozen
2 or 3 green onions, chopped
Mayonnaise to taste.
Salt and pepper to taste

1. Thaw peas under hot water.
2. Mix peas with green onions, mayonnaise, and salt and pepper. Refrigerate.

Nancy Kuempel
Cincinnati, Ohio

PEPPER-CHEESE SOUFFLÉ

Serves 6 to 8

Preparation 30 Minutes
Bake 1 Hour at 350°F

1 can (7-ounce) green chilies, chopped
2/3 cup chopped onions
1 pound sharp cheese, grated
3 eggs, beaten
3 cups milk
1 cup Bisquick
1 teaspoon salt

1. Layer in buttered 21/2- to 3-quart casserole half of chilies, onions, and cheese. Repeat.

2. To beaten eggs, add milk, Bisquick and salt (mixture will be thin). Pour into casserole. Bake at 350 degrees for 1 hour.

NOTE:

Bakes up like a souffle'. Good served with green salad.

Elizabeth James Luckow
Nederland, Colorado

MIGAS

Serves 2

Preparation 20 Minutes
Cook 10 Minutes

2 tablespoons butter
2 tablespoons finely chopped onion
2 tablespoons finely chopped green pepper
Dash Tabasco
4 eggs, lightly beaten
1/3 cup grated Cheddar cheese
Corn chips, crumbled
***Salsa Verde* or *Salsa Roja* (see Index)**

1. Melt butter in a large skillet. Allow to cool slightly, then return to heat. Add onions, peppers, and Tabasco, and saute' slightly over medium heat, stirring occasionally.
2. Add eggs and stir. When eggs are almost cooked, add cheese and turn heat to lowest setting. Stir in crumbled corn chips.
3. Serve hot with a side dish of *Salsa Verde* or *Salsa Roja,* if desired.

Ellen Doenges
Austin, Texas

BROILED BEEF
(*Carne Asada*)

Serves 4
Marinate Overnight

Preparation 15 Minutes
Cook 15 Minutes

1/2 cup plus 1 teaspoon lemon juice
1/4 cup Worcestershire sauce
1 medium onion, sliced
Broiling steak
1 cup finely shredded cabbage
1/4 teaspoon Tabasco
1/2 teaspoon salt
2 tomatoes, chopped

1. Mix 1/2 cup lemon juice, Worcestershire sauce, and onion. Pour over steak and marinate overnight.
2. Combine cabbage, Tabasco, 1 teaspoon lemon juice, and salt 2 hours before serving.
3. Broil steak and onions. Top with cabbage mixture and tomatoes and serve.

Maria Elena Brooks
San Francisco, California

Serve with a 1980 Concannon Zinfandel Rose'.

AVO-TACO PIE

Serves 6 to 8

Preparation 20 Minutes
Bake 25 Minutes at 375°F

1 pound lean ground beef
1/2 medium onion, chopped
1 can (8-ounce) tomato sauce
1 package (1 1/2-ounce) taco seasoning mix
2/3 cup sliced black olives
1 can (8-ounce) refrigerated crescent rolls
1 1/2 cups crushed corn chips
1 cup sour cream
4 ounces Cheddar cheese, shredded
Shredded lettuce, tomato, and avocado slices

1. In large frying pan, brown beef and onion. Drain fat and stir in tomato sauce, taco mix, and olives.
2. Separate crescent dough into 8 triangles, place in ungreased 9-inch pie pan and press to form a crust. (Or, line pan with pastry.)
3. Sprinkle 1 cup corn chips over crust and add meat. Spread sour cream over meat and top with cheese. Add remaining chips.
4. Bake at 375 degrees for 20 to 25 minutes or until crust is golden brown. Cut in wedges and top with shredded lettuce, tomato, and avocado slices.

Marge DeFries
Boulder, Colorado

Serve with Mexican beer.

CHICKEN BREASTS À LA RICHLIEU

Serves 4

Preparation 15 Minutes
Cook 10 Minutes

2 eggs
1 teaspoon oil
1 teaspoon salt
1/4 teaspoon pepper
4 chicken breasts, boned and skinned
1 cup Swiss cheese, grated
1 cup white bread crumbs
4 tablespoons butter

1. Beat eggs, oil, salt, and pepper.
2. Dip breasts in egg mixture. Roll in cheese and bread crumbs.
3. Melt butter in heavy skillet. Fry breasts over low heat for 7 to 10 minutes on each side.

Peg Pettit
Boulder, Colorado

Serve with a 1979 Parducci Sauvignon Blanc.

HUNTINGTON CHICKEN

Serves 12 to 14

Preparation 45 Minutes
Bake 30 Minutes at 350°F

- **2 pounds chicken**
- **1 1/2 cups diced green peppers**
- **1 1/2 cups diced celery**
- **8 ounces wide noodles**
- **3/4 pound American cheese, grated**
- **1 can (8-ounce) mushrooms**
- **1/2 can (10 3/4-ounce) cream of mushroom soup**
- **1 jar (2-ounce) chopped pimientos**

1. Stew chicken and remove meat from bones. Reserve broth.
2. Cover peppers and celery with water and soak.
3. Return broth to a boil and cook noodles 10 to 12 minutes. Drain.
4. Drain peppers and celery and toss with cooked noodles. Add 2/3 of cheese and all of the mushrooms, soup, and pimientos.
5. Pour into large casserole and cover with remaining cheese. Bake at 350 degrees until cheese melts and bubbles.

Mary Jane Husbands
Boulder, Colorado

Serve with a 1979 Parducci Chenin Blanc.

SOUTH-OF-THE-BORDER CHICKEN

Serves 10 to 12

Preparation 45 Minutes
Bake 1 1/2 to 2 Hours at 325°F

- **4 large chicken breasts**
- **4 to 6 chicken thighs**
- **1 can (10 3/4-ounce) cream of mushroom soup**
- **2 cans (10 3/4-ounce each) cream of chicken soup**
- **1 onion, grated**
- **1 bottle (7-ounce) green taco sauce**
- **2 cans (7-ounce each) chopped green chilies**
- **15 corn tortillas**
- **1 pound Longhorn cheese, grated**

1. Stew chicken in water to cover. Remove meat from bones and cut into chunks. Reserve broth.
2. Combine soups, onion, taco sauce, and chilies.
3. Cut tortillas in quarters and layer with chicken and sauce. Repeat layers and top with cheese.
4. Bake 1 1/2 to 2 hours at 325 degrees. If mixture becomes dry while baking, add some chicken broth.

NOTE:

Vary the chilies to suit your taste. This is a good use of leftover chicken or turkey and a good pot-luck dish.

Carol Barela
Boulder, Colorado

Serve with Mexican beer.

FILET OF SOLE PARMESAN

Serves 6

Preparation 20 Minutes
Bake 15 Minutes at 450°F

1 cup sour cream
2 tablespoons chopped parsley
2 tablespoons lemon juice
1 package green onion dip mix
6 medium filet of sole, fresh or defrosted
Seasoned salt
1/4 cup grated Parmesan cheese
Paprika

1. Combine sour cream, parsley, lemon juice, and dip mix.
2. Sprinkle filets with seasoned salt. Spread each with thin layer of sour cream mix. Roll up jelly-roll fashion and secure with toothpick.
3. Place in greased shallow baking dish or individual casseroles. Cover with remaining sour cream mixture. Sprinkle with cheese and paprika.
4. Bake in 450-degree oven for 15 minutes.

Janet Sparkman
Boulder, Colorado

Serve with a 1979 Sterling Fume' (Sauvignon) Blanc.

SHRIMP OLÉ

Serves 2

Preparation 15 Minutes
Bake 15 Minutes at 400°F

1/2 cup cheese and garlic croutons
1/2 cup grated Monterey Jack cheese
2 tablespoons diced green chilies
1 can (4 1/2-ounce) medium shrimp, drained and rinsed
2 tablespoons mayonnaise
1 tablespoon picante sauce (optional)

1. Cover bottom of individual casseroles or 1-quart baking dish with croutons and add 1/4 cup cheese.
2. Combine chilies, shrimp, mayonnaise, and picante sauce. Spread over crouton-cheese mixture.
3. Cover with remaining 1/4 cup cheese. Bake 15 minutes at 400 degrees.

Ray Imel, Jr.
Boulder, Colorado

Serve with Bohemia Mexican beer.

SHOESTRING CARROTS

Serves 6 to 8

Preparation 15 Minutes
Cook 15 to 20 Minutes

3 strips bacon, cut lengthwise in 1/2-inch strips
1 medium onion, chopped
1 1/2 pounds carrots, cut in julienne strips
1 teaspoon sugar
1 tablespoon flour
1 cup hot water
2 bay leaves
Salt and pepper to taste

1. Fry bacon until crisp and set aside. Saute' onion in bacon fat until light brown. Add carrots, sugar, flour, water, bay leaves, salt, and pepper.
2. Cover and cook gently until carrots are tender.
3. Place in serving dish and sprinkle with bacon bits.

Charlotte Griggs
Davenport, Iowa

CARROT CASSEROLE

Serves 8

Preparation 25 Minutes
Bake 1 Hour at 350°F

2 pounds carrots, cooked and mashed
1 tablespoon minced onion
1 tablespoon minced green pepper
1 cup milk
2 teaspoons lemon juice
2 eggs, slightly beaten
3 tablespoons butter
1 tablespoon flour
2 teaspoons salt
1 teaspoon sugar
Paprika to taste

1. Mix carrots, onion, green pepper, milk, lemon juice, eggs, butter, flour, salt, sugar, and paprika.
2. Pour into greased 1 1/2-quart casserole or ring mold. Set casserole in pan of hot water and bake 1 hour at 350 degrees.

NOTE:

If ring mold is used, buttered green peas may be served in center of ring.

Mildred Barrick
Boulder, Colorado

BLACK-EYED PEAS AND SPINACH

Serves 4

Preparation 10 Minutes
Cook 25 Minutes

2 tablespoons olive oil
1 large onion, quartered
1 can (15-ounce) black-eyed peas
1 package (10-ounce) frozen spinach, partially thawed
Juice of 1/2 lemon

1. Heat oil in 10-inch skillet. Add onion and cook for 5 minutes.
2. Add partially drained can of black-eyed peas. Cook 10 minutes.
3. Add partially defrosted spinach and cook 10 minutes longer. Add lemon juice, mix and serve.

Irene Roberts
Boulder, Colorado

SPINACH SURPRISE

Serves 4 to 6

Preparation 25 Minutes
Bake 20 Minutes at 350°F

2 packages (10-ounce each) frozen chopped spinach
1 jar (6-ounce) marinated artichoke hearts
8 ounces cream cheese, softened
1/4 cup grated Parmesan cheese

1. Prepare spinach according to package directions and drain.
2. Place artichoke hearts on bottom of a 1-quart casserole, and cover with cooked spinach.
3. Mix cream cheese and Parmesan cheese. Place cheese mixture over spinach.
4. Bake at 350 degrees for 20 minutes or until cheese mixture starts to brown.

Paul R. Flippen
Boulder, Colorado

ALMOND-POPPY SEED NOODLES

Serves 8 to 10

Preparation 25 Minutes

16 ounces wide noodles
Salted water
1 cup butter
1 1/2 cups blanched, slivered almonds
1/4 to 1/2 cup poppy seeds
1 teaspoon salt
Parsley to garnish

1. Cook noodles in salted water according to package directions.
2. Melt butter slowly in small skillet. Add almonds and saute' slowly until golden. Watch almonds closely to prevent burning. Stir in poppy seeds and salt.
3. When noodles are tender, drain thoroughly and return to pan. Add butter-almond mixture. Toss. Garnish with parsley.

Sylvia Barnett
Mobile, Alabama

NOODLE-HAM BAKE

Serves 4 to 5

Preparation 20 Minutes
Bake 30 Minutes at 300°F

1 cup milk
8 ounces cream cheese
1/2 teaspoon salt
1/2 teaspoon garlic salt
1/2 cup shredded Parmesan cheese
1 1/2 cups diced cooked ham
1/2 cup sliced celery
1/4 cup chopped green pepper
1/4 cup sliced ripe olives
1 package (4-ounce) crinkled noodles, cooked

1. Blend milk and cream cheese and heat, stirring to keep smooth.
2. Add salt, garlic salt, and half of Parmesan cheese. Stir in ham, celery, green peppers, olives, and noodles, and pour into a 9x9-inch casserole. Sprinkle the remaining Parmesan cheese on top.
3. Bake 25 to 30 minutes at 300 degrees.

Janet Desgalier
Boulder, Colorado

SOUR CREAM ONION PIE

Serves 6

Preparation 35 Minutes
Bake 25 Minutes at 375°F

9-inch pie crust (see Index)
1 pound onions, finely chopped
1 tablespoon butter
1/2 teaspoon salt
1/2 teaspoon pepper
1 cup sour cream
1 teaspoon flour
2 egg yolks

1. Line a 9-inch pie plate with dough and prick bottom with fork. Bake for 15 to 20 minutes at 350 degrees. Cool.
2. Saute' onions in butter until golden brown. Add salt and pepper.
3. Mix sour cream and flour and pour over onions. Bring mixture to boiling point and then cool.
4. Add egg yolks one at a time. Blend thoroughly.
5. Pour into pie crust and bake 20 to 25 minutes at 375 degrees.

QUICK HERB ROLLS

Serves 4

Preparation 30 Minutes
Bake 12 to 15 Minutes at 425°F

- 1/2 cup butter (not margarine)
- 2 tablespoons Parmesan cheese
- 1 1/2 teaspoon parsley flakes
- 1/2 teaspoon dill weed
- 1 tablespoon onion flakes
- 1 can (10-ounce) refrigerator biscuits, buttermilk variety

1. Melt butter in 9-inch pan. Mix cheese and herbs and onion flakes together and stir into butter. Let stand 15 to 30 minutes.
2. Cut biscuits into halves or fourths and dredge in herb butter to coat all sides.
3. Bake 12 to 15 minutes at 425 degrees. May be prepared several hours ahead and refrigerated.

Helen Wasley
Boulder, Colorado

SEVEN-LAYER CAKE

Serves 8 to 10

Preparation 20 Minutes
Refrigerate 2 Hours

- 6 ounces chocolate chips
- 1/2 cup butter
- 1/4 cup water
- 4 egg yolks
- 1/2 cup sugar
- 1 teaspoon vanilla extract
- 2 tablespoons rum (optional)
- 1 (10 3/4-ounce) frozen pound cake

1. Melt chocolate and butter with water over low heat in heavy saucepan. Remove from heat. Add slightly beaten egg yolks and stir well.
2. Add sugar, vanilla, and rum. Beat until smooth. Chill mixture until it is of spreading consistency.
3. While cake is frozen, use a sharp knife to cut 7 layers, lengthwise.
4. Frost each layer, stack, and frost top and sides. Make decorative pattern on top. Refrigerate several hours before serving in thin slices.

Pat Wright
Boulder, Colorado

ORANGE POPPYSEED CAKE

Serves 10 to 12

Preparation 15 Minutes
Bake 40 to 45 Minutes at 375°F

1 box yellow cake mix with added pudding
3 tablespoons flour
2 tablespoons poppy seeds
Grated peel of 1 orange
1/3 cup vegetable oil
3 eggs
1/2 cup orange juice concentrate
1/2 cup water
Orange Cream Cheese Frosting (see Index)

1. Combine cake mix, flour, poppy seeds, orange peel, oil, eggs, juice, and water. Mix until smooth.
2. Pour into greased and floured bundt pan and bake 40 to 45 minutes at 375 degrees. Cool slightly and remove from pan. Frost with Orange Cream Cheese Frosting.

Shirley Brown
Boulder, Colorado

VARIATION:

While cake is still warm, poke holes in it with a fork. Boil 1 cup orange juice and 2 tablespoons lemon juice for 3 minutes. Stir in 2 tablespoons rum and slowly pour over cake until all is absorbed. Omit frosting. Chill.

BUTTER BRITTLE COOKIES

Yields 3 1/2 to 4 Dozen

Preparation 15 Minutes
Bake 10 Minutes at 350°F

40 to 50 graham cracker squares
1 cup butter or 1/2 cup butter and 1/2 cup margarine
1/2 cup sugar
1 cup slivered almonds

1. Lay graham crackers on buttered cookie sheet.
2. Boil butter and sugar 2 minutes and spread over crackers. Sprinkle with almonds.
3. Bake for 10 minutes at 350 degrees. Caution: loosen from pan immediately after removing from oven.

Rae Kelly
Scottsdale, Arizona

SUGAR WAFERS

Yields 3 to 4 Dozen

Preparation 20 Minutes
Bake 6 to 8 Minutes at 375°F

1 cup butter
4 tablespoons sugar
2 cups flour (scant)
OPTIONAL TOPPINGS
Sugar crystals
Cocoa powder
Finely chopped nuts
Instant coffee crystals
Coconut

1. Cream butter with sugar then slowly work in the flour until dough can be easily handled.
2. Dusting palms of hands with sugar, form into balls the size of quarter. (If dough is difficult to handle, chill slightly before shaping.) Place on ungreased cookie sheet and press flat with the bottom of a glass dipped in sugar.
3. Leave plain or sprinkle with sugar crystals, cocoa powder, finely chopped nuts, instant coffee granules, or coconut. Bake 6 to 8 minutes at 375 degrees. Do not brown.

NOTE:

Quickly made in food processor. With steel blades in place, add flour, butter cut into 8 pieces, and sugar. Process, on and off, until ball begins to form. Continue as above.

Pat Wright
Boulder, Colorado

SOUTHERN FUDGE BARS

Yields 16

Preparation 10 Minutes
Bake 30 Minutes at 350°F

1 cup flour
1 cup sugar
1 teaspoon baking powder
3 tablespoons cocoa
1/4 teaspoon salt
2 eggs
1/2 cup butter, melted
1 teaspoon vanilla extract
1/2 cup chopped pecans
Powdered sugar

1. Mix flour, sugar, baking powder, cocoa, and salt.
2. Beat in eggs, butter, vanilla, and pecans. Mixture will be very stiff.
3. Spread in greased 8 x 8-inch pan and bake 30 minutes at 350 degrees.
4. While still warm, sprinkle with powdered sugar and cut into squares.

Joanne Thornton
Wheatridge, Colorado

MENUS AND NOTES • FROM • THE KITCHEN

BRUNCH

Wine Cooler

Glazed Sausage Ball

Chili-Cheese Bake

Blushing Apple Salad

Tomato Tangarine Salad

Sesame Wafers

St. Alban's Lemon Squares

Iowa Brownies

LUNCH FOR A CROWD

Cranberry Wine Punch

Orange Chicken Salad

Melon Wedges

Pickled Bell Peppers

Sesame Rolls

Fruit Ice

Sugar Wafers

SALAD LUNCHEON BUFFET

Mexican Layered Dip

Tabbouleh

Corn-Date Salad

Avocado Mousse

Herring Salad

Indonesian Bean Sprout Salad

Pineapple Fruit Salad

Sweet Potato Muffins

Cheese Bread

Champagne Punch

BRIDGE LUNCHEON

Wine Cooler

Hoi-sin Chicken Salad

or

Chinese Chicken Salad

Chocolate Toffee Angel Cake

WINTER PICNIC

Spanakopita

Sweet and Sour Pickled Beets

Celery and Carrot Sticks

Chicken Guava

North Farm House Bread

Carrot Cake

NEW YEAR'S DAY FOOTBALL PARTY FOR 12

Champagne Punch or The Longhorn

French Drip Beef with
Hot Mustard Sauce

or

Peppered Beef with Mustard
Horseradish Sauce

Red Ribbon Salad, Zucchini Salad

Billie's Oatmeal Bread

Graham Cracker Cake

Chocolate Mints

COCKTAILS FOR 8 TO 12

Scotch Eggs

Spanakopita

Indonesian Peanut Butter Dip
with raw vegetables

Spiced Nuts

Crab-Cheese Mushrooms

Marinated Green Olives

Chips and Flat Bread or crackers

PATIO COCKTAILS

Tomato Toasts

Spicy Cocktail Meatballs

Chinese Barbecued Baby Drumsticks

Mexican Eggroll

Guacamole

Pecan-Cheese Bites

DO AHEAD COCKTAILS FOR 12 TO 24

Bleu Cheese Cheesecake
with assorted crackers

Spinach Balls

Polynesian Meat Balls

Chicken Almond Puffs

Cereal-Nut Mix

Sesame Seed Wafers

Zucchini Finger Food

Raw Vegetable Assortment
with Boot's Dipping Sauce

COCKTAILS IN A HURRY

Artichoke Puffs
Apricot-Mustard Spread
Chili Con Queso Dip
Crackers, Tortillas, Nuts

VEGETARIAN COCKTAIL PARTY

Vegetarian Pâte'
Sesame Seed Wafers
Stuffed Artichokes
Greek Mushrooms
Pickled Bell Peppers
Greek Pastry Hors D'Oeuvres
Cheese Ball with assorted crackers
Egg Dip with raw vegetables
Greek *Skordalia* Sauce

SUMMER BUFFET

Spicy Ham Roll Ups
Stuffed Celery
Chicken and/or Ribs in Cecilia's Mama's Barbecue Sauce
Danish Potato Salad
Copper Pennies
Homemade Ice Cream with Scotch Shortbread

BUFFET FOR A CROWD 50 TO 100

Chicken Kapama
Fettucini with Avocado and Ham
Salad Italiano
French Rolls
Versatile Pound Cake
Black Bottom Cupcakes

CHRISTMAS BUFFET

Traditional Eggnog
Pecan Cheese Bites
Potato Frittata Squares
Christmas Eve Salad
Spicy Spinach Salad
Swedish Pickled Shrimp
Sliced Bake Ham with Wild Berry Sauce
Cheese Stuffed Zucchini
Barley Casserole
Refrigerator Rolls
English Toffee Bars, Date Rocks, Christmas Cake Cookies, German Bar Cookies, Layered Fudge Bars, Golden Fruit Cake, Almond Roca, Divinity

THANKSGIVING DINNER

Molded Cucumber Salad
Turkey With Rice-Vegetable Sausage Stuffing
Nan's 3-Vegetable Casserole
Sweet Potato Bake
Happy's Apple Skillet
Bubby's Cranberry Sauce
Special Yeast Dinner Rolls
Indiana Apple Pie

WINTER'S EVENING MENU

Hearts of Palm
Canard au Cidre
Baked Vegetable Puree
Wild Rice and Mushrooms
Gateau au Chocolat

PASTA PARTY

Assorted Stuffed Mushrooms
Marinated Red Pepper
Fresh Egg Pasta in a Variety of Flavors
White Clam Sauce
Eggplant Spaghetti Sauce
Bacon Spaghetti Sauce
Herb Bread
Lemon Sherbet

VEGETARIAN DINNER

Middle Eastern Cold Summer Soup
Zucchini Salad
Lasagne with Mushrooms
Green Beans with Garlic
Billie's Oatmeal Bread
Fruit Ice

FAST GOURMET

Baked Cheese Soup
Cashew-Nut Salad
Zesty Steak
Almond Poppy Seed Noodles
Quick Herb Rolls
Seven Layer Cake

BOUNTY OF SUMMER

Lamb Dijon
Marinated Mushrooms
Peas and Artichokes
Broiled Tomatoes
Herb Bread
Peaches with Sour Cream
and Strawberries
Sugar Wafers

SUMMER SIT DOWN DINNER

Greek Mushrooms
Salad Italiano
Breast of Chicken Parisienne
Carrots and Leeks Vichey
Rice Pepita
Dill Bread
Cold Raspberry Soup

AFRICAN DINNER

African Crunchy Appetizer Bits
Chilled Paw Paw Soup
Sudan Salad
Spinach with Coconut Milk
and Peanut Sauce
Guinean Chicken Stew
Ground Nut Muffins
Casava Cake
Fresh Fruit

BELGIAN DINNER

Mussels Marinière
Leek Soup
Carbonnades Flamande
Brussels Sprouts au Gratin
or
Belgian Endive
with Creamy Vinaigrette Dressing
Quick Homemade Bread
Butter Torte

BRAZILIAN DINNER

Feijoada
Collard Greens with Orange Slices
Brazilian Hot Sauce
Brazilian Rice
Mandioc
Fruit Ice

CENTRAL EUROPEAN DINNER

Korozott
Hungarian Pickled Beet Salad
Pork and Sauerkraut Goulash
or
Hungarian Paprika Pork
Green Beans with Herb Sauce
Cheese Bread
Nut Torte

CHINESE

Hot and Sour Soup
Sweet and Sour Radish Salad
Spiced Napa Cabbage
Sweet and Pungent Fish
Chinese Cashew Chicken
Rice or Chow Mein Fried Noodles

FRENCH COUNTRY DINNER

Lillet or Red or White Sweet Vermouth
Marinated Artichokes
Pheasant in Sour Cream-Mushroom Sauce
Shoestring Carrots
Fresh Pasta
Lettuce Varieties with Creamy Vinaigrette Dressing
Brie Quiche with Cheese and Fresh Fruit
Clafouti aux Framboises

LIGHT FRENCH SUPPER

Champignons à la Greque
Two-Cheese Quiche
Broiled Tomatoes
French Rolls
10-Minute Chocolate Mousse

GREEK

Tiropetes
Stifatho and/or *Pastichio*
Emallees Zucchini Casserole
Sliced Tomatoes with Tomato Marinade
Baklava

INDONESIAN

Indonesian Bean Sprout Salad
Shrimp with Coconut
Köfta Curry
Chicken in Lime
Indonesian Rice
Indonesian Mixed Vegetables with Peanut Butter
Tea
Fresh Fruit

MEXICAN DINNER

Tortilla Soup
Zucchini in Salsa Verde
Mexican Barbecued Lamb
Guacamole
Refried Beans
Tortillas
Lemon Sherbet and Mexican Meringues

SPANISH DINNER

Orange Sangria
Gazpacho
Arroz con Mariscos
Marinated Red Peppers
Mixed Salad Greens with Zesty Lemon Dressing
Lemon Crisp

TURKISH LUNCHEON

Iç Pilav
Şiş Köfte
Sliced Tomatoes with Tomato Marinade
Baklava
Tea

VIETNAMESE

Vietnamese Sour Soup
Vietnamese Cabbage Salad
Oriental Fried Rice
Spring Rolls with *Nuőc Mam* Sauce
Tea

GENERAL INFORMATION AND HINTS

1. HERBS AND SPICES – Fresh herbs are preferred in cooking. If using dried herbs, use about 1/2 as much. This depends on the age of the dried herb and how it was stored. Add herbs and spices to cooked foods during last part of cooking. Add herbs and spices to uncooked foods, such as salad dressings and marinades, long before use to allow flavors to develop.
2. To peel tomatoes easily, place them in a brown paper bag and pour in boiling water. By the time the bag drains, the tomatoes are ready to peel.
3. THE VERSATILE LEMON – Besides the fact that lemon juice is a mild bleach and keeps certain foods from discoloring, it has other interesting uses. Add lemon juice to boiling rice or potatoes to keep them fluffy and white. Add to poaching fish to keep it white and firm. Two teaspoons lemon juice to 1 cup fresh cream turns it to sour cream. Two tablespoons lemon juice added to 1 cup undiluted evaporated milk produces sour cream also. A few drops added to chilled cream speeds up the whipping process. The garlic smell on hands can be removed by rubbing them with a lemon quarter. Chill undiluted evaporated milk in the freezer and add 1 tablespoon lemon juice for whipping.
4. Shorten soaking time of dried beans by boiling them for 2 minutes, then soaking for 1 hour before cooking.
5. Remove garlic from your breath by chewing on a whole coffee bean.
6. One tablespoon unflavored gelatin will gel 1 pint liquid.
7. If a recipe calls for rice and you are out, be daring and different and substitute bulgar wheat or barley.

ALTITUDE

1. Lower deep-fat frying temperature 3 degrees per 1,000 feet of altitude. This prevents over browning the outside of the food and undercooking the centers.
2. The recipes for cakes, breads, biscuits, cookies, and quick breads in this book are suitable for both low and high altitudes.
3. Breads rise faster at high altitude. Follow the rule "let rise until double in bulk."
4. Use extra large eggs in baking at high altitude if you are having difficulty.

DRIED FOODS

1. Use bumper crops of fruit by making FRUIT LEATHER – uncooked method. Puree fruits, adding 1 to 2 tablespoons water if necessary, and spread evenly 1/4-inch deep on sided baking sheet. Bake at lowest setting (140 to 150 degrees) with the door ajar for 10 hours or until fruit peels loosely from the pan. One tablespoon sugar, corn syrup, or honey may be added to each 2 cups of tart fruit. For taste variety, add 1/4 teaspoon cinnamon or a dash of nutmeg or 1/4 cup

sesame, pumpkin, or sunflower seeds to each 2 cups of puree. Two cups of puree is enough to cover a 12- x 17-inch baking sheet. Store in cool, dry, dark place. Keeps for a year or more in freezer or several months in refrigerator and 3 weeks at room temperature.

2. BEEF JERKY – Slice very lean meat (partially frozen) very thin, 1/8- to 1/2-inch thick, with the grain. Lay the strips out in a single layer, and flatten the strips by pounding with a rolling pin so they are fairly uniform in thickness. Season meat, no more than 1 teaspoon salt per pound of meat, or marinate 2 hours or more in Spicy Beef Kebob Marinade (see Index). Dry by stretching strips across clean oven racks (fasten short ones together with wooden picks). Dry, with oven door ajar, at 140 to 150 degrees for about 11 hours.

FOOD PROCESSOR

1. Adapt quick bread recipes for the food processor. Do the fruit or nut chopping, if necessary, first. Remove. Cream shortening and sugar, and all other ingredients except flour. Mix. Add flour last and process until just mixed in. Bread will be tough if processed too long.
2. About 1/2 as much liquid is needed when making pastry in the food processor. Process flour and salt just to mix. Add liquid and process 1 to 2 quick on/offs. Remove pastry, press into a ball, sprinkle with water if too dry.
3. For finely ground nuts, process with part of flour and sugar from the recipe so that nuts do not turn to butter.
4. To chop candied fruit in processor: add 1/2 cup flour or sugar per cup of candied fruit to prevent blade from gumming up. The same holds true for dried fruits. Subtract the amount of flour or sugar used in processing from amount needed in recipe for baking.

MICROWAVE HINTS

1. Microwave cooking is moist cooking, liquids do not evaporate or thicken as well. Reduce liquids in recipes by 1/4, except when cooking rice or pasta which requires established amounts of liquid for rehydration.
2. Foods with a skin, such as tomatoes, potatoes, and eggplants, should be pierced before cooking.
3. Adapt favorite recipes to microwave cooking. Reduce cooking time by 1/3 to 1/4 of conventional cooking time. Always undercook food and add the necessary finishing time in seconds. Always allow food to stand a few minutes before testing for doneness.
4. Dry bumper crops of fresh herbs for winter use. Wash, dry, and remove leaves from stems. Place on paper toweling, and heat 1 1/2 to 2 minutes or until they feel dry. Cool and store in airtight containers.
5. To make unused portions of red wine last longer, refrigerate, then bring to drinking temperature in the microwave by heating 3 ounces for approximately 15 seconds.
6. To soften brown sugar, place in a glass dish with a slice of apple, cover with plastic wrap, and heat 15 seconds.

7. Sterilize jelly glasses by filling them half full of water. Heat until water comes to a full boil.
8. Foods that are going to be cooked for more than 5 minutes should not be covered with plastic wrap because it melts. Cover foods with a paper towel or waxed paper to allow steam to escape and to prevent popping of natural juices that soil the oven.

COOKING WITH WINE OR SPIRITS

1. Never use "cooking wine." It is heavily salted - which distorts the recipe.
2. Wine intensifies flavor of salt. Add salt to taste.
3. Wine is used in cooking to *enhance* flavor, not to overpower other ingredients. Better to use too little than too much.
4. When wine is added *before* the final period of cooking, the alcohol boils off and only the flavor remains.
5. If you wish to add wine at the *end* of cooking, as in soups and sauces, *reduce* the wine (before adding) by half—i.e., boil it down to half its volume. This gets rid of the alcohol.
6. Be very careful when adding brandy, cognac, Madeira, or Marsala to a sauce, they may overpower flavor of sauce. Use only a few drops at a time—or eliminate if you are satisfied with flavor of sauce.
7. The best wine to cook with is the one you will be serving to drink with the dish. If you feel it is too expensive to cook with, use a less expensive wine in the same family for cooking.
8. Flaming: most wines do not have enough alcohol content to flame. Fortified wines (sherry, Madeira, port) at 20% alcohol, can be flamed. Brandy and liquors—30% alcohol and up—can all be flamed. To flame, gently heat wine or brandy just until very hot, then ignite and pour over dish. Do not let spirits boil, or alcohol will boil off and it will not flame.

Nona Jahsman
Palo Alto, California

EQUIVALENT MEASURES

1/3 of 1/4 teaspoon	Pinch
1/3 of 1/2 teaspoon	Pinch
1/2 of 1/4 teaspoon	1/8 teaspoon
3 teaspoons	1 tablespoon
1/3 of 1 tablespoon	1 teaspoon
1/3 of 2 tablespoons	2 teaspoons
1/3 of 5 tablespoons	1 tablespoon + 2 teaspoons
1/3 of 7 tablespoons	2 tablespoons + 1 teaspoon
1/2 of 1 tablespoon	1 1/2 teaspoons
1/2 of 3 tablespoons	1 tablespoon + 1 1/2 teaspoons
1/2 of 5 tablespoons	2 tablespoons + 1 1/2 teaspoons
1/2 of 7 tablespoons	3 tablespoons + 1 1/2 teaspoons
2 tablespoons	1/8 cup

4 tablespoons	1/4 cup
5 tablespoons + 1 teaspoon	1/3 cup
10 tablespoons	5/8 cup
10 tablespoons + 2 teaspoons	2/3 cup
12 tablespoons	3/4 cup
16 tablespoons	1 cup
1/3 of 1/4 cup	1 tablespoon + 1 teaspoon
1/3 of 1/3 cup	1 tablespoon + 2 1/3 teaspoons
1/3 of 1/2 cup	2 tablespoons + 2 teaspoons
1/3 of 2/3 cup	3 tablespoons + 1 2/3 teaspoons
1/3 of 3/4 cup	1/4 cup
1/2 of 1/4 cup	2 tablespoons
1/2 of 1/3 cup	2 tablespoons + 2 teaspoons
British pint	20 ounces or 2 1/2 cups American
(Br) 1 tablespoon	4 teaspoons American

CONVERSION TABLES

The measurements used in this book are standard American. Some British units of measurement have the same names as American units but not all are equivalent. In general, weights are equivalent, but volumes are not. The American cup contains 8 fluid ounces and the British cup contains 10 fluid ounces.

We hope these charts will help you convert our recipes for your home use and enjoyment. The measurements are approximate.

LIQUID CONVERSION TABLE

AMERICAN	BRITISH (fluid ounces)	METRIC (milliliters)
1/8 teaspoon	pinch	0.6 ml
1/4 teaspoon	1/4 level U.K. teaspoon	1.2 ml
1/2 teaspoon	1/2 level U.K. teaspoon	2.5 ml
1 teaspoon	1/6 ounce, 1 U.K. level teaspoon	5.0 ml
1/2 tablespoon	1/4 ounce	7.5 ml
1 tablespoon	1/2 ounce, 1U.K. dessert spoon	15 ml
1/8 cup	1 ounce	30 ml
1/4 cup	2 ounces	60 ml
1/3 cup	2 2/3 ounces	80 ml
1/2 cup	4 ounces	125 ml
2/3 cup	5 1/3 ounces	160 ml
3/4 cup	6 ounces	180 ml
1 cup	8 ounces (average tea cup)	240 ml
2 cups (1 pint)	16 ounces	475 ml
4 cups (1 quart)	32 ounces	950 ml

DRY AND SOLID MEASURE CONVERSION TABLE

	AMERICAN	BRITISH (Ounces)	METRIC (Grams)
Flour	4 level tablespoons	1 ounce	30 grams
	1 cup	4 1/4 ounces	120 grams
Sugar			
Fine Granulated	1 level teaspoon	1/6 ounce	5 grams
	1 level tablespoon	1/2 ounce	15 grams
	1 cup	8 ounces	240 grams
Confectioners	1/4 cup	1 ounce (generous)	35 grams
Brown (packed)	1 tablespoon	1/3 ounce	10 grams
	1/2 cup	2 2/3 ounces	80 grams

Salt	1 teaspoon	1/16 ounce	6 grams
	1 tablespoon	1/2 ounce	15 grams
Baking Powder & Soda	1 teaspoon	1 teaspoon (approx.)	4 grams
Cornstarch	1 tablespoon	1/3 ounce	10 grams
Spices (ground)	1 teaspoon	1/12 ounce	2 1/2 grams
	2 tablespoons	1/4 ounce	15 grams
Breadcrumbs			
Dry	1 cup	3 1/4 ounces	90 grams
Fresh	1 cup	1 1/2 ounces	45 ounces
Rice	1 cup	8 ounces	240 grams
Nuts	1 cup	5 1/2 ounces	150 grams
Butter and Fat	1 tablespoon	1/2 ounce	15 grams
	1/2 cup	4 ounces	125 grams
	2 cups	1 pound	500 grams
Chopped Meat	1 cup	8 ounces	225 grams
Dried Fruit	1 cup	8 ounces	225 grams

Yeast packages in America, dry or cake weigh 1 ounce each.

EQUIVALENTS

Amount	Equals
CHEESE	
4 ounces Bleu cheese	1 cup crumbled
1 pound Cheddar cheese	4 cups grated, sieved or chopped
1 pound cottage cheese	2 cups
3 ounces cream cheese	6 tablespoons
4 ounces Parmesan cheese	1 cup grated
5 ounces prepared cheese spread	1/2 cup
CHOCOLATE	
1 ounce (1 square) chocolate	4 tablespoons grated
COFFEE	
1 pound coffee + 2 1/2 gallons water	50 servings
CRUMBS	
1 slice bread	1/4 to 1/3 cup dry crumbs 3/4 to 1 cup soft crumbs
19 chocolate wafers 15 ginger snaps 22 soda crackers 24 vanilla wafers	1 cup fine crumbs
16 to 18 graham crackers	1 1/3 cups crumbs = 1 pie crust
EGGS	
7 large eggs	1 cup egg whites
1 egg white (medium egg)	2 tablespoons
14 large eggs	1 cup egg yolks
1 egg yolk	1 tablespoon

FLOUR

1 pound cake	Almost 5 cups sifted
1 pound all-purpose	4 cups sifted
1 pound rye	4 1/2 to 5 cups sifted
1 pound wheat	3 1/2 cups unsifted

DRIED FRUIT

3 cups dried apricots (1 pound)	6 cups cooked
1 pound coconut	5 cups shredded
1 pound dates	1 3/4 cups chopped
1/2 pound prunes, whole	1 1/2 cups uncooked 2 cups cooked
1/2 pound raisins or currants	1 1/2 cups

FRUIT

1 pound apples (3 medium)	3 cups peeled, diced or sliced
1 apple	1 cup sliced or chopped
1 pound (3 medium) bananas	2 to 2 1/2 cups sliced or 1 3/4 cups mashed
1 medium banana	1/3 cup mashed
1 cup berries	1/2 cup puree
1 pound cherries	2 cups pitted
1 lemon (medium)	3 to 4 tablespoons juice 1 1/2 to 2 teaspoons grated rind
1 medium lime	2 tablespoons juice
3 to 4 medium oranges	1 cup juice
1 medium orange	2 tablespoons grated rind
1 piece 1-inch rind	1/8 teaspoon grated
1 large peach or nectarine	1 cup sliced
1 medium pear	2/3 to 3/4 cup sliced or chopped
3 to 4 pounds pineapple	3 cups chopped or sliced
1/2 pound rhubarb	2 cups sliced
2 cups whole strawberries	1 1/2 cups sliced
1 1/2 cups cut-up fresh fruit	1 can (16-ounce) fruit, drained

MEAT

1 pound cooked meat	3 cups chopped

NUTS

1 pound whole, shelled almonds	3 1/2 cups nut meats
1/2 pound whole, shelled almonds	1 1/2 cups ground
1 pound shelled peanuts	3 1/4 cups nut meats
1 cup shelled peanuts	1 cup coarsely or finely chopped
2 cups whole peanuts	1 cup peanut butter
1/2 pound pecans, shelled	1 3/4 cups nut meats 1 cup coarsely chopped

RICE, BEANS, PASTA

1 cup dried beans	2 1/2 cups cooked
1 cup macaroni (1/4 pound)	2 cups cooked
1 cup noodles (1/4 pound)	2 cups cooked
1 pound uncooked pasta	7 cups cooked
1 cup raw rice	3 cups cooked
1 pound spaghetti	7 cups cooked

SUGAR

1 pound brown	2 1/4 cups packed
1 pound granulated	2 1/2 cups
1 pound powdered	4 cups sifted 3 1/2 cups unsifted

VEGETABLES

4 medium beets	2 cups cooked and diced or julienned
1 pound cabbage	5 cups shredded
1 pound carrots (8 to 10)	2 3/4 to 3 cups sliced or diced
6 medium carrots	3 cups sliced or shredded
1 pound cauliflower	4 cups sliced
1 pound celery	4 cups diced
3 stalks celery	1 cup sliced or diced
1 medium cucumber	1 cup sliced or chopped
1 medium (8-ounce) eggplant	2 cups sliced 1 cup chopped 2 cups shredded
1 medium clove garlic	1/4 teaspoon chopped
1 pound green beans	3 cups cut
6 ounces green beans	1 1/3 cups cut
1 medium green pepper	3/4 cup sliced or chopped
8 ounces leeks	3 cups sliced
1/2 pound mushrooms	2 1/2 to 3 cups sliced 2 cups chopped
1 medium (5-ounce) onion	1 to 1 1/3 cups sliced 1/2 cup chopped
Parsley, 1 cup loosely packed sprigs or leaves	1/3 cup minced 1/2 cup coarsely chopped
1 pound peas in pods	1 cup shelled
1 pound potatoes (3 medium)	2 1/2 cups sliced, diced 2 cups cooked and mashed
1 small (4-ounce) potato	3/4 cup sliced 2/3 cup chopped 3/4 cup shredded
3 scallions	1/3 cup chopped 1/4 cup minced
2 pounds pumpkin	2 cups cooked and mashed
1 medium squash (1 pound = 4 cups sliced 3 cups chopped 3 cups shredded)	1 to 1 1/2 cups cooked

1 cup cooked squash	1 cup mashed
1 pound (3 medium) tomatoes	1 cup pulp and juice
1 1/4 cups cut-up fresh vegetables	1 10-ounce package frozen
1 cup cooked, drained vegetables	1/2 cup puree
1 can water chestnuts (8-ounce)	1 cup sliced or chopped

Ingredient Substitutions
Courtesy of Colorado State University Extension Service

Baking powder	1 tsp	• 1/4 tsp baking soda, 1/2 tsp cream of tartar and 1/4 tsp cornstarch • 1/4 tsp baking soda plus 5/8 tsp cream of tartar
Bay leaf, crushed	1 tsp	• 1 whole bay leaf
Cornstarch	1 Tbsp	• 2 Tbsp all-purpose flour
Corn syrup	1 cup	• 1 cup granulated sugar plus 1/4 cup water or other liquid called for in recipe
Catsup	1 cup	• 1 cup tomato sauce plus 1/2 cup sugar, 2 Tbsp vinegar (for use in cooking)
Chili sauce	1 cup	• 1 cup tomato sauce, 1/4 cup brown sugar, 2 Tbsp vinegar, 1/4 tsp cinnamon, dash of ground cloves and allspice
Chocolate		
unsweetened	1 oz	• 3 Tbsp cocoa plus 1 Tbsp butter or fat • 3 Tbsp carob powder plus 2 Tbsp water
semi-sweet	1 2/3 oz	• 1 oz unsweetened chocolate plus 4 tsp sugar
Cracker crumbs	3/4 cup	• 1 cup bread crumbs
Cream		
half & half, 10-12% fat	1 cup	• 1 1/2 Tbsp butter plus 7/8 cup milk • 1/2 cup coffee cream plus 1/2 cup milk
whipping, 36-40% fat	1 cup	• 1/3 cup butter plus 3/4 cup milk (for baking only, will not whip)
sour	1 cup	• 7/8 cup buttermilk, yogurt or sour milk plus 3 Tbsp butter
Cream of tartar	1/2 tsp	• 1 1/2 tsp lemon juice or vinegar

Ingredient	Amount	Substitute
Eggs		
whole, large	1 egg	• 3 1/3 Tbsp frozen egg yolks, thawed
		• 2 egg yolks (in baking)
whites	1 egg white	• 2 Tbsp frozen egg whites, thawed
yolks	1 egg yolk	• 2 Tbsp dried egg yolks plus 2 tsp water
		• 3 1/2 tsp frozen egg yolks, thawed
Flour		
pastry	1 cup	• 7/8 cup all-purpose or bread flour
cake	1 cup	• 7/8 cup all-purpose flour (1 cup less 2 Tbsp)
white, all-purpose for thickening	1 Tbsp	• 1/2 Tbsp cornstarch, potato starch, rice starch or arrowroot
white, all-purpose for baking	1 cup	• 1/2 cup barley flour
		• 1 1/2 cups bread crumbs
		• 1 1/8 cups cake flour (1 cup plus 2 Tbsp)
white, all-purpose, self-rising	1 cup	• 1 cup all-purpose flour plus 1 1/4 tsp baking powder and 1/4 tsp salt
Garlic	1 clove	• 1/8 tsp garlic powder or instant minced garlic
		• 1/2-1 tsp garlic salt (reduce amount salt called for in recipe)
Ginger		
candied or raw	1 Tbsp	• 1/8 tsp powdered ginger
Herbs, fresh	1 Tbsp	• 1/3 to 1/2 tsp dried herbs
Honey	1 cup	• 1 1/4 cup sugar plus 1/4 cup water or liquid called for in recipe
Horseradish		
grated fresh	1 Tbsp	• 2 Tbsp bottled horseradish
Lemon		
juice	1 tsp	• 1/2 tsp vinegar
grated rind	1 tsp	• 1/2 tsp lemon extract
Maple syrup	about 2 cups	• Combine 2 cups sugar and 1 cup water; bring to clear boil; take off heat; add 1/2 tsp maple flavoring
Milk		
buttermilk or sour	1 cup	• 1 cup sweet milk minus 1 Tbsp plus 1 Tbsp vinegar or lemon juice; let stand 5 minutes
		• 1 cup sweet milk plus 1 1/4-1 3/4 tsp cream of tartar
		• 1 cup yogurt
skim	1 cup	• 1/3 cup instant nonfat dry milk plus 7/8 cup water
whole	1 cup	• 1/2 cup evaporated milk plus 1/2 cup water
		• 1 cup reconstituted dry milk plus 2 1/2 tsp butter or margarine

sweetened, condensed	1 cup	• 1 cup plus 2 Tbsp dry milk plus 1/2 cup warm water plus 3/4 cup sugar; add dry milk to warm water, mix well; add sugar; may set bowl in pan of hot water to dissolve sugar
Mint leaves		
fresh chopped	1/4 cup	• 1 Tbsp dried mint leaves
Mushrooms, fresh	1 lb.	• 3 oz dried plus 1 1/2 cups water
		• 1 8-oz can
Mustard, dry	1 tsp	• 1 Tbsp prepared mustard
		• 1/2 tsp mustard seeds
Nuts	1 cup	• 1 cup rolled oats, browned (in baked products)
Onion	1 small	• 1 1/3 tsp onion salt
		• 1 to 2 Tbsp instand minced onion
		• 1 tsp onion powder
Orange	1 medium	• 6 to 8 Tbsp juice; 3/4 cup diced; 2 to 3 Tbsp grated rind
Parsley, fresh	2 tsp	• 1 tsp parsley flakes
Rum	1/4 cup	• 1 Tbsp rum extract plus enough liquid to make 1/4 cup
Sugar		
brown	1 cup	• 1 cup granulated sugar
		• 1 cup granulated sugar plus 1/4 cup unsulphured molasses
powdered	1 cup	• 3/4 cup granulated sugar
granulated	1 cup	• 1 cup firmly-packed brown sugar
		• 1 3/4 cup confectioners sugar (for uses other than baking)
Tomatoes		
packed	1 cup	• 1/2 cup tomato sauce plus 1/2 cup water
canned	1 cup	• 1 1/3 cups diced tomatoes simmered 10 minutes
Tomato juice	1 cup	• 1/2 cup tomato sauce plus 1/2 cup water
Tomato sauce	2 cups	• 3/4 cup tomato paste plus 1 cup water
Tomato soup	1 10 3/4-oz can	• 1 cup tomato sauce plus 1/4 cup water
Yogurt	1 cup	• 1 cup buttermilk
Sour Cream		• 6 oz cream cheese and 3 Tbsp milk

NOTES

NOTES

INDEX

NOTES

THE COLORADO COOK BOOK
Campus Box 184
University of Colorado
Boulder, Colorado 80309

Name ______________________________
Address ____________________________
City _______________________________
State ________________ Zip __________
Master Card __ VISA __ Exp. date _______
Card No. ___________________________
Signature __________________________

The proceeds from the sale of this book will purchase books for the University of Colorado Libraries-Boulder. Make checks payable to **"The Colorado Cook Book."**

Cook
Book(s) ___ copies x $13.95 $__________

Postage &
Handling ___ x $1.50 $__________

THE COLORADO COOK BOOK
Campus Box 184
University of Colorado
Boulder, Colorado 80309

Name ______________________________
Address ____________________________
City _______________________________
State ________________ Zip __________
Master Card __ VISA __ Exp. date _______
Card No. ___________________________
Signature __________________________

The proceeds from the sale of this book will purchase books for the University of Colorado Libraries-Boulder. Make checks payable to **"The Colorado Cook Book."**

Cook
Book(s) ___ copies x $13.95 $__________

Postage &
Handling ___ x $1.50 $__________

THE COLORADO COOK BOOK
Campus Box 184
University of Colorado
Boulder, Colorado 80309

Name ______________________________
Address ____________________________
City _______________________________
State ________________ Zip __________
Master Card __ VISA __ Exp. date _______
Card No. ___________________________
Signature __________________________

The proceeds from the sale of this book will purchase books for the University of Colorado Libraries-Boulder. Make checks payable to **"The Colorado Cook Book."**

Cook
Book(s) ___ copies x $13.95 $__________

Postage &
Handling ___ x $1.50 $__________

THE COLORADO COOK BOOK
Campus Box 184
University of Colorado
Boulder, Colorado 80309

Name ______________________________
Address ____________________________
City _______________________________
State ________________ Zip __________
Master Card __ VISA __ Exp. date _______
Card No. ___________________________
Signature __________________________

The proceeds from the sale of this book will purchase books for the University of Colorado Libraries-Boulder. Make checks payable to **"The Colorado Cook Book."**

Cook
Book(s) ___ copies x $13.95 $__________

Postage &
Handling ___ x $1.50 $__________